ZEW Economic Studies

Publication Series of the Centre for European Economic Research (ZEW), Mannheim, Germany

ZEW Economic Studies

Further volumes of this series can be found at our homepage: springeronline.com/series/4041

Vol. 11: K.L. Brockmann, M. Stronzik (Eds.)
Flexible Mechanisms for an Efficient Climate Policy
Cost Saving Policies and Business Opportunities
2000. VIII, 130 pp. ISBN 3-7908-1314-1

Vol. 12: W. Smolny
Endogenous Innovations and Knowledge Spillovers
A Theoretical and Empirical Analysis
2000. VIII, 277 pp. ISBN 3-7908-1320-6

Vol. 13: M. Lechner, F. Pfeiffer (Eds.)
Econometric Evaluation of Labour Market Policies
2001. X, 242 pp. ISBN 3-7908-1372-9

Vol. 14: M. Beise
Lead Markets
Country-Specific Success Factors of the Global Diffusion of Innovations
2001. XVI, 305 pp. ISBN 3-7908-1430-X

Vol. 15: O.H. Jacobs, C. Spengel
Effective Tax Burden in Europe
Current Situation, Past Developments and Simulations of Reforms
2002. X, 131 pp. ISBN 3-7908-1470-9

Vol. 16: U. Kaiser
Innovation, Employment, and Firm Performance in the German Service Sector
2002. X, 164 pp. ISBN 3-7908-1481-4

Vol. 17: J. Köke
Corporate Governance in Germany
An Empirical Investigation
2002. VIII, 184 pp. ISBN 3-7908-1511-X

Vol. 18: E. Wolf
What Hampers Part-Time Work?
An Empirical Analysis of Wages, Hours Restrictions and Employment from a Dutch-German Perspective
2003. X, 174 pp. ISBN 3-7908-0006-6

Vol. 19: P. Cecchini et al. (Eds.)
The Incomplete European Market for Financial Services
2003. XII, 255 pp. ISBN 3-7908-0013-9

Vol. 20: C. Böhringer, A. Löschel (Eds.)
Empirical Modeling of the Economy and the Environment
2003. VI, 326 pp. ISBN 3-7908-0078-3

Vol. 21: K. Rennings, T. Zwick (Eds.)
Employment Impacts of Cleaner Production
2003. VIII, 322 pp. ISBN 3-7908-0093-7

Vol. 22: O. Bürgel, A. Fier, G. Licht, G. Murray
The Internationalisation of Young High-Tech Firms
An Empirical Analysis in Germany and the United Kingdom
2003. XII, 291 pp. ISBN 3-7908-0120-8

Vol. 23: F. Hüfner
Foreign Exchange Intervention as a Monetary Policy Instrument
Evidence for Inflation Targeting Countries
2004. X, 175 pp. ISBN 3-7908-0128-3

Vol. 24: E. Lüders
Economic Foundation of Asset Price Processes
2004. XII, 121 pp. ISBN 3-7908-0149-6

Vol. 25: F. Reize
Leaving Unemployment for Self-Employment
An Empirical Study
2004. XII, 241 pp. ISBN 3-7908-0168-2

Vol. 26: Ch. Böhringer, A. Löschel (Eds.)
Climate Change Policy and Global Trade
2004. VIII, 381 pp. ISBN 3-7908-0171-2

Vol. 27: K. Jacob et al.
Lead Markets for Environmental Innovations
2005, XII, 273 pp.
ISBN 3-7908-0164-X

Vol. 28: L. Lammersen, R. Schwager
The Effective Tax Burden of Companies in European Regions
2005. XI, 251 pp. ISBN 3-7908-1562-4

Vol. 29: Ch. Elschner, R. Schwager
The Effective Tax Burden on Highly Qualified Employees
2005. VIII, 123 pp. ISBN 3-7908-1568-3

Charlotte Lauer

Education and Labour Markets Outcomes

A French-German Comparison

With 56 Figures
and 57 Tables

Physica-Verlag
A Springer Company

ZEW
Zentrum für Europäische
Wirtschaftsforschung GmbH
Centre for European
Economic Research

Series Editor
Prof. Dr. Dr. h.c. mult. Wolfgang Franz

Author
Dr. Charlotte Lauer
Centre for European Economic Research (ZEW)
Department of Labour Markets,
Human Resources and Social Policy
L 7,1
68161 Mannheim
lauer@zew.de

Cataloging-in-Publication Data
Library of Congress Control Number: 2004116632

ISBN 978-1-4419-3434-5 Physica-Verlag Heidelberg New York

Physica-Verlag is a part of Springer Science+Business Media

springeronline.com

Cover design: Erich Dichiser, ZEW, Mannheim
Cover image: including photo from TU Berlin/Public Relations and Public Information Office

SPIN 11365792 43/3135-5 4 3 2 1 0 – Printed on acid-free paper

Preface

This study is a comparison of French and German education and its impact on individual labour market outcomes. I am very grateful to my supervisor Prof. Dr. Dr. h.c. mult. Wolfgang Franz for finding interest in this topic, allowing me the freedom to write my doctoral dissertation on this subject. I would like to thank him for his helpful assistance throughout this work. I am also indebted to Prof. Dr. Walter Müller, from the Mannheim Centre for European Social Research, who kindly accepted to be my second supervisor.

This work has been made possible through the financial support of the Thyssen Foundation within the framework of the project "Qualifikation und Arbeitsmarkterfolg in Deutschland und Frankreich – Der Einfluss von bildungs- und familienpolitischen Maßnahmen im Vergleich" which I gratefully acknowledge. Moreover, I would not have been able to do this piece of research without Dr. Ali Skalli, from the University Panthéon-Assas in Paris, who accepted me as an associate researcher at his institute and gave me access to the French data.

Additionally, I would like to thank my colleagues from the Centre for European Economic Research (ZEW), in particular Prof. Dr. François Laisney who gave me precious advice on econometrics, Frank Reize for a fruitful exchange of ideas on methodological matters as well as Peter Jacobebbinghaus who always patiently discussed the most various issues with me. The nice atmosphere at the ZEW's Department of Labour Markets, Human Resources and Social Policy made me enjoy doing research and I would like to express my gratitude to all my colleagues from this department for the pleasant and constructive working environment.

Last but not least, I would like to thank my husband Bernd Lauer for following all the tiniest developments in my dissertation, the forward as well as the backward steps, with affection and support.

Mannheim, September 2004 Charlotte Lauer

Contents

1 Introduction

In Germany, the publication of the results of the latest PISA (Programme for International Student Assessment) study (OECD 2002) caused a genuine shock in public opinion and among policy makers. Indeed, German students performed significantly below OECD average in all three areas tested (mathematical, reading and scientific literacy) and in particular much worse than their European neighbours. For example, though French students were far from being brilliant at PISA, they performed significantly better than their German counterparts. Not only were the average results of German students comparatively poor, but they were also particularly strongly dispersed. The PISA results triggered an intense discussion on the equity and the efficiency of the German education system, on the causes and consequences of the poor educational performance. A major concern is the particular tightness of the link observed between the German students' PISA achievement and their social background compared to other countries. Because educational achievement conditions a larger number of outcomes in subsequent life, the strong link between education and social origin perpetuates existing economic and social inequalities across generations. The weaknesses observed today with respect to the level and the distribution of education will have far-reaching implications, not only for the cohorts observed presently but also for the following generations. Thus, it is not surprising that Germany was particularly concerned about the poor performance of its youths at PISA.

Potential causes of the poor German achievement and of its high dispersion at PISA have been seen in specific features of the German education system. For instance, as a rule, German pupils are streamed into different types of secondary schools according to their learning ability at a very early stage in their educational career, at the end of primary schooling, when the influence of the parental background is supposed to be stronger than at later stages. This early segregation is suspected to produce more social inequalities than a more egalitarian system such as the French one, where the first streaming of pupils takes place later on in the educational process and all pupils attend a single structure after primary school. Moreover, the late age of school start in

Germany as well as the half-day school model, as opposed to full-day school systems such as that prevailing in France for example, are typically mentioned as potential reasons for the comparatively poor educational achievement of German youths. Thus, France provides a good benchmark for comparison with Germany with respect to educational outcomes since its education system differs precisely in the features that are thought to be at the origin of the German PISA debacle.

The PISA tests provide a snapshot view of specific cognitive skills of youths at a given point in the educational process. In order to have a comprehensive measure of all the educational skills acquired throughout initial education, however, one should examine educational achievement after initial education has been completed and consider all types of skills acquired, not only literacy in three general subjects. Educational credentials should certify the skills acquired within the education system. Therefore, they provide a measure of the educational knowledge and skills possessed by the individual. Thus, the distribution of educational credentials obtained in the population gives an overview of the distribution of knowledge and skills produced by the education system and available to the country.

It is of particular interest for a country to assess its strengths and weaknesses with respect to the educational status of its population. As a matter of fact, within the course of economic development, qualifications of individuals have gained increasing importance as a production factor. In modern economies, firms' competitiveness depends largely on their innovation capacity and their ability to find a highly qualified workforce at an acceptable price. The increasing role for growth of what is called "human capital" in economic theory, in analogy to physical capital, has been well documented in the literature[1]. The output is seen as a function, beside other inputs, of the stock of human capital. The latter includes all the knowledge, skills and aptitudes relevant to production. A high level of human capital in the population is assumed to have a permanent effect on growth in so far as it favours more intensive research and development and a faster rate of technological progress[2].

Beyond mere economic reasons, a population with a high level of human capital has further advantages. Indeed, human capital is known to have a positive impact on a wide range of other outcomes. Because it favours the employability of individuals, it makes them less likely to have to rely on social solidarity or to fall into social exclusion. Though the causality is less directly assessable, societies with a high level of human capital are known to have a lower incidence of criminality or other social problems, a better health level, are more likely to have democracies and political stability. The initial educational achievement undoubtedly represents the essential component of individuals' overall human capital, even though it is complemented in

[1] See the detailed overview of the endogenous growth theory in Aghion and Howitt (1998).

[2] See among others Romer (1990).

the course of life by knowledge and skills acquired through work experience, on-the-job training or any other informal learning. Thus, it is hardly surprising that policy makers aim to foster education and that they pay particular attention to its distribution and its impact on various outcomes.

Public authorities intervene in various ways on education issues. They set the institutional design of the education system, decide on the organisation of educational careers, on subjects to be taught and on certification of skills. Moreover, they intervene by subsidising education, investing public resources in education, e.g. for teachers, material or real estate. From an economic point of view, public involvement is only required to the extent that private educational efforts would lead to sub-optimal outcomes, i.e. to the extent that there are market imperfections. There are some theoretical arguments why this should be the case for the educational good. A first argument relates to the presence of positive externalities, such as the positive effects of a highly educated society in terms of criminality, health etc. Individuals know that acquiring skills through education will improve their prospects in various aspects of life. However, because they do not directly reap the whole benefit of it due to the presence of positive externalities, they will tend to under-invest in their education compared to the socially optimal level of investment. Another argument relates to capital market imperfections. As e.g. Kodde (1988) argues, commercial institutions are likely to consider human capital to be a risky, nonliquid and intangible asset. As a consequence, in general, higher loans can only be obtained against higher borrowing rates. Besides, individuals may have different access to financial resources, and for some more than for other individuals, funds may be rationed at specific levels. In the presence of capital market imperfections, individuals of poorer background might not be able to invest in the optimal amount of education. To sum up, left to the mere market forces, individuals would tend to under-invest in their education, especially those individuals facing higher credit constraints.

This explains why countries generally invest a substantial proportion of their national resources in education. As a whole, OECD countries spent some 5.2 percent of their collective GDP on educational institutions in 2000 (OECD 2003). Germany spends somewhat less on education than in the OECD on average with about 4.5 percent of its GDP, while French expenditure on education is slightly above average, with about 5.8 percent of its GDP. The bulk of the educational expenditure stems from public funds. The share of public funds in total educational expenditure amounted to about 88.4 percent in 2000 on average in OECD countries, 81.1 percent in Germany and even 92.1 percent in France (OECD 2003). As a result, educational expenditure represents a considerable part of total public expenditure (mean of OECD countries in 2000: 13.0 percent, Germany: 9.9 percent, France: 11.4 percent, OECD 2003).

Such huge investments are an invitation for researchers to assess the performance of the education systems with respects to the aims pursued. This is what this study aims at for France and Germany, examining the situation in the past few decades. To be specific, the German side of the study focuses on the Western part of Germany. This is because East Germany would require a specific analysis since a large proportion of East Germans were educated and worked under the old regime under very different conditions. Moreover, throughout the 1990s, the economic conditions in the East remained very different from the West and influenced by the old system. In the remainder of the analysis, Germany therefore refers to West Germany.

France and Germany pursue similar objectives as far as education is concerned. They both strive to raise the level of education while reducing social inequalities in educational opportunities. Moreover, they both aim at endowing pupils with knowledge and skills that make them able to find a job on the labour market. Education is an essential determinant of employment prospects and these condition to a large extent social integration and success in life. Therefore, beyond the interest of education per se, it is one of the essential tasks of the education system to endow youths with qualifications that make them apt to integrate successfully into the labour market. In this respect, France and Germany are submitted to similar constraints. They share a similar level of economic development, are respectively the main competitor of the other and are both confronted with increasing international competition and rapid technological change. They both experience difficulties in adapting their workforce to the requirements of a changing economic environment, which is expressed in high unemployment rates, especially among the least qualified. In this context, it should be of interest to assess how efficient either country is in producing for its population educational skills that are relevant to the labour market.

Though the educational objectives as well as the constraints on the education system are common to France and Germany, the means employed to achieve these objectives and to adapt to the new environment differ largely. French and German policy makers have chosen different options for the organisation of their education system, the content of the education provided and the certification of cognitive skills. The first step of this study will therefore be to analyse the priorities in the production of education and in particular the nature of the qualifications produced by it and certified by the credentials provided by the education system. This is the object of chapter 2. The objective behind this exercise is to identify different aspects of educational policy and institutions that might affect the outcomes examined in the subsequent analyses. In other words, the aim is to prepare and provide elements of explanation for the analysis of the strengths and weaknesses in education policy and institutions in relation to the goals mentioned above. Moreover, from a practical point of view, this first step aims to construct a scale of educational attainment suited to the empirical comparison between France and Germany that will be undertaken in the subsequent analyses.

Based on the thorough understanding gained in chapter 2 on the nature of educational attainment as certified by the educational credentials in France and Germany, the distribution of educational attainment in either country will be examined in detail in chapter 3. In this chapter, evidence will be provided on how these competing countries stand with respect to this essential asset of their economy and society. Hereby, the focus is laid on comparing the level of education attained and its development over time, but also on the nature and the extent of social inequalities. In particular, it will be examined how strongly educational achievement depends on family background and gender, since, as has been argued above, inequalities in educational achievement have repercussions on a variety of outcomes in subsequent life. A specific modelling framework has been developed for this purpose, the aim being to provide an economic rationale to the empirical analysis of educational attainment. Moreover, the model allows us to estimate the impact of background factors at different stages of the educational career. In this way, some conclusions will be drawn on the nature and the extent of social inequalities at different stages of the educational process in France and Germany.

The rest of the study deals with the impact of the level of education attained on individual labour market success. Looking at the labour market outcomes of education is expected to provide some insights into the relative efficiency of the French and the German education systems as providers of qualifications to be used productively on the labour market. Observing the patterns prevailing both within and across countries makes it possible to disclose similarities and differences and thus to pinpoint the relationship between education and selected labour market outcomes. Using a differentiated measure of educational attainment, one can assess how different types and levels of general and vocational education are valued on the labour market. Comparing the relative labour market value of the various qualifications helps to characterise the link between education and success on the labour market as well as identifying some strengths and weaknesses in the respective education systems.

To be more specific, chapter 4 is concerned with the link between education and unemployment risk. The more "successful" qualifications are those which best protect against the unemployment risk. The concept of unemployment risk, however, is complex and dynamic in nature. People become unemployed at a certain point in time and after a certain period, they leave unemployment for another labour force state. This might never happen, happen once or several times in the working career. Thus, the unemployment problem can be viewed in terms of transition(s) into and out of unemployment. In this study, the various aspects of the dynamics of unemployment and the role of education on each component will be examined. The analysis distinguishes between the risk of entering unemployment, the risk of remaining in unemployment and the risk of recurrence of unemployment. Different types and levels of education might affect these dimensions of the unemployment problem in a different way. The starting point of this analysis will be a discrete time hazard rate model with competing risks and nonparametric unobserved heterogeneity, where the impact of education on the hazard rate into and out of unemployment is estimated. Based on these results, further computations will be performed to estimate the impact of education on the duration of unemployment episodes, on the occurrence of repeated unemployment and on the cumulated unemployment risk in a given period. Furthermore, the degree of concentration of the unemployment problem on certain qualification groups will be examined.

After having analysed whether individuals find a productive use for the qualifications they acquired within the education system, the question arises how "good" this employment is. The earnings provide a quantitative indicator of the labour market value of qualifications. Therefore, chapter 5 analyses the relationship between education and earnings. To be more specific, this chapter aims to assess the labour market value of different types and levels of education by estimating the additional earnings that can be expected from the attainment of a specific education level compared to a reference education level, everything else being kept constant. Hereby, not only the expected level of earnings will be considered, but also their dispersion. Indeed, the risk associated with the educational investment not only consists of the unemployment risk examined in chapter 4, but also of an earnings risk. The higher the dispersion of earnings to be expected from the completion of a certain education level, the riskier the investment. Based on estimates from an earnings equation with correction for selectivity and multiplicative heteroscedasticity, a so-called average earnings premium will be computed for various possible qualifications. This measures the average labour market value of qualifications if everything else remains constant. Moreover, the residual earnings dispersion, i.e. the variance of earnings that is unexplained by the explanatory factors, will be allowed to vary across education groups and gender. This way, one can estimate not only how much additional earnings can be expected from the completion of a higher level of education, but also how this affects the predictability of earnings, measured by the residual earnings variance.

Overall, this research aims at carrying out an in-depth analysis of the distribution of educational attainment and its consequences in terms of individual labour market outcomes. The extent and the nature of gender differences will be carefully examined throughout all partial analyses. The comparison of France and Germany, beyond its interest per se, makes it possible to identify some strengths and weaknesses with respect to the distribution of the human capital asset in two competing countries. Moreover, it allows us to draw some conclusions with respect to the relative efficiency of the French and German education systems as providers of qualifications to be used in the labour market. Looking at what functions better in another country should help to improve the own system.

2

The French and the German education systems

To be able to compare the distribution of educational attainment and its labour market outcomes in two countries, one needs to define an adequate and comparable measure of educational outcomes for both countries. All the difficulty consists in finding a measure for educational attainment which, on the one hand, accounts for the relevant hierarchies of credentials within each country while, on the other hand, being suited to highlight similarities and differences across countries. This necessitates a good understanding of the logic underlying the education systems, in particular with respect to the organisation of the education systems and the nature of the skills certified by the credentials delivered by the education system. This is why the first step of this chapter consists in providing a detailed description of the French and the German education systems, with a view to avoiding misinterpretations due to insufficient knowledge of the institutions. Building on this knowledge on the institutional context, the second step will seek to elaborate a comparative scale of educational attainment, with the practical imperative of being usable for empirical analyses on the basis of the data sets commonly available for research, and in particular of those used within the framework of the present research.

The chapter is organised as follows. Section 2.1 gives a brief overview of the administration of the education system, focussing on the distribution of competencies across the various actors and on funding aspects. Then, section 2.2 outlines in a comparative manner the essential features of the education system as it is organised in France and in Germany. Thereby, the organisation of the successive stages within the educational career are presented in detail. Based on this knowledge, a comparative and practically implementable typology of educational attainment will be elaborated and presented in section 2.3. This typology of educational attainment will be used in the subsequent chapters.

The description of the institutional features of the education systems is based on information drawn from diverse sources. The main source is the information provided by the organisation Eurydice (http://www.eurydice.org/), a European information network that publishes analyses of the education systems in Europe as well as specific studies on subjects of European interest related to education (see for instance Eurydice/Cedefop 1995 or European Communities 2002). A large part of this information is available online, in particular through Eurybase, the online database of Eurydice. This was supplemented by information from the European Commission (see, for the field of higher education, European Communities 1998), from the national ministries for education (http://www.bmbf.de/ for Germany and http://www.education.gouv.fr/ for France) as well as from various publications (essentially Rothe 1995; Moebus and Verdier 1997; Brauns, Müller and Steinmann 1997).

2.1 Administration of the education system

France and Germany differ a lot with respect to the distribution of responsibilities for educational matters. Broadly speaking, a very centralised education system in France may be opposed to a decentralised education system in Germany.

2.1.1 Distribution of responsibilities

Germany

The German education system is characterised by the federal structure of the Federal Republic of Germany, which counts sixteen *Länder* (federal states)[1], and about 16,000 towns. Each *Land* has its own constitution and Government. The Basic Law *(Grundgesetz)* stipulates that legislative powers basically fall to the *Länder*, unless the Basic Law confers them explicitly to the Federation *(Bund)*. Thus, education policy is primarily the responsibility of the *Länder*.

The Federal Government's responsibilities in educational matters include essentially the regulation of financial assistance for pupils and students, the promotion of research, the regulation of distance-learning courses and the passing of framework legislation on the general principles of higher education (*Hochschulrahmengesetz*). The Federal Government also provides the legal provisions for civil service employment (e.g. for teachers and professors). The *Länder* make the legal provisions set at the federal level more concrete by creating and implementing the relevant *Land* legislation.

The Basic Law also sets the framework for the cooperation between the Federation and the *Länder* in educational matters, which is necessary to guarantee a uniform fundamental structure of the school system in Germany. This cooperation takes place within the framework of the *Bund-Länder* Commission for Educational Planning and Research Promotion (*Bund-Länder-Kommission für Bildungsplanung und Forschungsförderung, BLK*), in which

[1] Five *Länder* were re-introduced after German unification in 1990.

the Federal Government and the governments of the *Länder* are represented. Furthermore, the *Länder* governments also cooperate among themselves within the framework of the Standing Conference of the *Länder* Ministers of Education and Cultural Affairs (*Ständige Kultusministerkonferenz*, KMK). The *Länder* have agreed upon, among other things, the designation and organisation of the various types of educational institutions and the mutual recognition of qualifications in all *Länder*.

In the segment of pre-primary education, about 70 percent of all institutions are run by the voluntary bodies of the youth services, mainly churches and welfare services, while the remaining 30 percent are administered by the towns. As far as primary and secondary education are concerned, the authority of the *Länder* extends not only to the organisation of the schools themselves, but also to the definition of teaching objectives and curricula and to the supervision of teachers. As a rule, higher education is provided by public institutions under the authority of the *Länder*. However, the higher education institutions have administrative autonomy in the limits of legal provisions. This autonomy includes both academic matters, such as the establishments of curricula, and administrative matters such as personnel, economic, budgetary and financial administration.

The responsibility for initial vocational training is shared by the *Länder* and the Federation. While the Federation is responsible for the regulation of in-company vocational training, the *Länder* are responsible for vocational schools and define among other things the curricula. The chambers (of commerce and industry, of agriculture etc.) control the practical implementation of national regulations in companies providing vocational training. All actors cooperate within the framework of the so-called "dual" education system.

France

The French education system is characterised by its high degree of centralisation, even though the process of decentralisation[2], initiated in 1982, has somewhat altered the distribution of responsibilities also in educational matters. Metropolitan France (i.e. without overseas *départements*) is composed of 22 regions, each of which containing two to eight *départements*, and counts about 36,000 towns.

Education policy remains primarily the responsibility of the central State. Thus, the Government is responsible for the definition and the implementation of education policy in accordance with the Constitution. The State defines educational guidelines, curricula and contents of examinations, the latter having national validity. Furthermore, it is responsible for the recruitment, the training, the administration and the salaries of teaching and administrative staff and is directly responsible for all matters concerning tertiary education as well as for initial vocational training.

[2] Decentralisation consists in transferring to regional authorities certain responsibilities which were previously exerted by the State.

For certain specific fields of education policy, however, regional and local authorities have been vested with new responsibilities. Thus, each level of authority is now responsible for a particular level of education: the regions are responsible for building and maintaining the *Lycées* as well as for specialised institutions, and have important powers regarding vocational training; the *départements* are responsible for building and maintaining *Collèges* (lower secondary schools) as well as for the provision of school transport; and the towns are responsible for building and maintaining pre-primary and primary schools.

Since 1985, the autonomy of *Collèges* and *Lycées* in teaching and educational matters has been recognised. However, this autonomy relates only to the definition of a specific school plan by which national objectives and curricula are to be implemented, taking into account the characteristics of the local socio-economic environment. Also universities have been granted administrative and academic autonomy since 1984, but this autonomy only gained a real meaning in 1989, when a contractual policy between the State and the higher education institutions[3] replaced the traditional annual grants of resources by the central administration.

2.1.2 Funding of education

Germany

Almost all schools – general, vocational and of higher education – are public institutions. Teachers at public schools are usually civil servants[4]. In principle, attendance at all public schools is free of charge. Schools run by voluntary bodies are also subject to state supervision and are supported financially by the *Länder* or the towns. For their school-leaving degrees to be recognised, they must comply with the relevant *Land* regulations concerning courses taught, teacher qualifications and examinations. Higher education is mostly free of charge. Only a low "social contribution" *(Sozialbeitrag)* or "contribution to the student administration" *(Studentenwerksbeitrag)* is charged for the use of social facilities. Despite the allocation of major public subsidies to *Kindergärten*, and of church tax receipts in the case of church-run *Kindergärten*,

[3] Each tertiary education institution defines a four-year development plan which leads to the negotiation and signature of a contract obliging the State to grant the required resources for the four-year period.

[4] The majority of teachers in the *Länder* in the former German Democratic Republic (GDR) currently hold the status of salaried employees. The KMK reached an agreement in May 1993 on the "Recognition of Teacher Training Courses in the former GDR and their Assignment to Conventional Career Paths" in order to clarify the salary groups of teachers who received their training in the former GDR. The agreement has helped to ensure that regulations are drawn up under which east German teaching staff can obtain civil servant status and be integrated into the salary structure of the *Länder* in Western Germany.

the parents have to pay fees for pre-primary institutions, which may depend on their income. Pupils in general and vocational education (from the tenth school year on) may obtain financial assistance in the form of a grant depending on parental income. Students who have few other means are entitled to receive financial assistance under the terms of the Federal Training Assistance (*Bundesausbildungsförderungsgesetz*, in brief BAFöG) partly in the form of an interest-free loan, partly as a grant.

France

The State covers the salaries of teaching and administrative staff at all levels of the education system. However, the local authorities are now responsible for investment and operational expenditure in their respective field of responsibility. Since the end of the 19th century, the State has guaranteed the availability of "compulsory, free and secular" public education. Nevertheless, private education is also allowed and present. Public education covers more than 80 percent of pupils up to upper secondary school. The bulk of private education is composed of Catholic institutions which signed a contract with the State. In so doing, these institutions are committed to the timetables and curricula applied in public education and are subject to State supervision. The school fees charged by private institutions vary from school to school and may depend on parental income. The cost of apprenticeship is covered from two sources: from an apprenticeship tax equivalent to 0.5 percent of the gross annual salary costs of companies[5] and from the regional apprenticeship fund. The latter is funded by state transfers and by the regional council's own resources. The regions also contribute to the financing of universities together with the State. Universities only charge low registration fees, but in other tertiary level public or private institutions, fees may be higher. Students may receive financial assistance in the form of grants provided on the basis of social criteria or on the basis of the institutions' own criteria as well as interest-free loans.

2.2 Organisation of the educational career

In France, education is compulsory from age 6 to age 16, i.e. for 10 years. Note that education and not school attendance is compulsory in France. In Germany, school attendance is compulsory for all children older than 6 for 9 years of full-time general education and 3 years of part-time education in vocational training schools for those pupils not willing to pursue further general or vocational full-time education after the end of compulsory general education. In the French education system, as a rule, all pupils follow a common core curriculum throughout primary and lower secondary education. A differentiation of educational tracks appears at the upper secondary level. By

[5] The liberal and agricultural professions are exempted from this requirement.

contrast, in Germany, differentiation already takes place after primary education (at age 10), when pupils are directed into different kinds of secondary schools according to their abilities.

The educational career can be broken down into a certain number of sequential stages: pre-primary education, primary education, secondary education and tertiary education. Figures 2.1 and 2.2 provide a synthetic overview of the education systems in both countries, which will be developed in the following sections.

2.2.1 Pre-primary and primary education

Germany

In Germany, the *Kindergarten* is the traditional form of pre-school provision for children aged between 3 and 6. This service does not come under an educational jurisdiction but under the authority of social services for children and young persons. Therefore, children in those institutions are looked after by trained educational and auxiliary staff, which are not teachers but educators. Beside *Kindergärten*, children over five may attend pre-school classes (*Vorschulen*) at primary schools, which aim to encourage children to learn by playing. Attendance at pre-school institutions takes place on a voluntary basis. As a rule, children attending pre-school institutions are not expected to achieve any specific level of intellectual attainment, even in the pre-school classes. The function of *Kindergärten* rather consists in the care and the general up-bringing of the child as well as the inculcation of basic social and behavioural rules.

Primary education is provided at primary schools (*Grundschulen*) and covers 4 years (6 years in Berlin and Brandenburg), generally on a half-day basis. It is common for all children. The *Grundschule* lays the foundations for secondary education and focusses on the acquisition of reading, writing and arithmetic skills.

France

In France, contrary to Germany, nursery schools (*écoles maternelles*) are an integral part of the education system. The teachers in nursery schools have the same qualifications as the primary school teachers. Children between the ages of 2 and 6 may attend the nursery schools, and in practice, almost all children aged 3 to 6 do so[6]. In order to provide a smooth transition from the pre-primary to the primary level, the upper class of the nursery school is part of the basic learning cycle which continues into the first two years of

[6] In the school year 1999/2000, about 35 percent of the children aged 2 and 100 percent of children aged 3 to 6 attended a (full-day) nursery school in France. As a comparison, only 56 percent of children aged 3 to 4, 83 percent of children aged 4 to 5 and 90 percent of children aged 5 to 6 did so in Germany (Eurybase 2003).

Fig. 2.1. The German education system

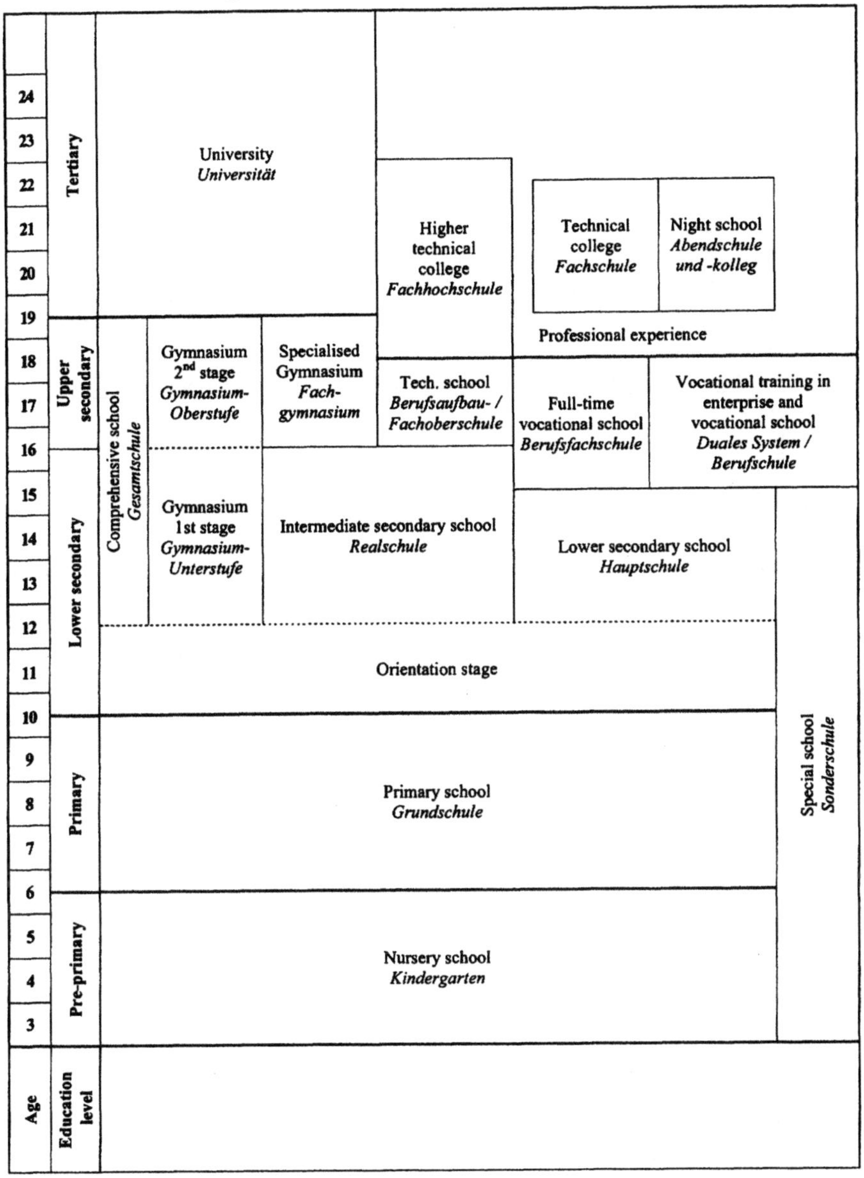

Fig. 2.2. The French education system

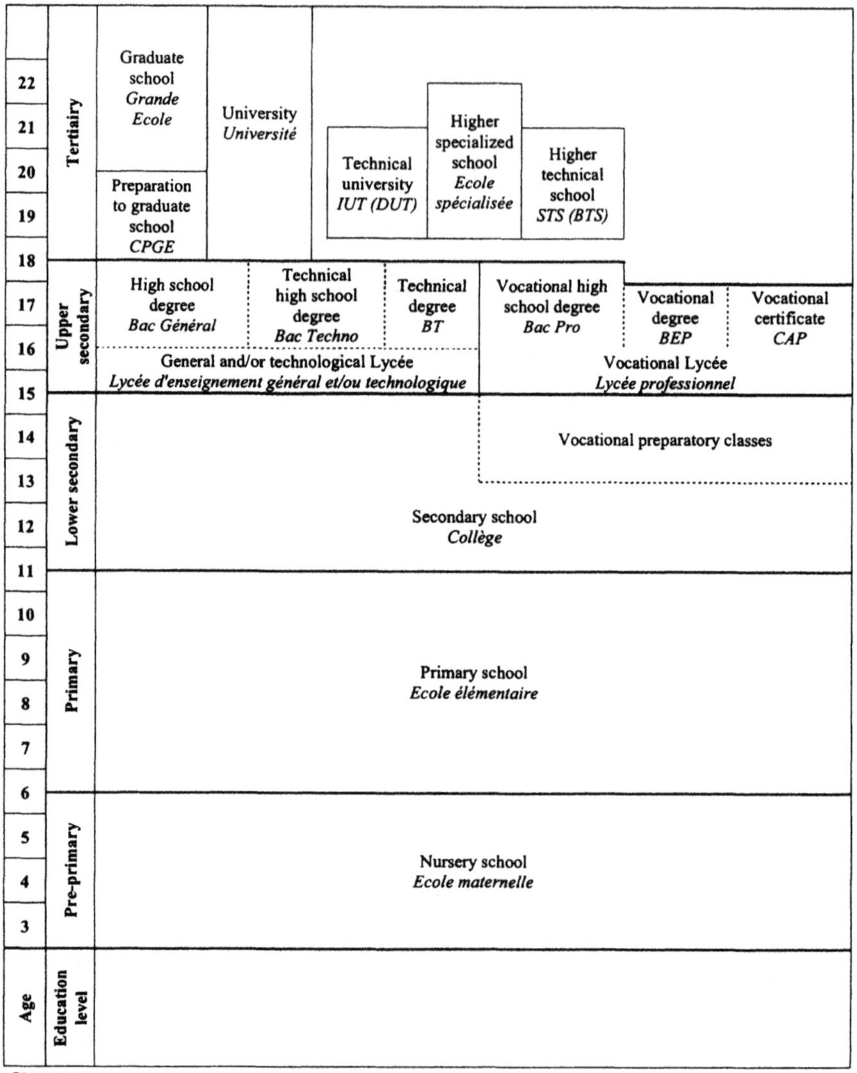

Glossary:

CPGE: Classe Préparatoire aux Grandes Ecoles
IUT / DUT: Institut / Diplôme Universitaire Technologique
STS / BTS: Section / Brevet de Techniciens Supérieurs
Bac Général: Baccalauréat Général
Bac Techno: Baccalauréat Technologique
Bac Pro: Baccalauréat Professionnel
BT: Brevet de Technicien
BEP: Brevet d'Etudes Professionnelles
CAP: Certificat d'Aptitude Professionnelle, part-time or full-time

primary education. These nursery schools aim at contributing to the child's development, but also prepare them for primary school. Therefore, there exists a specific curriculum for nursery education and teachers decide on the basis of the child's achievement whether to introduce him or her into the primary level.

Primary education is common for all children and spans 5 years. It is organised in two cycles: the basic learning cycle (*cycle des apprentissages fondamentaux*), which begins in the upper classes of nursery schools and continues for two years at the primary level, and the consolidation cycle (*cycle d'approfondissement*). The skills to be acquired are defined for each cycle. These include both disciplinary and general skills and a special emphasis is laid on the acquisition of language skills. The teaching load is significantly heavier in France than in Germany[7]. Until 1989, pupils could take the CEP (*Certificat d'Etudes Primaires*) examination at the end of primary education and receive the certificate of the same name if successful.

2.2.2 Secondary education

2.2.2.1 Lower secondary education

Germany

After primary education, pupils are directed into different types of secondary schools according to their abilities. In the 5th and the 6th years, regardless of the school type attended, there is a phase of observation and orientation towards a further choice of educational path. In some *Länder*, this orientation stage is established as a separate stage, independent of the type of school attended. From the 7th year onwards, the school types are increasingly differentiated in terms of courses offered and requirements according to the school-leaving certificates aimed at. In most *Länder*, the different school types are:

- the *Hauptschule* (lower secondary school), which provides pupils with a fundamental general education. It generally comprises 5 years (6 in some *Länder*). After obtaining their school-leaving certificate (*Hauptschulabschluss*), pupils may pursue vocational training or, for particularly able pupils, transfer to the *Realschule* to pursue general education;
- the *Realschule* (intermediate secondary school), which offers pupils an intermediate general education. It generally covers the 5th to the 10th grade (6 years), and after obtaining their school-leaving certificate (*Realschulabschluss* or *Mittlerer Schulabschluss*), pupils may pursue vocational

[7] In 1997/98, the annual teaching load for a seven-year-old pupil amounted to 615 hours in Germany compared to 846 in France, and for a ten-year-old pupil 713 hours in Germany compared to 846 in France (European Communities 2002).

studies or transfer to school types providing a higher education entrance certificate like the *Gymnasium* or the *Fachoberschule*;

- the *Gymnasium* (higher secondary school), which provides intensified general education and is designed to lead to a qualification entitling to pursue tertiary level studies (*Abitur*). The first stage of *Gymnasium* studies corresponding to lower secondary education covers the 5th to the 10th grade (6 years). At the end of the 6th year of *Gymnasium*, pupils who have achieved at least pass marks in all subjects are promoted to the upper level of *Gymnasium*;
- the *Gesamtschule* (comprehensive school), which combines (cooperative type) or merges (integrative type) the various forms of lower secondary education mentioned previously. In the *Gesamtschulen* of the cooperative type, pupils are streamed according to the final school-leaving certificate aimed at, whereas *Gesamtschulen* of the integrative type form one single entity where children are streamed according to their ability level in each subject.

In recent years, some *Länder* have introduced new types of schools designed by different names depending on the *Land* (*Mittelschule, Sekundarschule, Regelschule, Regionale Schule, Integrierte Haupt- und Realschule* etc.). These new schools combine the educational paths of the *Hauptschule* and the *Realschule*. Moreover, special education is offered to children with learning disabilities or with some other physical or mental handicap in so-called *Sonderschulen* (special schools).

The basic idea of the German system is to offer pupils a basic general education adapted to their needs and aptitudes. Under certain conditions, pupils may pass from one branch to another. For instance, not only pupils who have followed a *Gymnasium*-type course may be entitled to proceed to the upper level of *Gymnasium*. The entrance requirement may also be obtained by way of a *Realschulabschluss* of a certain merit or via qualifications from *Berufsaufbauschulen* (vocational extension schools), *Berufsfachschulen* (full-time vocational schools) or *Fachschulen* (technical schools). However, in practice, upward mobility is rather limited.

France

After primary education, as a rule, French pupils all attend a single structure, the *Collège*[8]. Education in *Collège* spans over 4 years and is subdivided into

[8] The *Collège unique* has been introduced by the Haby Law in 1975. Before this date, secondary education was divided – analogously to the German system – into three branches: the *Lycée* section, leading to the maturity certificate, the *Collège* section leading to short cycle secondary education and the *transition* section providing basic general education. The unification of the three branches at the lower secondary level followed two objectives: raising the general education level of the population and promoting social democratisation, the three-tiered system being viewed as too strictly segregated and unfavourable to poorer social groups.

two cycles: the observation cycle (1st and 2nd year) and the guidance cycle (3rd and 4th year). A national certificate (*Brevet National* or *Brevet d'Etudes du Premier Cycle*, BEPC) is awarded at the end of *Collège*, but pupils move up to the next level regardless of whether they pass or fail the BEPC. People who have failed the BEPC may request the DFEO (*Diplôme de Fin d'Etudes Obligatoires*) which attests that they have completed compulsory schooling.

At the end of the 2nd *Collège* year, pupils with great learning difficulties may be placed in smaller 3rd year classes (*classe d'integration*) which offer special assistance and take the place of a pre-vocational class. At the end of the 3rd *Collège* year, pupils may also choose a 4th year class leading to the vocational branch. Since 1992, this class has been gradually replacing the pre-apprenticeship class. Originally set up in vocational *Lycées*, the pre-vocational branch in the 3rd and 4th year has been progressively incorporated into the *Collèges* since 1990. At the end of *Collège*, i.e. after 4 years of lower secondary education, pupils are directed towards one of the three branches of upper secondary education: the general track, the technological track or the vocational track.

2.2.2.2 Upper general or technical secondary education

In both countries, one can distinguish at the upper secondary level between general and technical education.

Germany

General education at the upper secondary level is provided in the upper classes of the *Gymnasium* (*gymnasiale Oberstufe*) and is usually divided into a one-year introductory phase and a two-year qualification phase. Pupils study subjects in three areas: i) languages, literature and arts, ii) social sciences and mathematics, and iii) natural and technical sciences. At the end of the 3 years of *Gymnasium*, pupils take the *Abitur* examination. Though this examination is organised at the level of *Länder*, the *Länder* have largely standardised the requirements of the examinations and agreed upon uniform criteria for a large number of subjects, so that the *Abitur* is recognised throughout all of Germany. Pupils who pass the *Abitur* receive a certificate which grants access to any branch of higher education (called *allgemeine Hochschulreife*, meaning general higher education entrance qualification). The assessment is partly based on a continuous assessment of the last two years of *Gymnasium*, and partly on the results of the *Abitur* examination.

Technical education at the upper secondary level can be received at technical or specialised *Gymnasien*[9], which have no classes at the lower secondary level. Like in the general *Gymnasium*, the study course spans 3 years, but it emphasises career-oriented subjects, such as business and engineering. To be

[9] They are called *Berufliches Gymnasium* or *Fachgymnasium* depending on the *Land*.

admitted, a pupil must have qualified for the upper classes of general *Gymnasium*[10]. The specialised subjects may be chosen in place of general subjects for the *Abitur* examination. Pupils who pass the examination qualify for entry to any type of tertiary education (*allgemeine Hochschulreife*). In some *Länder*, it is possible to obtain at *Fachgymnasien* a double qualification, i.e. the right to pursue higher education and a vocational qualification. In that case, the courses take 4 years and involve two separate examinations for the vocational qualification and for the *Abitur*.

France

General or technological *Lycées* prepare pupils in 3 years for the *Baccalauréat*, a nationally centralised examination which entitles them to enter higher education. If the pupils fail this examination, they may request a secondary school leaving certificate which does not entitle them to pursue tertiary level studies (*Certificat de Fin d'Etudes Secondaires*, CFES). No continuous assessment enters the *Baccalauréat* results. The first year at the *Lycée* offers a common core curriculum followed by all pupils and is essential for pupil's educational orientation. Depending on preferences and abilities, the pupil chooses the type of courses he or she will attend in the following two years in accordance with the type of *Baccalauréat* aimed at. Thus, at the end of the first year in the *Lycée*, pupils may be directed to:

- 3 types of general *Baccalauréat* (*Bac Général*): L (literary), ES (economic and social) and S (scientific);
- 6 types of technological *Baccalauréat* (*Bac Techno* or BTn): STT (tertiary sciences and technologies), STI (industrial sciences and technologies), STL (laboratory sciences and technologies), SMS (medical and social sciences) and in the agricultural field STAE (agricultural and environmental sciences and technologies) or STPA (farm-produce industry sciences and technologies);
- the technical certificate (*brevet de technicien*, BT). This certificate provides a qualification as a technician specialised in a specific area, but is not really of the same standard as the *Baccalauréat*. Holders of the *brevet de technicien* can either enter employment in their specific area of specialisation or continue their studies, but only at the lower tertiary level (primarily in the higher technical classes STS or in a university institute of technology IUT, see below).

[10] The qualification is obtained either through a successfully completed lower secondary stage of *Gymnasium* or through a *Realschule* degree of a good level.

2.2.3 Initial vocational qualification

2.2.3.1 Part-time vocational tracks

Germany

Following full-time compulsory education, most young people in Germany pursue vocational education and training courses, mainly through the so-called "dual" system, the German apprenticeship training system. This training system is referred to as dual because it is carried out at two different places, namely at a vocational school (*Berufsschule*) and at a firm. Training is provided within the framework of a civil-law contract between a company and the young person. The contract covers all important aspects of the training, like the duration of the training (generally about three years), the skill profile of the chosen occupation, the level of the basic allowance granted to the trainee, the amount of time devoted to training in the company and to learning at the *Berufsschule* etc. Thus, the contract includes both the duty of the trainee to learn, in the workplace and at the *Berufsschule*, and the duty of the business to provide training.

The *Berufsschule* is not only attended by apprentices, but also by those pupils who have left general education but are still required to attend compulsory education at least on a part-time basis. The *Berufsschule* provides pupils with general and vocational education, paying special attention to meet the requirements of vocational training. Pupils have the possibility to receive basic vocational training in a separate first stage, either in the form of a year's full-time schooling or through a dual system arrangement (*Berufsgrundbildungsjahr*).

Pupils successfully passing the final examination receive a leaving certificate which proves that they have achieved the objectives of the dual training both in the workplace and at the *Berufsschule*. This certificate entitles them to admission to advanced vocational training, for example at a *Fachschule*, or enables them to work immediately as a qualified employee or worker in one of the many state-recognised occupations for which formal training is required[11].

France

Part-time vocational training (*formation en alternance*) is not the rule in France and has been developed as a measure against the particularly high youth unemployment. Thus, it is primarily an instrument of employment policy rather than of education policy and the aim is to facilitate integration in the labour market. Part-time initial vocational education combines theoretical training with practical training in a company. Like in Germany, the young person in part-time training receives a salary, the level of which depends on

[11] There exist about 370 recognised occupations, spanning almost all areas of the economy.

the type of contract, age and seniority. The main form of part-time vocational education is the apprenticeship, a special route of initial vocational training introduced in 1971[12], while the other training measures for young people between 16 and 25 have been developed since 1983 and are based on a concept of continuous training:

- The apprenticeship training (*apprentissage*)

  The apprenticeship training is based on an employment contract between a company and a young person (less than 26 years old). It combines the acquisition of know-how in a company with theoretical education in an apprenticeship training centre (*Centre de Formation des Apprentis*, CFA) with a view to acquiring a vocational degree of the upper secondary or tertiary education level. The duration of the apprenticeship ranges from one to three years. Employers are required to provide apprentices with practical training and to enrol them in a CFA providing instruction corresponding to the qualification called for in the contract. The great majority of apprentices are younger than 19, have a low level of qualification and prepare for a vocational certificate of the CAP/BEP type (about three quarters of the apprentices). However, the share of *Baccalauréat* holders undergoing an apprenticeship while preparing for a tertiary level degree (like a BTS, see below) is increasing.
  The successive governments created a large series of part-time training measures for 16-25-year-olds which aimed at facilitating the integration of young persons into working life while providing a qualification. The main types of integration contracts are the following:

- The guidance contract (*contrat d'orientation*)

  This training is offered to people aged up to 21 years who do not hold a technical or vocational certificate and have not completed secondary general education or to people aged up to 25 who have a certificate of the general or technological upper secondary level but no vocational certificate. In the former case, the maximum duration of the contract is 9 months, in the latter case, it is 6 months. This contract aims, by providing vocational guidance, at giving youngsters access to employment or to help them re-enter a qualification process by way of a further apprenticeship, a qualification contract or reintegration into the education system.

[12] In France, the guilds lost all privileges after the French Revolution in 1789. Successor organisations were not allowed to be constituted. Thus, after this date, in-company training was carried out within the framework of civil-law contracts. Models of part-time qualification in schools and companies were sporadically reintroduced during the 20th century (around 1920) but a legal anchorage was only achieved through the 1971 law.

- The qualification contract (*contrat de qualification*)

  This type of training is offered to young people up to 25 years of age who wish to complement their initial training with a vocational course. The duration of the contract ranges between 6 and 24 months. Employers commit themselves to providing young people with employment and vocational training leading to a recognised qualification or a certificate. At least 25 percent of the total time of the contract must be spent for general, vocational and technological training.

- The adaptation contract (*contrat d'adaptation*).

  These employment contracts are signed by a company and a young unemployed person up to 25 years of age and may be of limited or unlimited duration. As the name indicates, this contract is designed to provide training which allows the trainee to adapt to a specific kind of employment. It is a form of part-time training that links general, vocational and technological training and the acquisition of vocational skills during working time.

Interestingly, more and more *Baccalauréat* or tertiary level degree holders are engaged in qualification or adaptation contracts. There is a large number of other measures of part-time training, like the "individualised training credit" (*Crédit Formation Individualisé*, CFI), which was established in 1991 and gives young people the right to attend a personalised training leading to certification, or the "solidarity employment contract" (*Contrat Emploi-Solidarité*), introduced in 1990, which enables young persons with a qualification equivalent to a vocational *Baccalauréat* and having difficulty in finding employment to work half-time under a part-time employment contract. All these measures were introduced since the mid-1980s as a reaction to the high level of youth unemployment and should rather be seen as continuous rather than initial training.

2.2.3.2 Full-time vocational tracks

Germany

Beside the dual system, which involves the bulk of young people, vocational training may also be provided in full-time vocational schools. Broadly speaking, there are two types of full-time vocational schools:

- *Berufsfachschulen* (full-time vocational schools) and *Fachschulen* (technical colleges)

  These schools prepare students for entry into an occupation and provide them with initial vocational training while they continue general education. The *Berufsfachschulen* require only a lower or middle school leaving certificate (*Hauptschul-* or *Realschulabschluss*), while admission to the

Fachschulen requires previous completion of a relevant vocational training or evidence of work experience in the relevant field. The *Fachschulen* train specialised middle-level staff expected to assume relatively important responsibilities within clearly defined areas.

- *Berufsaufbauschulen* (vocational extension schools) and *Fachoberschulen* (technical secondary schools)

  These schools primarily confer entrance qualification for some kind of further studies rather than vocational skills as such. The *Berufsaufbauschulen* aim at students who have completed[13] vocational training and lead to the *Fachschulreife* certificate, which is equivalent to the intermediate certificate of the *Realschule*, a school entry requirement for certain vocational schools (*Berufsfachschule, Fachoberschule* and *Fachgymnasium*). The *Fachoberschule* allows pupils who have completed intermediate general education in a *Realschule* or *Berufsaufbauschule* to qualify for higher education via the *Fachhochschulreife* certificate, introduced in the late 1960s or via the (*fachgebundene Hochschulreife*). However, the *Fachhochschulreife* only opens access to lower tertiary institutions (*Fachhochschulen*, see below), not to universities. The *fachgebundene Hochschulreife* entitles to study at the *Fachhochschule* or at the university for specific courses of study.

France

In France, vocational education is essentially provided through the national education system on the basis of full-time vocational schooling in vocational *Lycées (Lycées Professionnels)*. There is a wide selection of vocational certificates, but here are the main ones:

- *Certificat d'Aptitude Professionnelle* or CAP (vocational aptitude certificate)

  The CAP may be completed in 3 years after completion of the 2nd *Collège* year, or in 2 years after the 4th year of *Collège* and is primarily designed to prepare students for a specific occupation. It can be obtained by full-time schooling at a vocational *Lycée*, or by means of an apprenticeship. Fewer pupils, nowadays, opt for a CAP after the second *Collège* year. This development is in line with the ambition of conducting all children to the end of upper secondary schooling and operating some streaming only after this stage (Brauns et al. 1997). The low-status option of a CAP is predominantly left to those pupils not being able to finish *Collège* education[14]. After the CAP, the most able pupils continue their studies

[13] Or are still completing it, in which case students attend the vocational school on a part-time basis.

[14] Until 1991, those pupils could also pass the CEP (*Certificat d'Education Professionnelle*) after a one year course.

and prepare for another vocational certificate, like the BEP (see below), or the *Brevet Professionnel*[15] (BP) or some other supplementary vocational certificates like the BEA/C/I/H/S (*Brevet d'Enseignement Agricole/Commercial/Industriel/Hôtelier/Social*).

- *Brevet d'Etudes Professionnelles* or BEP (vocational studies certificate)

  The BEP may be completed in 2 years after completion of the 4th year of *Collège* and covers a more extensive field than the CAP. Holders of the BEP can enter working life but the BEP is increasingly seen as a springboard to continue further studies and to prepare for a vocational (or technological for the most able pupils) *Baccalauréat*. In case the technological *Baccalauréat* is aimed at, holders of the BEP can improve their chances of success by following an "adapted" 2nd year of *Lycée* (*première d'adaptation*). Other pupils will pursue their vocational education and qualify for an advanced or supplementary vocational certificate like the *Brevet Professionnel* (BP), *Brevet de Technicien* (BT) or the BEA/C/I/H/S mentioned above.
  Both CAP and BEP courses request periods of on-the-job training (*stages*) and to a larger extent than in Germany, they also include a substantial amount of general education requirements in addition to technical and vocational education.

- *Baccalauréat Professionnel* or *Bac Pro* (vocational *Baccalauréat*)

  The vocational *Baccalauréat* was introduced in 1985 in order to enable the holders of a BEP to acquire a higher level of qualification. Unlike the technological *Baccalauréat*, the vocational *Baccalauréat* is primarily a vocational integration certificate leading directly to the exercise of an occupation, even though it also entitles pupils to enter university studies. Thus, it is targeted at specific occupations, whereas the technological *Baccalauréat* is much broader in scope.

2.2.4 Tertiary education

In Germany, the system of higher education is characterised by the traditional predominance of universities, even though there exist some other higher education institutions. Conversely, in the French system of higher education, there is a great variety of institutions, which may have different admission requirements and offer a wide variety of degrees.

---

[15] The BP can be obtained after at least 2 years of work experience in the respective occupation, or after at least 5 years of work experience for those people not holding a CAP. It is the master craftsmen certificate (corresponding to the German *Meisterbrief*).

2.2.4.1 University education

Germany

Universities (Universitäten) and equivalent institutions (*Technische Universitäten, Technische Hochschulen, Gesamthochschulen*) are the traditional place where academic education is provided in Germany. They offer study courses in the whole range of subjects. The prerequisite for starting a course of university studies is proof of having a general or subject-specific university entrance qualification (*Allgemeine* or *fachgebundene Hochschulreife*)[16]. Typically, university study programmes lead to academic examinations (*Hochschulprüfungen*) leading to degrees such as the *Diplom* or *Magister Artium*, but studies in specific fields (teaching careers, medicine or law) lead to *State examinations* (*Staatsexamen*) or also (theology) to church examinations (*kirchliche Prüfungen*).

The *Diplom* degree courses are divided into two cycles: a period of basic studies (*Grundstudium*) followed by advanced studies (*Hauptstudium*). Basic studies are generally concluded with an intermediate examination (*Zwischenprüfung* or *Vordiplomprüfung*), while advanced studies end up with the *Diplom* examination (*Diplomprüfung*). The duration of the basic studies cycle generally amounts to 2 years (4 semesters) and the overall study duration until *Diplom* examination theoretically spans over 8 to 10 semesters (4 to 5 years) depending on the type of studies chosen. However, the German university system leaves a large autonomy to the students, who may interrupt their studies for completing internships or stays abroad for instance, take on a part-time job to finance the studies or simply postpone the date of the examination. This often results, in practice, in a much longer study duration than the theoretical duration expected for the various study courses.

In the *Magister* degree programme, the students study two major subjects, or one major subject and two minors (e.g. German language and literature and history). The combination of different subjects aims at guaranteeing a broad study base. As a first degree, the *Magister* degree is usually awarded as *Magister Artium* (MA). The standard period of studies for a MA is 9 semesters (4.5 years). Studies are divided into foundation courses (*Grundstudium*) of 4 semesters ending with an intermediate examination and an advanced study cycle of 5 semesters including the *Magister* examination. The *Magister* degree is also conferred at the end of a 1 to 2-year postgraduate programme.

Study programmes in the fields of medicine (general medicine, veterinary, dentistry or pharmacy), of teaching careers and of law are sanctioned by *State examinations*. Training in law, for instance, comprises a course of study in law at university, culminating in the first State examination (*Erstes Staatsexamen*). This first State examination degree provides access to a further phase of training on the job. This probationary period ends up with the second

[16] In some disciplines (medicine, pharmacy, business etc.), however, demand far exceeds the number of student places available. Access to these disciplines is therefore restricted (*numerus clausus*).

State examination (*Zweites Staatsexamen*), which qualifies the holder to the qualification concerned (e.g. lawyer).

Students who passed the *Diplom* or *Magister* examination or the first State examination with at least a "good" grade may take postgraduate courses, such as a *Magister* or more typically a doctorate (*Promotion*).

France

Universities are public institutions admitting, as a rule without selection procedure[17], all applicants in possession of a *Baccalauréat* or a certificate judged equivalent. University education is organised in three successive cycles, each of which leads to nationally recognised qualifications.

The first cycle lasts 2 years (2 years of post-*Baccalauréat* education, in brief *Bac+2*) and leads to a certificate of general university studies (*Diplôme d'Etudes Universitaires Générales*, DEUG). At the end of this cycle, students not eligible for higher university degrees are selected out.

The second cycle may span 1 to 3 years. It may lead to the *licence* (DEUG plus 1 year, i.e. *Bac+3*) or to the *maîtrise* (*licence* plus 1 year, i.e. *Bac+4*). Moreover, universities also offer, as part of the second cycle, engineering degrees (*maîtrise* plus 1 year or DEUG plus 3 years, i.e. *Bac+5* level, *maîtrise* degrees from a university institute of professional education (*Institut Universitaire Professionnel* IUP), acquired in 3 years after a first year of DEUG or of a preparatory class for the *Grandes Ecoles*, i.e. *Bac+4* level, and degrees from the university teacher training institutes (*Institut Universitaire de Formation des Maîtres*, IUFM), which admit students who have completed 3 years of post-secondary education (*licence* or *Bac+3* level) and lasts 2 years. In addition to nationally recognised degrees, universities may offer certificates on their own authority.

The third cycle offers successful graduates of the second cycle highly specialised education: a professional specialisation of one year with a compulsory period of in-company training, leading to a certificate of advanced specialised studies (*Diplôme d'Etudes Supérieures Spécialisées*, DESS, *Bac+5* level) or a training in research leading at the end of the first year to an advanced research studies certificate (*Diplôme d'Etudes Approfondies*, DEA, *Bac+5* level) and then to the preparation over 3 or 4 years of a doctorate (*Doctorat*, *Bac+8* level).

2.2.4.2 Non-university education

Germany

In the late 1960s, a new kind of higher education institutions was established in Germany, the higher technical colleges (*Fachhochschulen*, FH). The *Fach-*

[17] Except in the fields of medicine and pharmacy, where the number of student places is limited (*numerus clausus*) and in which students are selected at the end of the first year on the basis of their performance.

hochschulen aim at preparing students for professional activities on the basis of praxis-related teaching, involving the practical application of scientific knowledge and methods. They are organised in the same way as universities and the courses offered cover predominantly the fields of engineering sciences, economics and business studies, and social sciences. The study programmes are particularly oriented towards practical applications and include periods of compulsory in-company training. To be admitted, students must hold a university entrance qualification (*allgemeine* or *fachgebundene Hochschulreife*) or the *Fachhochschule* entrance qualification (*Fachhochschulreife*). Studies at *Fachhochschulen* generally last 4 years and student's graduation time is more reliably predictable than at universities. While originally the *Fachhochschulen* were conceived as short-cycle institutions, there has been a continuous upgrading over time and many *Fachhochschulen* try to endow themselves for competition with universities[18].

In some *Länder* (Baden-Württemberg, Bavaria, Berlin, Lower Saxony and Schleswig-Holstein), some other short-cycle institutions were founded as less academic institutions, the *Berufsakademien*, which transpose the principle of the dual system to the tertiary level (2 to 3 years of part-time school training and firm-based training). In Baden-Württemberg, *Berufsakademien* are almost considered as being of the same level as *Fachhochschulen*, but in the other *Länder*, they are rather considered as coming in the category of the *Fachschulen*.

France

Beside universities, a large number of public and private institutions offer tertiary level education in France:

- Short-term higher education programmes

  They generally cover 2 years after *Baccalauréat* completion and lead to a certificate of technical or professional education. University institutes of technology (*Institut Universitaire de Technologie*, IUT) deliver after 2 years a university technology certificate (*Diplôme Universitaire de Technologie*, DUT) and entitle the holders to take on managerial positions in the secondary or tertiary sector. Admission to an IUT is subject to selection. Higher technical classes (*Sections de Techniciens Supérieurs*, STS) offer 2 years of highly specialised training which leads to an advanced technical certificate (*Brevet de Technicien Supérieur*, BTS). Admission to an STS is based on an applicant's dossier. Beside IUT and STS, students may prepare in 2 years for a certificate of scientific and technical *studies* (*Diplôme d'Etudes Universitaires Scientifiques et Techniques*, DEUST) or in up to 4 years a paramedical training, for which the admission procedure is based on a competitive examination.

[18] Some of them even strive to receive the university status.

- Long-term higher education programmes

  A wide selection of other higher education institutions, public or private, compete with universities in offering long-track study courses in the whole range of scientific disciplines. These very diverse institutions are known as *"Grandes Ecoles"* and have in common selective entrance procedures, generally based on competitive examinations for which students prepare in up to 3 years after *Baccalauréat* – depending on the type of institution –, in specific preparatory classes (*Classes Préparatoires aux Grandes Ecoles*, CPGE). Private institutions can request recognition by the State of the diploma they deliver. There are three types of private institutions: private engineering schools (*écoles d'ingénieurs*), schools of business administration (*grandes écoles de commerce et de gestion*) and Catholic institutes. There is also a variety of public institutions: institutes for political studies (*Instituts d'Etudes politiques*, IEP), scientific *Grandes Ecoles*, like the *Ecole Nationale des Arts et Métiers, Ecoles Normale Supérieures* (ENS), *Ecoles Supérieures*, like the *Ecole Nationale d'Administration* (ENA, public administration), the *Ecole Polytechnique* (engineering), the *Ecoles Nationales Vétérinaires* (ENV, veterinary), the *Ecoles d'architecture* (architecture). There is a well-known hierarchy of *Grande Ecoles* within their specific fields. The schools with the best reputation are extremely selective and have the vocation to train an "elite" expected to take on responsibilities in the key positions of the economy. If in the last decade, a variety of far less prestigious *Grandes Ecoles* have been founded, the elite, whether in the civil service, academia or in the private economy, is in large part still recruited from the traditional *Grandes Ecoles* (see Bauer and Bertin-Mourot 1995).

2.3 Comparing educational attainment

In empirical research, various measures of educational attainment are used, ranging from the number of schooling years to test scores or typologies based on the educational certificates. As a matter of fact, there is no consensus view on how to measure educational attainment and the relative merits of each measurement depend highly on the specific structure of the education system observed (Brauns et al. 1997) as well as on the specific purpose followed. Comparing educational attainment across countries requires an educational classification which accounts for the relevant hierarchies of credentials within each country while being suited to highlight similarities and differences across countries. Some international classifications of educational attainment have been developed, like the ISCED (OECD 2003) or the CASMIN (König, Lüttinger and Müller 1988) typologies, which enable to run comparative analyses on a broad range of countries and are quite detailed. Due to their international focus, these classifications need to be applicable to a large number of countries, and this implies that they are not specifically adapted to the peculiarities of the French and German education systems as well as of the data sets used in this analysis.

Therefore, I prefer here to construct an own classification scale – which builds on the CASMIN typology – specifically designed to capture institutional differences and similarities between the French and the German education systems in their distinctive features and suited to highlight the hierarchy of credentials. Hereby, the aim is not to construct some kind of ideal comparison scale for France and Germany, but rather a scale that can be implemented using the data sources available for empirical research. The first section describes the data available, the possibilities they offer and the limitations they impose, before I proceed in the next section to the elaboration of the classification scale itself.

2.3.1 The data

The empirical analyses of the educational distribution and its impact in terms of labour market outcomes in France and Germany in the subsequent chapters are based on three data sets: for Germany the German Socio-Economic Panel (GSOEP) and for France the *Formation et Qualification Professionnelles* (FQP) survey and the *Emploi* survey.

2.3.1.1 General description

The GSOEP

The German Socio-Economic Panel (GSOEP) is a longitudinal household survey conducted on an annual basis since 1984. In the first wave, some 12,000 individuals aged 16 and over, and distributed across roughly 6,000 households, were interviewed. The information available is drawn from the statements of the individuals. Individual and household identifiers make it possible to track individuals over time. Due to panel attrition, sample size diminishes somewhat every year, but in 1998, a refreshment sample of about 2,000 persons was added to the data base and in 2000, a further sample of about 11,000 new individuals was added. Initially, the sample only referred to residents in West Germany, but following German unification, the sample has been extended to the former German Democratic Republic in 1990. The GSOEP is representative of the population residing in Germany and contains a large number of socio-economic variables on demography, education, employment, income, housing and health. For further information on the GSOEP, see Haisken-DeNew and Frick (2000).

The Emploi survey

The *Emploi* survey is an annual household survey which is representative of the population residing in metropolitan France (without overseas *départements*). All the surveys from 1968 onwards are available for research. In the 1982-89 series, the survey covers about 150,000 individuals aged 15 and above, distributed across approximately 80,000 households. The information stems from the statements of the persons asked. From 1990 onwards, the sample size has been somewhat reduced and since then, the sample population counts some 135,000 individuals distributed across roughly 65,000 households. To avoid sample size reduction due to panel attrition, one third of the sample is renewed each year. This means that it is possible to track one third of the sample over time for a period of three years. The *Emploi* Survey contains detailed information on employment, job search, education and vocational mobility. For further information on the *Emploi* survey, consult the online information available under http://www.iresco.fr/labos/lasmas/enqempl.htm.

The FQP survey

The *Formation et Qualification Professionnelles* (FQP) survey is a cross-sectional survey which was drawn for the years 1964, 1970, 1977, 1985 and 1993. Only the 1993 wave is available for this research. This wave covers about 18,000 individuals aged between 20 and 64 and distributed across 14,000 households. The FQP survey contains detailed information on the current and past labour market situation of the individuals, very detailed information on their education and training as well as on their family background. For further information on the FQP survey, consult the online information available under http://www.iresco.fr/labos/lasmas/enqfqp.htm.

2.3.1.2 Information on educational attainment

Since the aim of this section is to establish a comparative measure of educational attainment for both countries, the information on education contained in these data sets is now examined into more detail.

Germany

In the GSOEP data, information related to education refers to the highest degree obtained in terms of secondary education, vocational training and higher education. Combining the information drawn from these three variables on secondary, vocational and higher education makes it possible to construct an indicator of final educational achievement. Alternatively, the information on the highest degree obtained in each of the educational fields may be used to build a quantitative estimator of educational achievement by estimating approximately the number of years of schooling attended, using standard or typical durations required to complete specific degrees. No information is available on the field of study of the highest degree obtained in the GSOEP.

France

The variables on education are defined in a very similar way in the *Emploi* and in the FQP data. Compared to the GSOEP data, the information on educational achievement is much more detailed in the French data sets. First, precise information is available regarding the age at which the person asked finished his or her education, which makes it possible to determine precisely the actual number of years of education received in case this is needed. Moreover, the data distinguishes between the highest degree obtained and the highest level of education attended regardless of whether the degree has finally been obtained or not. Since only the highest degree obtained is available for Germany, the information on the highest level of education attended without obtaining a degree should not be used for comparisons with Germany. Therefore, in the following, the notion of educational attainment or level of education will refer to the highest degree obtained. Like for Germany, French respondents are asked to indicate the highest degree they obtained in general, in technical/vocational and in higher education. This similar structure is helpful with a view to elaborating a classification for comparison purposes. However, the information on the type of educational credential obtained is more precise for France than for Germany. For example, the higher education variable contains more than 10 categories instead of the sole distinction between lower and upper tertiary degrees in the German data[19]. Beside the mere statistical priorities, this difference in the degree of precision partly reflects the different structure of the education system itself, since, as seen above, the German education system of higher education is less differentiated than the French one in terms of degree levels. Whatever the reasons, an unfortunate consequence is that part of the information has to be given up if a comparative classification is to be established. Indeed, by making things comparable, one automatically loses information when the information provided in one data source is more detailed than in the other one. Analogue to the German data, there is no information on the field of the completed studies in the *Emploi* Survey.

2.3.2 Typology of educational attainment

Based on the data available on the highest degree obtained in general, vocational and higher education, we can now construct a comparable typology of educational attainment which can be implemented using the GSOEP and the FQP or the *Emploi* data. By doing so, one has to be careful about the national terminology, which might be misleading. For instance, to what extent is the French maturity degree (*Baccalauréat*) really comparable with the German concept of *Abitur*, the German *Fachhochschule* comparable with a French short-track tertiary level certificate (two years after *Baccalauréat*)?

[19] However, the distinction between *Bac+3* and *Bac+4* or above is only available after 1992, when an additional question was introduced.

What should be done for instance with the French *Grandes Ecoles*, which have no equivalent in Germany? Finding answers to these questions requires a thorough understanding of the educational systems, but since the systems present obvious differences, there can be no perfect correspondence of diploma. The classification developed here gives priority to the internal consistency of the hierarchy of educational credentials rather than to strict comparability across countries. Indeed, the aim is not to define strictly identical educational categories, which would be neither possible nor desirable, but rather to provide a tool for comparative analyses of educational attainment or its outcome in France and Germany. Only these analyses will provide real evidence on the degree of comparability between France and Germany with respect to educational attainment. In the following parts, synthetic denominations of the credentials are used, but of course, also credentials of an equivalent level are meant. Please refer to the description of the credentials in section 2.2 and to the glossary in Appendix A in case more detailed information is needed.

A look at the national scales proves useful, for it reveals the logic underlying the hierarchical ordering of the educational credentials. In France, an official grid of qualification levels has been introduced in 1969:

- Level VI: completion of the first cycle of secondary education
- Level Vbis: completion of the second cycle of secondary education without achievement of a vocational certificate
- Level V: completion of basic vocational education (CAP, BEP or equivalent) without completion of the *Baccalauréat*
- Level IV: *Baccalauréat* (general, technological or vocational), BT, BP and equivalent
- Level III: diploma at *Baccalauréat+2* level (BTS, DUT, DEUG etc.)
- Level II: diploma at *Baccalauréat+3/4* level (*licence, maîtrise, diplôme de Grande Ecole* etc.)
- Level I: postgraduate degree, i.e. diploma at *Baccalauréat+5* level and beyond.

As appears from this grid, in France, the completion or not of the maturity degree (*Baccalauréat*) is a key discriminating factor with respect to educational attainment. This reveals French emphasis on general education and explains that three-level scales generally comprise:

- Levels VI, V bis, V: less than *Baccalauréat*
- Level IV: *Baccalauréat* (including vocational and technological *Baccalauréat* and certificates of equivalent levels)
- Levels III, II, I: more than *Baccalauréat.*

In Germany, no such official grid is available, but observing the education scales typically adopted in official statistics reveals that qualification levels are ranked according to the achievement in vocational education only, and not in general education. Typically, a four-level ranking is adopted:

Table 2.1. Franco-German typology of educational attainment

	Highest degree obtained
Level 1	**No vocational qualification**
10	No degree G: no degree F: no degree
11	Lower secondary education G: *Hauptschule* F: CEP/DFEO
12	Intermediate secondary education G: *Realschule* F: BEPC
Level 2	**Basic vocational qualification**
20	No or lower secondary education + basic vocational degree G: no degree/*Hauptschule* + *Lehre*/*Berufsfachschule* F: no degree/CEP/DFEO + CAP/BEP
21	Intermediate secondary education + basic vocational degree G: *Realschule* + *Lehre*/*Berufsfachschule* F: BEPC + CAP/BEP
Level 3	**Intermediate qualification**
30	Intermediate vocational degree G: *Fachschule*/*Gesundheitsschule*/*Beamtenschule* F: BP/BEA/BEC/BEH/BEI/BES
31	Vocational maturity degree G: *Fachhochschulreife* F: *Bac Techno*/*Bac Pro*/BT
32	General maturity degree G: *Hochschulreife* (*Abitur*) F: *Bac Général*
33	General maturity degree + vocational degree G: *Hochschulreife* + voc. qualification (*Lehre*/*Fachschule*) F: *Bac Général* + voc. qualification (CAP/BEP/BP/*Bac Pro*)
Level 4	**Tertiary level qualification**
40	Lower tertiary education G: *Fachhochschule*/*Ingenieurschule* F: *Bac+2* (DEUG/BTS/DUT)
41	Upper tertiary education G: *Universität*, *Technische Universität* F: *Bac+3/4* and beyond (*Licence*, *Maîtrise*, *Grande Ecole*, *Bac+5*)

Note: G=Germany, F=France.

- Unskilled: no vocational degree
- Low skilled: basic vocational qualification (e.g. *Lehrausbildung*, i.e. apprenticeship)
- Medium skilled: intermediate vocational qualification (e.g. *Fachschule*)
- High skilled: tertiary education graduates.

The high skilled category is often divided into lower tertiary education graduates (e.g. *Fachhochschulen*) and upper tertiary education graduates (university graduates). Interestingly, the completion or not of the maturity degree, the *Abitur*, is not reported. Note that the French level IV, which is referred to as *Baccalauréat* level, also includes some vocational types of *Baccalauréat* and other vocational or technical certificates considered as equivalent. Among these, the *Brevet Professionnel* is the master craftsmen certificate, which corresponds to the *Meisterbrief*, and is put in the *Fachschule* category in Germany.

Table 2.1 presents the typology proposed for measuring final educational attainment in France and Germany, using the information available in the GSOEP and in the *Emploi* and FQP surveys. As mentioned before, this typology can also be used with other data sets like *Mikrozensus* for Germany. The educational categories refer to the highest level of degree obtained and have been numbered in order to facilitate further analyses. For presentation reasons, only the most representative degrees of each category are reported here, but of course, the categories also include degrees of an equivalent level. To take into account the specific attributes of the German and the French education systems, special attention has been paid to the distinction, for a given level of educational attainment, between general and vocational education as well as to the position of the maturity certificate.

2.4 Summary and conclusions

The main elements of comparison of the French and German education systems are now summarised and put into perspective, with a special emphasis on the aspects relevant to the subsequent analyses.

The German education system is marked by the federal structure of the Federal Republic of Germany, as opposed to the traditional centralism prevailing in France for general and also educational matters. As far as the education system is concerned, the first difference that appears is the school character of pre-primary education in France as opposed to Germany, the earlier age at which French pupils are enrolled into primary education and the full-day character of schooling in France as opposed to half-day schooling in Germany. Thus, French children start learning at a younger age than their German counterparts and receive from the very beginning a larger amount of teaching. Moreover, French egalitarianism up to the lower secondary level contrasts with German differentialism. Indeed, the principle of the French system at the lower secondary level consists, analogue to the situation prevailing at the primary education level, in mixing up children of all abilities in the same classes in the hope that weaker pupils will be positively influenced by stronger ones. In contrast, the German system aims at offering a differentiated education adapted to the needs and aptitudes of children through pupils' early streaming into different types of institutions or classes according to their learning ability.

A further essential difference between France and Germany concerns the value placed on different types of education. In France, the ambition of education policy is basically to provide general education[20]. As a result, general education is more prized than vocational education. Typically, the objective of educational policy has been to help pupils reach the highest possible level of general education. This explains the key position of the maturity degree (*Baccalauréat*) in France. Only if pupils fail on the way to *Baccalauréat Général* will they opt for a deviant track, vocational education. In other words, vocational education is reserved to the "selected-out" of the general education system and qualifications like the CAP or BEP have a very low status. The reforms conducted in the last decades generally aimed at helping those pupils who have been selected out of the general education system and guided into vocational education to re-enter the school system and reach a higher level of general education, possibly the *Baccalauréat*. That is the sense of the introduction of the vocational *Baccalauréat* in the mid-1980s. This conception of the role of education also explains that more than in Germany, vocational degrees also entail a substantial amount of general education requirements, more than in corresponding vocational tracks in Germany. This is viewed as important as such, but is also meant to facilitate return to the general education system. The general skills acquired may be credited and they entitle to rejoin the general education system at a higher level ("gateways" or *passerelles*) in order, for instance, to prepare for the *Baccalauréat*.

In Germany, no comparable primacy of general education over vocational education is observable. An essential aim of educational policy in Germany is to prepare young people for labour market occupations and ensure a smooth transition from school to work. The craftsman ideal remains very present in German views (Rothe 1995). Vocational education, via the dual system inherited from the Middle Age, is an essential component of the education system, and that is the track most young persons choose. It is not a last resort like in France but is rather seen as an adequate way of providing pupils with specific vocational skills needed by the economy. This predominance of labour market considerations explains that companies are entrusted with part of the initial training duty within the framework of the "dual" system, whereas in France, even vocational education is typically provided on a theoretical basis

[20] Even though the rise in unemployment – especially among the least qualified – induced the successive governments to take labour market aspects increasingly into consideration.

in full-time schools. Even though the apprenticeship does exist in France, it is not really comparable to the German apprenticeship. Apprenticeship in France does not provide a qualification as such but is rather one of several forms under which pupils may prepare for some other educational certificates of various levels (CAP, BEP, *Bac Pro* or even tertiary level degrees), the more usual form being full-time school-based education. The other kinds of part-time vocational qualifications in France are primarily instruments of employment policy rather than of education policy. They are not considered as part of the initial education system as such but rather have the objective to facilitate labour market entry for those young persons experiencing difficulties in finding a job.

Thus, the German system of vocational education is oriented towards occupational training rather than towards levels of qualification like the French one. It is not primarily designed to help pupils re-enter the education system at a higher level, which is therefore more strenuous and time-consuming than in France. As a result, in Germany, the decision regarding the possible level of educational attainment is strongly pre-determined by the kind of secondary school attended[21], and this streaming of pupils according to their learning abilities takes place at a very early age compared to France.

At the tertiary level, there are also noticeable differences. The German system is relatively homogeneous. The bulk of German students attend universities or the more practically oriented *Fachhochschulen*. The French landscape of higher education is much more diverse and differentiated. Indeed, at a given education level, different types of private and public institutions (universities, *Grandes Ecoles*, institutes etc.) coexist and offer a wide range of study programmes with different purposes and approaches, some of them being more academic, other having a more practical focus. Moreover, the vertical stratification is also much more pronounced in France than in Germany. The universities themselves offer certificates at a larger number of levels: *Bac+2* (e.g. DEUG), *Bac+3* (e.g. *licence*), *Bac+4* (e.g. *maîtrise*), *Bac+5* (e.g. DESS), *Bac+8* (doctorate). Besides, there exists, on the one hand, a large number of short-track practically oriented tertiary level studies (BTS, DUT etc.) and, on the other hand, elite institutions, the so-called, *Grandes Ecoles*, which have no equivalent in Germany. The *Grandes Ecoles* are designed to form an elite destinated to occupy highly skilled positions in politics, sciences, business and engineering. As such, they have on average a more practical orientation than the universities. Thus, though the German education system is more oriented towards the needs of the labour market at the secondary level, the opposite seems to be true at the tertiary level.

Thus, France and Germany differ widely with respect to the design of their respective education systems, in particular with respect to the streaming of pupils, the possibility to re-enter the general education system once being in

[21] Not going to *Gymnasium*, for instance, reduces dramatically the chances of studying at university.

the vocational one, and more generally with respect to the balance between general and vocational education at the various levels of education. These different conceptions of the role and the organisation of the education system are likely to be reflected in the distribution of educational attainment among the population of both countries. Making use of the comparative typology of educational credentials established in this chapter, the next chapters gather some empirical evidence on the distribution of educational attainment in France and Germany as well as its determinants and consequences in terms of labour market outcomes.

3

Educational attainment in France and Germany

The level of education of the population is commonly viewed as an essential factor for a country's economic and social development. In modern economies, and particularly in the context of natural resources scarcity and global competition, output growth largely depends on the ability of firms to find a workforce disposing of the skills needed for their activity. This is the concept of "human capital" referred to in economic literature, in analogy to physical capital. The initial educational achievement undoubtedly represents an essential component of one's overall human capital, even though it is complemented in the course of life by skills acquired through work experience or on-the-job training. Moreover, education is known to have a positive impact on a wide range of other outcomes such as criminality, social exclusion, health etc. On an individual level, the educational achievement determines to a large extent the prospects in terms of employment and earnings (see chapter 4 and chapter 5), but also in terms of access to cultural goods and personal development in general.

Thus, it is not surprising that governments in advanced countries typically claim to pursue two essential objectives regarding education: raise the education level of the population, on the one hand, and reduce social inequalities in educational attainment, on the other hand. France and Germany share these key objectives, though they differ in the means employed to achieve them, judging from the different political options chosen to shape the education systems (see chapter 2). The question therefore arises how successfully these common objectives have been met in either country and how France and Germany, two competing economies that share a similar level of development, stand with respect to this long-term indicator of economic and social development.

In France and Germany alike, education has become a prominent issue in the political debate. In Germany, the latest PISA (Programme for International Student Assessment) study (OECD 2002), that reports the results of reading, mathematical and scientific literacy tests of students conducted in a wide range of countries in 2000, caused a genuine shock in public opinion and among policy makers. Indeed, German students performed significantly worse than the average of participating OECD countries and in particular worse than most other developed countries (Artelt et al. 2001). Though French students were far from being brilliant, they performed significantly better than their German counterparts. Their results were slightly above OECD-average in reading and natural sciences and they perform significantly better than average in mathematics. Moreover, the variance in the test results of German students turned out to be particularly large compared to the other countries and in particular compared to France. Commentators deplored the particularly large extent of social inequalities in PISA achievement in Germany. The link between PISA achievement and social origin was found to be tighter in Germany than in any other PISA-participating country, in particular much tighter than in France (Artelt et al. 2001). In both countries, the test results proved to vary across genders. Girls performed much better than boys in the reading literacy tests and boys were slightly better than girls in the mathematical tests. In the natural sciences tests, German boys were slightly better than girls, whereas in France, no gender differences were observed. Making a simple average of the three fields of competencies tested without weighting them, girls perform on average better than boys at PISA in both France and Germany.

The PISA results were at the origin of an intense discussion in Germany on the causes and remedies of the poor educational performance. Both the efficiency and the equity of the education system have been called into question. In the debate on the forces driving the poor German performance, a reason for the strong dispersion of test achievement and for the strong link between family background and test achievement has been seen in some specific features of the German education system. First, the early streaming of German pupils into secondary schools of different levels (see chapter 2) leads to social segregation and is suspected to produce more social inequalities in educational opportunities than a more egalitarian system such as the French one, where the first streaming of students takes place at a much later stage in the educational career, when the influence of family background is expected to be weaker (Artelt et al. 2001; Gottschall and Hagemann 2002). Moreover, the later school starting age and half-day school in Germany, as opposed to the French full-day school model, are typically mentioned as factors explaining the strong effect of social background in Germany (Veil 2002; Gottschall and Hagemann 2002). Thus, France provides a good benchmark for a comparison with Germany, since the education system there differs from the German one precisely in the features that are thought to explain the stronger dependence of the German results on family background.

Certainly, the PISA tests provide only a snapshot view of the cognitive skills of 15-year-old students who are still enrolled in education. They do not provide a picture of all the skills acquired through initial education, since the latter include more skills than those tested in PISA and can only be measured after initial education has been completed. Therefore, looking –

when initial education has been completed – at the level and the nature of the credentials obtained is expected to give a more precise measure of the skills acquired within the system of initial education, in so far as the educational credentials certify the acquisition of such skills. The question arises whether the same hierarchies with respect to level, dispersion and dependence on social background and gender of educational attainment are observed in terms of the educational credentials finally obtained as in terms of PISA skills at age 15 in France and Germany. This is why this chapter examines the impact of family background and gender on educational attainment as measured by the educational credentials obtained in the course of initial education.

Looking at the empirical evidence available so far, it appears that there is a lack of comparative studies on this topic for France and Germany. The studies available for each country do indicate the presence of a strong link between social background and educational attainment, but the methodologies used differ so that the results are hardly comparable. Thus, it is not possible to say on the basis of the empirical evidence available so far whether the German education system produces more or less social inequalities in terms of educational attainment than the French one which is supposed to foster more social equality. The first aim of this chapter will therefore be to gain some empirical evidence concerning the extent of social inequality in educational opportunities in France and Germany and to relate the findings to the current political debate on the performance of the respective education systems. The knowledge gained from chapter 2 will be used for this, in particular the differentiated measure of educational attainment elaborated for the specific purpose of a French-German comparison on the basis of the highest degrees obtained in general, vocational and higher education.

Moreover, the literature related to this topic often establishes the statistical link between social origin and educational achievement without relying on a theoretical model. On top of that, there is no consensus on the proper way to model the determination of educational outcomes empirically. Therefore, a second aim of this study will be to develop a model of educational attainment which makes sense in economic terms while being directly estimable empirically. Hereby, special attention will be paid to the economic meaning of the estimated coefficients and to modelling the sequential nature of the educational process.

This chapter is structured as follows. After providing a descriptive overview of the distribution of educational attainment in both countries in section 3.1, section 3.2 reviews the evidence available so far in the literature with regard to the analysis of the determinants of educational attainment, both in terms of methodology and also more specifically for France and Germany. In a next step, section 3.3 proposes a comparative analysis of the determinants of final educational attainment in France and Germany. Then, in section 3.4, a closer look is taken at the process of educational attainment. The educational career is viewed as being composed of two essential stages: school and post-school education, whereby a correlation between these stages is permitted. The model developed for this analysis is then applied to French and German data in order to gain empirical evidence on the impact of social background on both stages of the educational attainment. Finally, section 3.5 summarises the main findings and draws some conclusions.

3.1 Distribution of educational attainment

Given the importance of the level of education as a social and economic factor, the first step of the analysis will consist in examining how things stand with respect to this factor for France and Germany, two of the most influential countries in the European sphere that compete in terms of economy and social models. As a rule, it is difficult to compare aggregate figures drawn from national sources. The indicators are often defined in a different way, and the population under analysis might differ (age group considered, whole population or labour force, etc.). In this sense, the availability of individual data represents a considerable advantage, since it makes it possible to shape the samples in a way as similar as possible and to construct similar indicators. Thus, using the GSOEP and *Emploi* data presented in section 2.3.1 as well as the typology of educational attainment constructed in section 2.3.2, it is possible to provide a detailed description of the distribution of educational attainment in both countries.

Table 3.1. Delimitation of the working samples drawn from the GSOEP and the *Emploi* data sets

	Germany		France	
	Observations	(%)	Observations	(%)
Total	213,520		2,358,411	
Without:				
East German	168,601	(-21.0)	-	
Foreigners*	136,066	(-19.3)	2,239,696	(-5.0)
Beyond 65	116,936	(-14.1)	1,848,403	(-17.5)
Below 25	96,002	(-17.9)	1,387,113	(-25.0)
Enrolled	92,574	(-3.6)	1,370,765	(-1.2)
Education missing	91,576	(-1.1)	1,361,587	(-0.7)
Working sample	91,576		1,361,587	

* Foreigners born abroad only. The sample of foreigners is oversampled in the GSOEP data (see Haisken-DeNew and Frick 2000).

The data used covers the period from 1985 to 2000 for both countries. Table 3.1 reports the original number of observations available in the data for the waves 1985 to 2000 as well as the remaining number of observations after certain population groups have been successively dropped from the sample. The percentage values in table 3.1 indicate for each step of the sample delimitation by how much the sample has been further reduced by the exclusion of the group considered. Certain categories of population have been excluded from the sample for the following reasons:

- For Germany, the analysis is limited to the western part of country. This is because re-unification has taken place in 1990. Therefore, no data is available for East Germany before this date and including East Germany for the years after 1990 would introduce a structural break in the data. Moreover, the education system was different in the former German Democratic Republic and the comparison between East and West Germany would require a separate analysis.
- For both countries, only nationals and foreigners born in the country considered have been retained in the samples. Foreigners are problematic as far as they completed their education abroad. In the German data, information is available on whether a person obtained the degree in Germany or abroad. Therefore, it would be possible to keep in the sample only those foreigners who studied in Germany. Unfortunately, such information is not available in the French data. From 1992 onwards, it would be possible, however, to identify the foreigners' age of entry into France, but not for the previous years. Since the information should be consistent over time, one cannot make use of this information. One solution would be to only retain nationals for the analysis. However, the definition of nationality differs in both countries. Broadly speaking, the right to nationality is based on parentage in Germany whereas it is based on place of birth (and parentage) in France. Therefore, in order to make data as comparable as possible for both countries while keeping it consistent over time, individuals either having the French/German nationality or being born in these countries have eventually been kept in the sample to be analysed.
- The sample has been reduced to the population aged 25 to 65. The upper age limit is set at age 65 in order to avoid problems of mortality that might bias the composition of the sample if it depends on the education level and differs between France and Germany. The lower age limit is set at 25 to make sure that the bulk of the population has already finished initial education, even if they have attained a high level of education.
- The individuals who are still enrolled in education, though older than 25, have been dropped from the sample since the level they will finally achieve is unknown. As can be seen from table 3.1, this concerns a small proportion of the sample as defined above.
- Finally, the individuals for which no information on their educational attainment is available have also been dropped from the sample since this is the variable to be analysed.

The analysis of the distribution of educational attainment provides insights into the quantitative importance of the various qualifications offered by the respective education systems such as described in the previous chapter. In this overview, special emphasis is laid on similarities and differences between France and Germany with respect to the overall educational distribution, but also with respect to developments over time and gender differences.

3.1.1 Attainment in general secondary education

All pupils start with acquiring general education throughout primary education and secondary education. At some point, which depends on their abilities and preferences, as well as on the organisation of the education system, the pupils leave the general education system and turn to the acquisition of vocational or academic qualifications. The level attained in general secondary education is decisive for subsequent steps in the educational career. Indeed, advanced qualification courses (vocational or academic) generally have specific eligibility requirements in terms of general secondary education. Let us have a look at the distribution of attainment in general secondary education in France and Germany.

3.1.1.1 Structure and developments over time

Following the same logic as in the typology established in table 2.1, attainment in general secondary education is defined by the highest general school degree obtained, ranked in 4 levels as reported in table 3.2.

Table 3.2. Definition of attainment in general secondary education

School degree	Germany	France
No school degree	No school degree	No school degree
Low level	*Hauptschule* degree	CEP/DFEO
Intermediate level	*Realschule* degree	BEPC
High level	*Hochschulreife* (*Abitur*)	*Baccalauréat Général*

Table 3.3 shows how secondary school degrees are distributed in the French and German populations between 25 to 65 years of age, in 1985 and 2000. Since the developments in the distribution of educational attainment do not present erratic changes but rather follow a regular trend, comparing the first year of the period observed to the latest one provides a reliable overview of developments over this time period. In case more information is needed, the reader is referred to table B.2 in appendix B, which contains the corresponding figures for each year between 1985 and 2000. From one year to the next,

however, most of the population observed remains the same. Only a few young individuals enter thè population observed and a few old individuals disappear from it. Therefore, taking a look at the distribution of educational credentials for specific generations instead of the distribution in the whole population, all generations taken into account, puts a different perspective on the analysis of changes in the distribution of educational attainment. In particular, this should provide insights into the way the educational distribution is likely to develop in the future as long as new generations replace older ones in the whole population. For this reason, table 3.4 indicates how secondary eduction is distributed in one "old" birth cohort (1929-38) and one "young" cohort (1959-68)[1].

Table 3.3. Distribution of general secondary education by year

	Germany		France	
School degree	**1985**	**2000**	**1985**	**2000**
No degree	0.5	2.3	28.9	29.0
Low level	64.2	44.9	39.9	20.1
Intermediate level	23.8	32.6	16.8	25.4
High level	11.5	20.1	14.4	25.5

Table 3.4. Distribution of general secondary education by birth cohort

	Germany		France	
School degree	**1929-38**	**1959-68**	**1929-38**	**1959-68**
No degree	1.1	3.0	32.8	35.7
Low level	68.4	33.9	45.3	4.4
Intermediate level	21.4	39.9	10.9	32.4
High level	9.0	23.1	11.0	27.5

The following elements appear from the tables:

- There is a stronger dispersion in the distribution of secondary education degrees in France than in Germany.

  A striking feature is the very high proportion of individuals with no secondary education degree at all in France compared to Germany. At the same time, however, significantly more people hold the general maturity degree in France than in Germany. By contrast, the large majority of German people hold either the lowest or the intermediate school certificate. Thus, whereas there was a significantly higher dispersion in the PISA test scores distribution among German students than among French students, the general secondary education degrees, which are supposed to test more or

[1] The choice of these cohorts is motivated in section 3.3.2.

less the same skills, are on the contrary less dispersed in Germany than in France.

- In both countries, the level of secondary education has increased since the mid-1980s.

  This is the result of a strong drop in the proportion of individuals with only a low school degree[2]. At the same time, the proportion of individuals with an intermediate or a higher secondary school degree has increased steadily over the period. The rise in the level of secondary schooling is particularly obvious considering the developments across cohorts. Therefore, the educational attainment in general secondary education is expected to keep on improving in the French and German population as the younger generations replace the older ones.

- The rise in the level of secondary schooling attained by the population has been more pronounced in France than in Germany.

  The fall in the share of holders of a low school degree appears to be amazing in France, especially when considering the developments across cohorts[3]. As a counterpart, the increase in the share of intermediate and high-level school degrees has been particularly strong in France.

3.1.1.2 Gender differences

The developments described above hide significant differences between men and women, and these gender differences are not similar in France and Germany. Table 3.5 shows how attainment in secondary education is distributed among men and women in 1985 and 2000, and table 3.6 shows the educational structure in specific cohorts. Here are the key elements that can be observed from the tables:

- In France, women have a higher level of secondary education than men, while this is not true in Germany.

  In France, women have lower shares of no or low school degrees and higher shares of intermediate and maturity degrees compared to men. This is consistent with the findings of the PISA study, where girls performed better than boys on average. In Germany, women have a higher share of intermediate school graduates, but more men than women hold the general maturity certificate. Thus, it is not clear whether German men or women have a better secondary education achievement. Girls' lead in terms of literacy such as tested in PISA does not translate into a higher share of maturity degrees but into a higher share of intermediate school degrees.

---

[2] Note, however, that the share of people with no school degree at all has not dropped but rather increased.

[3] This drop is the reason why the CEP has been suppressed in 1989.

Table 3.5. Distribution of general secondary education by year and gender

School degree		Germany 1985	Germany 2000	France 1985	France 2000
No degree	Men	0.5	2.4	29.9	32.2
	Women	0.6	2.3	28.0	25.9
Low level	Men	62.3	46.3	40.8	20.3
	Women	66.0	43.5	39.1	20.0
Intermediate level	Men	22.3	29.6	15.0	24.0
	Women	25.1	35.6	18.5	26.8
High level	Men	14.9	21.7	14.3	23.5
	Women	8.4	18.6	14.5	27.4

Table 3.6. Distribution of general secondary education by birth cohort and gender

School degree		Germany 1929-38	Germany 1959-68	France 1929-38	France 1959-68
No degree	Men	1.0	3.2	32.8	40.6
	Women	1.2	2.9	32.8	31.0
Low level	Men	67.3	38.3	45.6	4.6
	Women	69.4	29.3	45.1	4.1
Intermediate level	Men	21.0	34.8	9.0	31.1
	Women	21.8	45.3	12.4	33.8
High level	Men	10.7	23.7	12.6	23.7
	Women	7.6	22.5	9.7	31.2

- In both countries, women have improved their position in terms of secondary schooling since the mid-1980s.

  French women have deepened their comparative advantage over time. This is particularly obvious considering the developments across birth cohorts. In particular, the proportion of women with no school degree has rather decreased, while it has significantly risen for men across cohorts. Moreover, the increase in the share of general maturity degrees has been particularly strong among French women, so that in the young generation, the gap in favour of women in terms of general maturity completion is quite large. In Germany too, women have improved their position compared to men. The drop in the share of low school (*Hauptschule*) degree holders has been much stronger for women than for men (see table 3.6). However, the strong decrease in the share of low school degree holders among women has been matched by a particularly strong increase in the share of intermediate certificates (*Realschule*), while men have conserved the advantage in terms of maturity degrees, though it has reduced. In the end, whereas French and German men have the same rate of general maturity completion in the youngest generations observed, French women do significantly better than their German counterparts in terms of secondary education.

3.1.2 Final educational attainment

The distribution of secondary education degrees largely influences the distribution of final educational attainment, and so do its developments, with a time lag. In particular, because the proportion of maturity holders is higher in France than in Germany, the share of tertiary education graduates is expected to be higher in France. Furthermore, since gender differences are larger in Germany than in France at the secondary school level, they are also likely to be greater in Germany than in France in terms of final educational attainment.

3.1.2.1 Structure and developments over time

Here again, the developments in the distribution of final educational attainment do not present erratic changes, and comparing 1985 to 2000, such as in table 3.7, provides an overview of the developments that have taken place in the time span between these dates. Detailed information for each year between 1985 and 2000 is given in tables B.3 to B.6 in appendix B. Moreover, in table 3.8, the distributional attainment of the 1929-38 birth cohort is compared to that of the 1959-68. This should provide further insights into the developments across generations and thus into the way the educational distribution is likely to develop in the future as long as new generations replace older ones in the whole population. The level of education finally attained is defined according to the typology proposed in table 2.1

Looking at the educational distribution in both countries, the following key elements can be observed.

- The distribution of final educational attainment is more dispersed in France than in Germany.

  In France, there is both a higher proportion of individuals with a low level of education and a higher proportion of tertiary level graduates. In contrast, the distribution of educational attainment is strongly concentrated around basic and intermediate vocational qualifications in Germany. Thus, Germany is in a better position than France at the bottom of the educational scale but France has an advantage at the upper end of the educational distribution.
  Looking more into detail, it can be observed that not only is the share of people with no vocational qualification significantly higher in France, but half of those do not even dispose of a secondary school degree, while

this is very unusual in Germany. At the other end of the distribution, it appears that the higher share of tertiary level graduates in France is entirely attributable to the lower tertiary level, which is more than twice as high as in Germany[4], while the share of upper tertiary level graduates has the same order of magnitude in France and in Germany[5].

- At the intermediate qualification level, the level of general education attained is higher in France.

  In Germany, the overwhelming majority of the intermediate skill group has an intermediate vocational qualification below the maturity level (typically a *Fachschule* or technical college degree). Conversely, in France, the large

Table 3.7. Distribution of final educational attainment by year

		Germany		France	
	Education level	**1985**	**2000**	**1985**	**2000**
1	**No vocational degree**	**24.7**	**15.5**	**56.5**	**36.0**
10	No degree	0.4	0.7	23.3	17.6
11	Lower secondary	22.1	11.3	25.9	11.0
12	Intermediate secondary	2.3	3.5	7.4	7.4
2	**Basic vocational degree**	**49.0**	**48.0**	**21.7**	**29.4**
20	Lower secondary + basic voc.	37.4	30.6	17.0	19.1
21	Interm. secondary + basic voc.	11.6	17.4	4.7	10.3
3	**Intermediate qualification**	**15.5**	**20.0**	**9.3**	**12.8**
30	Intermediate voc.	11.0	10.6	2.1	1.8
31	Vocational maturity	1.8	3.6	1.8	4.1
32	General maturity	0.6	1.3	4.3	6.0
33	General maturity + voc.	2.1	4.6	1.1	0.9
4	**Tertiary level degree**	**10.8**	**16.4**	**12.4**	**21.9**
40	Lower tertiary	3.7	5.2	6.3	11.1
41	Upper tertiary	7.1	11.2	6.2	10.9

[4] Note, however, that the level of the German *Fachhochschule* qualification is higher than that of French *Bac+2* qualifications and is closer to a *Bac+3* level qualification, which is classified as upper tertiary qualification in France (see chapter 2).

[5] Making use of the more detailed information available in the French data (see table B.1 in Appendix B), we observe that the majority of the *Bac+2* holders has a BTS/DUT degree, the rest being equally distributed among the university first cycle degrees (DEUG and the like) and paramedical qualifications. At the upper tertiary level, more than 70 percent have a university degree, while the remaining 30 percent have a *Grande Ecole* degree and less than 5 percent of the upper tertiary level graduates hold a degree from one of the most prestigious *Grandes Ecoles*.

Table 3.8. Distribution of final educational attainment by birth cohort

		Germany		France	
	Education level	**1929-38**	**1959-68**	**1929-38**	**1959-68**
1	**No vocational degree**	**27.4**	**9.2**	**67.6**	**28.5**
10	No degree	0.9	1.0	29.3	18.8
11	Lower secondary	24.2	6.1	31.8	2.0
12	Intermediate secondary	2.3	2.2	6.5	7.7
2	**Basic vocational degree**	**50.6**	**45.5**	**17.1**	**34.3**
20	Lower secondary + basic voc.	39.1	24.6	14.6	18.4
21	Interm. secondary + basic voc.	11.4	20.9	2.5	15.9
3	**Intermediate qualification**	**11.9**	**24.7**	**6.6**	**13.5**
30	Intermediate voc.	7.9	11.7	1.9	1.4
31	Vocational maturity	2.2	5.0	0.6	4.5
32	General maturity	0.8	1.4	3.7	6.5
33	General maturity + voc.	1.0	6.6	0.4	1.1
4	**Tertiary level degree**	**10.2**	**20.6**	**8.7**	**23.8**
40	Lower tertiary	4.2	7.4	3.7	12.5
41	Upper tertiary	6.0	13.3	5.0	11.3

majority of people in this skill group has completed the maturity certificate, either the vocational one or even more often the general one. This reflects the key position of the *Baccalauréat* in France, unlike in Germany, where the completion of vocational qualification seems to be the socially accepted norm and general education alone poorly valued. For instance, it is very uncommon in Germany to stop studying after having obtained the *Abitur*[6], while a nonnegligible proportion of French people does so.

- The level of final educational attainment has strongly increased since the mid-1980s in both countries, but particularly in France.

  In both France and Germany, the proportion of individuals without any vocational degree has decreased markedly since 1985 and considering the developments across cohorts, the drop is even more amazing. In both countries, this decrease mainly reflects a significant drop in the share of individuals with the lowest secondary school degree as the highest degree, but in France, the very high percentage of people without any school degree has also decreased substantially.
  This drop has been matched by an increase in intermediate and tertiary level qualifications, but in France, the share of individuals with a basic vocational qualification has increased too. The expansion in intermediate

[6] Most people who possess the German *Abitur* pursue further studies, either a vocational qualification – which is, in turn, very unusual in France – or tertiary level studies.

level (level 3) qualifications is particularly obvious when considering developments across cohorts. In both countries, it has more than doubled from the 1929-38 cohort to the 1959-68 cohort. The expansion of higher education has been just as strong as that of intermediate qualifications in Germany, but even stronger in France. This is essentially the result of a particularly strong progression of lower tertiary level degrees in France compared to Germany, while the expansion rate of upper tertiary level degrees is similar in scope for both countries[7]. The progression of tertiary level degrees is stronger when looking at specific generations than when looking at the whole population, at the lower and at the upper tertiary level alike. This suggests that the expansion of higher education is likely to continue in the future.

- The level of general education attained for a given level of vocational education has increased over time.

  Within the group of people with no vocational degree (level 1), the proportion of intermediate school certificates has increased over time. This is particularly true in France, judging from the developments across cohorts. Among the graduates of basic vocational education (level 2), too, an increasingly large share of people holds an intermediate secondary education certificate in both countries. However, in France, the share of level 20 qualifications has also increased – though to a lesser extent – in response to the decrease in the share of level 1 qualifications, whereas in Germany, level 20 qualifications have become less frequent and seem to be increasingly replaced by level 21 qualifications. The increase in the proportion of individuals with an intermediate qualification observed previously has been mainly driven by the expansion of the maturity degrees, both vocational and general (levels 31 and 32). In Germany, however, the share of individuals not studying at the tertiary level after obtaining their general maturity degree has also increased over time. Thus, while the share of maturity holders has increased over time in both countries, the propensity

[7] Note that in Germany, the expansion of university degrees has been significantly stronger than that of the *Fachhochschule* degrees, while lower and upper tertiary level qualifications have expanded at a similar path in France. In France, the impressive expansion of lower tertiary degrees is essentially attributable to the rise in BTS/DUT degrees among the *Bac+2* holders since the mid-1980s (see table B.1 in Appendix B). At the upper tertiary level, the relationship between university and *Grandes Ecoles* has remained rather stable since the mid-1980s (approximately 70 percent against 30 percent of upper tertiary level graduates). However, among holders of a *Grande Ecole* degree, fewer have nowadays a degree from a top *Grande Ecole*. This development is due to the creation of a large number of new *Grandes Ecoles* which are less selective or less prestigious than the traditional ones and drive the relative share of top *Grandes Ecoles* down. If the share of postgraduates has risen until the mid-1990s, it has been following a decreasing trend since then.

to undertake tertiary level studies when possessing the maturity degree seems to have somewhat decreased in Germany.

3.1.2.2 Gender differences

In both countries, there are significant gender differences in the qualification structure of the population. Table 3.9 shows the gender-specific distribution of educational attainment in France and Germany in 1985 and 2000, and table 3.10 shows how the distribution of educational attainment among men and women has changed over generations. Tables B.3 to B.6 in appendix B provide additional details. The key elements that appear from these tables can be summarised as follows:

- Gender differences in final educational attainment are much more pronounced in Germany than in France.

  In Germany, men undoubtedly have a higher educational attainment than women. A larger share of women has no or only a basic vocational degree and a smaller share of women has completed intermediate or higher education. In France, however, the differences between men and women are much smaller and men perform better in some respects, women in other respects.
  A striking feature is that in 2000, almost twice as many women as men have no vocational degree in Germany, while only less than 20 percent more women than men have no vocational qualification in France. Looking more in detail, it appears that in Germany as in France, the proportion of individuals with neither a school nor a vocational degree is nearly the same for men and women. Thus, the gender gap in this category mainly stems from the fact that among people with no vocational qualification, more women than men with a lower or intermediate school degree stop studying.
  At the other end of the educational distribution, the difference between France and Germany is amazing. While the share of higher education graduates is slightly higher among women than among men in France in 2000, there is a huge gap in favour of men in Germany. A closer look reveals that the latter is true at the lower tertiary level and at the upper tertiary level alike. However, in France, the gap in favour of women is due to the lower tertiary level, whereas men still have the advantage in terms of upper tertiary level degrees[8].

[8] As can be seen from table B.1 in appendix B, at the lower tertiary level, almost three quarter of French men and almost half of French women have a BTS/DUT qualification, which provides an advanced technical degree, in 2000. A much larger share of women than men pursues paramedical studies. At the upper tertiary level, a much larger share of men graduated from a *Grande Ecole* (40 percent of men against 15 percent of women) in 2000, and if 6.5 percent of French men held a degree of a top *Grande Ecole*, only 2.5 percent of women did so.

Table 3.9. Distribution of final educational attainment by year and gender

	Education level		Germany 1985	Germany 2000	France 1985	France 2000
1	**No vocational degree**	**Men**	**11.5**	**11.6**	**51.6**	**32.8**
		Women	**36.7**	**19.3**	**61.2**	**39.0**
10	No degree	Men	0.3	0.7	22.5	17.7
		Women	0.5	0.8	24.0	17.6
11	Lower secondary	Men	10.4	9.0	22.9	9.0
		Women	32.6	13.6	28.8	12.9
12	Intermediate secondary	Men	0.8	1.9	6.2	6.2
		Women	3.6	4.9	8.5	8.5
2	**Basic vocational degree**	**Men**	**53.5**	**46.2**	**26.0**	**33.9**
		Women	**45.0**	**49.7**	**17.7**	**25.0**
20	Lower secondary + basic voc.	Men	44.2	33.0	21.9	24.1
		Women	31.3	28.3	12.4	14.3
21	Interm. secondary + basic voc.	Men	9.3	13.3	4.1	9.8
		Women	13.8	21.3	5.3	10.7
3	**Intermediate qualification**	**Men**	**19.6**	**21.8**	**9.4**	**11.9**
		Women	**11.8**	**18.4**	**9.2**	**13.6**
30	Intermediate voc.	Men	14.9	13.0	2.6	1.9
		Women	7.5	8.3	1.7	1.6
31	Vocational maturity	Men	2.0	3.6	2.1	4.2
		Women	1.6	3.6	1.6	4.0
32	General maturity	Men	0.5	1.5	3.7	5.0
		Women	0.7	1.1	4.9	7.0
33	General maturity + voc.	Men	2.1	3.8	1.0	0.8
		Women	2.1	5.3	1.1	1.1
4	**Tertiary level degree**	**Men**	**15.4**	**20.0**	**13.0**	**21.4**
		Women	**6.6**	**13.1**	**11.9**	**22.4**
40	Lower tertiary	Men	5.4	7.2	5.1	9.4
		Women	2.2	3.5	7.4	12.5
41	Upper tertiary	Men	10.0	12.8	7.9	11.9
		Women	4.4	9.7	4.5	9.8

Table 3.10. Distribution of final educational attainment by cohort and gender

Education level			Germany		France	
			1929-1938	1959-1968	1929-1938	1959-1968
1	**No vocational degree**	**Men**	**10.7**	**7.7**	**60.9**	**27.6**
		Women	**41.2**	**10.8**	**73.3**	**29.4**
10	No degree	Men	0.5	1.1	28.3	19.2
		Women	1.2	0.8	30.2	18.4
11	Lower secondary	Men	9.6	5.4	27.6	1.7
		Women	36.3	6.7	35.3	2.4
12	Intermediate secondary	Men	0.6	1.3	5.0	6.7
		Women	3.8	3.2	7.8	8.6
2	**Basic vocational degree**	**Men**	**57.4**	**42.6**	**20.7**	**38.9**
		Women	**44.9**	**48.4**	**14.0**	**29.7**
20	Lower secondary + basic voc.	Men	48.9	27.1	18.8	23.3
		Women	31.0	21.8	10.9	13.6
21	Interm. secondary + basic voc.	Men	8.5	15.4	1.8	15.7
		Women	13.9	26.6	3.1	16.2
3	**Intermediate qualification**	**Men**	**16.5**	**24.8**	**7.8**	**11.2**
		Women	**8.0**	**24.6**	**5.7**	**15.6**
30	Intermediate voc.	Men	11.9	14.9	2.7	1.3
		Women	4.5	8.4	1.2	1.4
31	Vocational maturity	Men	3.5	3.9	1.1	4.2
		Women	1.1	6.2	0.2	4.9
32	General maturity	Men	0.5	1.3	3.6	5.0
		Women	1.2	1.4	3.8	8.0
33	General maturity + voc.	Men	0.7	4.7	0.4	0.7
		Women	1.3	8.5	0.4	1.4
4	**Tertiary level degree**	**Men**	**15.4**	**24.8**	**10.7**	**22.3**
		Women	**5.9**	**16.3**	**7.0**	**25.3**
40	Lower tertiary	Men	7.0	10.0	3.1	10.6
		Women	1.9	4.7	4.1	14.5
41	Upper tertiary	Men	8.4	14.9	7.6	11.7
		Women	3.9	11.6	2.9	10.8

In the middle range of the educational distribution, it appears that in France significantly more men than women hold a basic vocational degree whereas in Germany, slightly more women than men do so in 2000. At the intermediate qualification level, too, the situation differs in France and in Germany. More men than women have an intermediate qualification level in Germany, while the reverse is true in France, even though the gap is rather small there.

- In both countries, women have a higher level of general education for a given level of final vocational education.

  Among people with no vocational education (level 1), for instance, more women than men have an intermediate school degree, especially in Germany in the youngest cohort. This is also obvious for completers of a basic vocational degree (level 2). In both countries, more men completed only the low school degree at most and more women hold the intermediate school certificate. At the intermediate level (level 3), too, the level of general education attained is higher for women in both countries. Indeed, more women hold the general maturity degree in this skill group, while more men hold an advanced vocational certificate, particularly in Germany.

- Women have improved their position since the mid-1980s in both countries, but particularly in France.

  In both countries, the drop in the share of individuals with no vocational degree has been much stronger for women than for men. This is essentially the effect of the drop in the share of individuals with a low school degree which was particularly strong for women in both countries.
  This stronger drop of level 1 qualifications among women translates into a comparatively stronger progression in the share of basic and above all of intermediate qualifications in both countries. Thus, whereas the share of individuals with at most a vocational degree has decreased over time for men in Germany, it has increased for women in the same period[9]. In France, there has been a progression of level 2 qualifications for both men and women, but it was stronger for women. The expansion of intermediate qualifications has been far more pronounced for women than for men, essentially due to the particularly strong progression of maturity certificates, general or vocational, among women.
  As mentioned before, gender differences – in favour of men – are far more pronounced in Germany than in France as far as higher education is concerned. The figures show that there are no clear signs of significant convergence between genders in Germany. Instead, the expansion rather seems to have followed a similar path and the gap remains similar in absolute

[9] This stronger progression of level 2 qualifications is essentially due to the particularly strong increase in the proportion of women holding an intermediate school degree beside their vocational certificate in Germany.

terms, both at the lower and at the upper tertiary level. In France, however, women have improved their position compared to men, both at the lower[10] and at the upper tertiary level. In the youngest cohort observed, the share of French female university graduates is almost as high as that of men.

Overall, it is striking that whereas there is a higher dispersion in Germany than in France in terms of numerical and literacy skills such as measured in the PISA study, the distribution of attainment in secondary and post-secondary education is, on the contrary, much *less* dispersed than in France. Moreover, whereas girls were found to perform better on average than boys in terms of the general skills tested in PISA, this does not translate into better educational achievement, especially in Germany. As mentioned in the introduction, France and Germany share the fundamental objective to attain the largest possible extent of social equality in educational opportunities. The remainder of this chapter therefore examines whether the impact of social background on educational achievement is stronger in Germany than in France, as could be assumed given certain features of the education systems and given the results of the latest PISA study. Moreover, it examines the extent and the nature of gender differences.

3.2 Determinants of the level of education: overview of the literature

Let us have a look at what has been done in the literature on this topic so far. The overview of the literature provided in this section first focusses on the modelling framework typically used in the literature for analyses of the determinants of educational attainment and then presents the state of the empirical evidence available for France and Germany, in particular with respect to the effects of social origin.

3.2.1 Modelling strategies

Both the various theoretical frameworks and the empirical approaches adopted in the literature to model and estimate the determinants of educational outcomes are reviewed here.

3.2.1.1 Theoretical framework

The bulk of the work related to the modelling of educational outcomes is more or less explicitly imbedded in the human capital theory, which dates back to

[10] This is mainly the result of a very strong progression of women holding a degree of the BTS/DUT level, see figures in table B.1 in appendix B.

Becker (1964) and Mincer (1974). According to the human capital approach, individuals decide on the optimal amount of education they want to invest in by weighing up the costs and the returns of additional schooling. The acquisition of education generates costs, in any case opportunity costs in the form of foregone earnings during the time education is taken and possibly also direct costs (e.g. books, tuition fees etc.). On the other hand, education is assumed to raise one's productivity, which will be rewarded in terms of earnings in the subsequent working career. Therefore, an optimising individual will choose the level of education which maximises his net return and continue to invest in further education until the marginal cost of additional investment equals the marginal return. This theory implies that human capital investment differs among individuals due to differences in either return or cost conditions. The human capital theory has been criticised for privileging mere monetary considerations, mainly regarding education as a monetary investment and disregarding nonmonetary utility aspects or consumption motives. As a matter of fact, education may contribute to nonmonetary utility in the short run as well as in the long run. In response to this objection, some economists extended the model and included the consumption motive in the human capital approach, assuming that education increases the efficiency of allocating leisure (see Heckman (1976) and Kodde (1988), who show that the demand for education is higher if one integrates consumption motives).

Another extension of the human capital model can be found in the household production model, introduced by Becker (1965), which insists on the necessity of viewing the process of educational attainment as an aspect of family behaviour rather than individual behaviour. According to this approach, children's educational attainment is a commodity which enters the household utility production. The household is viewed as a production unit which generates utility for its members using some market inputs (e.g. school quality) as well as household inputs (e.g. time, family characteristics). Adults in the family, typically parents, make decisions regarding the generation and the use of household resources. Parental decisions may affect children's outcomes directly, through for instance the amount of resources allocated to the children, the nature of these resources or their timing, but also indirectly, through for instance decisions related to the family structure or the location the children grow up in. The household production model has been continuously refined and complemented. Among others, Taubman (1976) stresses the importance of genetic inheritance, since scholastic abilities are to some extent passed on from one generation to the next. Also Becker and Tomes (1986), and more recently Ermisch and Francesconi (2001), insist on the inheritability of certain endowments like ability or preferences, which translate into human capital. Hanushek (1992) points to the fact that there is a trade-off for the parents between the number and the "quality" of the children, here measured by their scholastic performance, because parents maximise the household utility, a function of the quantity and the quality of the children, subject to a budget constraint and a time constraint. More recently, Wilson (2001) tries to integrate in a model of educational attainment aspects of both the human capital theory and the production function model.

Another vein of literature has a sociological focus and seeks to provide hypotheses to explain why the various social groups do not have the same educational prospects. For instance, the socialisation approach emphasises the transmission by peers or role models, typically the parents, to the child of a pattern of behaviour. Another example is the life course development hypothesis which highlights the role of the age at which educational decisions occur. Indeed, as Müller (1990) states, as students grow older, they will increasingly be able to make their own choices and will be less dependent on their family background. An interesting consequence of this hypothesis is that if this turns out to be true that the timing of educational decisions in the life course matters, educational policy could reduce social inequality in terms of educational prospects by delaying the moment when educational decisions are to be made (see the formulation of alternative hypotheses in Shavit and Blossfeld (1993) to explain differences in educational attainment across countries).

3.2.1.2 Empirical implementation strategies

As far as empirical evidence is concerned, the major part of the literature does not primarily aim at establishing causal relationships but rather focusses on the nature and extent of correlations between parental and child's outcomes, without being primarily interested in the process by which these correlations arise. In many studies, empirical analyses are only loosely related to a theoretical model, even though other studies do imbed their empirical analysis in a more or less explicit theoretical framework (see the overview of Haveman and Wolfe 1995). More concretely, a typical approach has been, following Blau and Duncan (1967), to estimate the impact of selected variables on ultimate educational attainment, measured by completed years of schooling. Such an approach assumes that there exists a linear relationship between the explanatory factors – typically family background variables – and years of schooling.

By contrast, Mare (1980), after Boudon (1974), points to the usefulness, as a complement to the traditional approach, of viewing final educational attainment as the result of a process which can be decomposed into a finite number of stages at which the student makes decisions. In other words, educational attainment can be viewed as a sequence of transitions within the education system, and the product of the transition probabilities generates the probability of final educational attainment. Beyond the interest of analysing specific transitions per se, Mare (1980) argues that restricting the analysis to the determinants of final educational attainment only is not informative with respect to the stage at which the explanatory factors exert an influence, whether they affect the probability of transiting to the highest level of education attained or the probability of successfully completing some earlier transition. The approach he proposes therefore consists in analysing school continuation decisions. Given information on the highest grade finally completed, the school continuation decisions at each grade can be deduced, i.e. the probability that a person attended a particular grade of schooling, given that the person completed the previous grade. Beside empirical studies which focus on one particular transition in isolation from other transitions (e.g. Willis and Rosen 1979; Manski and Wise 1983 examine the transition from high school to college attendance), many studies (among others Shavit and Blossfeld 1993) are directly based on the schooling-transition model of Mare (1980).

In a recent work, however, Cameron and Heckman (1998) have criticised the schooling-transition model as applied in the empirical literature and questioned the empirical conclusions usually drawn from the application of this model, in particular the decline in the impact of family background across transitions. Their main objection relates to educational selectivity. Indeed, schooling transition models generally ignore that factors which are not observable to the scientist might influence transitions, such as ability or motivation. Thus, after each transition, only a certain type of students – in terms of these unobserved factors – remains in the sample that will form the basis for the next transition. When ignoring the progressive selectivity of sample composition with respect to unobserved heterogeneity as one moves along the educational career, one might wrongly attribute an effect to an explanatory variable whereas it is in fact the effect of the nonrandomly distributed unobserved factors. The direction and the size of this dynamic selection bias depends on the nature of the correlation of the unobserved factors across transitions (Cameron and Heckman 1998). The model of Cameron and Heckman (1998) has, however, the drawback of modelling the educational decision in terms of schooling years and as if the decision was taken once for all at the beginning of the educational career (see further details in sections 3.3.1 and 3.4.1).

Overall, there is no consensus on the proper way to model educational decisions and there seems to be scope for research in this area.

3.2.2 Evidence for France and Germany

Given the political relevance of the educational issue in France and Germany, it is not surprising that the extent of social inequalities in educational opportunities has been the object of a large number of empirical studies in these countries.

Germany

Kristen (1999) provides a detailed review of studies related to educational decisions and educational inequality for Germany. A number of sociological studies examine transitions within the education system, particularly the transition from primary to secondary education, an essential stage in the German education system. The first studies date back to the 1970s, in the context of a strong educational expansion. Among others, Baur (1972) analysed the transition rates from one class to the next within and between the school types, laying special emphasis on differences across social groups. The 1980s see the emergence of new studies that rely on multivariate statistical methods (e.g. Wiese 1982; De Graaf 1988). More recently, Blossfeld (1993) but also Müller and Haun (1994) examined the issue of educational inequality across social groups and its changes over time in Germany. They find evidence of strong links between social origin and educational attainment and that social inequalities have not reduced significantly over time. Also Dustmann (2001) shows that parental background is closely related to the secondary track children follow, which, in turn, is strongly correlated with subsequent educational achievement. In recent years, the extent of inequalities across ethnic groups in Germany in terms of educational attainment has gained much interest in empirical research. Büchel and Wagner (1996), as well as Bender and Seifert (1996) and Gang and Zimmermann (1999), examine for instance the extent of the disadvantage experienced by children of immigrants in terms of educational outcomes, while Kristen (2000) concentrates on the transition from primary to secondary schooling of immigrants compared to native German children.

France

In France also a great interest for social inequalities in educational matters arose along with the educational expansion of the 1970s. The works of Bourdieu and Passeron (1970) and Boudon (1973) are seen as the reference in this respect and in the debate on this topic, equality in educational opportunity is viewed as the main means to attain the meritocratic ideal (see also Goux and Maurin 1997). Throughout the 1980s, it remained a topic investigated by French sociology, with for instance the studies of Duru-Bellat and Mingat (1987) and Duru-Bellat, Jarousse and Mingat (1993). In the past decade, Goux and Maurin (1997) and Thélot and Vallet (2000) used the representative *Formation et Qualification Professionnelles* (FQP) data (see section 2.3.1) to examine whether social inequalities at school have reduced over time. The authors of the latter study find out that social inequalities have reduced since the beginning of the century, but considering only the past few decades, the authors of the former study conclude that social inequality in terms of education has not reduced much, like in many other countries – including Germany (see Shavit and Blossfeld 1993).

Overall, the literature available for France and Germany leads to the conclusion that there is indeed a strong link between social background and educational achievement in both countries. However, the results are hardly comparable because the studies available generally have a national focus rather than a comparative one, do not define educational attainment in a similar way and use different methodological frameworks. Therefore, it is not possible to say, based on the empirical evidence available so far, whether Germany faces a particularly high degree of social inequalities in educational achievement, and in particular whether social inequalities are higher there than in France, where the education system, more than the German one, is supposed to foster social equality. The examination of this question is the aim of the following econometric analysis.

3.3 Determinants of final educational attainment

First of all, a methodological framework has to be chosen to analyse the impact of social background on educational achievement. As mentioned in section 3.2.1, there is no consensus in the literature on the right way to model educational outcomes and the models available present certain drawbacks which make them problematic for the present study. Therefore, one of the objectives of this work is to develop an own model of educational attainment that fulfills the following requirements. First, the model should be written in such a way that it provides a theoretical foundation to the subsequent empirical analyses. Thus, it should be applicable directly to the French and German data, so that the interpretation of the parameters can be drawn from the theoretical modelling. Furthermore, it should allow to model also the sequential nature of the educational process and the differential options faced by students at certain points of the educational career given the institutional features of the education system. In a first step (3.3.1), a model of final educational attainment is formulated which draws on the model of Cameron and Heckman (1998). In a second step (3.4.1), the model will be extended to decompose educational achievement into attainment in secondary and in post-secondary education.

3.3.1 Formulation of the model

The basic model presented here differs less in terms of economic content than in terms of formulation from that of Cameron and Heckman (1998). It is reformulated in such a way that it can be directly implemented and interpreted empirically. The model will then be applied to French and German data with a view to providing evidence on the impact of social background on educational outcomes in France and Germany while illustrating the empirical opportunities offered by the model.

Let us suppose that each individual chooses, given some constraints, how much he wants to invest in education, i.e. chooses the education E he wants to acquire among J educational alternatives E_j of increasing levels, with $j \in \{1...J\}$[11]. Let E^* be the desired educational level. The desired level of ed-

[11] Cameron and Heckman (1998) express the educational decision in terms of years of schooling.

ucation is not observable, but only the actual decision E_j of the individual[12] i.e. the education level j actually chosen.

The decision is assumed to be rational in the sense that it maximises the perceived utility for the individual, subject to some constraints. The perceived utility is defined as the expected net returns, i.e. the difference between expected returns and expected costs of each educational alternative E_j, given some characteristics. The concept of utility may cover monetary as well as nonmonetary aspects such as life satisfaction, access to cultural goods, leisure etc. Consequently, the terms "returns" and "costs" are used for ease of language, but may also be nonpecuniary. They should be understood as a positive and a negative utility respectively. Thus, the optimal educational decision for an individual with a given vector of characteristics x is given by:

$$Max_{j \in \{1 \ldots J\}} \; r(E_j \mid x) - c(E_j \mid x) \qquad (3.1)$$

where r denotes the expected return and c the expected cost associated with educational level E_j. x includes both personal and familial characteristics[13] observable to the scientist that may influence the – perceived or real – utility of the educational options, either positively, through the return function or negatively through the cost function. As an example of personal characteristic, the cohort an individual is born in might affect the perception of the utility of completing a certain level of education due to social or economic context prevailing at the time educational decisions were made. Familial characteristics might also affect the expected utility of education, through the availability of financial resources for instance, but also through the transmission of abilities and preferences[14]. The return function is assumed to be strictly positive, weakly convex and increasing with the education level. The cost function is assumed to be positive, concave and increasing with the education level. The cost function starts with the value zero, while the return function is strictly positive. These assumptions ensure that the net expected return, i.e. the utility, will be concave and positive for at least the lowest possible education level.

The costs and returns of education are allowed to differ across individuals and it is assumed that they are affected by personal and familial characteristics

[12] Within the framework of this model, it does not matter who in fact makes the decision, whether it is the individual himself or somebody else (the parents, for instance). What counts is the outcome of the decision among the possible alternatives. For ease of presentation, I will speak of the individual rather than of the decision-maker, since the outcome concerns the individual.

[13] The year of birth, parental education, income or occupation, for instance, can be such characteristics. See section 3.3.2 for further details on the mechanisms through which these variables might affect the net utility of education.

[14] See in section 3.2.1 the theoretical rationale for personal and family characteristics affecting educational decisions, as well as more detailed explanations of the channels through which the variables should exert their influence on educational outcomes in section 3.3.2.

observable to the scientist and by some other unobserved factors. They can be decomposed in the following way[15]:

$$r(E_j \mid x) = r(E_j)\,\varphi_r(x)\,\varepsilon_r \qquad (3.2)$$
$$c(E_j \mid x) = c(E_j)\,\varphi_c(x)\,\varepsilon_c$$

where $\varphi_r(x)$ is a positive function defining the effects of the personal and familial characteristics on the expected returns to education and ε_r is a random variable accounting for the effect of unobserved individual heterogeneity on the expected returns[16]. Similarly, $\varphi_c(x)$ is a positive function which defines the effects of the observed personal and familial characteristics on the expected costs of education and ε_c is a positive random variable representing the impact of unobserved individual heterogeneity.

Thus, both obwerved characteristics and unobserved individual heterogeneity may affect the expected returns and the expected costs in different ways[17]. However, the personal shifters φ_r, φ_c, ε_r, and ε_c are assumed not to depend on the specific education level. Without loss of generality, it is assumed that $E(\varepsilon_r) = E(\varepsilon_c) = 1$, meaning that unobserved heterogeneity has on average a neutral effect on the return as well as on the cost expectations.

The optimal educational decision E_{j^*} is such that the expected utility is maximised, i.e. the net return associated with the optimal decision E_{j^*} must be positive, larger than the net returns expected from the next lower education level E_{j^*-1} and at least as large as those expected from the next higher education level E_{j^*+1}[18]:

$$r(E_{j^*})\,\varphi_r(x)\,\varepsilon_r - c(E_{j^*})\,\varphi_c(x)\,\varepsilon_c > 0$$
$$r(E_{j^*})\,\varphi_r(x)\,\varepsilon_r - c(E_{j^*})\,\varphi_c(x)\,\varepsilon_c > r(E_{j^*-1})\,\varphi_r(x)\,\varepsilon_r - c(E_{j^*-1})\,\varphi_c(x)\,\varepsilon_c$$
$$r(E_{j^*})\,\varphi_r(x)\,\varepsilon_r - c(E_{j^*})\,\varphi_c(x)\,\varepsilon_c \geq r(E_{j^*+1})\,\varphi_r(x)\,\varepsilon_r - c(E_{j^*+1})\,\varphi_c(x)\,\varepsilon_c$$

---

15 Cameron and Heckman (1998) assume on their part that the return only depends on the education level and only let the cost function depend on observed and unobserved heterogeneity.

16 Due to the multiplicative structure of the model, $\varphi_r(x) > 1$ (< 1) implies that the observed characteristics of an individual, taken together, increase (decrease) the return expectations. Similarly, $\varepsilon_r > 1$ (< 1) means that the unobserved factors increase (decrease) the return expectations.

17 A high scholastic ability, for instance, a typically unobserved factor, reduces the cost of educational investment, but might not increase to the same extent the return to educational investments, since the way the acquired knowledge is "transformed" into wages depends on another kind of ability.

18 If the net return is equal for E_j and E_{j+1}, the individual is assumed to choose E_j.

This is equivalent to:

$$\varphi_c(x)\varepsilon_c\left[r(E_{j^*})\,\frac{\varphi_r(x)\varepsilon_r}{\varphi_c(x)\varepsilon_c}-c(E_{j^*})\right]>0$$
$$\varphi_c(x)\varepsilon_c\left[r(E_{j^*})\,\frac{\varphi_r(x)\varepsilon_r}{\varphi_c(x)\varepsilon_c}-c(E_{j^*})\right]>\varphi_c(x)\varepsilon_c\left[r(E_{j^*-1})\,\frac{\varphi_r(x)\varepsilon_r}{\varphi_c(x)\varepsilon_c}-c(E_{j^*-1})\right]$$
$$\varphi_c(x)\varepsilon_c\left[r(E_{j^*})\,\frac{\varphi_r(x)\varepsilon_r}{\varphi_c(x)\varepsilon_c}-c(E_{j^*})\right]\geq\varphi_c(x)\varepsilon_c\left[r(E_{j^*+1})\,\frac{\varphi_r(x)\varepsilon_r}{\varphi_c(x)\varepsilon_c}-c(E_{j^*+1})\right]$$

Let us define: $\varphi(x)=\frac{\varphi_r(x)}{\varphi_c(x)}$ and $\varepsilon=\frac{\varepsilon_r}{\varepsilon_c}$.

$\varphi(x)$ measures the net impact of personal and familial characteristics x and ε the net effect of unobserved individual heterogeneity on the expected relation of returns to costs. Since $\varepsilon_r>0$, $\varepsilon_c>0$, $\varepsilon>0$, $\varphi_r(x)>0$ and $\varphi_c(x)>0$, one obtains after simplification:

$$r(E_{j^*})\,\varphi(x)\,\varepsilon-c(E_{j^*})>0$$
$$r(E_{j^*})\,\varphi(x)\,\varepsilon-c(E_{j^*})>r(E_{j^*-1})\,\varphi(x)\,\varepsilon-c(E_{j^*-1})$$
$$r(E_{j^*})\,\varphi(x)\,\varepsilon-c(E_{j^*})\geq r(E_{j^*+1})\,\varphi(x)\,\varepsilon-c(E_{j^*+1})$$

or

$$0<\frac{c(E_{j^*})}{r(E_{j^*})}\,\frac{1}{\varphi(x)}<\varepsilon$$
$$\frac{c(E_{j^*})-c(E_{j^*-1})}{r(E_{j^*})-r(E_{j^*-1})}\,\frac{1}{\varphi(x)}<\varepsilon\leq\frac{c(E_{j^*+1})-c(E_{j^*})}{r(E_{j^*+1})-r(E_{j^*})}\,\frac{1}{\varphi(x)}$$

Consequently, the probability that an individual chooses E_j is given by:

$$Pr(E_j|x)=Pr\left[\frac{c(E_j)-c(E_{j-1})}{r(E_j)-r(E_{j-1})}\,\frac{1}{\varphi(x)}<\varepsilon\leq\frac{c(E_{j+1})-c(E_j)}{r(E_{j+1})-r(E_j)}\,\frac{1}{\varphi(x)}\right]\quad(3.3)$$

To simplify the notation, let us call:

$$\mu_j=\ln\left(\frac{c(E_{j+1})-c(E_j)}{r(E_{j+1})-r(E_j)}\right)\quad\text{and}\quad\gamma_j=\mu_j\frac{1}{\varphi(x)}\quad(3.4)$$

The probability that an individual chooses exactly education level E_j is therefore given by the probability that the error term is comprised between two thresholds γ_{j-1} and γ_j. To put it in words, for each educational level, there is a threshold for going from one level of education to the next. The higher the threshold is, the lower the probability to attain the next higher education level will be. If an individual, for instance, has a higher threshold γ_j than another, given their respective personal and familial characteristics x, this means that the relation of the additional cost to opt for education level E_{j+1} rather than E_j to the additional return of doing so is more unfavourable for the first individual than for the second one and that the probability that the first individual attains education level E_{j+1} at least[19] will be lower.

Thus, any difference in the personal and familial characteristics x may affect educational decisions to the extent that it affects the expected ratios μ_j of marginal costs to marginal returns from the next lower level to the next higher level. Note that in this model, it is not necessary to assess the *actual* costs and returns of each educational alternative, but it is enough to determine how the observed characteristics influence the *perceived* ratios of costs to returns. Taking the logarithm of the expression in brackets in equation (3.3) and assuming that $\varphi(x) = \exp[\beta x]$, we obtain:

$$Pr(E_j \mid x) = Pr\left[\mu_{j-1} - \beta x < \ln \varepsilon \leq \mu_j - \beta x\right] \tag{3.5}$$

If $\ln \varepsilon$ is assumed to be normally distributed with mean 0 and variance σ^2, equation (3.5) may be rewritten as

$$Pr(E_j \mid x) = \Phi\left(\frac{\mu_j - \beta x}{\sigma}\right) - \Phi\left(\frac{\mu_{j-1} - \beta x}{\sigma}\right) \tag{3.6}$$

where Φ is the cumulative standard normal distribution function.

This expression takes the familiar form of an ordered probit model, where the μ_j's are the cut values[20]. The ordered probit model written above can only be identified up to some factor of proportionality. Since it is the ratio of the parameters to σ which matters, it is convenient to normalise σ to 1 (Maddala 1983: 23). The parameters β and the cut values μ_j can be estimated by maximising the likelihood function for this model:

$$\mathcal{L} = \prod_{i=1}^{n} \prod_{j=1}^{J} \left[\Phi(\mu_j - \beta x_i) - \Phi(\mu_{j-1} - \beta x_i)\right]^{I_{ij}} \tag{3.7}$$

where I_{ij} is an indicator variable equal to 1 if the individual i, $i \in \{1...n\}$ opts for educational level E_j and 0 otherwise. Maximising $\mathcal{L}$ boils down to maximising $\ln \mathcal{L}$, since $\mathcal{L}$ is a positive function and $\ln \mathcal{L}$ a monotone increasing transformation of $\mathcal{L}$.

---

19 Note that if one wants to determine the impact of a change or difference in x on the probability of completing exactly E_j – and not at most or at least –, one needs to consider the impact of x on both bounds and to know the distribution function of ε.

20 Note that given the assumptions made for the cost and return functions, we have at the extremes $\mu_0 = -\infty$ and $\mu_J = +\infty$.

Therefore, the model can be easily estimated by maximising the following log-likelihood function[21]:

$$\ln \mathcal{L} = \sum_{i=1}^{n} \sum_{j=1}^{J} I_{ij} \ln \left[\Phi(\mu_j - \beta x_i) - \Phi(\mu_{j-1} - \beta x_i) \right] \tag{3.8}$$

This model can be directly applied to the case of France and Germany, using individual data. After providing details on the data as well as on the choice and definition of the variables used for the estimation in section 3.3.2, section 3.3.3 presents the estimation results.

3.3.2 Data and variables

For France, the *Formation et Qualification Professionnelles* (FQP) data is more appropriate than the *Emploi* survey for the purpose of this study because it contains a series of variables depicting social origin[22] (see the description of the data sets in section 2.3.1). Moreover, comparable information is available in the German data. Therefore, the following estimations are based on the GSOEP data for Germany and on the FQP data for France.

Table 3.11. Delimitation of the working samples drawn from the GSOEP and the FQP data sets

	Germany		**France**	
	Observations	**(%)**	**Observations**	**(%)**
Total	9,426		16,226	
Without:				
East German	7,944	(-15.7)	-	
Foreigners*	6,162	(-22.4)	15,298	(-5.7)
Enrolled	6,079	(-1.4)	15,227	(-0.5)
Education missing	6,005	(-1.2)	15,037	(-1.2)
Working sample	6,005		15,037	

* Foreigners born abroad only. The sample of foreigners is oversampled in the GSOEP data (see Haisken-DeNew and Frick 2000).

As in the descriptive analysis and for the same reasons (see section 3.1, only West Germans are analysed for Germany and the sample is reduced to nationals or foreigners born in the country, not enrolled in education and for which we have complete information on their educational attainment. Moreover, the sample selected here consists of the cohorts born between 1929 and

[21] It can be estimated directly with a standard statistical package such as Stata 7.0, which includes a command for the estimation of ordered probit models.

[22] The *Emploi* data only contains information on father's occupation.

1968. Limiting the sample to the cohorts born between 1929 and 1968 makes sure that the French individuals observed are aged between 25 and 65, since all the information is drawn from 1993, the single FQP wave available. Extending the analysis to cohorts born after 1968 would increase dramatically the percentage of individuals still enrolled in education. For Germany, one could also take all the information from the 1993 wave, just as for France, but in order to maximise the (limited) number of observations, the cohorts born before 1948 are taken from the 1985 wave of the panel, where they are more numerous, while cohorts born after 1948 are drawn from the 1999 wave. In the end, this selection leaves us with an estimation sample of about 6,000 individuals for Germany, and around 15,000 individuals for France. Table 3.11 reports the number of observations remaining after each step of the sample selection and indicates the corresponding sample reduction in percentage.

The educational decision as such cannot be observed, since there is no information on what motivates individuals in their educational choices, but one can observe the educational outcome, i.e. the result of the decision. The educational outcome, and therefore the dependent variable, is defined here as the highest degree obtained in 5 levels E_1 to E_5 to follow model notation, based on the typology presented in table 2.1 and aggregated as in table 3.12[23].

Table 3.12. Definition of dependent variable: final educational attainment

Education level			**Germany**	**France**
Denomination	*Model*	*Typology*		
No voc. degree	E_1	Level 1	No voc. degree	No voc. degree
Basic voc. degree	E_2	Level 2	*Lehre*	CAP/BEP
Interm. qualification	E_3	Level 3	*Fachschule/Abi*	*Baccalauréat* level
Lower tertiary	E_4	Level 40	*Fachhochschule*	*Bac+2* level
Upper tertiary	E_5	Level 41	*Universität*	Above *Bac+2* level

The next step is to specify the personal and familial characteristics contained in the vector x. The choice of the explanatory variables is restricted by the fact that they need to be available in both data sets if the effects are to be compared. Thus, one has to give up information which is available in one data set but not in the other[24]. The analysis concentrates on the effects of variables which are common in both data sets: birth cohort and gender as per-

[23] For further information on the construction of the education levels, the reader is referred to chapter 2.

[24] For instance, information on the size of the city the individual grew up in would be available for Germany, but not for France. Information on mother's occupation is available for France but not for Germany. Including these variables when available proved to somewhat improve the fit but had only a minor impact on the other coefficients.

sonal characteristics, parental education and father's occupation as familial characteristics.

Beyond possible differences between men and women in certain types of abilities and preferences that might affect the actual costs and returns of educational alternatives, gender might also affect the perception of the utility of attaining a certain education level. Indeed, women are likely to have representations of their role with respect to parenthood and working career that differ from those of men. For instance, it is well known (e.g. Marry, Kieffer, Brauns and Steinmann 1998; Lauer and Weber 2003) that there is a more traditional division of work in West Germany, with mothers staying at home to raise the kids while fathers are the "bread-winners", than in France, where mothers more often work and even full-time. If German women expect this traditional division of work, they might view it as less essential, i.e. associate a lower return or utility, to attain a high level of education than men or than French women and adapt their educational investment accordingly.

The year of birth might also affect the ratio of cost to return of education, since the generation one belongs to implies that educational decisions were made at the same time and the context prevailing at that time – social norms, economic context – might have an influence. The birth year appears in the form of birth cohort dummies: born between 1929 and 1938, which serves as the reference category, born between 1939 and 1948, born between 1949 and 1958 and born between 1959 and 1968[25].

Parental background might affect children's educational outcomes through various channels. First, the availability of financial resources within the family may affect the educational prospects of the children. In the presence of imperfect capital markets, investment in education might be limited by credit constraints (Rosenzweig and Wolpin 1993). Neither the GSOEP nor the FQP Survey contain information on parental income. However, the occupational situation of the father during the childhood of the individual can serve as a proxy for the financial situation of the household the individual grew up in, which may affect cost to return expectations, especially through the cost side. The information on father's occupation in the FQP data is available at different aggregation levels, so that it proved possible to aggregate the German information so as to build a comparable set of dummy variables for both countries. Thus, the occupational position of the father is defined as worker (as the reference category), farmer, self-employed, senior manager, intermediate manager or employee (see table B.7 in appendix B).

Beyond mere financial aspects, family background may also affect children's educational prospects through the transmission of certain endowments, like abilities or preferences. Indeed, scholastic abilities are to some extent passed on from one generation to the next, reducing the "cost" of acquiring education and therefore lowering the thresholds. A high level of ability

[25] Since the French data dates back to 1993, one cannot examine a cohort born after 1968 if one wants the individuals observed to be older than 25.

might also help to better convert education into utility (e.g. wages, free time use) and thus increases the return, which further lowers the thresholds. But also the transmission of preferences and values (parental background as a role model) will affect the perception of the costs and returns of education. Highly educated parents generally place greater value on education and are therefore more likely to encourage their children to pursue further studies. Information on the education level of both mother and father – defined in 4 categories: no vocational education, basic vocational education, intermediate qualification and higher education, see table 3.12 – is used as an indicator for this potential transmission of ability and preferences. Dummies for missing information on the father's occupation and parent's education have been included in order to avoid problems of selective sample composition due to nonrandom missing information.

3.3.3 Estimation results

Specification tests

Table 3.13 presents overall statistics as well as the results of specification tests[26]. A Wald test performed on the hypothesis that all coefficients except the threshold values are zero is rejected at the 1 percent significance level for France as for Germany. Then, another series of tests aims at examining whether the parameters differ significantly between men and women, in which case the specification should account for this. The tests on gender differences are based on an estimation of the model developed in section 3.3.1, with the five-level dependent variable described above, which includes in addition to the explanatory variables further dummies constructed by interacting all the explanatory variables with a dummy variable for gender (1 if the individual is a female, 0 if he is a male). The coefficient of the interaction term, if it proves significant, indicates the additional impact of the variable for women.

For Germany, the null hypothesis that all the gender interaction dummies for one set of variables are not jointly significantly different from zero is only rejected for the birth cohort variables (at a 1 percent significant level). For the other variables, the null hypothesis cannot be rejected at the 10 percent level, which means that gender differences in the impact of the family background variables are not significant in a statistical sense. A significance level of at least 10 percent has been retained as a criterion for the interaction dummies to be included in the final specification. Thus, only the interaction terms between the birth cohort and gender have been retained in the final specification for Germany. For France, however, the test results show that there are noticeable gender differences in the cohort effects, like in Germany, but also in the impact of father's education and occupation on the child's educational prospects. Therefore, I include interaction dummies for the cohort variables, but also for the father's background in the final estimation for France.

[26] The formula of these χ^2-tests is given in equation (4.13) in chapter 4.

Table 3.13. Test results and overall statistics

Null hypothesis	Germany χ^2	Germany p> χ^2	France χ^2	France p> χ^2
Tests on coefficients				
Overall Wald test	1,436.25	0.00	3,833.30	0.00
Female * Birth cohort = 0	61.59	0.00	74.54	0.00
Female * Mother's education = 0	2.52	0.64	6.93	0.14
Female * Father's education = 0	7.37	0.12	11.82	0.02
Female * Father's occupation = 0	1.82	0.94	23.80	0.00
Tests on thresholds				
μ_1: Male = Female	227.86	0.00	79.71	0.00
μ_2: Male = Female	182.69	0.00	19.35	0.00
μ_3: Male = Female	154.67	0.00	26.58	0.00
μ_4: Male = Female	114.82	0.00	73.64	0.00
Male - Female = constant for all μ	10.12	0.02	172.17	0.00
Observations	6,005		15,037	
Log-likelihood	-7,122.45		-17,919.69	

In the empirical literature, it is common practice either to simply include a gender dummy as an additional explanatory variable to account for potential gender differences in levels[27] or to estimate the model separately for men and women. The drawback of the latter approach is that one cannot test whether the differences observed are significant or not. The former approach makes it possible to test for gender differences in levels, but its drawback is the implicit assumption that gender has a similar impact – if any – on all threshold values, e.g. being a female raises all the thresholds by the same amount. It is conceivable, however, that gender does not affect all thresholds in the same way[28]. Since there is no a priori reason to assume that this is the case, I tested it in the following way. I ran a regression of educational attainment on the explanatory variables – including the gender interaction terms that proved significant to account for gender differences in slope coefficients – and allowed the threshold values to differ between men and women[29]. The first series of tests reported in table 3.13 indicate for each threshold whether the hypothesis that the threshold is the same for men and women can be rejected

[27] That is, differences across genders that do not stem from a different impact of certain variables on the outcome, the latter being captured by interaction dummies such as presented before.

[28] For instance, the difference between men and women might be higher at the threshold to university than at previous thresholds.

[29] This cannot be estimated directly with the ordered probit command of Stata 7.0 but is easily programmable within the framework of maximum likelihood estimation (see Gould and Sribney 1999).

or not. If it is not rejected, then it is more efficient to estimate only a single threshold for men and women. The second test consists in testing whether the difference between men and women is the same for all thresholds, in which case it would be more efficient to include a gender dummy as an additional regressor and estimate common thresholds for men and women. The tests show that, for France and for Germany alike, the thresholds differ significantly across genders. Moreover, the gender gap in the thresholds is not constant. Therefore, gender differences are better accounted for by estimating separate thresholds for men and women rather than by including a gender dummy variable as an additional regressor.

Results

Table 3.14 reports the estimation results. A positive and significant coefficient means that a value of one for the dummy variable is associated with a higher educational attainment than if the dummy variable was zero[30].

The impact of the birth cohort on educational outcomes presents obvious similarities in France and Germany. In both countries, the cohort coefficients are significant, positive and also increasing for all except for German men. It means that, all else equal, the cost to return ratio associated with education has decreased compared to the reference cohort. As can be seen from the significantly positive and increasing interaction terms, educational expansion has been much more marked among women than among men[31], all other things equal. This phenomenon is particularly pronounced in Germany.

In both countries, parental education has a significant impact on children's educational outcomes. The higher the education of the parents is, the higher the education of their children will be. As mentioned in section 3.3.2, this might reflect a certain inheritance of scholastic abilities that drives the "cost" of acquiring education down in terms of effort, or the transmission of certain norms and preferences (role models) with respect to the utility of education. To be more specific, having parents who hold a higher education degree seems to particularly favour educational prospects, especially in Germany, where there is a big jump in the coefficient from parents with an

---

30 It also means that the variable increases the probability of achieving the highest education category E_5 and decreases that of achieving only the lowest category E_1. For the intermediate categories, a positive coefficient increases the probability of holding *at least* E_2 or of holding *at least* E_3. In order to obtain a precise measure of the impact of a variable on the probability of achieving exactly one specific intermediate education level, one needs to compute equation (3.6), which takes the effect of β on the lower and upper bounds and on the outcome of the distribution function.

31 For men, the effect of belonging to a specific cohort rather than the reference cohort 1929-38 can be directly read from the coefficient of the simple cohort dummies. For women, however, one needs to add the coefficient of the simple cohort dummy to that of the same cohort dummy interacted with the gender dummy.

Table 3.14. Determinants of final educational attainment

Variable	Germany coef.	(s.e)	France coef.	(s.e)
Birth cohort (ref.: 1929-38)				
1939-48	0.27**	(0.06)	0.43**	(0.04)
1949-58	0.34**	(0.06)	0.47**	(0.04)
1959-68	0.22**	(0.06)	0.50**	(0.04)
Female * 1939-48	0.14†	(0.08)	-0.05	(0.06)
Female * 1949-58	0.45**	(0.09)	0.21**	(0.06)
Female * 1959-68	0.60**	(0.08)	0.36**	(0.06)
Mother's education (ref.: No voc. degree)				
Basic voc. degree	0.22**	(0.03)	0.21**	(0.04)
Intermediate qualif.	0.36**	(0.09)	0.64**	(0.05)
Higher education	0.96**	(0.13)	0.53**	(0.06)
Missing	0.05	(0.06)	-0.02	(0.07)
Father's education (ref.: No voc. degree)				
Basic voc. degree	0.27**	(0.05)	0.20**	(0.04)
Intermediate qualif.	0.40**	(0.06)	0.53**	(0.06)
Higher education	0.87**	(0.08)	0.96**	(0.07)
Missing	0.13†	(0.07)	-0.35**	(0.08)
Female * Basic voc. degree			0.13*	(0.06)
Female * Interm. qualif.			0.07	(0.09)
Female * Higher education			-0.11	(0.09)
Female * Missing			0.11	(0.10)
Father's occupation (ref.: Worker)				
Farmer	0.18**	(0.07)	-0.08†	(0.04)
Self-employed	0.48**	(0.06)	0.36**	(0.05)
Senior manager	0.89**	(0.06)	0.69**	(0.06)
Middle manager	0.56**	(0.05)	0.46**	(0.05)
Employee	0.34**	(0.07)	0.37**	(0.05)
Missing	0.14**	(0.04)	0.38**	(0.04)
Female * Farmer			0.23**	(0.06)
Female * Self-employed			0.25**	(0.06)
Female * Senior manager			0.11	(0.09)
Female * Middle manager			0.16*	(0.07)
Female * Employee			0.11	(0.07)
Female * Missing			0.08	(0.06)

to be continued...

...table 3.14 continued

Variable		Germany coef.	Germany (s.e)	France coef.	France (s.e)
Thresholds					
μ_1	Male	-0.55**	(0.06)	0.51**	(0.04)
	Female	0.44**	(0.06)	1.00**	(0.04)
μ_2	Male	1.07**	(0.06)	1.47**	(0.04)
	Female	1.98**	(0.07)	1.73**	(0.04)
μ_3	Male	1.82**	(0.06)	1.97**	(0.04)
	Female	2.74**	(0.07)	2.28**	(0.04)
μ_4	Male	2.13**	(0.07)	2.35**	(0.05)
	Female	2.97**	(0.07)	2.92**	(0.05)

Significance level : † : 10% * : 5% ** : 1%

intermediate qualification to parents with higher education. In France, this is also the case – though to a lesser extent for mothers – but having parent's with a *Baccalauréat* degree means already a decisive improvement for children's educational prospects. The impact of the father's education has the same order of magnitude as that of the mother's education – except for a stronger effect of higher education of fathers than of mothers in France – even though the occupational position of the father is controlled for and not that of the mother[32]. Having a father with a basic vocational degree compared to one with no degree improves the educational prospects slightly more for women than for men in France. Otherwise, there does not seem to be any other gender differences in the impact of parent's education on children's educational outcomes, neither in France nor in Germany.

As far as the occupational position of the father is concerned, France and Germany prove very similar. Almost all coefficients are positive and significant for both countries[33], which means that the children of blue collar workers (the reference category) have the worst educational prospects. The order of magnitude of the coefficients is surprisingly similar. The best educational opportunities, all other things equal, have children of senior managers, followed by those of intermediate level managers (0.46 for men and 0.46+0.16=0.62 for women in France) and self-employed (0.36 for men and 0.36+0.25=0.61 for women in France). Children of farmers have only a slight advantage in terms of educational attainment compared to worker's children, but are significantly

[32] Thus, the influence of mother's education may include an indirect effect and partly stem from the correlated, but unobserved effect of the mother's occupational position. The coefficient for father's education is cleaned from this indirect effect since the impact of father's occupation appears separately.

[33] Except that in France, having a farmer rather than a worker as a father is only an advantage for women, while sons of farmers face more unfavourable educational prospects than workers' children, though only slightly.

disadvantaged compared to children of employees. These results might be the consequence of financial constraints which raise the costs of investing in education and thus enhance the cost to return ratio. This could also reflect different systems of preferences, e.g. worker families place less value on education than others and children growing up in those families would expect a lower utility from education or higher costs than other families. In Germany, there are no significant differences between men and women, contrary to France, where daughters of farmers and self-employed (and to a lesser extent of middle staff managers) have somewhat better relative prospects compared to their male counterparts.

As seen before, there are significant differences in the threshold values between men and women in both countries. To be more specific, women have systematically higher thresholds than men, at all education levels and in both countries, even though the gap is not constant across all thresholds. This means that for a given family background and a given cohort, women expect higher costs or lower returns to education and invest less in education than their male counterparts. Interestingly, the gap between men and women in the value of the thresholds is larger in Germany than in France, which means that, all else equal, women are more at a disadvantage in Germany than in France in terms of educational attainment. This might be due to the fact that women anticipate a more traditional division of tasks with respect to family and work in Germany and attach less importance to attaining a high level of education than in France.

To sum up, it seems that the observed differences between France and Germany in the distribution of educational attainment cannot be explained so much by a difference in social inequality in terms of family background or cohort. In fact, both countries have faced an educational expansion of the same order of magnitude and more pronounced for women, and the family background variables exert a rather similar impact. Moreover, an important difference between France and Germany appears. While women have, for a given social background, poorer educational prospects in both countries, women's handicap turn out to be much greater in Germany, as the larger gap in the thresholds show. Thus, the particularly strong impact of family background found for Germany as well as the better performance of women in terms of PISA test scores are not observed in terms of highest degree obtained. Of course, the generations observed here are older than that covered by PISA and educational credentials, in particular vocational ones, do not certify exactly the same skills as those tested in PISA. A more detailed analysis will be run in the next section (section 3.4) to distinguish between school and post-school education. The skills certified by the school degrees are expected to be more closely related to those tested in PISA.

3.4 Decomposition of the educational career

The model described and applied above is very simple to implement empirically – though the differentiation of the thresholds for men and women requires self-programming of the estimator – and provides a convenient interpretation framework for the analysis of the determinants of educational attainment. In particular, it allows an interpretation of the cut values obtained by the ordered probit estimation which makes sense in economic terms. In this section, an extension of this model is proposed in order to allow the analysis to go into the details of the educational process. Indeed, after having determined the overall impact of certain factors on final educational achievement, it may be of interest to examine at which stage of the educational career which factors exert an influence. As a matter of fact, some factors might influence educational decisions more decisively (or exclusively) at an earlier stage of the educational career, others at a later stage or exert a different influence at either stage. For instance, does parental background play a more important role for earlier or for later stages of the educational process? Has the observed educational expansion taken place at all levels? Are gender differences similar throughout the educational career? Moreover, changes in the environment at a given stage, such as a reform in the educational system or changing economic conditions, changing situation of the parents, new information, or simply personality development over time, might modify the appreciation of returns and costs and therefore induce a reorientation of decisions for subsequent stages. Finally, at certain stages of the educational career, explicit decision-taking is required, which implies that a reorientation is possible, under the constraints of a new context and of previous choices which might have limited the possible subsequent alternatives.

In order to examine these issues, the educational career is now decomposed into successive stages: primary education, general secondary education and post-secondary education. This decomposition is general enough to be applicable to most educational systems. Given that all individuals are assumed to receive primary education, the final educational outcome is the result of two decisions: the decision upon general secondary education and that upon post-secondary education, given the level attained in general secondary education.

3.4.1 Formulation of the model

This section proposes an extension of the model defined in section 3.3.1 which consists in decomposing educational attainment into school attainment and post-school attainment. An appealing approach owing to its simplicity would be to consider that for each transition, the model defined in section 3.3 applies, i.e. after having completed secondary education, individuals decide on their post-secondary education, given the new set of variables and the choices available, independently of their previous choices. Practically, this would result in a sequential-response model, which only differs from the textbook models as presented in Amemiya (1986), Maddala (1983) or Gouriéroux (1989) through the fact that we have an ordered choice instead of a binary choice. However, this approach is only valid under the assumption that the conditional probability of the choice at the second decision point is independent of the choice at the first point, i.e. that the random factors influencing responses at various stages are independent. Otherwise, the estimated coefficients will be biased. Since a selection with respect to unobservable factors may take place, as Cameron and Heckman (1998) argue, I do not want to impose a priori such a restriction and will therefore estimate the correlation between the first and the second stage along with the other parameters instead of a priori assuming it equal to zero.

Let us call E^S the level of general secondary education attained by an individual among K alternatives E^S_k of increasing levels, with $k \in \{1...K\}$, and E^{S*} the unobservable desired secondary school attainment. Furthermore, let us define K variables E^{Fk}, with $k \in \{1...K\}$, which represent the final educational level an individual attains given that he holds a secondary school degree of level k, and E^{Fk*} the corresponding unobservable desired educational attainment. Given his secondary school degree of level k, the individual may choose one of L_k educational alternatives E^{Fk}_ℓ of increasing levels, with $\ell \in \{1...L_k\}$. To sum up, we have the following variables:

$$\begin{aligned} \text{Secondary schooling: } E^S &= E^S_k &&, k \in \{1...K\} \\ \text{Final education: } E^{F1} &= E^{F1}_\ell &&, \ell \in \{1...L_1\} \\ E^{F2} &= E^{F2}_\ell &&, \ell \in \{1...L_2\} \\ \dots \\ E^{FK} &= E^{FK}_\ell &&, \ell \in \{1...L_K\} \end{aligned}$$

As in section 3.3, we can define K+1 functions $\varphi^S(x^S)$, $\varphi^{F1}(x^{F1})$, ..., $\varphi^{FK}(x^{FK})$, and K+1 error terms ε^S, ε^{F1}, ..., ε^{FK}. Furthermore, we assume that $\varphi^t(x^t) = \exp[\beta_t x_t]$, with $t \in \{S, F1...FK\}$ and, analogue to equation (3.5), we obtain for all $k \in \{1...K\}$ and $\ell \in \{1...L_k\}$:

$$\begin{aligned} &Pr(E^S_k \mid x^S, E^{Fk}_\ell \mid x^{Fk}) = \\ &Pr[\mu^S_{k-1} - \beta^S x^S < ln\varepsilon^S \leq \mu^S_k - \beta^S x^S, \\ &\qquad \mu^{Fk}_{\ell-1} - \beta^{Fk} x^{Fk} < ln\varepsilon^{Fk} \leq \mu^{Fk}_\ell - \beta^{Fk} x^{Fk}] \end{aligned} \tag{3.9}$$

where

$$\mu^S_j = \ln\left(\frac{c(E^S_{j+1}) - c(E^S_j)}{r(E^S_{j+1}) - r(E^S_j)}\right) \text{ and } \mu^{Fk}_j = \ln\left(\frac{c(E^{Fk}_{j+1}) - c(E^{Fk}_j)}{r(E^{Fk}_{j+1}) - r(E^{Fk}_j)}\right) \tag{3.10}$$

If one knew for sure that the school decision $E_k^S \mid x^S$ and the post-school decision $E_\ell^{Fk} \mid x^{Fk}$ were independent from each other, one would have

$$Pr(E_k^S \mid x^S,\ E_\ell^{Fk} \mid x^{Fk}) = Pr(E_k^S \mid x^S)\ \ Pr(E_\ell^{Fk} \mid x^{Fk})$$

and one could consider that the model explained in section 3.3 applies first for the school decision and then for the post-school decision, given the new set of background variables and the choices available. However, this approach is only valid under the assumption that the choice at the second decision point is independent of the choice at the first point, conditional on the background variables x, i.e. that the random factors influencing choices at various stages are independent. Otherwise, the estimated coefficients will be biased (dynamic selection bias, see Cameron and Heckman 1998). Since a selection with respect to unobservable factors may take place, I do not want to impose a priori such a restriction. I therefore estimate the correlation between the first and the second stage along with the other parameters instead of assuming it *a priori* zero. The error terms are assumed to follow a multivariate normal distribution of the following form[34]:

$$\begin{pmatrix} ln\varepsilon^S \\ ln\varepsilon^{F1} \\ ln\varepsilon^{F2} \\ \vdots \\ ln\varepsilon^{FK} \end{pmatrix} \sim \mathcal{N}\left(\begin{pmatrix} 0 \\ 0 \\ 0 \\ \vdots \\ 0 \end{pmatrix}, \begin{pmatrix} 1 & \varrho_1 & \varrho_2 & \cdots & \varrho_K \\ \varrho_1 & 1 & 0 & \cdots & 0 \\ \varrho_2 & 0 & 1 & & \vdots \\ \vdots & \vdots & & \ddots & \vdots \\ \varrho_K & 0 & \cdots & 0 & 1 \end{pmatrix} \right)$$

As in section 3.3, only the ratio of the β's to the σ's can be identified, therefore the σ's can be normalised to 1 without loss of generality. We have K correlation parameters $\varrho_k, k \in \{1...K\}$, corresponding to the correlation between secondary school choice and final educational choice given the secondary school degree obtained, for each secondary school degree.

To simplify the presentation, let us define, similarly to equation (3.4):

$$\gamma_k^S = \mu_k^S - \beta^S x^S \qquad \text{and} \qquad \gamma_\ell^{Fk} = \mu_\ell^{Fk} - \beta^{Fk} x^{Fk}$$

Thus, equation (3.9) becomes:

$$Pr(E_k^S \mid x^S,\ E_\ell^{Fk} \mid x^{Fk}) = Pr\left[\gamma_{k-1}^S < ln\varepsilon^S \le \gamma_k^S\,,\ \gamma_{\ell-1}^{Fk} < ln\varepsilon^{Fk} \le \gamma_\ell^{Fk}\right]$$

Given the assumptions on $\ln \varepsilon^S$ and $\ln \varepsilon^{Fk}$, one obtains:

$$Pr(E_k^S \mid x^S,\ E_\ell^{Fk} \mid x^{Fk}) = \tag{3.11}$$

$$\Phi_2(\gamma_k^S, \gamma_\ell^{Fk}, \varrho_k) - \Phi_2(\gamma_k^S, \gamma_{\ell-1}^{Fk}, \varrho_k) - \Phi_2(\gamma_{k-1}^S, \gamma_\ell^{Fk}, \varrho_k) + \Phi_2(\gamma_{k-1}^S, \gamma_{\ell-1}^{Fk}, \varrho_k)$$

where Φ_2 is the bivariate standard normal distribution. The probability corresponds to the grey area in figure 3.1:

[34] See the general overview of bivariate and multivariate probit models in Greene (2000), Ronning (1991) or Gouriéroux (1989).

Fig. 3.1. Joint probability of E_k^S and E_ℓ^{Fk}

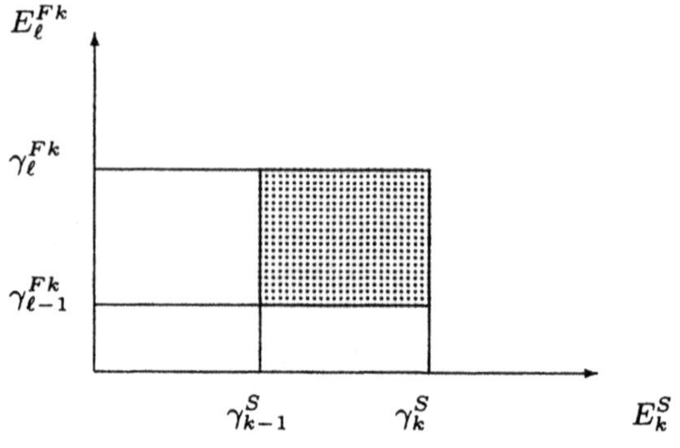

Thus, the log-likelihood for this model may be written as:

$$\ln \mathcal{L} = \sum_{i=1}^{n} \sum_{k=1}^{K} \sum_{\ell=1}^{L_k} I_{ik\ell} \ln \left[Pr(E_k^S \mid x_i^S, E_\ell^{Fk} \mid x_i^{Fk}) \right] \tag{3.12}$$

where $Pr(E_k^S \mid x_i^S, E_\ell^{Fk} \mid x_i^{Fk})$ is defined as in equation (3.11) for all individuals i, $i \in \{1...n\}$ and $I_{ik\ell}$ is an indicator variable equal to 1 if individual i obtained school degree k and post-school degree ℓ.

The estimation of this sequential model is not as straightforward as that of the single-equation version in section 3.3, but it remains reasonably feasible. As a matter of fact, since the expression of the log-likelihood function to be maximised has been determined (in equations (3.12) and (3.11)), one just needs to find a maximisation procedure to be able to recover the parameters (the β's, μ's and ϱ's). Using Stata 7.0, the maximisation can be done numerically with the help of the Newton-Raphson iterative procedure[35]. However, this numerical maximisation may be quite time-consuming.

3.4.2 Data and variables

The model is applied to the GSOEP and the FQP data, the purpose being both to gain evidence of social inequalities in terms of educational attainment in France and Germany and to provide an illustration of how the model functions in practice. The ultimate educational outcome is, following the model,

[35] The principle of the Newton-Raphson procedure is the following. Starting with a vector of initial values b_0, the algorithm calculates a new vector b_1 such that $b_1 = b_0 + g(-H)^{-1}$, where g is the gradient vector and H the matrix of second derivatives, then calculates $b_2 = b_1 + g(-H)^{-1}$ and repeats the procedure until convergence is achieved (see details in Gould and Sribney 1999).

the result of two decisions. The first decision is about attainment in general secondary education, and the second one is about post-school educational achievement. Here again, it is assumed that the educational outcome observed is the result of the decision of the individual given some constraints.

The dependent variables are defined by the highest degree obtained in general secondary education and in post-school education for each specific school degree. Attainment in general secondary education has been defined by three levels E_k^S, $k \in \{1...3\}$: low (E_1^S), middle (E_2^S) and high (E_3^S). For post-school attainment, the definition of the dependent variable depends on the level attained in general secondary education. Since there are three possible levels of attainment in secondary education, there are three different variables E_ℓ^{Fk} for post-school attainment, one for each school degree $k \in \{1...3\}$, the categories $\ell \in \{1...L_k\}$ of each (number and type) depending on the value of k, i.e. on the type of secondary school degree possessed. In the end, I therefore estimate, through the maximisation of the log-likelihood function defined in equation 3.12, a model of four simultaneous equations (the secondary school equation – low, middle or high – on the one hand, and the post-low secondary, the post-middle secondary and the post-high secondary equations on the other hand) see table 3.15), with as many correlations ϱ_k, $k \in \{1...3\}$ between attainment in secondary education and subsequent achievement as there are secondary school degrees. Figure 3.2 represents graphically the system of equations which has been estimated for both countries.

Table 3.15 precises which educational degrees are included in the various categories of the dependent variables of each equation for France and Germany. The educational levels thereby defined are basically an aggregation of the typology of table 2.1. Only the most typical degrees of each category are reported here, but also credentials of a similar levels are meant. Note that the school variable depicts attainment in *general* secondary education. Therefore, the highest category consists of the general maturity degree holders, whereas holders of a vocational type of maturity certificate are affected to the intermediate level of general secondary education[36]. For further details, consult the description of French and German educational credentials in chapter 2.

One issue to be examined is whether social background plays a more important role in the school stage or in the post-school stage of the educational career. Therefore, the same variables on family background as in section 3.3 (parental education and father's occupation) have been included in the school and in the the post-school equations. Moreover, the model allows time-variant factors to influence educational choices. Ideally, one would like to use information on e.g. the financial situation of the household, on changes in the

[36] For the group of individuals with an intermediate level of general secondary education, access to higher education has been obtained via the vocational maturity. Only a negligible number of individuals with the lowest level of general secondary education managed to get a higher education degree in the end. The few cases observed got access to (lower) higher education through the achievement of the vocational maturity degree.

Fig. 3.2. System of equations estimated

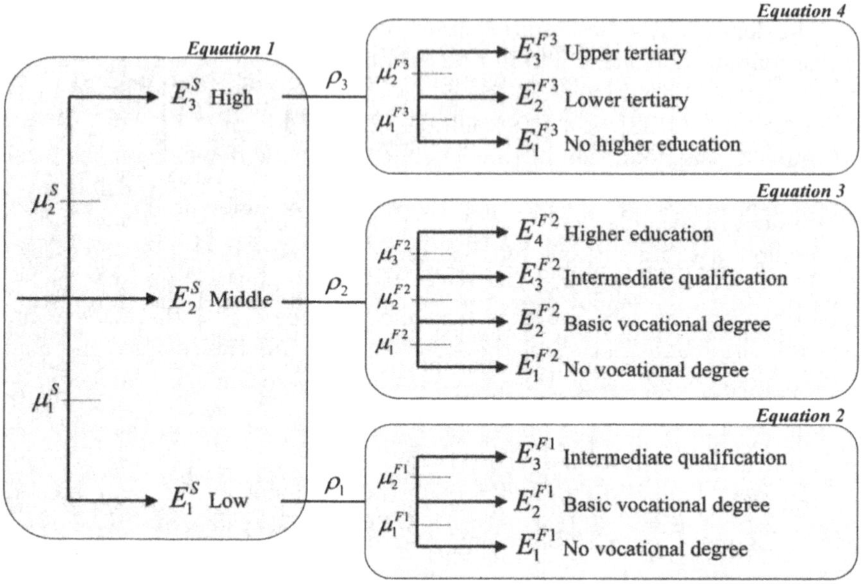

household structure etc. at the time when the individual decided upon his secondary education and when he decided upon his post-secondary education. Since this kind of information is not available, the approach adopted here was the following. I assume that the decision concerning the next educational stage is made at the end of the immediately preceding stage. For Germany, it is the end of primary schooling, at the age of 10, since this is the stage at which pupils are streamed into different types of secondary schools. For France, it is the end of lower secondary schooling – approximately at age 14 –, since, as mentioned in section 2.2.2, pupils attend a single structure throughout lower secondary education. Therefore, one can examine the effect of the context prevailing at that time by looking at the effect of finishing the previous step in that year rather than in this other year. Concretely, a set of dummy variables indicating in which year the individual finished the previous stage (primary education for Germany, lower general secondary education for France), grouped in five-year dummies has been included in the secondary school equation.

Similarly, the decision concerning post-secondary education is assumed to take place at the end of secondary education. Thus, one can examine the effect of finishing secondary education at a specific point in time rather than at another point in time and include in the post-school equations a set of dummy variables indicating the year in which the person finished general secondary

Table 3.15. Definition of dependent variables

Education level	Germany	France
General secondary education (equation 1):		
E_1^S Low	*Hauptschule* degree or less	CEP/DFEO or less
E_2^S Middle	*Realschule* degree	BEPC
E_3^S High	*Abitur*	*Bac Général*
Post-(general) secondary education of:		
Low second. graduates (equation 2)		
E_1^{F1} No voc. degree	No voc. degree	No voc. degree
E_2^{F1} Basic voc. degree	*Lehre*	CAP/BEP
E_3^{F1} Interm. qualif.	*Fachschule/Fachoberschule*	BP/*Bac Pro*/*Bac Techno*
Middle second. graduates (equation 3)		
E_1^{F2} No voc. degree	No voc. degree	No voc. degree
E_2^{F2} Basic voc. degree	*Lehre*	CAP/BEP
E_3^{F2} Interm. qualif.	*Fachschule/Fachoberschule*	BP/*Bac Pro*/*Bac Techno*
E_4^{F2} Higher education	*Fachhochschule*/University	*Bac+2* and beyond
High second. graduates (equation 4)		
E_1^{F3} Interm. qualif.	No higher education	No higher education
E_2^{F3} Lower tertiary	*Fachhochschule*	*Bac+2*
E_3^{F3} Upper tertiary	University	*Bac+3* and beyond

education, grouped in five-year secondary school cohorts. The computation of the year in which the individual ended secondary education is based on information on the type of secondary education completed and its duration. This approach makes it possible to model institutional differences in the organisation of the educational stages, in particular concerning their duration. From a technical point of view, having different variables in the equations avoids that the identification of the model relies on the distributional assumption only.

The estimation results of this system of four equations are given and commented in section 3.4.3 and 3.4.4.

3.4.3 Determinants of secondary education

Specification tests

Table 3.16 presents overall statistics as well as specific test results for the secondary school equation for both countries[37].

The overall Wald test is run on the null hypothesis that all slope coefficients of all equations are jointly insignificant. The null hypothesis is rejected at a

[37] The tests are χ^2-tests, the formula is given in equation (4.13) in chapter 4.

Table 3.16. Overall statistics and test results for secondary education equation

	Germany		France	
Tests	χ^2	p> χ^2	χ^2	p> χ^2
Tests on coefficients				
Overall Wald test	2,230.26	0.00	4,432.38	0.00
Partial Wald tests	1,484.41	0.00	3,906.70	0.00
Female * End previous stage	45.32	0.00	26.90	0.00
Female * Mother's education	2.44	0.68	0.72	0.95
Female * Father's education	1.03	0.90	5.84	0.21
Female * Father's occupation	5.66	0.46	20.68	0.00
Tests on thresholds				
μ_1^S: Male = Female	4.11	0.04	3.15	0.08
μ_2^S: Male = Female	37.19	0.00	3.85	0.07
Male - Female = constant for all μ^S	47.07	0.00	6.24	0.01
Observations	5,857		15,037	
Log-likelihood	-10,031.73		-25,226.79	

1 percent significance level for both countries. The specific Wald test for the secondary school equation (named here partial Wald test) is also rejected at a 1 percent significance level for France and for Germany alike and attests that the slope parameters of this equation are jointly significant for both countries. Gender differences in the coefficients as well as in the threshold values and in the correlations have also been tested in the same way as in section 3.3.3. Only the significant interactions with gender (at a 10 percent significance level at least) have been retained in the final specification, since it would be inefficient to estimate more coefficients than necessary. Likewise, the secondary school thresholds were allowed to differ between men and women. As a matter of fact, the tests show that the thresholds differ significantly across genders and that the gender gap in the thresholds is not constant across thresholds. Thus, gender differences are better accounted for by estimating separate thresholds for men and women rather than by including a gender dummy variable as an additional regressor (see section 3.3.3 for a more detailed explanation of what these tests measure).

Estimation results

Observing table 3.17, it appears that there has been a strong educational expansion at the secondary school level. Indeed, the primary school cohort dummies for Germany and the lower secondary cohort dummies for France all prove extremely significant for the determination of attainment in secondary education and exhibit an increasing pattern. In other words, the later the previous stage was completed, the higher the attainment in general secondary education is, which means that the net utility of a high-level secondary

Table 3.17. Determinants of secondary school attainment

Variable	Germany coef.	Germany (s.e)	France coef.	France (s.e)
End of previous education stage (ref.: 1939-1950)				
1951-55	0.29**	(0.08)	0.25**	(0.07)
1956-60	0.39**	(0.08)	0.45**	(0.06)
1961-65	0.42**	(0.08)	0.55**	(0.05)
1966-70	0.57**	(0.07)	0.72**	(0.05)
1971-78	0.49**	(0.06)	0.75**	(0.04)
Female * 1951-55	-0.22*	(0.11)	-0.03	(0.08)
Female * 1956-60	-0.19**	(0.08)	0.02	(0.07)
Female * 1961-65	0.24*	(0.11)	0.13*	(0.06)
Female * 1966-70	0.20*	(0.10)	0.16*	(0.08)
Female * 1971-78	0.34**	(0.09)	0.25**	(0.04)
Mother's education (ref.: No voc. degree)				
Basic voc. degree	0.26**	(0.04)	0.20**	(0.04)
Intermediate qualif.	0.40**	(0.10)	0.72**	(0.05)
Higher education	0.90**	(0.14)	0.69**	(0.06)
Missing	0.05	(0.07)	-0.10	(0.08)
Father's education (ref.: No voc. degree)				
Basic voc. degree	0.21**	(0.06)	0.21**	(0.03)
Intermediate qualif.	0.33**	(0.07)	0.62**	(0.05)
Higher education	0.80**	(0.09)	0.88**	(0.05)
Missing	0.02	(0.09)	-0.23**	(0.06)
Father's occupation (ref.: Worker)				
Farmer	0.10	(0.08)	-0.00	(0.05)
Self-employed	0.65**	(0.06)	0.59**	(0.05)
Senior manager	1.12**	(0.07)	1.02**	(0.07)
Middle manager	0.68**	(0.05)	0.74**	(0.05)
Employee	0.38**	(0.08)	0.57**	(0.05)
Missing	0.28**	(0.05)	0.52**	(0.05)
Female * Farmer			0.21**	(0.07)
Female * Self-employed			0.08	(0.07)
Female * Senior manager			-0.17*	(0.09)
Female * Middle manager			-0.00	(0.07)
Female * Employee			0.00	(0.07)
Female * Missing			-0.08	(0.06)
Thresholds				
μ_1^S Male	1.15**	(0.07)	1.46**	(0.04)
Female	1.28**	(0.07)	1.36**	(0.04)
μ_2^S Male	2.10**	(0.07)	2.25**	(0.06)
Female	2.56**	(0.08)	2.13**	(0.05)

Significance level : † : 10% * : 5% ** : 1%

school degree has increased over time in both countries. The level of secondary schooling has expanded at a faster rate in France than in Germany. In both countries, the expansion of secondary schooling has been stronger for women than for men, especially for the generations finishing the previous stage in 1961-65 and after.

In both countries, mother's education is strongly significant for achievement at school, like father's education. Moreover, neither in France nor in Germany are there any significant gender differences in the effects of parental education. Roughly speaking, the coefficients have the same order of magnitude for both countries and show a similar pattern: the higher parental education is, the higher the probability is that children will be successful at school. However, there is in France, as opposed to Germany, an obvious threshold effect for having parents (particularly a mother) with an intermediate qualification, meaning in particular the *Baccalauréat*. As a result, the positive impact on school performance of having parents (mother or father) with an intermediate qualification is significantly stronger in France than in Germany. This highlights the key role of the *Baccalauréat* in France. In Germany, the jump takes place between intermediate qualification (which is, unlike in France, often an advanced technical degree rather than a maturity degree) and a tertiary level degree.

Father's occupation also proves to have a significant impact on children's school performance, both in France and in Germany, and the coefficients follow a similar pattern. All the significant coefficients are positive in both countries, which means that individuals in the reference category, the children of workers, are the least successful in terms of general secondary education. Another common feature is that in both countries, sons and daughters of farmers do not have significantly better prospects at school compared to workers' children[38], while sons and daughters of senior managers achieve best, followed by the children of middle staff managers and of self-employed. A dissimilarity between France and Germany concerns the fact that children of French employees seem to perform comparatively better at school than their German counterparts[39]. Another difference is that father's occupation has a slightly different impact across men and women for secondary education in France, while this is not the case in Germany: French females benefit more in terms of secondary education from having a farmer as a father and slightly less from being the daughter of a senior manager compared to males.

As far as the threshold values are concerned, the difference between France and Germany is striking. As a matter of fact, the thresholds are significantly higher for females than for males in Germany, while the reverse is true in France. This implies that for the same other characteristics and coefficients,

---

38 Except for French females.

39 A possible explanation for this could be that, compared to blue collar jobs, white collar jobs yield a larger earnings premium in France than in Germany (see Kaukewitsch and Rouault 1998).

the cost to return ratio of completing a high-level secondary school degree will be higher for women than for men, while it is higher for men than women in France, all other things equal. In other words, all else equal, achievement at school should be poorer for women than for men in Germany, while it will be better for women than for men in France. The gap in the thresholds in favour of men seems to be more pronounced in Germany than it is in France in favour of women.

Overall, the impact of family background on general secondary education achievement is not significantly stronger in Germany than in France, which contradicts the findings from the PISA study found for 15-year-olds in 2000. Moreover, females' lead in terms of PISA skills translate into higher achievement in general secondary in France even when controlling for social background, but not in Germany. The latter results, however, could be due to the fact that older generations are observed here and it is not sure how men and women would have performed had they done the PISA tests.

3.4.4 Determinants of post-secondary education

Specification tests

Table 3.18 (Germany) and table 3.19 (France) report test results for the three post-secondary equations.

Table 3.18. Test results for post-secondary education equations – Germany

	Level of secondary school attained:					
	Low		**Middle**		**High**	
Null hypothesis	χ^2	p> χ^2	χ^2	p> χ^2	χ^2	p> χ^2
Tests on coefficients						
Partial Wald tests	757.48	0.00	366.36	0.00	159.56	0.00
Female * End prev. stage	35.03	0.00	11.05	0.09	9.61	0.21
Female * Mother's educ.	2.63	0.45	5.15	0.16	2.04	0.73
Female * Father's educ.	9.44	0.01	5.27	0.26	3.35	0.50
Female * Father's occ.	10.31	0.19	1.57	0.95	2.80	0.83
Tests on thresholds	$k = 1$		$k = 2$		$k = 3$	
μ_1^{Fk}: Male = Female	77.91	0.00	24.97	0.00	4.76	0.03
μ_2^{Fk}: Male = Female	57.00	0.00	36.39	0.00	2.29	0.11
μ_3^{Fk}: Male = Female			38.61	0.00		
Male - Female = constant	0.09	0.77	0.68	0.71	3.42	0.06
Tests on correlations	$k = 1$		$k = 2$		$k = 3$	
ϱ_k: Male = Female	0.30	0.59	0.45	0.50	0.05	0.82

Table 3.19. Test results for post-secondary education equations – France

	Level of secondary school attained:					
	Low		Middle		High	
Null hypothesis	χ^2	p> χ^2	χ^2	p> χ^2	χ^2	p> χ^2
Tests on coefficients						
Partial Wald tests	424.95	0.00	112.73	0.00	87.44	0.00
Female * End prev. stage	39.61	0.00	6.20	0.40	16.15	0.01
Female * Mother's educ.	9.17	0.03	4.06	0.26	4.50	0.34
Female * Father's educ.	3.95	0.41	4.29	0.37	1.34	0.85
Female * Father's occ.	13.61	0.03	5.69	0.46	3.64	0.73
Tests on thresholds	$k = 1$		$k = 2$		$k = 3$	
μ_1^{Fk}: Male = Female	109.73	0.00	0.29	0.59	14.67	0.00
μ_2^{Fk}: Male = Female	39.09	0.00	0.11	0.73	30.63	0.00
μ_3^{Fk}: Male = Female			0.05	0.83		
Male - Female = constant	12.77	0.00	0.67	0.72	32.45	0.00
Tests on correlations	$k = 1$		$k = 2$		$k = 3$	
ϱ_k: Male = Female	3.40	0.17	1.00	0.32	0.53	0.47

Partial Wald tests on the coefficients of each equation separately are all rejected at a 1 percent significance level and attest that the slope parameters are jointly significant in all post-school equations for both countries. For France like for Germany, however, the value of the χ^2-statistics is all the lower since the level of education is higher. This suggests that the variables used have more explanatory power at earlier stages of the educational career, in particular at the secondary level. Here again, only the significant interactions with gender, at a 10 percent significance level at least, have been retained in the final specification.

For Germany, all the thresholds prove to differ significantly between men and women. However, the gender gap in the thresholds appears to be constant across thresholds for the post-secondary education of low and intermediate school graduates. Therefore, for these two equations, it is preferable to opt for a specification with a dummy variable as an additional regressor instead of differentiated thresholds. For France, the thresholds differ significantly across genders and the gap is not constant across thresholds, except for the group of intermediate school graduates. Therefore, in the specification finally retained, different thresholds are estimated for men and women for the low and high school degree holders. For intermediate school degree holders, however, the equality of the thresholds for men and women cannot be rejected, like the hypothesis that the difference across genders is constant (e.g. zero) across thresholds. Thus, for this equation, common thresholds are estimated and no gender dummy variable is included since it would be insignificant (and a test shows that this is indeed the case).

In France and in Germany alike, there are no significant differences between males and females in the correlation between secondary school attainment and post-secondary achievement. Therefore, only one single correlation coefficient has finally been estimated for both countries.

Estimation results

The estimation results of the three post-school equations are reported in table 3.20 for Germany and table 3.21 for France.

In France as in Germany, the educational expansion has not only concerned secondary education, but also post-secondary education, though not at all levels. The post-school achievement of poorly educated men has rather stagnated after an initial improvement compared to generations who finished their secondary education in the decade immediately after World War II, but there has been a strong improvement among women, as the positive and increasing gender interaction dummies show, especially in Germany. For intermediate school degree holders, the situation differs somewhat in France and in Germany. In France, there has been a similar expansion in the post-school achievement of male and female intermediate school degree holders, whereas in Germany, the improvement has been significantly stronger among women. The post-school achievement of high school graduates has developed in the opposite way compared to that of more poorly educated individuals. In Germany, the propensity to study among those entitled to do so has declined over generations, for both men and women. In France also, a similar phenomenon of declining propensity to study is observable, but only among men and to a lesser extent, whereas among female *Baccalauréat* holders, there has been, by contrast, an increase over time in the propensity to pursue tertiary level studies.

Parental education continues to exert an influence at the level of post-school education, though to a lesser extent than for secondary schooling. Here again, the pattern is very similar for France and Germany. In both countries, mother's education[40] plays a less important role compared to father's education at the post-school level, though it remains significant. Having a university graduate as a father is a particularly determining factor for the post-school educational prospects of individuals with low or intermediate school degree, especially for *Hauptschule* graduates in Germany. At a higher level of secondary education, however, the influence of parental education attenuates strongly. Mother's education has virtually no influence on the educational decisions of general maturity holders, except if the mother is a university graduate, but even there, the effect is very small in scope. The educational attainment of the father has more influence on the probability to undertake

[40] The too small proportion of mothers with a higher education degree made it necessary to aggregate the categories "intermediate qualification" and "higher education" into one single category for the post-school attainment of people with low or middle general education.

Table 3.20. Determinants of post-secondary school attainment – Germany

	Level of secondary school attained:					
	Low		Middle		High	
Variable	coef.	(s.e)	coef.	(s.e)	coef.	(s.e)
End of secondary education (ref.: 1945-1955)						
1956-60	0.25**	(0.10)	0.22†	(0.13)	0.23	(0.18)
1961-65	0.23**	(0.10)	0.25†	(0.15)	-0.04	(0.16)
1966-70	0.16*	(0.11)	0.12†	(0.07)	-0.21	(0.15)
1971-75	0.13†	(0.12)	0.39**	(0.15)	-0.39*	(0.16)
1976-80	0.24**	(0.11)	0.15*	(0.08)	-0.61**	(0.14)
1981-86	0.09	(0.13)	0.08	(0.08)	-0.81**	(0.12)
Female * 1956-60	0.22†	(0.13)	0.02	(0.18)		
Female * 1961-65	0.23†	(0.13)	-0.04	(0.20)		
Female * 1966-70	0.72**	(0.13)	0.50**	(0.19)		
Female * 1971-75	0.51**	(0.14)	0.35*	(0.17)		
Female * 1976-80	0.63**	(0.13)	0.56**	(0.16)		
Female * 1981-86	0.71**	(0.17)	0.51**	(0.16)		
Mother's education (ref.: No voc. degree)						
Basic voc. degree	0.26**	(0.05)	0.22**	(0.07)	-0.07	(0.08)
Intermediate qualif.	0.46**	(0.16)	0.49**	(0.13)	-0.13	(0.15)
Higher education					0.08*	(0.04)
Missing	0.00	(0.07)	0.22*	(0.11)	0.00	(0.19)
Father's education (ref.: No voc. degree)						
Basic voc. degree	0.20**	(0.08)	0.15†	(0.09)	0.08	(0.14)
Intermediate qualif.	0.52**	(0.12)	0.24*	(0.12)	0.09*	(0.05)
Higher education	1.22**	(0.25)	0.64**	(0.18)	0.37†	(0.20)
Missing	0.15	(0.11)	-0.02	(0.14)	-0.46†	(0.24)
Female * Basic voc. degree	0.27**	(0.10)				
Female * Interm. qualif.	0.10	(0.16)				
Female * Higher educ.	-0.28	(0.30)				
Female * Missing	0.18	(0.14)				
Father's occupation (ref.: Worker)						
Farmer	0.12	(0.08)	0.39**	(0.14)	0.05	(0.20)
Self-employed	0.48**	(0.09)	0.42**	(0.12)	0.30†	(0.16)
Senior manager	0.64**	(0.16)	0.78**	(0.19)	0.36*	(0.18)
Middle manager	0.50**	(0.09)	0.48**	(0.13)	0.19	(0.15)
Employee	0.31**	(0.10)	0.38**	(0.12)	0.17	(0.20)
Missing	0.08	(0.06)	0.15†	(0.09)	0.07	(0.13)
Female	-1.16**	(0.11)	-0.91**	(0.14)		

to be continued...

...table 3.20 continued

		Level of secondary school attained:					
		Low		Middle		High	
Variable		**coef.**	**(s.e)**	**coef.**	**(s.e)**	**coef.**	**(s.e)**
Thresholds		$k=1$		$k=2$		$k=3$	
μ_1^{Fk}	Male	-0.72**	(0.08)	-0.47	(0.52)	2.31**	(0.36)
	Female					2.47**	(0.29)
μ_2^{Fk}	Male	1.09**	(0.14)	0.91**	(0.32)	2.50**	(0.33)
	Female					2.74**	(0.27)
μ_3^{Fk}	Male	.		1.79**	(0.20)		
	Female						
Corr. second./post-second.		$k=1$		$k=2$		$k=3$	
ϱ_k		0.59**	(0.15)	0.59**	(0.20)	0.83**	(0.12)

Significance level : † : 10% * : 5% ** : 1%

tertiary level studies, but the effect is weaker than for those individuals with a general education below the maturity level. The interaction terms in the post-low secondary equation show that the educational attainment of the father (in Germany) and mother (in France) seems to have more importance for women. The fact that the father has completed an apprenticeship (in Germany) or that the mother has an intermediate qualification (in France) improves more the prospects in vocational education for females than for males. However, the other interaction terms are not significant in statistical terms.

In France as in Germany, the effect of father's occupational position is strongest for secondary education, and tends to decrease as the education level already attained gets higher (with the exception of *Realschule* graduates in Germany, for which the impact of father's occupation remains particularly strong). The impact of father's occupation is weakest for holders of the maturity degree. In this group, only individuals with a senior manager (or a self-employed in Germany) as a father achieve significantly better than the reference category of workers' children. Overall, in both countries, like for secondary schooling, sons and daughters of senior managers have undoubtedly the best educational prospects with respect to post-school education, while workers' children have the worst educational outcomes. Also children of middle staff managers and of self-employed achieve significantly better than workers' children. It is worth noticing that self-employment seems to have a somewhat stronger positive impact in Germany than in France, especially at higher education levels (achievement after middle or high secondary education). Children of farmers perform better than those of workers at the post-school level if they succeed in having an intermediate level of general

Table 3.21. Determinants of post-secondary school attainment – France

	Level of secondary school attained:					
	Low		Middle		High	
Variable	coef.	(s.e)	coef.	(s.e)	coef.	(s.e)
End of secondary education (ref.: 1945-1955)						
1956-60	0.42**	(0.06)	0.32**	(0.11)	-0.00	(0.17)
1961-65	0.42**	(0.06)	0.39**	(0.10)	-0.16	(0.17)
1966-70	0.39**	(0.06)	0.50**	(0.11)	-0.07	(0.19)
1971-75	0.43**	(0.07)	0.68**	(0.12)	-0.37†	(0.20)
1976-80	0.42**	(0.07)	0.74**	(0.12)	-0.37†	(0.21)
1981-86	0.39**	(0.08)	0.91**	(0.12)	-0.41†	(0.21)
Female * 1956-60	-0.11	(0.09)			0.21	(0.23)
Female * 1961-65	0.17*	(0.08)			0.29	(0.21)
Female * 1966-70	0.25**	(0.08)			0.33	(0.21)
Female * 1971-75	0.19*	(0.09)			0.47*	(0.21)
Female * 1976-80	0.38**	(0.10)			0.49*	(0.22)
Female * 1981-86	0.58**	(0.11)			0.61**	(0.22)
Mother's education (ref.: No voc. degree)						
Basic voc. degree	0.24**	(0.08)	0.17*	(0.07)	0.02	(0.10)
Intermediate qualif.	0.15	(0.15)	0.28*	(0.12)	0.10	(0.19)
Higher education					0.10*	(0.18)
Missing	0.00	(0.11)	0.02	(0.17)	-0.11	(0.20)
Female * Basic voc. degree	0.11	(0.12)				
Female * Interm.	0.57**	(0.18)				
Female * Missing	-0.10	(0.17)				
Father's education (ref.: No voc. degree)						
Basic voc. degree	0.36**	(0.04)	0.16**	(0.06)	0.09	(0.11)
Intermediate qualif.	0.36**	(0.10)	0.35**	(0.11)	0.12*	(0.19)
Higher education	0.60**	(0.14)	0.45**	(0.15)	0.31*	(0.25)
Missing	-0.23**	(0.07)	-0.17	(0.12)	-0.24	(0.19)
Father's occupation (ref.: Worker)						
Farmer	-0.18**	(0.05)	0.21**	(0.07)	0.10	(0.12)
Self-employed	0.36**	(0.07)	0.21*	(0.10)	0.06	(0.22)
Senior manager	0.55**	(0.15)	0.47**	(0.14)	0.30**	(0.29)
Middle manager	0.36**	(0.09)	0.27*	(0.11)	0.08	(0.24)
Employee	0.43**	(0.07)	0.16	(0.10)	0.02	(0.20)
Missing	0.16*	(0.07)	0.24**	(0.09)	0.43*	(0.20)
Female * Farmer	0.17*	(0.08)				
Female * Self-employed	0.21*	(0.09)				
Female * Senior manager	0.09	(0.17)				
Female * Middle manager	0.31**	(0.11)				
Female * Employee	0.07	(0.10)				
Female * Missing	0.21**	(0.08)				

to be continued...

...table 3.21 continued

Variable		Low coef.	Low (s.e)	Middle coef.	Middle (s.e)	High coef.	High (s.e)
		Level of secondary school attained:					
Thresholds		$k=1$		$k=2$		$k=3$	
μ_1^{Fk}	Male	0.41^{**}	(0.05)	0.68^{**}	(0.24)	0.35^{**}	(0.13)
	Female	1.07^{**}	(0.07)			0.96^{**}	(0.13)
μ_2^{Fk}	Male	1.91^{**}	(0.10)	1.52^{**}	(0.21)	0.92^{**}	(0.13)
	Female	2.39^{**}	(0.13)			1.82^{**}	(0.13)
μ_3^{Fk}	Male			2.17^{**}	(0.19)		
	Female						
Corr. second./post-second.		$k=1$		$k=2$		$k=3$	
ϱ_k		0.38^{*}	(0.16)	$0.23^{\dagger}$	(0.14)	$0.10^{\dagger}$	(0.06)

Significance level : † : 10% * : 5% ** : 1%

education[41]. There are no differences between men and women with respect to the impact of father's occupation in Germany, whatever the educational stage observed, and only slight differences in France for secondary education and post-CEP/DFEO (low-level secondary) education[42].

At the post-secondary level, French women have higher thresholds than men, except among BEPC (intermediate school degree) holders, for which there are no differences across genders in the post-school attainment thresholds. This implies that French women have only an advantage in terms of cost to return ratio as far as school education is concerned. For post-school education, however, men are in a better position, as in Germany, where either the dummy variable for being a female is significantly negative[43] or the thresholds for females are significantly higher than for males. On the other hand, however, the gender gap in favour of men among holders of the general maturity degree seems to be more pronounced in France than in Germany.

Even with this rather simple specification in terms of variables included, the correlations between the secondary school equation and the post-secondary equations all prove significant for both countries. This implies that the decisions at the different stages are not independent and that a purely sequential model – or a model focussing on one specific transition within the educational career in isolation from previous transitions – would be inappropri-

41 The negative impact of having a farmer as a father found for the further education of men with no or only a poor school degree in France is compensated by a positive impact of the same extent for women.

42 As mentioned previously, French females benefit more from having a farmer as a father, but also from having a self-employed father or an intermediate-level manager in terms of post-school education after a low-level school.

43 Which corresponds to higher thresholds for females by the amount of the female dummy.

ate. Therefore, the additional computational burden resulting from a time-intensive maximisation procedure seems to be worthwhile[44]. Secondary and post-secondary attainments are positively related. This is in line with the interpretation of unobserved factors such as motivation or ability playing a similar role at all educational stages. The correlations seem to be stronger in Germany than in France, both in terms of the size of the correlation and in terms of significance of the correlations[45].

3.5 Summary and conclusions

In times of global competition and technological progress, education is more than ever an essential factor of productivity and social development. This is why the publication of the results of the PISA study provoked a genuine shock in public opinion in Germany and triggered an intense debate on the causes of the poor performance of German students compared to students from other countries. France is a good benchmark for a comparison with Germany for several reasons. First, France has a similar level of economic development as Germany and it is useful to know how Germany stands compared to one of its most important competitors in Europe with respect to this essential factor. Furthermore, France shares with Germany the objective to raise the average education level while reducing social inequalities in educational achievement, but differ in the political options chosen to reach these goals regarding the organisation of the education system[46]. Moreover, French students performed better than their German counterpart in the PISA study. They attained a higher test score level on average, with a lower dispersion and a weaker dependence on social origin. Because PISA tested only specific skills at a given age, an essential aim of this chapter is therefore to examine whether the patterns observed in PISA persists when considering final educational attainment measured by the degrees obtained. Indeed, not only the PISA skills are essential to assess the educational situation of a country, but all the skills acquired within the education system and the educational credentials obtained provide a good indicator of these.

[44] If the correlations had proved to be insignificant, the estimations should rather be run separately, because it would be more efficient in the sense that fewer parameters are estimated.

[45] This is not really surprising if one considers that the sequences defined by the model depict very well the German education system, while the stages within the French education system are more loosely interrelated and more reorientations are possible.

[46] In particular, the early streaming of German students into different types of secondary schools, as opposed to the *collège unique* in France, as well as the late school starting age and half day school in Germany, as opposed to the French full-day school model are prominent explanations for the poor success of German students in PISA.

A look at the literature available so far reveals a lack of comparative evidence on this issue for France and Germany, but also points to the need for linking empirical research to a theoretical framework. A further aim of this work was therefore to develop a methodological framework suited to such an analysis, the ambition being to develop a theoretical model of educational attainment that can be implemented directly, and in this way to confer an economic rationale on the empirical analysis of the determinants of educational achievement. In the model developed here, the individual chooses, given his personal and familial characteristics, the education level that maximises his expected utility. In its simplest version, the formalisation of these assumptions leads to an ordered probit model where the threshold values are given by the expected ratio of the marginal "costs" of attaining the next higher education level to the marginal "returns" of doing so. The higher the thresholds, the lower is the probability that the individual will opt for the next higher education level. In an extension of the model, the ultimate educational outcome is broken down into two stages: school and post-school achievement. The same utility maximisation framework as described above applies at both stages, but a correlation between the stages is permitted and estimated along with the other parameters in order to avoid the bias due to selectivity with respect to unobserved factors from one stage to the next.

Looking at the distribution of educational attainment, a striking feature is the stronger dispersion in France compared to Germany. This is obvious at the secondary level, but also in terms of final educational attainment. Thus, the higher dispersion in the PISA test results in Germany compared to France does not have for corollary a higher dispersion in the degrees obtained. In particular, whereas the share of German students with particulary low levels of reading and mathematical literacy was found to be much higher than in France, the percentage of individuals with no school degree at all is on the contrary very much higher in France. This raises the question of the certification of skills by the credentials issued by the respective education systems. It seems that in Germany, even when students fail at the most elementary level of reading and mathematical skills, they nevertheless manage to obtain a school degree, whereas the same people in France would fail at obtaining any school degree. The same holds for vocational degrees. Here again, many more French people fail to obtain any vocational degree, even the basic degrees which are known to have a low status in France. An explanation for this – consistent with the PISA findings – is that the requirements in terms of general skills (mathematics and French) are higher in France even for low-level vocational qualifications. Fulfilling these minimum requirements in general subjects is a necessary condition for the student to be given the vocational degree. In Germany, it is very unusual that people fail to obtain an apprenticeship degree because they were too bad in mathematics or German. The concentration of educational degrees with at the same time a large dispersion of test results suggests that the variance in the skill levels for a given degree is particularly large in Germany. Thus, there seems to be scope for further research on the link between skill level and educational credentials, how it developed over time and how meaningful the degrees are in terms of the skills they certify. Of course, this can only be done if data including both skill measures and degrees obtained are made available to scientists.

Another central finding is that France and Germany prove to be remarkably similar with respect to the impact of family background on the educational outcomes. Roughly speaking, the higher the education of the parents, the higher is the educational outcome of their children. Also the influence of father's occupation exhibits a more or less similar pattern in France and Germany. Thus, the stronger dependence of the PISA test results on family background in Germany compared to France does not translate into stronger social inequalities in terms of educational credentials. Here again, this suggests that the correspondence between skills and degrees does not work in the same way in both countries and that the German education system is more lenient with students having poor results in general skills, who typically stem from poorer social backgrounds in terms of parental education and occupation.

Furthermore, the variables turn out to exert a different influence depending on the educational stage observed. The educational upgrade phenomenon across cohorts, for instance, occurred at the secondary level, but at the post-secondary level, maturity holders experienced a decline in their propensity to study, anything else equal. The influence of parental education and paternal occupation is stronger for the achievement at secondary school than for post-school achievement, especially if the level of secondary education attained is high. This has important implications for education policy. To be more efficient, measures designed to reduce social inequalities in educational achievement should be targeted at early stages of the educational process. For the subsequent education of maturity holders, for instance, family background is found to have virtually no significant influence. The effect of gender differs radically when distinguishing between school and post-school achievement. Thus, decomposing the educational career into different stages made it possible to gain more insights into the channels through which background characteristics affect educational outcomes. The model developed for this purpose proved particularly useful, since there is indeed a significant correlation between the unobserved factors determining school and post-school attainment, which justifies the computational burden of the simultaneous estimation.

Finally, the analysis reveals huge differences between France and Germany with respect to gender differences. The impact of parental background does not differ between genders, or only in a minor way. This is true in both countries. However, for a given social background and cohort, women appear to have higher educational thresholds than men for attaining the next higher education level, especially in Germany[47]. This means that for a given cohort

[47] Indeed, an originality of the estimations conducted here is that the threshold values have been allowed to differ between men and women in a nonsystematic way.

and family background, access to education is more difficult for women than for men. Looking in more detail into the educational career, it appears that, at the school level, French women have lower thresholds than French men, which means a better school achievement in terms of school degrees. Thus, the better performance of girls at PISA translates into women having higher school degrees than men. In Germany, however, girls' lead in terms of the general skills tested at PISA does not translate into better school achievement for a given background, since the estimated thresholds to higher school levels are higher for women than for men. One explanation for this could be that German women anticipate a more traditional division of tasks with respect to family and work and attach less importance to attaining a high level of education than in France. There seems to be scope for further research with repect to secondary school choice of boys and girls in Germany, for given schooling ability. At the post-secondary level, however, French women have, like German women though to a lesser extent, higher thresholds than men[48]. This indicates a certain specialisation or preference of women for general education while men perform comparatively better in more vocational fields.

Overall, the differences observed in the distribution of educational attainment in France and Germany seems to stem less from differences in terms of social inequality as measured by the family background than from differences in inequality across genders. Moreover, it proved worthwhile to look in more detail into the educational process, since family background, gender and cohort proved to exert a different influence at the school level and at the post-secondary level. The results point to the necessity of looking into more detail at the link between skills and degrees, provided appropriate data is available. Beyond the interest of the analysis of educational attainment per se, being aware of these specific features should help analyse and interpret education-related outcomes in France and Germany, in particular labour market outcomes. This is the aim of the following chapters.

[48] Except for the group of individuals with an intermediate school degree, for which there are no significant gender differences.

4

Education and unemployment in France and Germany

In chapters 2 and 3, the nature of the qualifications obtained in the French and German systems of initial education as well as the distribution of educational attainment and its determinants in either country were analysed in detail. These chapters were rather directed at the analysis of the internal efficiency of the respective education systems in producing skills of different types, beyond any original social inequalities. In the subsequent chapters, the study moves on to the analysis of the way final educational attainment is "rewarded" or "valued" by the labour market in either country. Indeed, though the education system does not have as sole mission to endow pupils with skills that will enable them to be successful in the labour market, this is nevertheless one of its essential tasks. Two outcomes are considered here as measures of the labour market reward of education: the unemployment risk (chapter 4) and labour earnings (chapter 5). Comparing the labour market outcomes of the qualifications issued by the respective education systems as certified by the credentials obtained should give insights into the external efficiency of the education systems in terms of labour market opportunities and help to identify the relative strengths and weaknesses of either system in this respect.

As many European countries, France and Germany are plagued with high levels of unemployment, the reduction of which having invariably been at the top of the political agenda for the past few years or even decades. The educational attainment is an essential determinant of the employability of individuals in so far as it constitutes an essential part of the human capital they can offer on the labour market. Therefore, it is hardly surprising that policy-makers look, among other things, into the education system for solutions to their unemployment problem. In order to reform the education system so as to contribute to the alleviation of the unemployment problem, however, one needs to know which parts of the education system are more successful than others, which types of skills produced by the education system turn out to be employed on the labour market and which do not. This, in turn, requires that the precise pattern of dependence of unemployment on the type and level of educational attainment be known. Cross-country comparisons can prove very helpful in this respect. Indeed, if another country sets different priorities on its education system, looking at the success of this system in terms of unemployment compared to the success of the own education system can give ideas how to design more efficiently the own education system. As the previous chapters showed, France and Germany appear to have chosen different options for their education systems, in particular with respect to the degree of consideration of the needs of the labour market or more generally speaking with respect to the balance between general and vocational education. How this different prioritisation in the various educational tracks performs in terms of unemployment risk will be examined here in detailed.

Thus, the aim of this chapter is to analyse the extent to which the skills obtained in the course of initial education protect against the unemployment risk, and to find out which qualifications prove more successful than others. The concept of unemployment risk, however, is a complex notion that covers different dimensions. Basically, unemployment should be viewed as a dynamic problem. People become unemployed at a certain point in time and after a shorter or longer period, they get out of unemployment. This might never happen, happen once or several times. Put it differently, one can distinguish between the risk of entering unemployment and the risk of remaining in unemployment, as well as the risk of recurrence of unemployment. Educational attainment might affect these dimensions in a different way. Certain types of qualifications might prove particularly efficient in protecting against the risk of entering unemployment, others might be more successful in getting people out of unemployment, for instance. This is what this chapter seeks to analyse on the basis of the patterns observed within each country and across them. Moreover, special attention will be given to gender differences, since the labour market outcomes are typically gender specific.

Looking at the evidence from the literature (see section 4.1), it appears that the link between education and unemployment is far from being clear-cut from a theoretical point of view. The empirical evidence available so far do not point either to conclusive results in so far as the studies available come to different – if not contradictory – conclusions with respect to the role of education for unemployment depending on the country observed, the methodology used, the aspect of unemployment focussed on and the degree of precision of the measure of educational attainment. Moreover, there are no comparative studies of the education-unemployment link in the French and German adult populations, even though, as argued before, the differences in the education systems of these countries might help identify the link between certain types of qualifications and the unemployment risk. Thus, this study tries to use the knowledge on the French and the German education systems gained in the previous chapters and in particular the differences across them to identify the nature of the education-unemployment link. Moreover, it considers for this purpose the various aspects of the dynamics of unemployment in a single consistent framework rather than focussing on one specific aspect of the unemployment problem only (e.g. the unemployment duration as is frequent in the literature). From a methodological point of view, the unemployment problem is decomposed in its various components in an original manner, starting from a discrete time competing risks hazard rate model applied to the analysis of transitions into and out of unemployment. The formal presentation of the model proposed here demonstrates that the multinomial logit implementation that has been applied in the recent empirical literature without being derived formally can be rationalised from an econometric point of view.

The chapter is organised as follows. First, section 4.1 looks into the literature for explanations of the link between education and unemployment. The attempt is made to derive from various theories some theoretical elements of explanation of the possible link between education and unemployment, but also the empirical evidence available so far on this topic will be reviewed and the value added of this study will be put forward. Then, section 4.2 presents as a starting point a static descriptive analysis of the link between education and the unemployment rate in France and Germany, since the unemployment rate is the most widely used indicator of the labour market performance. This descriptive analysis is based on representative microdata sets which make it possible to distinguish between unemployment, non-employment and employment in a way as similar as possible for both countries. Then, the chapter moves on to an econometric analysis of the impact of education on the various dimensions of the dynamics of unemployment. Section 4.3 motivates the choice of a discrete-time competing risks hazard rate model with nonparametrically modeled unobserved individual heterogeneity and proposes a rigorous formulation of the model that will be estimated. The estimations require an extensive preparation of the microdata, all the more since the French and the German data sets on which the analysis is based need to be put in comparable form first. The construction of the spell data and of the variables used for the analysis is explained in section 4.4.

The rest of the chapter presents the results of the econometric analysis. First, section 4.5 presents the results with respect to the risk of entering unemployment. The estimations focus on the impact of education on the risk of transiting from employment to unemployment. Then, section 4.6 examines the chances, once unemployed, to exit unemployment and how education affects them. In particular, I look at the reemployment prospects of the unemployed and derive from the estimation results an estimate of the unemployment duration employees can expect if they enter unemployment, accounting for the possible censoring of the unemployment spells. Following this, the results established in sections 4.5 and 4.6 will be combined in section 4.7 to compute a synthetic indicator of the total unemployment risk employees can expect to face given their education level, taking into account the risk of experiencing unemployment at all, the expected duration of unemployment episodes and the occurrence of multiple spells. Building on this indicator, a simple concentration index will illustrate the extent to which the unemployment problem is unevenly distributed across certain population groups. Finally, some conclusions will be drawn in section 4.8 with respect to the nature of the unemployment problem in France and German and to the relative efficiency of the qualifications issued by the respective education systems to protect against the unemployment risk in its various dimensions.

4.1 Education and unemployment: overview of the literature

4.1.1 Theoretical background

Different theoretical veins might be thought of to explain the relationship between education and unemployment: the human capital theory, the job search theory, the job competition model and the matching model.

According to the *human capital theory* (Becker 1964; Mincer 1974), education can be viewed as an investment in human capital, and the optimal amount of education is chosen so as to maximise lifetime earnings or more generally utility. A higher level of education entails costs in the short run, but is expected to be associated with a higher level of life-cycle earnings. In this framework, unemployment represents a constraint on choice rather than an element of it, and additional schooling is expected to alleviate this constraint (see for instance Ashenfelter and Ham 1979). Moreover, due to complementarity effects, there is a positive relationship between the level of education and the acquisition of further qualification through training or learning by doing (Nickell 1979). Insofar as part of this human capital is firm-specific, the more human capital an individual possesses, the less likely he is to quit or to be made redundant by the employer (Nickell 1979; Forgeot and Gautié 1997). Therefore, the human capital theory provides arguments why the level of education should reduce the probability of entering unemployment. The impact of education on the duration of unemployment is less clear-cut from a human capital theoretical point of view. On the one hand, more skills are expected to increase the chances of finding employment (at or below market wages). On the other hand, however, periods of unemployment represent an interruption in the accumulation of human capital. Since, as was just mentioned, highly educated individuals tend to accumulate more human capital on the job, they are expected to be more heavily penalised in relative terms by periods of inactivity. Unemployment might not only represent an interruption in the accumulation of the human capital, but also a depreciation of the stock of human capital, which needs to be maintained and updated (Polachek and Siebert 1993). Here again, it is expected that highly educated workers face a larger depreciation of their human capital due to the convexity of the depreciation rate.

Heckman (1979) was the first to point to the fact that relating the observed distribution of earnings to the level of education, such as stipulated in the human capital theory, is not an appropriate way to determine the true relationship between education and wages for the whole population because the working population might be a nonrandom sample of the whole population. This is what he refers to as sample selection bias. The *job search theory* (see e.g. Mortensen 1986) focusses on this selection process and aims at providing theoretical explanations on the matching process between workers and jobs. In a search theoretical framework, the unemployed will opt for leaving unemployment if the utility (that might be expressed as the expected wage minus the cost of being employed) of the job offer he or she is facing lies above his reservation wage, i.e. the minimum earnings that he or she will request to give up the unemployment benefit and take paid employment. Education is expected to have a positive influence on job opportunities, since it is assumed that the individual can accept a job below his education level but cannot find a job requiring a higher level of education. At the same time, however, well educated individuals have higher wages, and therefore a higher reservation wage, which has a negative impact on the probability of exiting unemployment. It is also assumed that well educated people have higher costs of becoming employed, which has a negative impact on the unemployment exit probability. This is because the jobs requiring a high level of education are typically sparsely located and finding a new high-level job often implies moving or commuting costs (Kettunen 1997). Thus, greater education increases the arrival rate of offers, but it is also expected to decrease the acceptance rate of these offers. The overall effect of education on the unemployment exit probability remains unclear on theoretical grounds. The same reasoning can be applied to those persons of active age who have withdrawn from the labour market, typically women with children. These women will only opt for employment if the costs of re-entering the labour market (e.g. child care costs) are below the benefits, i.e. if the wage they expect is sufficiently high.

The search theory implicitly assumes that inactivity is supply-led and more or less voluntary (Nicaise 2001), suggesting that unemployed people are in the position to afford to refuse all the jobs that are too lowly paid in their views. This sounds somewhat counter-intuitive in times of massive involuntary unemployment. In such a context, one would expect inactivity to be forced by constraints on the demand side of the labour market. One would expect individuals to compete for the same scarce jobs by bidding down on wages or by accepting jobs below their qualification level. This type of argument insists on the demand side of the labour market and is known as the *job competition* or *job queuing model*, in reference to Thurow (1975). In this model, wages are tied to jobs instead of persons, because productivity is viewed as a characteristic of the job rather than of the individual worker. The labour market is represented as consisting of two queues. One queue contains the jobs, ranked according to the skills they require, the other queue contains the individuals, ranked according to their qualifications. Job seekers try to find the best jobs, and employers always prefer the highest educated among the candidates to a posted job because everyone is paid the same wage on a given job and the more highly educated workers are trained at a lower cost. As a result, the best jobs go to the higher educated, while the lower educated, due to their less favourable position in the job queue, are forced to accept less attractive jobs. In a context of a vast supply of labour relative to more scarce labour demand, the higher educated who do not find suitable employment will look for a job further down the queue, thereby crowding out the less educated. This crowding out phenomenon implies that the least educated face the greatest unemployment risk, all the more since the supply of educated labour increases conditional on the structure of labour demand. In this framework, education plays essentially a filtering role. The degree obtained does not primarily guarantee that the individual disposes of productive skills, but rather signals to the employer potential trainability and serves to position the individuals in the queue.

While the human capital theory and the search theory focus on the supply side of the labour market and job competition models rather focus on the demand side, *matching models* (see Mortensen 1976; Jovanovic 1979; Pissarides 1990; Layard, Nickell and Jackman 1991; Franz 1999) aim to treat both sides explicitly. The demand side of the labour market is assumed to consist of jobs with different skill requirements. The supply side consists of individuals who have acquired skills by means of education. Vacant jobs are filled according to a matching process where both the individual and the employer search for the ideal partner. The search process includes some search costs due to imperfect information on both sides. It also depends on labour market tightness in the respective sector, i.e. on the relative stocks of vacancies and unemployment. The matching model accounts for the fact that unemployment might co-exist with vacancies in the labour market. In this model, the effect of education is a priori unclear, since there is no ranking like in the job queuing model. The effect depends on the relative demand and supply in the various skill sectors. The rising earnings differentials by education have received considerable attention in the United States and have been interpreted as being the consequence of changes in the relative demand for skilled workers, typically as a result of skill-biased technological change (e.g. Katz and Murphy 1992; Juhn, Murphy and Pierce 1993). Given the lesser wage flexibility in Europe, unemployment differentials by education levels may be viewed as the quantity adjustment counterpart of the American price adjustment.

Note that the job competition/crowding out hypotheses are not incompatible with the reservation wage hypothesis of the job search theory, neither do they contradict the human capital theory or the matching model. All these effects might be at work and these theories should be seen as complementary, though a single theory encompassing all these aspects is still missing[1].

[1] Some attempts have been made, e.g. Muysken and Ter Weel (2000) extend a matching model so as to capture the ingredients of both human capital and labour queue theories.

4.1.2 Empirical findings

Since the impact of education on the unemployment risk is far from being clear-cut from a theoretical point of view, let us now have a look at the empirical evidence available so far. The main studies are described below as well as the value added of the present study.

International evidence

The first study directly devoted to the link between education and unemployment is probably that by Nickell (1979). The author examines the impact of education on unemployment incidence, understood as the probability of being unemployed at a given time, then analyses the impact of education on the duration of unemployment based on a simplified version of a hazard rate model. Combining the information on the impact of education on the duration and on the incidence of unemployment enables him to derive education-specific probabilities of inflow into unemployment. The results show for Great Britain that the level of education strongly influences the probability of becoming unemployed during working life, but rather weakly affects the expected duration of unemployment spells.

Jacob Mincer also explored this relationship for men (Mincer 1991b) as well as for women (Mincer 1991a), though with a different methodology. His analysis is based on the decomposition of the unemployment rate into different components: the probability of having separated from the previous job, the probability of experiencing unemployment when separated, the duration of unemployment for job separators and the labour force rate as well as the labour force participation rate (for women). He then tries to identify the impact of education, net of other characteristics, on the components in a term by term multivariate analysis. As in the study of Nickell (1979) for the United Kingdom, Mincer concludes that in the United States, educational unemployment differentials are far more attributable to the fact that the higher education reduces the incidence of unemployment than to the fact that it reduces the duration of unemployment.

Kettunen (1997) explored the link between education and the duration of unemployment on the basis of a Weibull duration model with discrete mixing distribution for Finland. Education is found to have a strong effect on the duration of unemployment. Up to a certain level, a higher level of education increases the hazard of exiting unemployment, but beyond the bachelor's degree, the re-employment probability decreases again, and unemployed individuals with a master's or doctor's degree have the lowest probability of re-employment. This study, however, says nothing about the risk of entering unemployment.

More recently, Wolbers (2000) examined the effect of education on the mobility between employment and unemployment for the case of the Netherlands. The study applies a single risk discrete hazard rate model to assess on the one hand the impact of the education level on the probability that an employed individual enters unemployment, and on the other hand the effect of education on the probability to exit unemployment and to get re-employed. Contrary to the evidence found for the United Kingdom by Nickell (1979) and for the United States by Mincer (1991b), Wolbers (2000) finds out that in the Netherlands, education affects both entry into unemployment and unemployment duration. Broadly speaking, lower levels of education are associated with higher risks of entering unemployment and poorer chances of exiting unemployment, but the link is not linear. For instance, university graduates have a greater probability of encountering unemployment than individuals with higher vocational education, but there are hardly any differences in the unemployment exit rates of people with secondary and tertiary education. The author concludes that the results only partly supports the job competition model. Furthermore, he points to the usefulness of making the distinction between different types of education – in particular general versus vocational types of education – rather than only levels.

Evidence on France and Germany

A study that is specifically targeted at the relationship between education and unemployment while covering both France and Germany is that by Brauns, Gangl and Scherer (1999)[2]. The authors analyse the educational stratification of unemployment in early career in the United Kingdom, France and Germany. Based on simple logit estimates, the analysis concludes that Germany is characterised by a fairly smooth access to initial employment, but that once initial employment has been found, education plays a negligible role for the risk of unemployment. In contrast, in France (and in the United Kingdom), access to first employment is found to be more difficult and to depend less on education, but education seems to conserve a more important role than in Germany with respect to securing employment. However, this study focusses on early labour market career only and does not consider the duration of unemployment[3].

The topic of youth unemployment has been the object of several studies in France and Germany. Franz (1982) and later on Franz et al. (2000) and Zimmermann (2000), for instance, analysed youth unemployment in Germany, and the studies by Fougère, Kramarz and Magnac (2000) and D'Addio (1998) examine this issue for France[4]. France is characterised by a much higher youth unemployment than Germany. When measured roughly (through the number of years of schooling or through binary variables), education is found to have

[2] This study builds on previous studies by Müller, Steinmann and Ell (1998) and Goux and Maurin (1998) that examined the transition from school to work and drew some conclusions on the link between education and first (un)employment.

[3] Only the transition probability within a given period of time is examined.

[4] See also Franz and Zimmermann (2002) and Bonnal, Mendès and Sofer (2002), that concentrate on the initial employment situation of basic vocational education graduates.

a unemployment-reducing effect for youth. However, all these studies argue that the youth employment market is a specific issue that requires particular analysis, because the mechanisms at work differ from those at work in the adult labour market. In particular, the institutional aspects of the transition from school to work play an essential role. Moreover, focussing on the age group 15-25 implies that a large proportion of the sample is still enrolled in education, in particular those youths that strive for a higher education degree. Therefore, these studies cannot really examine the situation of higher education graduates. In the present analysis, the focus is not on transition from school to work or youth unemployment but rather on the impact of the level of education finally attained on adult unemployment. This is why the focus is laid on people aged between 25 and 55, so that the overwhelming majority of this sample has finished initial education and that the sample composition is not biased with respect to educational attainment.

There are many other studies on France or Germany that analyse unemployment with another focus of interest than education. These studies do not refer explicitly to education, but education generally appears as an explanatory factor for unemployment. Most articles examine the duration of unemployment, i.e. the probability of exiting unemployment rather than the probability of entering unemployment. A general analysis of the determinants of unemployment duration is for instance provided by Wurzel (1993) or Hunt (1999) for Germany and Bonnal and Fougère (1990) or Cases and Lollivier (1994) for France. However, most papers focus on one particular aspect of unemployment duration. The impact of unemployment benefits, for instance, has been analysed by Steiner (1997) or Plaßmann (2002) for Germany and by Florens, Gérard-Varet and Werquin (1989) or Dormont, Fougère and Prieto (2001) for France. The impact of business cycle has been examined, for instance, by van den Berg and van der Klaauw (2001). Other papers have a rather technical focus like e.g. the distinction between state dependence and individual heterogeneity (e.g. Steiner 1997; Magnac 1998) or the impact of measurement error (Magnac and Visser 1999). These papers are useful for the present study from a methodological point of view but the impact of education is often hardly commented upon. Because it is not the focus of interest, education is generally defined quite broadly and generally a positive impact is found on the protection against unemployment risk. However, the evidence available for other countries (e.g. Wolbers 2000) shows that when using a more differentiated measure of education, the patterns observed are not so simple.

An important aspect raised by some scientists, in response to the numerous papers on unemployment duration that do not consider the risk of experiencing unemployment, is the necessity to analyse the occurrence of multiple spells of unemployment, arguing that the duration of unemployment spells tells only one side of the story if specific population groups are more likely to experience repeated spells of unemployment than others. Joutard and Ruggiero (2000), for instance, examined this for France and Karr and John (1989) for Germany, though with different methodologies[5]. Joutard and Ruggiero (2000) estimate a structural model of unemployment duration in which the job seekers may anticipate the possible recurrence of unemployment spells[6], but they do not really analyse the entry into unemployment as such and the impact of education on it. Karr and John (1989) decompose the cumulated unemployment duration of those individuals who have been registered as unemployed at the labour office at least once into the duration of unemployment per spell and the average number of spells experienced. They observe that individuals with a low qualification level face more often repeated unemployment, but do not differentiate much the level and type of education. The issue of repeated unemployment will be addressed in this study, though with a somewhat different methodology, for the reasons explained in section 4.7.1.

Value added of the present study

This chapter aims at complementing the empirical literature in several ways. First, it adds to the empirical evidence on the relationship between education and unemployment. Indeed, as has just been shown, the evidence available points to somewhat contradictory results, with some studies stating an impact of education on the unemployment entry risk, others on unemployment duration, some finding a linear impact, others not. In particular, the impact of education seems to depend on the aspect of the unemployment problem considered and on the degree of aggregation with which the level of education is defined.

Second, this study reconciles in a single study elements of analysis of the empirical relationship between education and unemployment that have only been addressed separately in the literature. Thus, it studies two countries in a comparative manner, distinguishes between differentiated levels and types of education, it analyses both the risk of entering unemployment and the chances of exiting unemployment, distinguishes between different exit destinations and computes an estimate of unemployment duration taking censoring into account. Moreover, it deals with the issue of multiple spells in an innovative manner, proposes a synthetic indicator of total unemployment risk and addresses the issue of the concentration of the unemployment problem on certain population groups. From a methodological point of view, this chapter brings a rigorous formulation of a competing risks model in a discrete time framework and demonstrates that the multinomial logit estimations which have been applied in the recent literature can be rationalised from an econometric point of view. Though time-consuming, up-to-date techniques have

[5] The same methodology as Karr and John (1989) has been used again later on by Franz et al. (2000) with a focus on youth unemployment in Germany, see above.

[6] They find out that in France, the highest degree obtained plays an all the more important role since the occupational position is of a high level. Moreover, the level of education attained turns out to be a more discriminating factor for women than for men, a fact which is not confirmed by the present study.

been used to model unobserved heterogeneity in a flexible – nonparametric – way.

Finally, such a comparison of France and Germany, which had not been done before, makes it possible to draw some conclusions regarding the impact of different levels and types of qualifications on various dimensions of the unemployment risk, based on the patterns observed both within and across countries and thus help uncover the strengths and weaknesses of the respective education systems in terms of unemployment risk.

4.2 Unemployment, non-employment and employment

The most widely used indicator on the performance of the labour market is the unemployment rate, which gives the proportion of the active labour force unemployed at a given point in time. Because both France and Germany are plagued with high levels of unemployment, policy makers in both countries search for the causes and remedies of unemployment and aim to know which groups of workers are more hit than others. The first step of the analysis therefore consists in providing an overview of the structure of unemployment depending on the education level in France and Germany. The aim of this descriptive overview is to identify where the problems are, i.e. for which qualification groups the unemployment risk is more acute, measured by the indicator of the unemployment rate[7]. In a further step (from section 4.3 onwards), an econometric analysis will go further into detail and seek to examine the precise nature of the unemployment problem and to isolate the effect of education. To this end, a dynamic view will be adopted: Instead of considering the risk of being unemployed at a given point in time, the analysis will examine the risk of entering unemployment, on the one hand, and the risk of not getting out of unemployment, on the other hand.

It is difficult to talk about the unemployment rate without talking about labour force participation. Indeed, the unemployment rate is the ratio of the unemployed to the active labour force. If labour force participation differs across educational groups or across countries, this will explain for a part the measured level of the unemployment rate. As a matter of fact, it is well known that the level of labour force participation differs largely in France and Germany (see e.g. Lauer and Weber 2003). Therefore, the detailed pattern of labour force participation by education will be examined here, too. A further indicator of the labour market performance is the employment rate, which relates the number of individuals in employment to the total population instead of relating it to the active labour force only. These three indicators –

[7] The distinction between risk of entering unemployment and duration of unemployment is not done at the descriptive level because of the problem of incomplete spells (censoring) which causes the duration of the observed unemployment spells to be underestimated. The econometric analysis will allow censoring to be taken into account and compute estimates of the unemployment duration.

unemployment rate, non-employment rate and employment rate – give first insights into the basic relationship between education and (un)employment.

4.2.1 Data and definition of the employment status

The aggregate data available within each country is often not comparable in terms of the definition of the concepts and of the sample populations observed. As far as international sources such as OECD are concerned, they aim to harmonise the definition of concepts (e.g. unemployment rate) and samples to make them comparable across a wide range of countries. However, as argued in chapter 2, the classification of educational attainment is also designed to be applicable to a large number of countries and it seems more advantageous to use the detailed educational typology established in chapter 2 and targeted at capturing the specific features of the German and the French education systems. Therefore, I follow the approach of Schmidt (1999) and Cohen, Lefranc and Saint-Paul (1997) to provide basic descriptive evidence on the basis of monthly microdata. This has additionally the advantage that the subsequent econometric analysis will rely on the very same data and variables.

The data used for the analyses is drawn from the GSOEP for Germany and from the *Emploi* survey for France (see the description in section 2.3.1). In both data sets, the respondents are requested to report their labour market status in each month of the year preceding the interview[8]. This monthly information makes it possible to retrace the labour market history of the respondents. In the *Emploi* survey, the interview takes place in March every year and the retrospective information refers to the 12 months immediately preceding the interview month[9]. Consequently, there is double information for March, since each wave yields information for March of the previous year until March of the current year. Because there might be some recall errors (see Magnac and Visser 1999), the information of the current year is retained for March. In the GSOEP, the month of the interview might vary across individuals and across waves, even though the bulk of the interviews take place at the beginning of the year. The retrospective information on the employment status does not depend on the interview month, though, since it refers to the calendar year preceding the year of the interview, i.e. it goes from January to December of the preceding year, whatever the interview month is.

In the GSOEP, the individuals are re-interviewed each year from 1984 onwards and leave the sample only because of attrition. This means that it is theoretically possible to track individuals in each month from January 1983 at the earliest (or from the first time they appear in the sample) to at most

[8] For France, the retrospective information is only collected from the 1990 wave onwards.

[9] In 1990, as an exception, the households were interviewed in January instead of March. This means that data for February 1990 is missing, since the 1990 wave provides information from January 1989 to January 1990, while the subsequent wave provides information from March 1990 to March 1991.

December 1999, since the most recent wave available at the time of this study is 2000. However, the *Emploi* survey collects information only from the 1990 wave onwards, and, as mentioned in footnote 9, the data for February 1990 is missing. Moreover, because the *Emploi* survey is a rotating panel in which one third of the sample is renewed each year, we can track the employment status of an individual for at most three consecutive years (i.e. for a maximum of 37 consecutive months). Therefore, the subsequent empirical analyses will basically rely on the data drawn from the latest three waves available, i.e. 1998, 1999 and 2000[10], and cover, broadly speaking, the period 1997 to 1999. As in chapter 3 and 5, the analysis focusses on West German residents and only nationals or individuals born in the country (see motivation for this in section 3.1). Moreover, the analysis focusses on individuals aged between 25 and 55. This age restriction aims to limit the problems related to retirement, on the one hand, and those related to the fact that too young individuals may not have finished their education yet, on the other hand.

For the analysis, three labour market states are distinguished: employment, unemployment and non-employment[11]. For Germany (GSOEP), the employment state comprises the categories full-time employment, part-time employment, short-time employment or training at work. For France (*Emploi*), it comprises permanent employment, fixed-term employment or training at work[12]. In the GSOEP data, the unemployment state refers to unemployment registration at the Federal Labour Office. This definition may give rise to both under- and overreporting of the true extent of unemployment[13]. In the

---

10 This has the practical advantage of making it possible to use the data from the GSOEP refreshment sample which was collected for the first time in 1998.

11 In the *Emploi* data, the respondents are requested to indicate a unique labour force state for each month, as opposed to the GSOEP, where individuals may report more than one state per month. For the analyses, however, one needs a unique labour market state. In case of multiple answers, it was therefore decided to choose which state applies for a specific month according to the priority: unemployment, employment, non-employment. For example, if one person indicates, for one specific month, having been both unemployed and employed, this person will be considered having been predominantly unemployed in that month. If a person reports having been employed and non-participating in a specific month, this person will be considered predominantly employed. Admittedly, this choice is arbitrary, but it is unavoidable that an arbitrary decision is taken and this decision rule has the advantage of keeping all the precious unemployment spells in the sample. Multiple answers concern 10.2 percent of the monthly observations.

12 The French and the German data do not distinguish between the same types of employment – full-time versus part-time, or permanent versus fixed term –, therefore, one cannot further differentiate the employment category in the same way for both countries.

13 Registering at the Labour Office is a necessary condition for being eligible for unemployment benefits, and registered unemployed do not need to search actively for a job on their own, even though in principle, the Labour Office will search on their behalf. Thus, some individuals may be registered as unemployed even

French data, by contrast, a respondent may assign himself to unemployment even if he is not registered as unemployed. What characterises unemployment is not defined more precisely, but because the monthly labour market state questions are asked at the end of the survey and because at an earlier stage of the survey, a clear reference to the ILO conditions[14] is established to define the current labour market situation of the respondent at the date of the interview, the perceived definition of unemployment in the monthly data is likely to be close to the ILO definition (see van den Berg and van der Klaauw 2001). The non-employment state is the remaining category and includes, for Germany as for France, retirement, maternity leave, education, military service, housewife and other nonspecified states out of the labour force.

Table 4.1. Typology of educational attainment – reminder

	Highest degree obtained
Level 1	**No vocational qualification**
10	No degree
11	Lower secondary education
12	Intermediate secondary education
Level 2	**Basic vocational qualification**
20	No or lower secondary education + basic vocational degree
21	Intermediate secondary education + basic vocational degree
Level 3	**Intermediate qualification**
30	Intermediate vocational degree
31	Vocational maturity certificate
32	General maturity certificate
33	General maturity certificate + vocational degree
Level 4	**Tertiary level qualification**
40	Lower tertiary education
41	Upper tertiary education

Thus, the concept of unemployment differs somewhat in the French and German data, but this difference is likely to affect the height of unemployment more than its structure or the impact of education on it, which is the main outcome of interest in the present analysis. Both data sets contain comparable information on completed degrees in general, vocational and higher education. This information can be combined to define a comparable variable for educa-

though they are not searching for a job. On the other hand, some other people might not be registered as unemployed at the Labour Office – for instance because they are not entitled to unemployment benefits any longer – even though they are available and searching for a job.

[14] An individual is unemployed if i) without employment, ii) seeking employment and iii) currently available for employment (International Labour Office 1989).

tional attainment based on the highest degree obtained such as established in section 2.3 (further details in chapter 2) and reminded in table 4.1.

4.2.2 Unemployment rates

Figure 4.1 shows the level of the unemployment rate depending on the educational attainment for the time period 1997 to 1999 in France and Germany (pooled samples) and figures 4.2 and 4.3 differentiate across genders. Figures C.1 to C.4 in appendix C provide further insights into the developments over the 1990s.

Fig. 4.1. Unemployment rate by education level (1997-99)

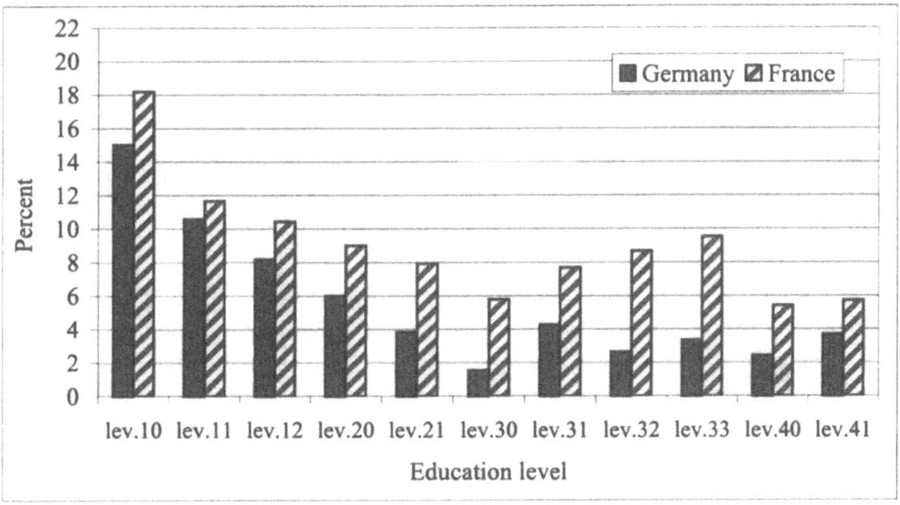

The unemployment rate is defined as the proportion of the labour force (i.e. employed plus unemployed persons) which is unemployed in the sense specified in section 4.2.1. Comparing the figures with the official statistics, the unemployment rates reported here appear quite low, especially for Germany. This has also been remarked by Schmidt (1999), who ran an extensive analysis of monthly labour market stocks and flows on the basis of the GSOEP retrospective monthly data. One reason for the low figures here is that the sample of observation consists of West German natives, whereas foreigners typically have higher unemployment rates. The same holds for France. Moreover, the sample only covers individuals aged 25 to 55 and not the whole labour force. This undoubtedly drives the unemployment rates down for France, since young people have comparatively higher unemployment rates. A further reason lies in the definition of unemployment used here, which includes in the denominator the self-employed and the military personnel. Finally, the employment

Fig. 4.2. Unemployment rate by education level and gender (1997-99) – Germany

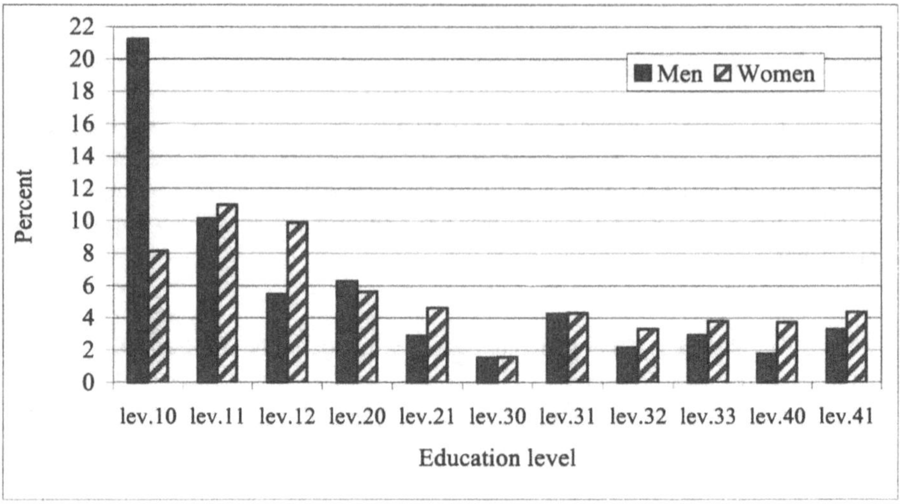

Fig. 4.3. Unemployment rate by education level and gender (1997-99) – France

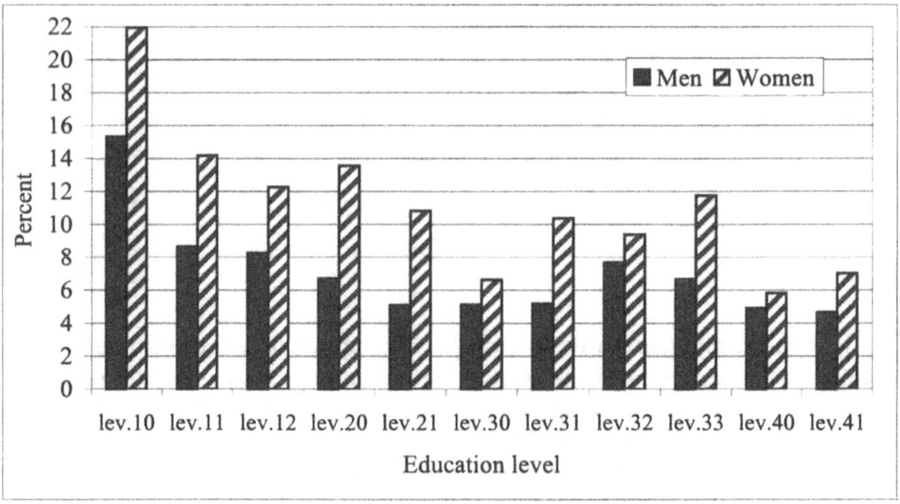

state is self-reported and as such not exempt from reporting errors or recall biases. The following elements appear from the figures.

- In both countries, the unemployment rate tends to decrease with the education level, but only up to a certain level (figure 4.1).

  In both countries, the unemployment rate decreases continuously with the education level until level 30, which corresponds to an advanced vocational qualification below the maturity level. The unemployment rate is by far highest for those individuals without any degree at all (level 10). Having at least a school degree, even below the maturity level, already reduces considerably the unemployment risk. Basic vocational education and above all intermediate vocational qualifications further protect from unemployment. However, the unemployment rate becomes again significantly higher for qualifications at the maturity level, especially in France. Even tertiary level qualifications are associated with an unemployment risk of the same level (France) or of a higher level (Germany) than advanced vocational qualifications.

- The unemployment rate is higher in France than in Germany at all education levels, but the gap is not constant across the educational distribution (figure 4.1).

  The gap is particularly large for basic vocational and intermediate qualifications (level 2 and 3), while it is smaller for low and high qualification levels. The level of unemployment of people with no degree at all, i.e. neither a school nor a vocational degree – is also significantly higher in France than in Germany[15]

- In both countries, women face a higher unemployment risk than men, but the gender gap is significantly larger in France than in Germany[16] (figure 4.2 and 4.3).

  Gender differences in the unemployment rate are much more marked in France than in Germany at all education levels. In Germany, as an exception, men with no degree at all (level 10) are more heavily penalised than women in terms of unemployment, but this concerns only a minor part of the population. At certain education levels, however, there is only a small difference between German men and women (level 11, level 20, level 30 and level 31). By contrast, in France, women face a higher unemployment risk than men, whatever their education level. The gender gap is lower at the higher education level.

4.2.3 Non-employment rates

Of course, the level and the structure of the unemployment rate might be influenced by the extent and the structure of labour force participation or the degreee of non-participation. The non-participation or non-employment rate is defined as the proportion of individuals in the total sample population being neither employed nor unemployed in the sense defined in section 4.2.1, i.e. it

[15] Note that the proportion of level 10 is much higher in France than in Germany (17.6 percent versus 0.7 percent in 2000, see table 3.7 in section 3.1.2, chapter 3).

[16] Remember from chapter 3 that, by contrast, gender differences in educational attainment – in favour of men – proved more marked in Germany than in France.

is defined as: number of non-participating persons / number of employed + unemployed + non-participating persons.

Fig. 4.4. Non-employment rate by education level (1997-99)

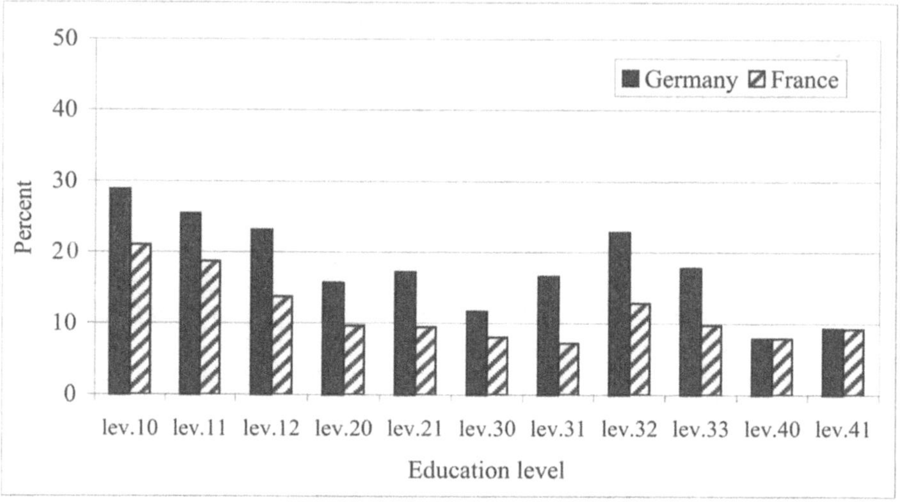

Figure 4.4 depicts the level of the non-employment rate by education level over the period under observation in France and Germany, and figures 4.5 and 4.6 present for each country the gender-specific non-employment rates. Further information on the developments over the 1990s are available in appendix C (figures C.5 to C.8). The following features can be observed.

- In both countries, labour force participation tends to increase with the education level, but only up to a certain level (figure 4.4).

  Non-employment is highest at the lowest education levels. It then tends to decrease with the education level, up to level 30 (advanced vocational qualification). However, in both countries, people having the maturity certificate, especially the general one, as the highest degree tend to be less likely to participate in the labour market. In Germany, higher education graduates exhibit the lowest non-employment propensity, particularly the *Fachhochschule* graduates (level 40). In France, however, level 3 qualifications or above exhibit a more or less similar participation behaviour (except for the general maturity holders).

- There is a weaker labour force participation in Germany than in France (figure 4.4).

  This is true at all education levels, except higher education, where the non-employment rates are equal in France and Germany. The difference in non-employment is largest at the maturity level (levels 31, 32, 33).

Fig. 4.5. Non-employment rate by education level and gender (1997-99) – Germany

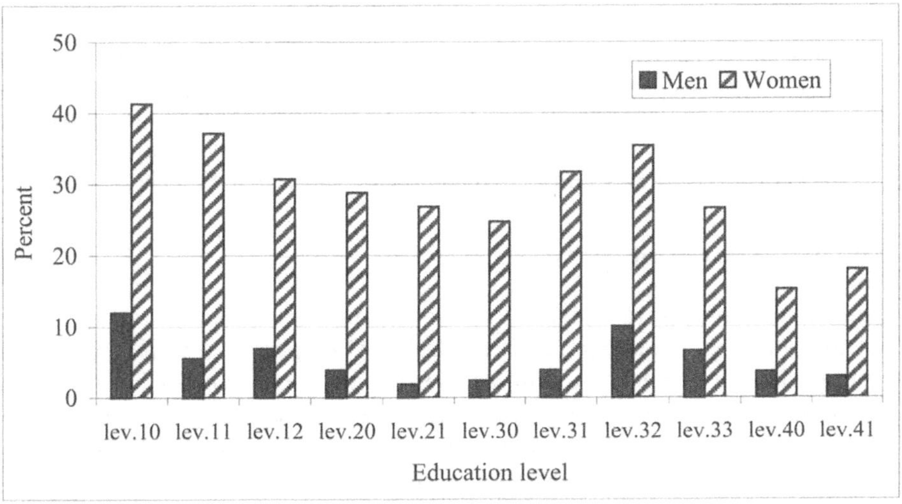

Fig. 4.6. Non-employment rate by education level and gender (1997-99) – France

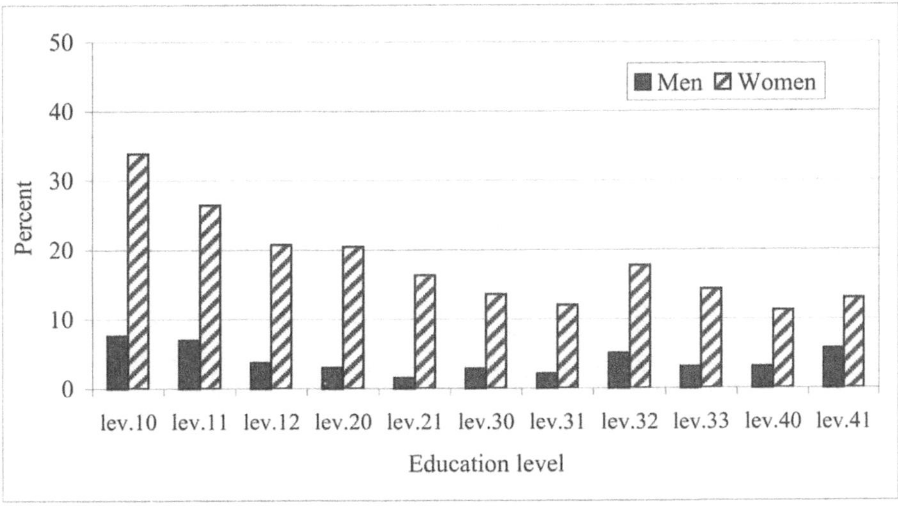

- The non-employment rate is low and rather similar among German and French men, but it is much higher for German women than for French women (figures 4.5 and 4.6).

  Not surprisingly, the level of non-employment is much higher for women than for men in both countries. The difference between France and Germany mainly stems from differences among women of these countries.

The same pattern holds for men and women regarding the dependence of non-employment on the education level, though the differences are more marked for women than for men. Note, however, that whereas the overall labour force participation of tertiary level graduates was found to be equal in France and Germany, this hides that German female graduates do have a higher non-employment rate compared to their French counterparts, but this is offset by the fact that German male university graduates have on the contrary a lower non-employment rate than their French counterparts.

4.2.4 Employment rates

The employment rate is defined as the proportion of the total sample population which is in employment, i.e. number of employed persons / number of employed + unemployed + non-participating persons. The higher the unemployment rate and the non-employment rates are, the lower the employment rate will be. Here again, in addition to figures 4.7, 4.8 and 4.9, further details on time developments are provided in appendix C (figures C.9 to C.12).

Fig. 4.7. Employment rate by education level (1997-99)

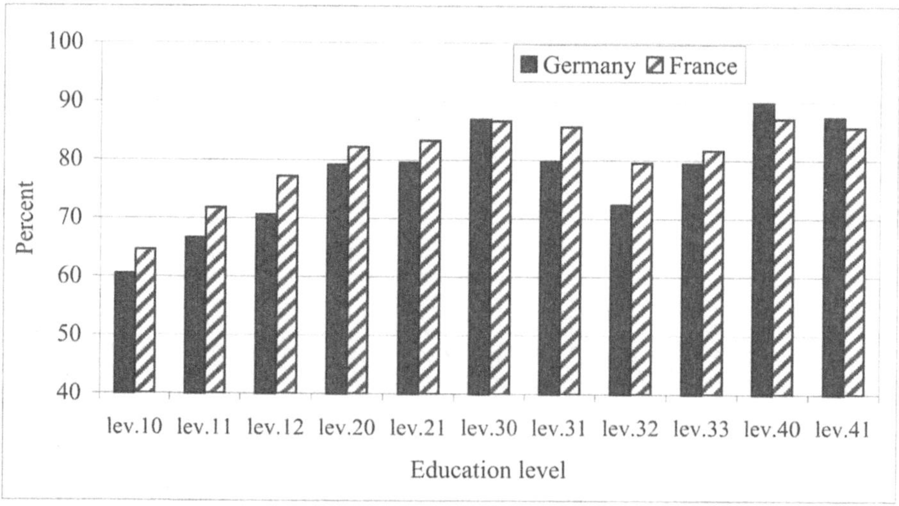

- The differences between France and Germany are much smaller for the employment rate than they are for the unemployment and the non-employment rates (figure 4.7).

  As we have seen, the unemployment rate is higher in France than in Germany, but the labour force non-employment rate is lower. Therefore, on the sole basis of information on unemployment and non-employment, it is not

Fig. 4.8. Employment rate by education level and gender (1997-99) – Germany

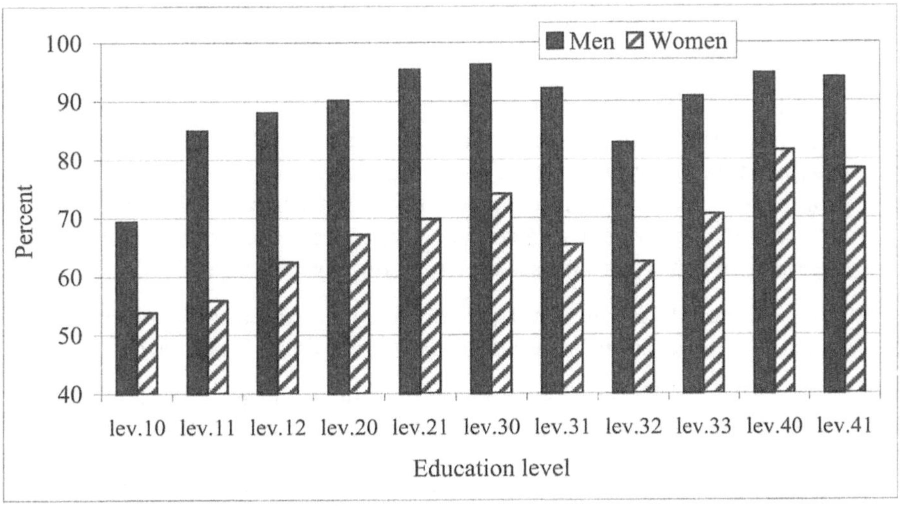

Fig. 4.9. Employment rate by education level and gender (1997-99) – France

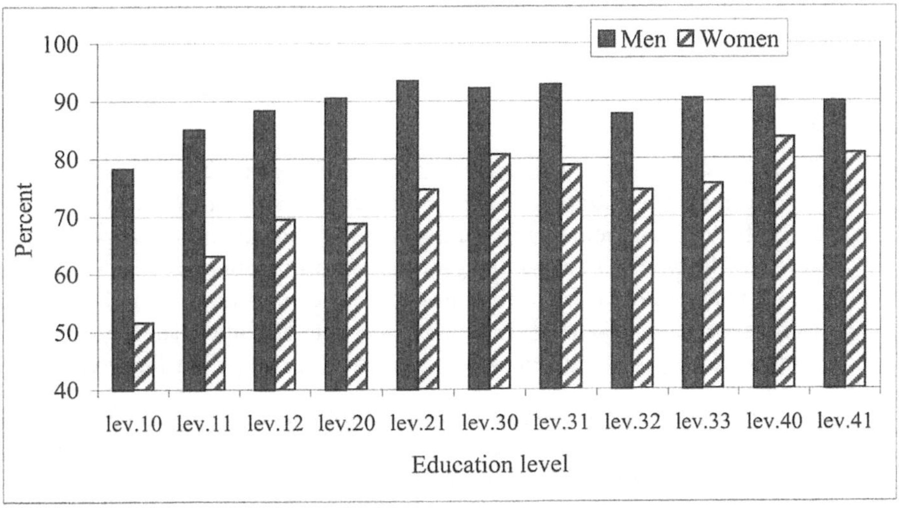

possible to conclude how the French employment rate should compare to the German one. Figure 4.7 shows that the differences between France and Germany are indeed much smaller for the employment rate than they are for the unemployment and the non-employment rates, because the effects go in opposite directions.

- The employment rate is higher in France than in Germany at lower education levels, but for tertiary level graduates, it is higher in Germany (figure 4.7).

  For qualifications up to the intermediate level 3, the employment rate is higher in France than in Germany. This is the result of a much higher labour force participation in France, which is only partially offset by the higher unemployment rate. For tertiary level graduates, however, the employment rate is lower in France than in Germany. This is entirely due to the unemployment differential, unfavourable to France, while the non-employment rate is similar in either country (see figure 4.4).

- In both countries, the employment rate increases almost linearly with education, but only up to a certain education level (figure 4.7).

  The employment rate increases with education up to level 30 (advanced vocational qualification). Holders of the maturity certificate, in particular of the general maturity certificate (level 32), however, have a comparatively lower employment rate than qualifications below that level, due to the combined effect of a high unemployment rate and a comparatively lower labour force participation. The university graduates have the highest employment rate, as a result of their comparatively low unemployment rate combined with a high labour force participation.

- Men have a significantly higher employment rate than women in both countries, but the gender gap is larger in Germany than in France (figures 4.8 and 4.9).

  Thus, the effect on the employment rate of the larger unemployment rate among men than among women in France is more than compensated by the effect of a much larger gender gap in the labour force participation rate in Germany. The gender gap in the employment rate is observed at all education levels. In both countries, it is more marked at lower education levels and lowest at the tertiary level. For men, the pattern of the employment propensity depends less on education than for women.

This overview of the incidence of unemployment and (non-)employment depending on the education level showed that the relationship between education and unemployment is far from being straight-forward when educational attainment is defined in a precise way. The relationship is not monotonous. There proved to be common features in France and Germany (e.g. in the pattern of dependence of the unemployment rate on education), but also significant differences (e.g. extent of differences between France and Germany across the educational distribution). This suggests that the educational credentials do not offer the same relative protection against the unemployment risk in either country. Besides, judging from the descriptive analysis, the impact of labour force participation should be taken into account, since it proves to differ significantly between France and Germany, at least for women, and affects the measured level of unemployment risk.

The unemployment rate is only a static indicator of the labour market performance, but as argued in the introduction, unemployment has a dynamic dimension. Therefore, the notion of unemployment will now be examined in more detail, exploring its dynamic dimension. Thus, instead of considering the risk of being unemployed at a given point in time, the rest of the analysis will examine the risk of entering unemployment, on the one hand, and the risk of not getting out of unemployment, on the other hand. Indeed, a higher unemployment risk, for instance, might be the result of a higher risk of entering unemployment or of a longer unemployment duration when unemployed. These are two different problems that the level of educational attainment might affect in different ways (see section 4.1). Looking more precisely at the impact of education on the various dimensions of the unemployment problem should help to find out the strengths and weaknesses of each education system in terms of external labour market efficiency. This should be examined in a multivariate framework, where the effect of education can be isolated from the effect of other factors that might affect the unemployment risk through their correlation with the education level.

4.3 Modelling framework

The aim of the subsequent econometric analysis is to estimate the impact of the educational attainment on the risk of entering unemployment and on the duration of unemployment, i.e. on the risk of not exiting unemployment. To be more specific, the analysis lays particular emphasis on the transitions from employment to unemployment and from unemployment to employment. Based on these first analyses, further dimensions of the unemployment problem such as the recurrence of unemployment or the total unemployment duration a person might expect in a given period will be investigated. However, an adequate methodological framework has to be found first to model labour market transitions.

4.3.1 A discrete time competing risks hazard rate model

As is well known, the analysis of transition data requires a specific modelling. The main reason relates to censoring (Jenkins 2002, Petersen 1995). A spell is said to be censored if the start date or the end date of the spell is not observed, if the spell is incompletely observed. As a result, the exact length of the spell is unknown. Most data sets contain both complete spells (both entry and exit dates are known) and incomplete spells, either right-censored (exit date is unknown) or left-censored (entry date is unknown). Treating censored spells as if they were uncensored, i.e. treating incomplete spells as if they were complete, would result in underestimating the average spell duration and bias the estimate of its determinants[17]. To make matters worse, long spells are more likely to be censored than short spells, particularly if the observation period is short. The basic idea of hazard rate models is that instead of focussing on the duration spent in a state (e.g. unemployment), one divides this duration into a certain number of time intervals and looks for each time interval whether the state the person was in has been left or not. This way, censoring is taken into account and the estimated effects of the covariates are unbiased (see section 4.3.2 for more details).

Single risk versus competing risks formulation

In their simplest form, hazard rate models consider the time spent in one specific state, i.e. the time elapsed until exit from this state occurs, whatever the destination state is. This is referred to as a *single risk* formulation. For instance, one would study the time spent in unemployment or the hazard of exiting unemployment, regardless whether the destination after unemployment is employment or non-employment. This may be a problem if the factors influencing the transition from unemployment to employment differ from those influencing the transition from unemployment to non-employment. Flinn and Heckman (1983) showed indeed that unemployment and non-employment should be considered behaviourally distinct states. Moreover, the descriptive analysis presented in section 4.2 showed that France and Germany differ widely with respect to the extent of labour force participation. Therefore, it seems a priori more adequate to distinguish employment from unemployment and non-employment and opt for a *multiple risks* or *competing risks* formulation[18]. Nevertheless, the hypothesis that the different outcome categories may be combined will be tested formally (see sections 4.5.1 and 4.6.1).

Discrete time versus continuous time formulation

The origin of hazard rate models is to be found in medical studies, which typically examine the impact of certain factors on life expectancy or on the incidence of certain diseases. This heritage from the medical sciences largely explains that hazard rate ("survival") models are commonly modelled in continuous time rather than in discrete time (see among others Kalbfleisch and Prentice 1980, Lancaster 1990). With the extension of survival models applications to the field of social sciences (in particular for demographic and labour market studies, see for instance Florens et al. 1995), however, discrete time formulations[19] have gained increasing interest, since in many cases, either the

[17] The same effect is produced if one decides, alternatively, to exclude censored spells from the sample.

[18] So-called "competing risks" models distinguish between different possible destinations which compete among each other in the sense that only the first risk realisation counts.

[19] The discrete time formulation has two drawbacks. First, the estimated coefficients depend on the length of the time interval. This means that the results will not be

process analysed is intrinsically discrete, or – more often – the data is only available in discrete time intervals. This is the reason why Petersen (1995) and Jenkins (1995), among others, propose a discrete time formulation for single risk models which has the practical advantage of being estimable in the end as a logit model.

However, most of the literature for competing risks relies on continuous time modelling, while the literature on competing risks models in a discrete time framework, however, is extremely scarce. Allison (1982) and more recently Petersen (1995) postulate that the discrete time competing risks case can be estimated as a multinomial logit model, by extension of the single risk case, but do not formalise this assumption. Jenkins (2002) proposes a discrete formulation for two competing risks that are assumed to be independent and finds that, under these assumptions, the two destination specific hazards can be modelled separately as logits, where the other destination is considered censored. Looking at the applied literature, recent studies (e.g. Zimmermann 2000, Steiner 2001 or Reize 2002) run multinomial logit estimations but do not formally derive the likelihood function corresponding to the estimated multinomial logit model. To my knowledge, the only attempt to model formally the multicategorical case in discrete time has been done by Fahrmeir and Tutz 2001, but it is done within the framework of generalised linear models. The next section therefore complements the literature by proposing a formal presentation of the competing risks model in a discrete time framework that demonstrates that the multinomial logit estimations which have been applied in the recent literature can be rationalised from an econometric point of view. Moreover, it models unobserved heterogeneity in a flexible – nonparametric – way.

4.3.2 Formal presentation of the model: basic concepts

Let us assume that T_{ij}^s describes the time that individual i, $i \in \{1...N\}$, spent in the sth, $s \in \{1...\Omega_{ij}\}$, spell of state type j, $j \in \{1...J\}$, before transition to another state or censoring[20] occurs. T_{ij}^s is a discrete random variable taking

comparable if the length of the time interval differs. However, this is not problematic here since this problem concerns primarily the constant term, whereas the other coefficients are generally less affected by the length of the time interval (Petersen 1995), and anyway, the data available for France and Germany, fortunately, are both available in monthly form. The second drawback is of a practical nature: to estimate a hazard rate model in discrete time, one needs to reorganise the data set so as to create one record per observed time unit and spell instead of having only one record per spell. This means that the data set will be considerably expanded, and computation time as well as memory requirements will increase accordingly.

[20] Censoring refers here to right-censoring. It is assumed that the start date of the spell is known.

positive integer values[21]. Now assume that T^s_{ij} may be partitioned into a discrete number of intervals I_t, $t \in \{1...T^s_{ij}\}$. If transition or censoring occurs in interval I_t, then, by definition, $t = T^s_{ij}$. If it has not yet occurred in interval I_t, i.e. if the individual survives in that state until the end of interval I_t, then $t < T^s_{ij}$.

The destination-specific hazard rate h^s_{ijk} is the probability that individual i leaves his sth spell of state type j for state k, $k(\neq j) \in \{1...J\}$, during interval I_t, given that the spell j lasted until the beginning of interval I_t, and given a vector of covariates $x_{ijk}(t)$[22] and some unobserved factors ε_{ij}[23]:

$$h^s_{ijk}(t|x_{ijk}(t), \varepsilon_{ij}) = Pr(T^s_{ij} = t, \delta^s_{ijk} = 1|T^s_{ij} \geq t, x_{ijk}(t), \varepsilon_{ij}) \tag{4.1}$$

where

$$\delta^s_{ijk} = \begin{cases} 1 \text{ if the } s\text{th spell of individual } i \text{ in state } j \text{ ends in state } k \\ 0 \text{ otherwise (spell is censored or ends in another state than } k) \end{cases}$$

In each time interval, only one state may be observed (the original state j or one of the other k states). Since the different exit states are mutually exclusive, the overall probability H^s_{ij} of ending the sth spell of state type j for any other state in interval I_t, conditional on the fact that the spell j lasted until the beginning of interval I_t, can be expressed as the sum of the transitions from j to each specific other state:

$$\begin{aligned} H^s_{ij}(t|x_{ij}(t), \varepsilon_{ij}) &= Pr(T^s_{ij} = t|T^s_{ij} \geq t, x_{ij}(t), \varepsilon_{ij}) \\ &= \sum_{k \neq j}^{J} h^s_{ijk}(t|x_{ijk}(t), \varepsilon_{ij}) \end{aligned} \tag{4.2}$$

On the contrary, the probability that individual i does *not* leave his sth spell in state j in time interval I_t, conditional on the fact that the spell j lasted until the beginning of interval I_t is given by:

$$1 - H^s_{ij}(t|x_{ij}(t), \varepsilon_{ij}) = Pr(T^s_{ij} > t|T^s_{ij} \geq t, x_{ij}(t), \varepsilon_{ij}) \tag{4.3}$$

Consequently, the unconditional probability that an individual i who was in his sth spell of state j remains in this state until the end of interval I_t (i.e. that he "survives" interval I_t) can be expressed by the so-called survivor function S^s_{ij}:

---

[21] T^s_{ij} is only observed for individuals who experience state j at least one interval and can therefore not be zero.

[22] The vector of explanatory variables may vary according to the origin state j, but also according to the destination state k.

[23] The unobserved individual factors affect the decision to exit the original state for choosing another state.

$$S_{ij}^s(t|x_{ij}(t),\varepsilon_{ij}) = Pr(T_{ij}^s > t|x_{ij}(t),\varepsilon_{ij}) \\ = \prod_{z=1}^{t}(1 - H_{ij}^s(z|x_{ij}(t),\varepsilon_{ij})) \tag{4.4}$$

Finally, the unconditional probability p_{ijk}^s that individual i leaves his original state j into state k exactly in interval I_t can be expressed by the probability that he survives time interval I_{t-1} and that he leaves state j in interval I_t, given he had survived until I_{t-1}:

$$p_{ijk}^s(t|x_{ijk}(t),\varepsilon_{ij}) = Pr(T_{ij}^s = t, k|x_{ijk}(t),\varepsilon_{ij}) \\ = h_{ijk}^s(t|x_{ijk}(t),\varepsilon_{ij}) \;\; S_{ij}^s(t-1|x_{ij}(t-1),\varepsilon_{ij}) \\ = h_{ijk}^s(t|x_{ijk}(t),\varepsilon_{ij}) \prod_{z=1}^{t-1}(1 - H_{ij}^s(z|x_{ij}(z),\varepsilon_{ij})) \tag{4.5}$$

Thus, the probability that spell number s of type j is complete and ends in state k is given by $p_{ijk}^s(T_{ij}^s)$, and the probability that it is censored is given by $S_{ij}^s(T_{ij}^s)$. Assuming that all spell observations, conditional on the explanatory variables and the unobserved factors, are independent and that censoring is random, the sample likelihood function for the original state j may be written as follows[24]:

$$\mathcal{L}_j = \prod_{i=1}^{N}\prod_{s=1}^{\Omega_{ij}}\left[\prod_{k\neq j}^{J} p_{ijk}^s(T_{ij}^s)^{\delta_{ijk}^s}\right] S_{ij}^s(T_{ij}^s)^{\gamma_{ij}^s} \tag{4.6}$$

where δ_{ijk}^s is defined as above and

$$\gamma_{ij}^s = \begin{cases} 1 \text{ if the } s\text{th spell of individual } i \text{ in state } j \text{ is censored} \\ 0 \text{ otherwise (spell ends in any state } k(\neq j) \in \{1...J\}) \end{cases}$$

Note that:

$$\gamma_{ij}^s + \sum_{k\neq j}^{J} \delta_{ijk}^s = 1 \tag{4.7}$$

The first factor of $\mathcal{L}_j$ corresponds to the contribution of the completed spells, the second factor represents the contribution of the censored spells. Using equations (4.4) and (4.5), the likelihood function may be rewritten as:

[24] The conditioning on $x_{ijk}(t)$ and ε_{ij} has been dropped temporarily to simplify notation.

$$\mathcal{L}_j = \prod_{i=1}^{N}\prod_{s=1}^{\Omega_{ij}}\left[\prod_{k\neq j}^{J}\left[h_{ijk}^{s}(T_{ij}^{s})\prod_{t=1}^{T_{ij}^{s}-1}(1-H_{ij}^{s}(t))\right]^{\delta_{ijk}^{s}}\right]\left[\prod_{t=1}^{T_{ij}^{s}}(1-H_{ij}^{s}(t))\right]^{\gamma_{ij}^{s}}$$

$$= \prod_{i=1}^{N}\prod_{s=1}^{\Omega_{ij}}\left[\prod_{k\neq j}^{J} h_{ijk}^{s}(T_{ij}^{s})^{\delta_{ijk}^{s}}\right]\left[\prod_{t=1}^{T_{ij}^{s}-1}(1-H_{ij}^{s}(t))\right]^{\sum_{k\neq j}^{J}\delta_{ijk}^{s}}\left[\prod_{t=1}^{T_{ij}^{s}}(1-H_{ij}^{s}(t))\right]^{\gamma_{ij}^{s}}$$

$$= \prod_{i=1}^{N}\prod_{s=1}^{\Omega_{ij}}\frac{\prod_{k\neq j}^{J} h_{ijk}^{s}(T_{ij}^{s})^{\delta_{ijk}^{s}}}{(1-H_{ij}^{s}(T_{ij}^{s}))^{\sum_{k\neq j}^{J}\delta_{ijk}^{s}}}\left[\prod_{t=1}^{T_{ij}^{s}}(1-H_{ij}^{s}(t))\right]^{\gamma_{ij}^{s}+\sum_{k\neq j}^{J}\delta_{ijk}^{s}}$$

Using equation (4.7), one obtains:

$$\mathcal{L}_j = \prod_{i=1}^{N}\prod_{s=1}^{\Omega_{ij}}\frac{\prod_{k\neq j}^{J} h_{ijk}^{s}(T_{ij}^{s})^{\delta_{ijk}^{s}}}{(1-H_{ij}^{s}(T_{ij}^{s}))^{1-\gamma_{ij}^{s}}}\prod_{t=1}^{T_{ij}^{s}}(1-H_{ij}^{s}(t)) \tag{4.8}$$

This likelihood is too complicated to be maximised directly, but, extending the method proposed by Jenkins (1995) for binary models to the multinomial case, one can derive an easier estimation method. The trick consists in defining new indicator variables which depend on the censoring indicators in the following way:

$$y_{ijkt}^{s} = \begin{cases} 1 \text{ if } \delta_{ijk}^{s} = 1 \text{ and } t = T_{ij}^{s} \\ 0 \text{ otherwise } (\gamma_{ij}^{s} = 1 \text{ or } \delta_{ijk}^{s} = 0 \text{ or } \delta_{ijk}^{s} = 1 \text{ and } t \neq T_{ij}^{s}) \end{cases}$$

$$z_{ijt}^{s} = \begin{cases} 1 \text{ if } \gamma_{ij}^{s} = 0 \text{ and } t = T_{ij}^{s} \\ 0 \text{ otherwise } (\gamma_{ij}^{s} = 1 \text{ or } t \neq T_{ij}^{s}) \end{cases}$$

where $t \in \{1 ... T_{ij}^{s}\}$.

One has:

$$z_{ijt}^{s} = \sum_{k\neq j}^{J} y_{ijkt}^{s}$$

To put it in words, for people staying in state j in all time intervals observed (censored observations), y_{ijkt}^{s} is zero for all intervals. For people making the transition to any k, y^s_{ijkt} is zero for all intervals except the interval of transition (the last one), when it is equal to 1. z^s_{ijt} is zero if the spell is censored and if it is not censored, it is zero for all intervals except the last one when transition occurs. Table 4.2 gives an example of how the data could look for an individual i who has Ω spells of different lengths, the first one being censored, the second one exiting to state 1, the second to state 2 and the Ωth one to state k (the subscripts i and j have been dropped for reasons of readability).

Table 4.2. Example of data set

s	t	γ	δ_1	δ_2	...	δ_k	y	y_1	y_2	...	y_k	z
1	1	1	0	0		0	0	0	0		0	0
1	2	1	0	0		0	0	0	0		0	0
1	3	1	0	0		0	0	0	0		0	0
2	1	0	1	0		0	0	0	0		0	0
2	2	0	1	0		0	0	0	0		0	0
2	3	0	1	0		0	0	0	0		0	0
2	4	0	1	0		0	1	1	0		0	1
3	1	0	0	1		0	0	0	0		0	0
3	2	0	0	1		0	2	0	1		0	1
⋮												
Ω	1	0	0	0		1	0	0	0		0	0
Ω	2	0	0	0		1	0	0	0		0	0
⋮	⋮	⋮	⋮	⋮		⋮	⋮	⋮	⋮		⋮	⋮
Ω	T^Ω	0	0	0		1	k	0	0		1	1

Using these indicator variables, the likelihood may be rewritten as:

$$\mathcal{L}_j = \prod_{i=1}^{N}\prod_{s=1}^{\Omega_{ij}}\left[\prod_{t=1}^{T^s_{ij}} \frac{\prod_{k\neq j}^{J} h^s_{ijk}(t)^{y^s_{ijk}}}{(1-H^s_{ij}(t))^{z^s_{ij}}}\right]\left[\prod_{t=1}^{T^s_{ij}}(1-H^s_{ij}(t))\right]$$

$$= \prod_{i=1}^{N}\prod_{s=1}^{\Omega_{ij}}\prod_{t=1}^{T^s_{ij}}\prod_{k\neq j}^{J} h^s_{ijk}(t)^{y^s_{ijk}}(1-H^s_{ij}(t))^{1-z^s_{ij}}$$

To put it differently:

$$\mathcal{L}_j = \prod_{i=1}^{N}\prod_{s=1}^{\Omega_{ij}}\prod_{k\neq j}^{J}\prod_{t=1}^{T^s_{ij}} h^s_{ijk}(t)^{y^s_{ijk}}\left(1-\sum_{k\neq j}^{J} h^s_{ijk}(t)\right)^{1-\sum_{k\neq j}^{J} y^s_{ijk}} \tag{4.9}$$

Thus, after this transformation, the likelihood function boils down to a standard multinomial likelihood function where the y^s_{ijt} is the dependent variable and the censored observations enter the likelihood function as an additional category[25]. In practical terms, one needs to rearrange the data so that the spell month (if the month is the time unit for intervals) is the unit of analysis instead of the spell and construct the indicator variables as described above.

4.3.3 Further specification choices

For equation (4.9) to be estimable empirically, one needs to make further choices.

Functional form of the hazard function

The hazard rate is assumed to have a multinomial logit form[26], with censoring as the base category:

$$h^s_{ijk}(t|x_{ijk}(t), \varepsilon_{ij}) = \frac{exp\left[\alpha_{jk}(t) + \beta^{'}_{jk} x_{ijk}(t) + \varepsilon_{ij}\right]}{1 + \sum\limits_{\ell \neq j}^{\Omega} exp\left[\alpha_{j\ell}(t) + \beta^{'}_{j\ell} x_{ij\ell}(t) + \varepsilon_{ij}\right]} \tag{4.10}$$

The multinomial logit form, however, is an adequate specification only if the so-called Independence of Irrelevant Alternatives (IIA) assumption is fulfilled, i.e. if the odds ratio for a subset of alternatives is independent of the remaining alternatives. This follows from the initial assumption required for modelling the decision problem as in (4.10) that the disturbances are uncorrelated between the states. The validity of the IIA assumption will be tested by means of two tests: the Hausman test and the Small Hsiao test.

The idea of the Hausman test (Hausman and McFadden 1984) is that if a subset of alternatives is truly irrelevant for the choice between the other alternatives, then, omitting it from the model will not change the parameter estimates systematically and will be more efficient. *A contrario*, if the IIA is not fulfilled, the parameter estimates will be affected by the omission of these alternatives and be inconsistent. This can be tested by the usual Hausman's specification test.

---

25 The last category of a multinomial decision problem may always be picked out and written the way the censored observation enters the likelihood function in equation (4.9).

26 This corresponds to a "proportional odds" model, which does not imply the rather restrictive assumption of the "proportional hazard" models that absolute differences in the covariates imply proportionate differences in the hazards, regardless of spell duration. See Kalbfleisch and Prentice (1980) and Lancaster (1990) for a discussion of the properties of the different functional forms for the hazard rate.

The test statistic is given by[27]:

$$\chi^2_{HM} = (\hat{\beta}_r - \hat{\beta}_u)'[\hat{V}_r - \hat{V}_u]^{-1}(\hat{\beta}_r - \hat{\beta}_u) \tag{4.11}$$

where β_r denotes the vector of parameter estimates resulting from the restricted model, i.e. the model with the restricted choice set, and β_u is the vector of parameter estimates resulting from the unrestricted model. $\hat{V}_r$ and $\hat{V}_u$ are the estimated variance-covariance matrices of the restricted and unrestricted models respectively. The null hypothesis is that IIA is fulfilled. χ^2_{HM} has asymptotically a chi-squared distribution with the corresponding degrees of freedom. Because the number of observations in the restricted and in the unrestricted models might differ, $[\hat{V}_r - \hat{V}_u]$ might not be positive definite, which would result in χ^2_{HM} turning negative, in which case the Hausman test is not valid.

An alternative is the Small-Hsiao test (Small and Hsiao 1985). The test statistic is given by:

$$\chi^2_{SH} = -2(\mathcal{L}(\hat{\theta}_u) - \mathcal{L}(\hat{\theta}_r)) \tag{4.12}$$

where $\hat{\theta}_u = \frac{\sqrt{2}}{2}\hat{\beta}^A_u + (1 - \frac{\sqrt{2}}{2})\hat{\beta}^B_u$ and $\hat{\theta}_r = \hat{\beta}^B_r$

The $\hat{\beta}^A$ and $\hat{\beta}^B$ denote the parameter estimates obtained from two distinct sub-samples A and B that are randomly drawn from the whole sample of observations and sum up to it. The subscripts u and r denotes, just like before, the unrestricted and the restricted model respectively. Thus, $\hat{\beta}_u$ is a weighted vector of the parameter estimates obtained from the two samples for the unrestricted model while $\hat{\beta}_r$ is the vector of parameter estimates for the restricted model for the second sub-sample B. $\mathcal{L}(\hat{\theta}_u)$ and $\mathcal{L}(\hat{\theta}_r)$ are the corresponding values of the likelihood function. χ^2_{SH} is asymptotically chi-squared distributed and therefore, the null hypothesis that IIA is fulfilled can be tested.

Furthermore, Wald tests (Judge, Hill, Griffiths and Lee 1985) will be run to test whether some of the outcome categories should be combined. The test statistic is given by:

$$\chi^2_W = (R\hat{\beta} - r)'(RVR')^{-1}(R\hat{\beta} - r) \tag{4.13}$$

where $\hat{\beta}$ is the vector parameter estimates and V the variance-covariance matrix. $R\hat{\beta} = r$ denotes the set of linear restrictions, meaning here the equality of the parameter estimates for two of the outcome categories. χ^2_W is asymptotically chi-squared distributed and the null hypothesis that the restrictions are valid, i.e. here that parameter estimates do not differ significantly across outcome categories, can be tested.

---

[27] The subscripts j and k have been dropped to simplify notation.

Functional form of the baseline hazard

In equation (4.10), $\alpha_{jk}(t)$ is the so-called baseline hazard function, which describes the pattern of duration dependence, i.e. the way – common to all persons since the baseline hazard does not depend on the (un)observable characteristics – the hazard rate depends on process time.

Basically, the baseline hazard can be specified parametrically or nonparametrically. A parametric specification of the baseline hazard function would imply that the duration dependence is the randomised outcome of a certain distribution function which has to be chosen (e.g. a polynome of order 2 or 3, or an exponential function of process time). However, the choice of the functional form imposes strong restrictions on the form of the hazard rate and of course more directly on the pattern of duration dependence. Alternatively, one might opt for a fully nonparametric specification, i.e. one would make no functional form assumption but estimate the baseline hazard for each process time unit instead.

Here, a semi-parametric specification has been chosen. The baseline hazard function is assumed to be piecewise constant, i.e. constant within fixed time spans. This allows for a flexible pattern of duration dependence and avoids misspecification biases, while it increases efficiency by permitting us to aggregate process time units where the duration effect is found to be constant or the number observations too small.

Specification of unobserved heterogeneity

It remains to specify the unobserved heterogeneity ε_{ij}. If one ignores unobserved heterogeneity, one implicitly assumes that all the individual heterogeneity is captured by the observed characteristics $x_{ijk}(t)$. However, there might be unobserved, and possibly unobservable factors, which affect the hazard rate. The effect of ignoring unobserved heterogeneity is well documented (see among others Heckman and Singer 1984, Lancaster 1990, Petersen 1995). The most well-known problem is that the degree of negative duration dependence is over-estimated if unobserved heterogeneity is present and not controlled for. This occurs because, by definition, individuals with an above-average exit rate will leave the population at risk on average at an earlier month than those individuals with below-average exit rate. As a result, the remaining sample will contain an increasingly high fraction of individuals with below-average exit rate as time passes. Therefore, the exit rate in the population remaining at risk will decline over time, i.e. there is negative duration dependence, even though the hazard rate of each of the subgroups might not show any negative duration dependence. Besides, the other coefficients might also be affected if these unobserved factors are correlated with the observed characteristics (usual omitted variable bias).

Here again, the question arises how to model unobserved heterogeneity, whether parametrically or nonparametrically. A common procedure is to impose a specific distribution on ε_{ij}, for instance a normal, a log-normal or a gamma distribution. Heckman and Singer 1984 have sharply criticised such a parametric approach, arguing that functional form assumption for unobserved heterogeneity might seriously affect the parameter estimates, and the economics provide little guidance for choosing one specific distribution rather than another. Even though Han and Hausman (1990) as well as Narendranathan and Stewart (1993) claim that with a nonparametric specification of the baseline hazard, the sensitivity of the estimates to the parametric heterogeneity is significantly lower, the problem remains. For this reason, unobserved heterogeneity will be specified nonparametrically using the mass point approach.

The idea of the mass point approach is that instead of imposing a specific parametric distribution on ε_{ij}, one assumes a discrete probability distribution for ε_{ij}, i.e. one assumes that ε_{ij} may be partitioned into a limited number M of mass points or location parameters ε_{mj}, $m \in \{1...M\}$, with a given probability $Pr(\varepsilon_{mj})$. In other words, it is assumed that there are M types of individuals in the sample which cannot be determined by the observed variables, and the mass points probabilities are the shares of these groups. The mass points and their probabilities have the following properties:

$$\sum_{m=1}^{M} Pr(\varepsilon_{mj}) = 1 \tag{4.14}$$

$$\sum_{m=1}^{M} Pr(\varepsilon_{mj})\varepsilon_{mj} = 0 \tag{4.15}$$

$$E(\varepsilon_{mj} x_{ijk}(t)) = 0 \tag{4.16}$$

To put it in words, the probabilities of the ε_{mj} sum up to one, their expectation is assumed to be zero and they are assumed to be uncorrelated with the covariates. Hence, the likelihood function (4.9) may be rewritten as[28]:

$$\mathcal{L}_j = \tag{4.17}$$
$$\sum_{m=1}^{M} Pr(\varepsilon_{mj}) \left[\prod_{i=1}^{N} \prod_{s=1}^{\Omega_{ij}} \prod_{k \neq j}^{J} \prod_{t=1}^{T_{ij}^s} h_{ijk}^s(t|x_{ijk}, \varepsilon_{mj})^{y_{ijkt}^s} \left(1 - H_{ij}^s(t|x_{ij}, \varepsilon_{mj})\right)^{1-z_{ijt}^s} \right]$$

Note that it is not necessary to estimate all of the M mass points and their corresponding probabilities. It is enough to estimate $M-1$ mass points and mass points probabilities, and to calculate the remaining mass point and its probability using deterministic relations (4.14) and (4.15). Indeed, using relation (4.14) the last mass point probability is given by:

[28] Note that, as Steiner (2001) argues, the model allows the observations to be correlated for a given individual, both within and between the spells. Therefore, the case where an individual experiences repeated spells j is indirectly accounted for by the model.

$$Pr(\varepsilon_{Mj}) = 1 - \sum_{m=1}^{M-1} Pr(\varepsilon_{mj}) \tag{4.18}$$

Then, using this result and relation (4.15), the last mass point can be computed:

$$\varepsilon_{Mj} = -\frac{1}{Pr(\varepsilon_{Mj})} \sum_{m=1}^{M-1} Pr(\varepsilon_{mj})\varepsilon_{mj} \tag{4.19}$$

The number of mass points remains to be determined. I will follow the approach of Baker and Melino (2000), which consists in choosing between different models on the basis of information criteria drawn from the estimation results of the different models. Thus, a first model without unobserved heterogeneity is estimated and the information criteria are computed. Then, the model is re-estimated with two heterogeneity groups (i.e. 2 mass points), and the resulting information criteria are compared with those obtained from the model without unobserved heterogeneity. If the model with 2 mass points offers an improvement according to the information criteria, the model is re-estimated with an additional mass point and again, the corresponding information criteria is calculated and compared with those obtained from the preceding model. The procedure is renewed until the addition of a further mass point stops improving the model. Information criteria have the general form:

$$IC = ln\mathcal{L}_j^* - cp \tag{4.20}$$

where $\mathcal{L}_j^*$ is the value of the log-likelihood function obtained after maximisation, p is the number of parameters estimated and c a penalty function. One option would be to set c to zero and simply compare the values of the log-likelihood, but doing so, one would neglect the fact that more parameter estimates are estimated when mass points are added and that the estimation loses in efficiency. This solution is therefore rejected. Instead, three alternative information criteria are used here, with different functions c as penalty for additional parameters, IC_A (Akaike Information Criterion), IC_B (Baysian Information Criterion) and IC_H (Hannan-Quinn Information Criterion):

$$\begin{aligned} &\text{For } IC_A, \quad c = 1 \\ &\text{For } IC_B, \quad c = ln(O)/2 \\ &\text{For } IC_H, \quad c = ln(ln(O)) \end{aligned} \tag{4.21}$$

where O is the number of observations. This makes it possible to see whether the number of mass points found as optimal is robust towards the choice of the penalty function.

4.4 Data and variables

In the following analysis, three employment states are distinguished, i.e. $J = 3$. State $j = 1$ corresponds to employment, state $j = 2$ corresponds to unemployment and state $j = 3$ to non-employment such as defined in section 4.2.1. The time intervals are of equal length and consist of months. The analysis concentrates on the impact of education on two outcomes: the risk of entering unemployment (section 4.5) or more precisely the hazard h_{i12}^{s} of losing one's job for entering unemployment, on the one hand, and when employment was lost the duration of subsequent unemployment (section 4.6), on the other hand. The latter aspect is derived from estimations of the hazard of exiting unemployment for employment (h_{i21}^{s}) or for non-employment (h_{i23}^{s}). Special attention will be paid to the impact of education on the reemployment prospects (h_{i21}^{s}).

4.4.1 Construction of the spell data

The data sets used and the limitation of the population observed have already been described in section 4.2.1. The first step is to construct the appropriate spell data. The data on the employment history is brought into person-month format as explained in section 4.2.1 and the variables necessary to the implementation of the model are constructed, in particular the spell identifiers, the censoring indicators and the hazard rates. Table 4.3 provides a summary of the composition of the sample.

For the analysis of entry into unemployment, the focus is on the transition from employment to unemployment. Therefore, one needs to identify employment spells. As mentioned previously, the *Emploi* data is a rotating panel and the individuals are interviewed only in three consecutive years, after which they leave the panel. I select those individuals interviewed for the first time in 1998 and use the information drawn from the two subsequent waves (1999 and 2000) to reconstitute their employment history over a period of 37 months (from March 1997 to March 2000). In order to make things comparable, the same restrictions have been adopted for the German sample, even though a longer panel would be available. Thus, for the German sample, the employment history is reconstituted over 37 months from December 1996 to December 1999[29]. Given the data sets and the restrictions on the sample population presented above, one can isolate about 5,600 spells of employment for Germany and some 18,200 for France (see upper part of table 4.3). Because

[29] Remember that in the GSOEP, the retrospective information refers to the preceding calender year and not to the 12 months preceding the interview. If the interview takes place in March 2000, the person is asked to retrace her employment history from January 1999 to December 1999. This implies that the employment information for the first months of 2000 will only be gathered in the next wave. Here, it was decided to cover the same period length of 37 months.

Table 4.3. Sample composition

Spells of:	Employment		Unemployment	
	Germany	France	Germany	France
Total sample				
Numb. spells	5,579	18,175	2,053	4,888
complete	495 (8.9%)	2,044 (11.3%)	1,541 (75.1%)	2,406 (49.2%)
right-censored	931 (16.7%)	1,964 (10.8%)	286 (13.9%)	974 (19.9%)
left-censored	759 (13.6%)	1,694 (9.3%)	207 (10.1%)	1,117 (24.1%)
left-right censored	3,394 (60.8%)	12,473 (68.6%)	19 (0.93%)	331 (6.8%)
Sample of analysis				
Numb. observations	136,948	490,848	15,089	23,112
Numb. spells	4,791	15,734	1,827	3,380
complete	252 (5.3%)	660 (4.2%)	1,541 (84.4%)	2,406 (71.2%)
right-censored	649 (13.6%)	1,944 (12.4%)	286 (15.6%)	974 (28.8%)
left-censored	582 (12.1%)	935 (5.9%)		
left-right censored	3,308 (69.0%)	12,195 (77.5%)		
Not right-censored spells ending in				
employment			1,308 (84.9%)	2,248 (93.4%)
unemployment	342 (41.0%)	1,109 (69.5%)		
non-employment	492 (59.0%)	486 (30.5%)	233 (15.1%)	156 (6.6%)
Numb. individuals	4,498	15,000	1,198	2,157
with 1 spell	4,220 (93.8%)	14,303 (95.3%)	812 (67.7%)	1,430 (66.3%)
with 2 spells	263 (5.9%)	660 (4.4%)	245 (20.5%)	416 (19.3%)
with 3 spells	15 (0.3%)	37 (0.3%)	90 (7.5%)	188 (8.7%)
with 4 spells			27 (2.3%)	77 (3.4%)
with 5 spells			11 (0.9%)	35 (1.6%)
with 6 spells			4 (0.3%)	7 (0.3%)
with 7 spells			5 (0.4%)	3 (0.1%)
with 8 spells			3 (0.2%)	1 (0.0%)
with 9 spells			1 (0.1%)	
Numb. months	37	37	107	36

employment spells are typically rather long, only a small proportion of them are complete: 9 percent for Germany and 11 percent for France.

Left-censored spells are problematic to handle. It is common practice to exclude them from the sample (see among others Steiner 2001, Reize 2002), especially when duration dependence – for which one needs to know the start date of the spell – is to be examined. This is the option chosen for the analysis of the duration of unemployment, since the process time, i.e. the time already spent in unemployment at the month of observation is known to be an essential explanatory factor of the hazard rate out of unemployment (duration dependence). However, it would be problematic for the analysis of entry into unemployment to exclude left-censored spells, first because the proportion of left-censored spells is quite large, secondly because keeping only not left-censored employment spells would boil down to selecting a very specific sample, with a high proportion of labour market entrants or career breakers. Therefore, it was decided to keep the left-censored spells in the sample for the analysis of entry into unemployment. It implies that there is assumed to be no duration dependence in the hazard rate out of employment (Jenkins 1995). In the present context, this should be a minor problem because the focus of the analysis is not on employment duration dependence and because both firm tenure and the censoring status appear as control variables in the regression.

A further selection needs to be done for the analysis of entry into unemployment. Indeed, the information on employment characteristics (see below) is not available from the monthly calendar data but only from the yearly interviews. This means that this information is only available if the individual was employed in the month of the interview. To make it possible to use this information, only those employment spells extending over the interview month have been retained for the analysis. In the end, we are left with about 4,800 employment spells for Germany and 15,700 for France (see the distribution of the spells with respect to censoring in table 4.3).

For the analysis of the reemployment prospects of the unemployed, one needs to identify unemployment spells. Because there are much fewer unemployment spells than employment spells and because the size of the German sample is much smaller than that of the French sample, it proved not to be feasible to reduce the observation period of individuals in the German sample to only 37 months as for the analysis of employment spells, due to an insufficient number of observations at the monthly level. Therefore, for Germany, the analysis uses information from the waves 1992 to 2000 and thus covers a total of 108 months (from January 1991 to December 1999). The data contains about 2,000 unemployment spells for Germany and slightly less than 4,900 unemployment spells for France. As a result, a comparatively larger proportion of these spells are complete in the German sample (76 percent for Germany against 49 percent for France). The sample of analysis is therefore reduced to about 1,800 unemployment spells for Germany and some 3,400 for France, 16 percent and 29 percent of which, respectively, being right-censored (see table 4.3).

Individuals might experience repeated spells. As far as employment spells are concerned, about 4,500 individuals experienced up to a maximum of 3 employment spells in Germany, while 15,000 French individuals experienced up to 3 employment spells (see lower part of table 4.3) in the three years observed. For unemployment spells, we have 1,200 persons in the German sample experiencing up to 9 unemployment spells within the 9 years observed, and 2,200 persons in the French sample encountering up to 8 times unemployment in an observation period of 3 years. Because an important proportion of the spells is censored, the observed duration of the unemployment spells underestimates the true duration of unemployment episodes, especially in France where the observation period is shorter and a larger share of spells censored.

Therefore, instead of taking the observed duration of unemployment spells, I will estimate the expected duration of unemployment – and the impact of education on it – on the basis of the results of the econometric analysis (section 4.6.3).

Given the selection procedure and the definition of the samples, the statements made in the subsequent analyses cannot be considered strictly applicable for the whole population in France and Germany, but they give useful insights into the factors affecting unemployment dynamics and highlight in particular the role played by education.

4.4.2 Explanatory variables

Most explanatory variables are taken from the yearly interviews and have been merged with the monthly data on employment history. As a rule, the information drawn from the interview month is assumed to apply for the period extending from the month after the interview month of the preceding wave[30] until the interview month of the current wave[31]. For the information on employment characteristics used for the analysis of entry into employment, however, the information is assumed to apply to the employment spell the interview month falls in.

Table 4.4 provides a synthetic overview of the explanatory variables used. For both the analysis of entry into unemployment and that of unemployment duration, the primary variable of interest in this study is the education level of the individuals observed. The education level is defined as in table 4.1, except that, because of an otherwise insufficient number of observations at the monthly level, education levels 30 and 31 have been aggregated into a single category, as well as level 32 and level 33[32].

Further variables have been included in the regressions to control for observed heterogeneity. Here again, the analysis limits to those variables that can be constructed in a comparable way for both countries. Sex, marital status and the number of children below 6 years of age in the household have been included since these variables are known to be essential factors affecting employment decisions, in particular with respect to labour market participation. Home ownership has been added as a further control variable as it might affect the extent to which labour earnings are necessary. Employment outcomes, and in particular the risk of entering unemployment or not getting out

[30] Remember that in the *Emploi* survey, the interview takes place in March every year, while the interview month differs from year to year in the GSOEP.

[31] An alternative would be to consider that the information drawn from the interview month applies partly to a certain period before the interview month, partly to a certain period after the interview month (e.g. for half of the time extending from the current interview month to the next one). This approach was not retained because it would have implied that we lose the first 6 months for France, which is problematic in view of the short overall period of observation available.

[32] For further details, please consult section 2.3.

Table 4.4. Explanatory variables

Variables	Definition
Variables common to both analyses	
Education level	7 categories: level 1; level 20; level 21; level 30/31; level 32/33; level 40; level 41 (see table 4.1)
Sex	2 categories: female; male
Marital status	2 categories: married; not married
Children<6	Number of children below 6 years of age
Home ownership	2 categories: owner of the house/appartment living in (himself or spouse); not owner
Age	6 categories: age 25 to 30; age 31 to 35; age 36 to 40; age 41 to 45; age 46 to 50; age 51 to 55
City size	3 categories: fewer than 20,000 inhabitants; between 20 and 100,000 inhabitants; 100,000 inhabitants or more
Unempl. rate	Monthly regional unemployment rate
Current quarter	4 categories: 1st quarter (January to March); 2nd quarter (April to June); 3rd quarter (July to September); 4th quarter (October to December)
Variables specific to the analysis of entry into unemployment	
Tenure	9 categories: <1 year; 1-1.5 years; 1.5-2 years; 2-3 years; 3-4 years; 4-7 years; 7-10 years; 10-15 years; ≥15 years
Firm size	6 categories: <5 employees; 5-19 employees; 20-199 employees; 200-1,999 employees; ≥2,000 employees; missing
Industry	9 categories: industry (mechanical and electrical engineering stone, iron, steel and chemical industry, paper, textile, food industry, other); agriculture/energy (agriculture, forestry, fishing, energy, mining); construction; trade (wholesale and retail); banking (banking, insurance, real estate); transports (transports and communications); private services (personal services, eating and drinking, other services to professionals or private households); public services (welfare services, government, non-profit institutions, other); missing
Prev. employment	3 categories: non-employed; employed; missing
Time trend	Month variable

to be continued...

...table 4.4 continued

Variables	Definition
Variables specific to the analysis of unemployment duration	
Duration	9 categories: 1 month; 2 months; 3 months; 4-6 months; 7-9 months; 10-12 months; 13-15 months; 16-18 months; ≥19 months
Prev. employment	2 categories: non-employed; employed
IRR	Predicted ratio of unempl. compensation to labour earnings
Quarter spell begin	4 categories: same as current quarter
Time trend	For Germany: 10 year dummies for 1991 to 2000. For France: month, month squared, month cubed

of unemployment, might also depend on the age of the individual, described here by 6 age groups.

Furthermore, local conditions might also matter. These are depicted by two variables: city size[33] and regional monthly unemployment rate. The latter information was obtained from the online time-series service of the Federal Office for Statistics for Germany and computed on the basis of the *Emploi* data for France. In addition, seasonal effects are expected to be captured by a set of dummy variables depicting the quarter in which the observation falls. Finally, time trend is controlled for by a month variable. For the analysis of entry into unemployment, it proves enough to only include a linear trend, whereas for the analysis of exit out of unemployment, a polynome of order 3 yielded better results. For Germany, however, which covers a longer period, time trend is accounted for by year dummies.

Furthermore, specific control variables have been added for either analysis. For the analysis of the risk of quitting employment for entering unemployment, a series of variables depicts the characteristics of the job occupied such as described in table 4.4. First, tenure is represented by a set of dummy variables. The information on tenure is drawn from the yearly interview and therefore applies to the interview month. It has then been incremented by one for each month pertaining in the employment spell, provided the person has reported in the subsequent wave to have incurred no job change in that year. The information on the following wave makes it possible to cross-check this variable. Then, comparable sets of dummies could be constructed for firm size and industry. Moreover, the employment state before the currently observed employment spells is captured as either non-employed, unemployed or missing (the latter category corresponding to the left-censored employment spells).

[33] A further differentiation of city size, in particular for cities over 100,000 inhabitants, proved not to be feasible because the city size classes in the French data does not correspond to those in the German data.

For the analysis of exit out of unemployment, the baseline hazard, which represents the spell duration elapsed until the month of the observation, is specified, as explained in section 4.3.3, as piecewise constant. To be more specific, it is defined by a set of dummy variables. Because the number of observations declines as the elapsed spell duration increases, the month dummies have been aggregated for longer elapsed durations such as described in table 4.4. Here also, a variable depicting the employment status occupied before the current unemployment spell has been added. However, because left-censored spells have been excluded from the sample, this variable only consists of two categories: non-employed or employed. The quarter in which the unemployment spell began is controlled for by a set of dummy variables.

Finally, a last variable aims at capturing to some extent the effect of the unemployment compensation system on the hazard of exiting unemployment, through its effect on the reservation wage in accordance with the job search theory (see section 4.1.1). An indicator of the income replacement ratio (IRR) is constructed, i.e. the ratio of the expected unemployment compensation to the expected labour earnings. The idea is that the higher the unemployment compensation is compared to the potential earnings to be obtained from working, the lower the probability that the individual leaves unemployment will be. The IRR is constructed in a similar way for both countries. In a first step, a reduced-form wage equation[34] has been run on the basis of the yearly data[35], with gender, education, age and age squared, the number of children below 6 years of age, region, city size and year dummies as explanatory variables. Then, using the estimation results (see table C.1 in appendix C), the income that could be potentially earned by the unemployed individuals in the sample of analysis can be predicted ("out-of-sample" prediction). Since the logarithm of the (monthly gross) wage has been used as a dependent variable, the prediction is given by $exp(\hat{\beta} + 1/2\hat{\sigma}^2)$, where $\hat{\beta}$ is the vector of estimated coefficients and $\hat{\sigma}$ is the standard error of the estimation (see Greene 2000).

In a second step, the unemployment benefits need to be computed. Unfortunately, the information on the unemployment benefits perceived is available on a monthly basis neither in the French nor in the German data. For France, the information on the perceived unemployment compensation available for the month of the yearly interview for those unemployed during that month is used. The logarithm of the unemployment compensation is regressed on gender, education, age and age squared, number of children below 6, region, city size, year dummies, but also on the duration of the current unemployment episode, the latter information being given by the unemployed in the yearly interviews (see estimation results in table C.1 in appendix C). For Germany,

[34] The sample used for the estimation has the same selection criteria (nationality, age, period considered) as the sample used for the analysis of unemployment spells.

[35] The wage earned is available at the monthly level neither for Germany nor for France.

there is information on the average monthly unemployment compensation[36] received in the previous year for people who were unemployed that year. This information is matched to the unemployment spells, and the logarithm of the unemployment compensation is regressed on the basis of this data set on the same variables as for France, and on the duration of the unemployment spells up to the month observed, which has been constructed from the spell data. As for wages, the predicted unemployment benefits is computed. The IRR is then the ratio of the predicted wage to the predicted unemployment compensation. Table C.3 in the annex provides descriptive statistics for the variables used for the analysis of entry into and exit out of unemployment, on the basis of the estimation samples.

4.5 Education and risk of entering unemployment

The first part of the analysis concentrates on the impact of education on the risk of entering unemployment, to be more specific, on the risk of transiting from employment to unemployment. Thus, the econometric modelling framework described in section 4.3 is applied to the estimation of the hazard of exiting employment for either unemployment (h^s_{i12}) or for non-employment (h^s_{i13}) as opposed to remaining in employment. Using the estimation results, one can compute estimates of the expected (monthly) risk of transiting from employment to unemployment given one's education level, but also of the expected risk that a person experiences at least one unemployment episode within a given period of time. The latter information will be used for the analysis of the expected unemployment duration in section 4.6.

4.5.1 Estimation results

Table 4.5 presents the results of specification tests with respect to the choice of the variables to be included in the regression and table 4.6 presents some further specification tests related to the functional form assumptions.

A first series of χ^2-tests (table 4.5) aims at examining whether there are some gender differences in the impact of certain variables on the hazard rate out of employment into unemployment and into non-employment[37]. These tests are based on an estimation of the model where some (sets of) variables have been interacted with the female dummy. The interactions which proved not to be significant at the 10 percent level at least were dropped from the specification. In a second step, the (joint) significance of the (sets of) variables themselves has been tested, on the basis of a specification including the

[36] Defined here as unemployment benefits (*Arbeitslosengeld*) plus unemployment assistance (*Arbeitslosenhilfe*).

[37] In these tests, the null hypothesis is that the variable(s) considered is (are) not significantly different from zero. The figure in parentheses gives the probability with which the null hypothesis can be rejected.

Table 4.5. Tests on coefficients: χ^2 (p> χ^2)

	Germany		France	
Hazard rate into:	**Unempl.**	**Non-empl.**	**Unempl.**	**Non-empl.**
Tests on gender interactions				
Female * Education	6.57 (0.36)	22.69 (0.00)	4.52 (0.60)	5.71 (0.46)
Female * Married	3.25 (0.07)	31.25 (0.00)	0.60 (0.44)	20.28 (0.00)
Female * Children<6	1.12 (0.29)	79.80 (0.00)	7.91 (0.00)	120.89 (0.00)
Female * Age	4.41 (0.49)	24.06 (0.00)	6.76 (0.24)	15.50 (0.00)
Female * City size	1.06 (0.59)	0.87 (0.65)	1.25 (0.54)	0.85 (0.65)
Female * Unempl. rate	0.05 (0.83)	0.73 (0.39)	0.16 (0.69)	0.16 (0.69)
Tests on specific coefficients (with only significant gender interactions)				
Education	18.03 (0.00)	31.77 (0.00)	76.37 (0.00)	18.63 (0.00)
Female	1.28 (0.26)	4.06 (0.04)	9.99 (0.08)	2.74 (0.09)
Tenure	83.76 (0.00)	37.83 (0.00)	59.20 (0.00)	38.05 (0.00)
Firm size	26.68 (0.00)	7.49 (0.19)	106.44 (0.00)	97.11 (0.00)
Industry	15.43 (0.05)	143.49 (0.00)	24.88 (0.00)	5.81 (0.67)
Prev. empl. status	55.83 (0.00)	4.05 (0.04)	237.77 (0.00)	29.41 (0.00)
Married	5.56 (0.06)	42.18 (0.00)	14.31 (0.00)	21.85 (0.00)
Children<6	1.68 (0.43)	0.17 (0.68)	0.03 (0.86)	1.70 (0.19)
Owner	3.51 (0.06)	0.01 (0.91)	15.20 (0.00)	1.10 (0.29)
Age	3.49 (0.62)	20.25 (0.00)	13.12 (0.22)	97.30 (0.00)
City size	5.97 (0.05)	7.18 (0.03)	1.20 (0.55)	3.61 (0.05)
Unemployment rate	5.02 (0.03)	1.44 (0.49)	7.19 (0.01)	4.36 (0.04)
Current quarter	1.68 (0.64)	57.51 (0.00)	90.20 (0.00)	162.50 (0.00)
Month	6.33 (0.01)	5.98 (0.01)	118.6 (0.00)	12.68 (0.00)
Tests on overall significance (finally retained specification)				
Overall Wald test	1,366.3 (0.00)		3,825.8 (0.00)	
Partial Wald tests	498.5 (0.00)	875.6 (0.00)	2,663.5 (0.00)	1,174.8 (0.00)

significant gender interaction terms. Here again, only the (sets of) variables significant at the 10 percent level at least have been retained for the final specification. Given that the computation time increases exponentially with the number of parameters to be estimated, it proved particularly desirable to drop the insignificant variables from the model. The variables included in the equation of the hazard into unemployment are allowed to differ from those retained for the equation of the hazard into non-employment. Finally, the overall Wald test, on the basis of the final specification with respect to the variables included, tests the hypothesis that all the slope coefficients of both equations are jointly insignificant, which is strongly rejected. The so-called partial Wald tests are used to test the joint significance of the explanatory variables for each destination state separately and the null hypothesis also proves to be always strongly rejected.

Moreover, the validity of the IIA assumption has been tested (table 4.6). The tests results show that for both countries, the IIA assumption is fulfilled,

Table 4.6. Other specification tests

		Germany	France
Tests for IIA		χ^2 (p> χ^2)	χ^2 (p> χ^2)
Hausman	Omitted: unempl.	5.21 (1.00)	1.46 (1.00)
	Omitted: non-empl.	7.36 (1.00)	25.76 (1.00)
Small Hsiao	Omitted: unempl.	59.61 (0.42)	47.56 (0.65)
	Omitted: non-empl.	51.69 (0.71)	47.81 (0.64)
Wald test for combining outcomes		χ^2 (p> χ^2)	χ^2 (p> χ^2)
Comb. unempl. and non-empl.		393.55 (0.00)	732.66 (0.00)
Comb. unempl. and empl.		508.97 (0.00)	2,663.53 (0.00)
Comb. non-empl. and empl.		875.43 (0.00)	1,174.76 (0.00)
Test for number of mass points		*IC*	*IC*
IC_A	No mass point	-5,154.6	-9,228.5
	2 mass points	-5,154.7	-9,230.5
IC_B	No mass point	-5,582.1	-9,672.1
	2 mass points	-5,592.0	-9,684.8
IC_H	No mass point	-5,282.6	-9,356.4
	2 mass points	-5,285.6	-9,361.5

both on the basis of the Hausman tests and on the basis of the Small Hsiao tests (see the explanation of these tests and on the testing procedure in section 4.3.3). Furthermore, a Wald test examines the hypothesis that some of the alternatives might be combined or aggregated into a single category, in which case the specification should be binomial rather than multinomial. In other words, the hypothesis is tested that the coefficients of two categories do not differ significantly from each other, for all the possible combinations. As the results in table 4.6 show, the multinomial specification seems to be appropriate for France as well as for Germany, since none of the categories should be combined.

Finally, the number of mass points describing unobserved individual heterogeneity had to be determined. Table 4.6 reports the value of the three information criteria defined in section 4.3.3. The preferred model is that yielding the lowest IC value. As can be seen, all three information criteria lead to the same conclusion. For France as for Germany, accounting for individual unobserved heterogeneity by distinguishing two mass points does not improve the fit of the model, which means that the best model should not include any mass point.

Table 4.7 presents the full estimation results of the model finally retained to estimate the determinants of the hazard rate from employment into unemployment and non-employment respectively for both countries. The focus of the analysis is here on the impact of education on the risk of entering unemployment. Therefore, the transition from employment to non-employment will

Table 4.7. Determinants of hazard rate from employment

	Germany		France	
Hazard rate into:	**Unempl.** coef. (s.e)	**Non-empl.** coef. (s.e)	**Unempl.** coef. (s.e)	**Non-empl.** coef. (s.e)
Education level (ref.: Level 1)				
Level 20	-0.35* (0.17)	-0.06 (0.18)	-0.24** (0.08)	0.14 (0.13)
Level 21	-0.46** (0.12)	-0.74** (0.00)	-0.37** (0.10)	-0.13 (0.16)
Level 30 or 31	-0.62** (0.14)	-0.01 (0.00)	-0.62** (0.14)	-0.38† (0.22)
Level 32 or 33	-0.67** (0.17)	-0.29** (0.00)	-0.55** (0.12)	-0.13 (0.19)
Level 40	-0.57** (0.19)	-0.68* (0.30)	-0.80** (0.12)	-0.27† (0.16)
Level 41	-0.32** (0.17)	-0.50* (0.24)	-0.73** (0.13)	-0.60** (0.19)
Fem. * Level 20		0.07 (0.20)		
Fem. * Level 21		0.62* (0.31)		
Fem. * Level 30 or 31		0.62* (0.28)		
Fem. * Level 32 or 33		0.64** (0.24)		
Fem. * Level 40		0.50 (0.36)		
Fem. * Level 41		0.45 (0.37)		
Female		0.77* (0.38)	0.17** (0.07)	0.36† (0.22)
Tenure (ref.:<1 year)				
1-1.5 years	-0.17 (0.11)	0.22 (0.10)	-0.53** (0.09)	-0.25 (0.21)
1.5-2 years	-0.16 (0.12)	0.20 (0.11)	-0.77** (0.11)	-0.98** (0.29)
2-3 years	-0.23* (0.11)	-0.21† (0.13)	-0.91** (0.11)	-0.66** (0.24)
3-4 years	-0.47** (0.13)	-0.28† (0.16)	-0.91** (0.15)	-0.63* (0.28)
4-7 years	-0.89** (0.22)	-0.33* (0.17)	-1.63** (0.14)	-0.61** (0.22)
7-10 years	-1.28** (0.27)	-0.58** (0.19)	-2.03** (0.16)	-0.90** (0.23)
10-15 years	-1.32** (0.28)	-0.48** (0.18)	-2.36** (0.18)	-1.32** (0.25)
≥15 years	-1.67** (0.28)	-0.89** (0.22)	-3.06** (0.16)	-0.93** (0.21)
Firm size (ref.: <5 employees)				
5-19 employees	0.49** (0.11)		0.27** (0.10)	-0.32† (0.19)
20-199 employees	0.18* (0.09)		0.24** (0.10)	-0.23 (0.16)
200-1,999 employees	0.01 (0.96)		0.18† (0.10)	-0.35* (0.15)
≥2,000 employees	-0.32* (0.14)		-0.05 (0.11)	-0.11 (0.14)
Missing	0.42† (0.22)		0.99** (0.10)	1.10** (0.14)
Industry branch (ref.: Industry)				
Agriculture, energy	-0.36 (0.26)	-0.31 (0.21)	-0.04 (0.16)	
Construction	0.18 (0.12)	0.54* (0.24)	-0.17 (0.17)	
Trade	-0.09 (0.11)	0.15 (0.16)	0.09 (0.12)	
Banking	-0.36* (0.15)	0.01 (0.20)	0.13 (0.20)	
Transports	-0.32† (0.18)	0.45* (0.23)	-0.35† (0.19)	
Private services	-0.12 (0.17)	0.70** (0.20)	0.15 (0.11)	
Public services	-0.29** (0.10)	-0.01 (0.14)	-0.16 (0.11)	
Missing	1.69** (0.00)	1.70** (0.18)	-0.82† (0.44)	

to be continued...

...table 4.7 continued

Hazard rate into:	Germany Unempl. coef. (s.e)	Germany Non-empl. coef. (s.e)	France Unempl. coef. (s.e)	France Non-empl. coef. (s.e)
Previous employment status (ref.: Non-employed)				
Unemployed	1.19** (0.00)	-0.42* (0.21)	1.29** (0.08)	-1.17** (0.22)
Missing	0.36** (0.00)			-0.86** (0.29)
Marital status (ref.: Not married)				
Married	-0.26† (0.14)	-0.50** (0.19)	-0.24** (0.06)	-0.51** (0.18)
Female * Married	0.28† (0.16)	1.35** (0.24)		1.03** (0.23)
Number of children				
Female* Children<6		0.69** (0.08)	0.33** (0.12)	0.98** (0.09)
Home ownership	-0.24† (0.13)		-0.25** (0.06)	
Age (ref.: Age 25-30)				
Age 31-35		-0.48† (0.27)		
Age 36-40		-0.63** (0.19)		
Age 41-45		-0.45* (0.14)		-0.20 (0.31)
Age 46-50		-0.28 (0.29)		-0.27 (0.30)
Age 51-55		0.69** (0.17)		1.56** (0.21)
Female * Age 31-35		0.37* (0.18)		
Female * Age 36-40		-0.11 (0.22)		
Female * Age 41-45		-0.29† (0.19)		-0.16 (0.16)
Female * Age 46-50		-0.38† (0.23)		-0.48 (0.33)
Female * Age 51-55		-1.32** (0.20)		-1.00** (0.33)
City cize (ref.: <20,000 inh.)				
20-100,000 inh.	-0.32* (0.14)	-0.03 (0.11)		
≥100,000 inh.	-0.26† (0.15)	-0.28* (0.11)		-0.19† (0.10)
Unemployment rate				
Unempl. rate/10	0.60** (0.27)		0.26** (0.10)	0.32* (0.15)
Current quarter (ref.: 1st quarter)				
2nd quarter		0.20† (0.12)	-0.82** (0.09)	-1.55** (0.14)
3rd quarter		0.15 (0.13)	-0.43** (0.08)	-1.01** (0.13)
4th quarter		-0.20 (0.14)	-0.26** (0.09)	-0.97** (0.15)
Month/10	0.15** (0.06)	0.11* (0.06)	-0.25** (0.06)	0.17** (0.05)
Constant	-7.04** (0.44)	-6.19** (0.37)	2.98* (1.44)	3.88** (1.21)
Number of observations	136,948		490,848	
Number of spells	4,791		15,734	
Number of individuals	4,498		15,000	
Log-likelihood	-5,067.6		-9,145.5	

Significance level : † : 10% * : 5% ** : 1%

not be specifically commented upon, but the results are reported in table 4.7 for the sake of completeness. Similarly, the impact of the variables other than education on the risk of entering unemployment can be read from the table but will not be commented here. The estimation results will be used to derive indicators of the impact of education on the risk of entering unemployment as showed in the following sections.

4.5.2 Expected monthly hazard of entering unemployment

First, an estimate of the expected hazard rates from employment into unemployment h^s_{i12} in France and Germany is computed for employees with average characteristics using formula (4.10), both overall and distinguishing by gender.

Fig. 4.10. Expected monthly hazard of leaving employment for unemployment

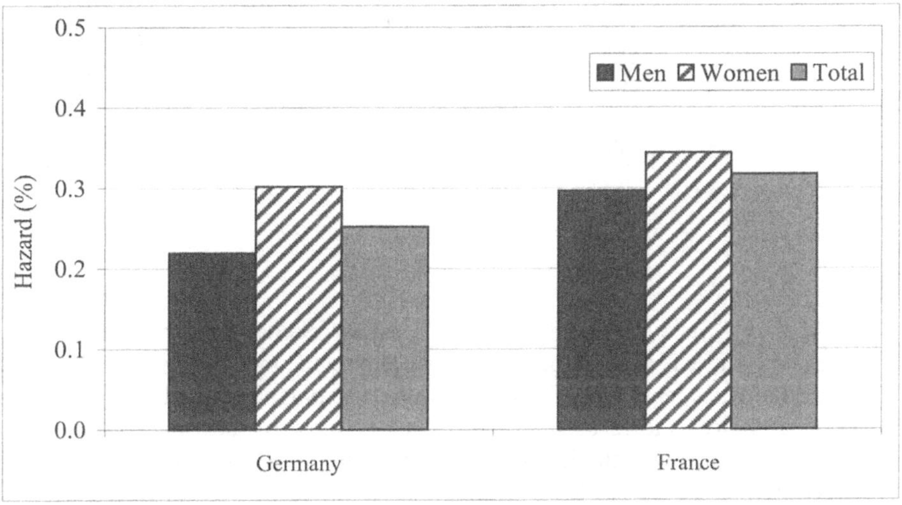

As appears from figure 4.10, the overall monthly risk of exiting employment for entering unemployment is significantly higher in France than in Germany. Moreover, in both countries, the risk of losing one's job for entering unemployment is higher for women than for men given their respective average characteristics. However, the gender gap is significantly larger in Germany than in France.

In table 4.7, it can be observed that the impact of education on the monthly hazard of transiting from employment to unemployment, anything else equal, does not vary across genders, judging from the insignificant interaction terms. The impact of education on the risk of transiting into unemployment can be best illustrated by computing the expected hazard rate into unemployment for employees with different levels of education, holding the other characteristics constant. Here, the other characteristics are set to population averages and only the education level was allowed to vary. The impact of education on the expected monthly hazard rate into unemployment in both countries is depicted in figure 4.11.

Fig. 4.11. Impact of education on the expected monthly hazard out of employment into unemployment by education level

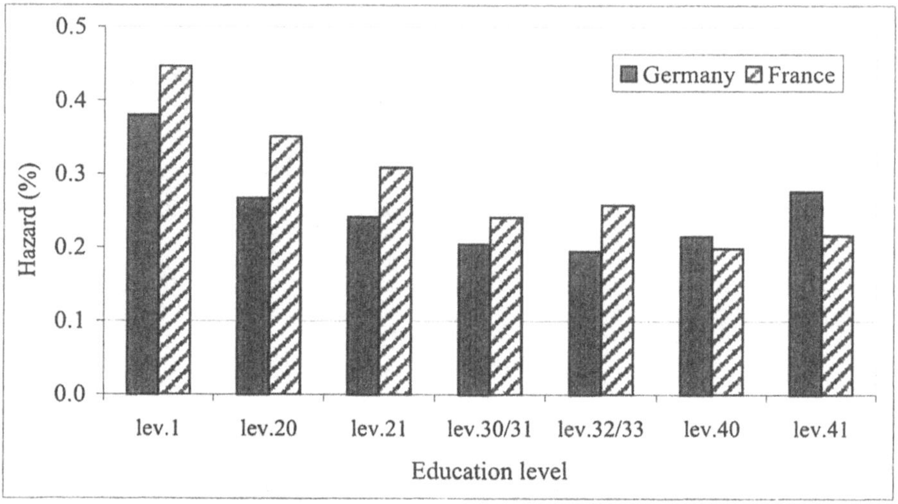

At first glance, there seems to be a rather negative relationship between education and the risk of entering unemployment, but the relationship is not monotonous, especially in Germany where the pattern is rather U-shaped. In both countries, the least qualified (level 1) have by far the highest risk of entering unemployment. However, in Germany, it is not true that the higher the education level, the lower the risk of entering unemployment. There, the best protection against the unemployment risk is given, all else equal, by vocational qualifications of intermediate level (level 3), whereas tertiary level graduates face a comparatively higher unemployment risk[38]. In France, tertiary level graduates do face the lowest unemployment risk, but the advantage is minor compared to advanced technical (level 3) qualifications. Thus, it is a good insurance against the unemployment risk to attain a minimum level of education. Beyond this level, however, the further advantage of attaining a higher level is either minor (France) or even negative (Germany).

A further feature emerging from the results is that beyond this threshold educational level, vocational skills that are strongly oriented towards the needs of the labour market seem to offer a comparatively better protection

[38] Note that Wolbers (2000) observes the same phenomenon for the Netherlands.

than more general education – even of a higher level – against the risk of being made redundant and entering unemployment. This interpretation would explain that the unemployment risk is highest for individuals without any kind of vocational education and that basic and above all intermediate vocational education reduces the unemployment risk, whereas higher education especially at the upper tertiary level does not reduce to the same extent the unemployment risk, especially in Germany. Looking at the tertiary level only, this interpretation is also consistent with the observation that lower tertiary qualifications better protect against the unemployment risk than upper tertiary qualifications in both countries[39]. Indeed, lower tertiary qualifications typically have a more practical focus, while upper tertiary education is more theoretical and also includes subjects like philosophy or languages that are less directly oriented towards the needs of the economy.

Thus, the risk of entering unemployment is higher in France than in Germany at lower qualification levels, but is lower at the tertiary education level. This suggests that the German system of vocational education performs better than the French one, while the French system of higher education proves more efficient than the German one with respect to the risk of entering unemployment. Again, this can be explained by the different options chosen by the respective education systems. Indeed, at level 2 and 3, the German education system is characterised by its high level of practical orientation through the dual system and its inherent firm-based training. Thus, these qualifications include a large amount of firm-specific human capital, which makes workers less likely to be made redundant. By contrast, vocational education is school-based as a rule in France, takes place on a rather theoretical basis and even the level 2 qualifications encompass a significantly larger amount of general subjects (see chapter 2). As such, they provide fewer labour-market specific skills, not to mention firm-specific skills.

At the tertiary level, however, education is more connected to the needs of the labour market in France than in Germany. Indeed, level 40 qualifications (lower tertiary) consists mainly of rather technically oriented tracks that deliver very specific skills (BTS, DUT, see chapter 2 and glossary in appendix A), while the level 40 qualifications in Germany consist of *Fachhochschulen* who are somewhat more general. At the upper tertiary level, a large share of the French graduates (about 30 percent, see chapter 3 and table B.1 in appendix B) come from the *Grandes Ecoles* which are specifically designed to meet the demand of the (elite of the) economy. Even at university, the link with the world of work is stronger than in the more academic German universities. The stronger practical orientation on average of the French system of higher education compared to the German one could explain that the risk of entering unemployment is lower there.

---

[39] A simple χ^2-test shows that the hypothesis of equality of the coefficients is rejected at the 1 percent level.

Thus, the interpretation that specific practical skills oriented towards the needs of the labour market offer a better protection than more academic knowledge is able to explain the pattern of hierarchies observed both within France and Germany and across them.

4.5.3 Expected risk of experiencing unemployment at least once within a given period

The hazard rate expresses the risk of transiting into unemployment in the next month, given that one was employed until that month. Thus, for every month of employment, the risk of becoming unemployed cumulates. Using this information, one can compute the overall risk of experiencing unemployment (at least once) within a certain period of time as an alternative indicator of the unemployment risk. This information will be useful for the subsequent analysis of unemployment duration if one wants to take the occurrence of multiple spells into account (see section 4.7.1).

The risk of experiencing unemployment at least once within a given period of time does not only depend on the transition probability into unemployment, but also on the probability of exiting to other states, here summarised as non-employment. Let T be the duration of the period considered, expressed in number of months. Considering a population of employees in a specific month ($j = 1$), the risk of experiencing unemployment ($k = 2$) at least once within the next T months equals the risk that one enters unemployment either in the first possible month, or in the second one, or in the third one etc. or in the Tth one. Put it more formally, the expected risk $\widehat{r}^s_{i12}(T)$ that an employed individual i experiences unemployment at least once within the next T months is:

$$\widehat{r}^s_{i12}(T) = \sum_{t=1}^{T} \widehat{p}^s_{i12}(t) \tag{4.22}$$

where p_{i12} is the probability that individual i leaves his sth spell of employment for unemployment exactly in month t, i.e. it is the probability that the individual remains in employment until $t-1$ and exits employment for unemployment in t. Using formulas (4.5) and (4.2), one obtains:

$$\widehat{r}^s_{i12}(T) = \widehat{h}^s_{i12}(1) + \sum_{t=2}^{T} \widehat{h}^s_{i12}(t) \prod_{\tau=1}^{t-1} (1 - \widehat{h}^s_{i12}(\tau) - \widehat{h}^s_{i13}(\tau)) \tag{4.23}$$

Because the expected hazard rates from employment are assumed to be constant across months and spells, i.e. $\widehat{h}^s_{ijk}(t) = \widehat{h}_{ijk}$ for all t and s, the expression above simplifies to:

$$\widehat{r}_{i12}(T) = \widehat{h}_{i12} \sum_{t=1}^{T} (1 - \widehat{h}_{i12} - \widehat{h}_{i13})^{t-1} \tag{4.24}$$

Using the fact that $\sum_{k=0}^{K} x^k = 1 + x + x^2 + ... + x^K = (1 - x^{K+1})/(1 - x)$, one finally obtains:

$$\widehat{r}_{i12}(T) = \widehat{h}_{i12} \left[\frac{1 - (1 - \widehat{h}_{i12} - \widehat{h}_{i13})^T}{\widehat{h}_{i12} + \widehat{h}_{i13}} \right] \tag{4.25}$$

Fig. 4.12. Expected risk of leaving employment for unemployment at least once within the next 36 months

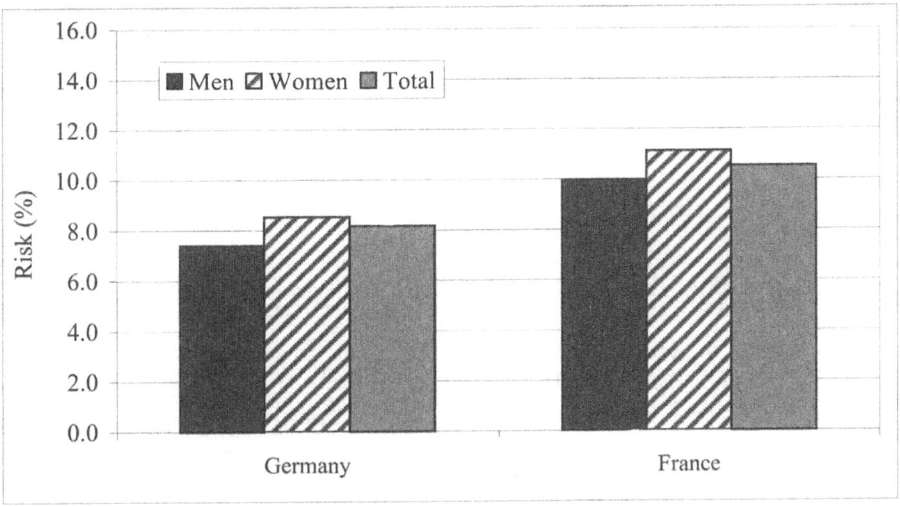

Figure 4.12 depicts the overall risk of encountering unemployment for men and women given their respective average characteristics, as well as for all persons, over a period of 36 months (3 years). As can be seen, the overall risk of experiencing unemployment is, again, higher in France than in Germany, but the gender differences are far less pronounced than when considering only the monthly hazard rate into unemployment. This is true in both countries, but particularly for Germany. The explanation for this is that the higher hazard rate into unemployment for females is somewhat offset by their higher hazard rate into non-employment, which drives the incidence of transitions from employment to unemployment down. Table C.4 in appendix C reports the expected hazards into non-employment and shows that indeed, transitions into non-employment are much more frequent for women than for men, particularly in Germany.

Setting the other variables to population averages, the overall risk of experiencing unemployment within 3 years by education (figure 4.13) does not change patterns significantly compared to the monthly hazard rates (figure 4.11). Therefore, the conclusions drawn above apply.

Fig. 4.13. Impact of education on the expected risk of leaving employment for unemployment at least once within the next 36 months

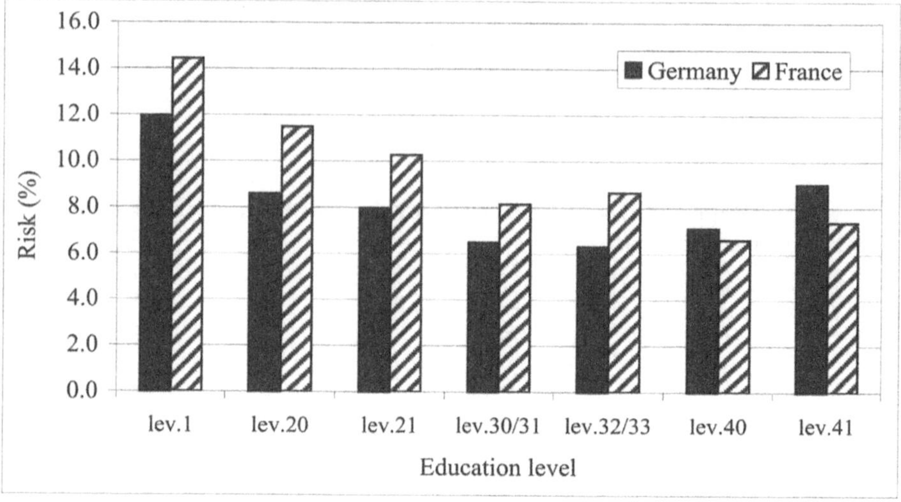

4.6 Education and duration of unemployment episodes

After having analysed the impact of the education level on the risk of leaving employment for unemployment, I examine in this section how education affects the chance of reemployment after an episode of unemployment and more generally how it affects the duration of unemployment episodes. In other words, the model of section 4.3 is now used to estimate the determinants of the monthly hazard rate from unemployment into either employment (h^s_{i21}) or non-employment (h^s_{i23}), as opposed to remaining unemployed. Drawing on these results, one can compute the expected duration of unemployment episodes given some characteristics.

4.6.1 Estimation results

Analogue to the approach followed in section 4.5.1, the first step consists in determining an adequate specification of the model. Given the extremely long computation time of the estimation with the mass points (about 5 days), the specification tests are based on estimations with no modelling of unobserved heterogeneity.

Table 4.8 reports the results of χ^2-tests on the coefficients of the variables, with a view to determining the variables to be included in the equations. Only the gender interactions significant at the 10 percent level at least have been kept in the finally retained specification. Then, on the basis of the equations including the significant interaction terms only, further tests on the variable coefficients have been run, and here again, only the significant ones at the 10

Table 4.8. Tests on coefficients: χ^2 (p> χ^2)

	Germany		**France**	
Hazard rate into:	**Empl.**	**Non-empl.**	**Empl.**	**Non-empl.**
Tests on gender interactions				
Female * Education	5.75 (0.45)	8.34 (0.21)	9.22 (0.17)	10.01 (0.12)
Female * Duration	7.26 (0.40)	10.95 (0.14)	10.19 (0.25)	11.93 (0.15)
Female * Married	5.05 (0.02)	32.93 (0.00)	0.12 (0.73)	1.29 (0.26)
Female * Children<6	4.03 (0.04)	10.19 (0.00)	24.56 (0.00)	4.65 (0.03)
Female * Age	7.11 (0.21)	6.42 (0.27)	8.02 (0.15)	5.07 (0.28)
Female * City size	6.29 (0.04)	1.00 (0.60)	16.44 (0.00)	3.89 (0.15)
Female * Unempl. rate	0.53 (0.47)	1.47 (0.22)	14.74 (0.00)	4.51 (0.03)
Tests on specific coefficients (with only significant gender interactions)				
Education	51.83 (0.00)	13.07 (0.36)	13.30 (0.04)	6.44 (0.32)
Female	3.72 (0.05)	0.55 (0.46)	0.76 (0.38)	0.01 (0.92)
Duration	95.28 (0.00)	18.34 (0.02)	166.85 (0.00)	17.47 (0.03)
Previously employed	35.07 (0.00)	7.01 (0.01)	68.89 (0.00)	6.72 (0.01)
Married	8.78 (0.01)	0.17 (0.86)	3.41 (0.18)	2.37 (0.31)
Children<6	0.13 (0.72)	14.67 (0.00)	29.99 (0.00)	15.35 (0.00)
Owner	0.90 (0.34)	5.47 (0.02)	0.82 (0.37)	0.36 (0.55)
Age	54.66 (0.00)	17.71 (0.00)	48.21 (0.00)	16.20 (0.00)
City size	15.80 (0.00)	0.30 (0.86)	26.18 (0.00)	4.74 (0.09)
Unemployment rate	12.79 (0.00)	0.32 (0.57)	0.01 (0.99)	0.50 (0.60)
IRR	11.01 (0.00)	0.06 (0.81)	9.68 (0.00)	0.20 (0.65)
Current quarter	11.70 (0.01)	7.07 (0.07)	63.40 (0.00)	126.80 (0.00)
Quarter of spell begin	3.94 (0.27)	0.29 (0.96)	10.32 (0.02)	5.49 (0.14)
Year	19.54 (0.01)	35.05 (0.00)		
Month			141.80 (0.00)	57.61 (0.00)
Tests on overall significance (finally retained specification)				
Overall Wald test	641.7 (0.00)		1,231.5 (0.00)	
Eq. specific Wald tests	447.5 (0.00)	190.9 (0.00)	915.5 (0.00)	313.9 (0.00)

percent significance level at least have been retained. The variables included are allowed to differ for the equation of the hazard from unemployment into employment and for the equation of the hazard into non-employment. The overall Wald test and the equation specific Wald tests are run on the basis of the final equations in terms of the variables included and give a measure of the fit of the model.

Table 4.9 reports the results of further tests aiming at determining the appropriate functional form. For both countries, the multinomial logit specification seems to be appropriate since the IIA assumption is fulfilled on the basis of both Hausman and Small Hsiao tests (see details on these tests in section 4.3.3). The Wald tests reported in table 4.9 show that it is adequate to distinguish between exit into employment and exit into non-employment and that none of the outcome categories should be combined. Moreover, all

Table 4.9. Other specification tests

		Germany	France
Tests for IIA		χ^2 (p> χ^2)	χ^2 (p> χ^2)
Hausman	Omitted: empl.	17.16 (0.97)	22.67 (0.54)
	Omitted: non-empl.	2.44 (1.00)	-1.37 (-.-)
Small Hsiao	Omitted: empl.	43.58 (0.49)	32.84 (0.71)
	Omitted: non-empl.	48.96 (0.28)	33.00 (0.70)
Wald test for combining outcomes		χ^2 (p> χ^2)	χ^2 (p> χ^2)
Comb. empl. and non-empl.		352.42 (0.00)	392.64 (0.00)
Comb. empl. and unempl.		447.46 (0.00)	915.50 (0.00)
Comb. non-empl. and unempl.		190.92 (0.00)	313.88 (0.00)
Tests for number of mass points		*IC*	*IC*
IC_A	No mass point	-5,344.6	-7,668.6
	2 mass points	-5,331.1	-7,696.8
	3 mass points	-5,333.1	-7.698.8
IC_B	No mass point	-5,619.0	-7,926.1
	2 mass points	-5,613.1	-7,862.4
	3 mass points	-5,622.7	-7,872.5
IC_H	No mass point	-5,435.7	-7,752.3
	2 mass points	-5,424.6	-7,683.1
	3 mass points	-5,429.2	-7,687.7

three information criteria (see section 4.3.3) lead to the conclusion that the optimal number of mass points is two.

The full estimation results for both countries are reported in table 4.10. The effects of the various covariates on both possible exits can be read from the table and will not be further commented here. The focus of the subsequent sections is on the reemployment probability of those unemployed persons who were previously employed and lost their job with a risk estimated in section 4.5[40]. Furthermore, the estimates of the hazard of entering unemployment and non-employment will be used to compute an estimate of the unemployment duration, taking the censoring problem into account, and assess the impact of education on it. Finally, the occurrence of multiple spells as well as the degree of concentration of unemployment on certain qualification groups will be examined.

[40] A dummy variable indicating whether the person was previously employed was included in the equations. About 80 percent of the unemployment spells follow an employment spell (see table 4.2 in appendix C). The estimations were not restricted to those spells only but rather include all unemployment spells including those following non-employment in order to gain precious observations.

Table 4.10. Determinants of hazard rate from unemployment

	Germany		France	
Hazard rate into:	**Empl.** coef. (s.e)	**Non-empl.** coef. (s.e)	**Empl.** coef. (s.e)	**Non-empl.** coef. (s.e)
Education level (ref.: Level 1)				
Level 20	0.33** (0.11)		0.15† (0.09)	
Level 21	0.57** (0.12)		0.23** (0.11)	
Level 30 or 31	0.57** (0.14)		0.34** (0.15)	
Level 32 or 33	0.78** (0.17)		0.35** (0.16)	
Level 40	0.94** (0.19)		0.42** (0.15)	
Level 41	0.90** (0.17)		0.45** (0.16)	
Female	-0.23† (0.13)			
Duration (ref.: 1 month)				
2 months	0.08 (0.11)	-0.55† (0.30)	-0.06 (0.10)	-0.17 (0.48)
3 months	0.13 (0.12)	-0.35 (0.30)	0.14 (0.15)	0.71† (0.40)
4-6 months	-0.04 (0.11)	-0.18 (0.24)	0.03 (0.15)	1.07** (0.35)
7-9 months	-0.00 (0.13)	-0.07 (0.26)	-0.12 (0.16)	1.57** (0.36)
10-12 months	-0.11 (0.15)	0.26 (0.27)	-0.13 (0.17)	1.41** (0.37)
13-15 months	-0.11 (0.18)	0.80** (0.28)	-0.29† (0.18)	0.61 (0.52)
16-18 months	-0.47* (0.22)	0.01 (0.41)	-0.27† (0.17)	1.53** (0.44)
≥19 months	-0.51** (0.17)	0.04 (0.28)	-0.35* (0.17)	0.61 (0.56)
Previously employed	0.52** (0.10)	-0.40** (0.15)	0.74** (0.11)	-0.41* (0.21)
Marital status (ref.: Not married)				
Married	0.27** (0.10)			
Female * Married	-0.31* (0.14)	0.85** (0.16)		
Number of children				
Children<6		-1.08** (0.42)	0.30** (0.07)	-0.80 (0.65)
Female* Children<6	-0.22* (0.11)	1.39** (0.44)	-0.54** (0.12)	1.37* (0.67)
Home ownership		0.35* (0.15)		
Age (ref.: Age 25-30)				
Age 31-35	0.03 (0.09)	-0.29† (0.18)	-0.26** (0.11)	-0.32 (0.23)
Age 36-40	-0.10 (0.11)	-0.64** (0.24)	-0.25* (0.13)	-0.84** (0.29)
Age 41-45	-0.09 (0.12)	-0.38† (0.24)	-0.50** (0.14)	-1.48** (0.38)
Age 46-50	-0.57** (0.14)	-0.85** (0.30)	-0.42** (0.15)	-0.17 (0.27)
Age 51-55	-0.92** (0.16)	-0.89** (0.27)	-1.00** (0.15)	-0.81* (0.33)
City cize (ref.: <20,000 inh.)				
20-100,000 inh.	-0.32** (0.12)		-0.04 (0.12)	-0.57* (0.29)
≥100,000 inh.	-0.35** (0.11)		-0.37** (0.09)	-0.36† (0.19)
Female * 20-100,000 inh.	0.28† (0.17)		-0.36† (0.20)	
Female * ≥100,000 inh.	0.30† (0.16)		0.31** (0.13)	

to be continued...

...table 4.10 continued

Hazard rate into:	Germany Empl. coef. (s.e)	Germany Non-empl. coef. (s.e)	France Empl. coef. (s.e)	France Non-empl. coef. (s.e)
Unemployment rate				
Unempl. rate/10	-0.62** (0.19)			
Female * Unempl. rate/10			-0.27** (0.09)	0.30* (0.14)
IRR	-1.39** (0.58)		-1.46** (0.52)	
Current quarter (ref.: 1st quarter)				
2nd quarter	-0.18* (0.09)	-0.35† (0.20)	-0.51** (0.08)	-3.04** (0.44)
3rd quarter	-0.07 (0.09)	-0.21 (0.19)	-0.39** (0.07)	-2.42** (0.32)
4th quarter	-0.25** (0.09)	0.07 (0.18)	-0.40** (0.07)	-1.81** (0.25)
Quarter of spell begin (ref.: 1st quarter)				
2nd quarter			-0.22** (0.09)	
3rd quarter			-0.05 (0.08)	
4th quarter			-0.14† (0.08)	
Time trend (ref. G: 1991)				
1992	-0.07 (0.22)	1.18* (0.55)		
1993	-0.42* (0.22)	0.61 (0.56)		
1994	-0.34 (0.22)	0.19 (0.57)		
1995	-0.14 (0.22)	0.92† (0.55)		
1996	-0.29 (0.23)	0.21 (0.56)		
1997	-0.15 (0.23)	-0.11 (0.57)		
1998	0.04 (0.23)	0.76 (0.55)		
1999	-0.18 (0.24)	0.16 (0.58)		
Month			-0.22** (0.04)	-0.82** (0.22)
Month squared/10			0.15** (0.02)	0.49** (0.11)
Month cubed/100			-0.03** (0.00)	-0.09** (0.02)
Constant	-2.31** (0.50)	-4.54** (0.58)	-1.09* (0.47)	-0.61 (1.39)
Mass points				
ε_1	1.21** (0.14)		1.73** (0.10)	
ε_2	-0.52		-0.58	
$Pr(\varepsilon_1)$	0.30** (0.08)		0.25** (0.04)	
$Pr(\varepsilon_2)$	0.71		0.75	
Number of observations	15,089		23,112	
Number of spells	1,827		3,380	
Number of individuals	1,198		2,157	
Log-likelihood	-5,257.1		-7,530.8	

Significance level : † : 10% * : 5% ** : 1%

4.6.2 Expected monthly hazard of reemployment

In the previous section (4.5), the risk of leaving employment for unemployment has been analysed. This section examines the chance of finding reemployment after such a job loss that ended in unemployment. Using the estimation results presented above, I compute an estimate of the expected hazard rates from unemployment into employment h_{i21} in France and Germany for males, females and overall, given the average characteristics in their respective groups using formula 4.10 and given that they were employed immediately before the unemployment spell. Note that it is necessary to correct for the longer period of observation in the German estimation, the latter being required due to an otherwise insufficient number of observations (see section 4.4.1). To predict the German hazard rates, the means of the explanatory variables has been computed over the last 36 months, i.e. from January 1997 to December 1999 to cover the same period as for the French estimation. The coefficients of the year dummies correct for the time restriction.

As mentioned previously, the optimal number of mass points amounts to two for both countries. This means that the French and the German samples can be divided into two heterogeneity groups respectively. The first group has, for some unobserved reason, an above average probability of exiting unemployment (positive mass point), while the second group has a slightly below average propensity to leave unemployment. In both countries, the probability of belonging to the former group is significantly lower than that of belonging to the latter group (see table 4.10). One hazard rate is computed for each of the identified heterogeneity groups and the overall hazard rate is calculated as the sum of the heterogeneity group specific hazard rates, weighted by the estimated probabilities of belonging to the respective heterogeneity group.

On the whole (see figure 4.14), once unemployed, the reemployment probability is higher in France than in Germany. Thus, the French have a higher risk of becoming unemployed than the German, but once unemployed, they have better chances of getting reemployed. This is particularly true for men while the difference between France and Germany in the reemployment prospects of unemployed women – poorer than those for men – is minor.

As for entry into unemployment, the education level is not found to exert a different impact for men and women on the exit out of unemployment into employment. The impact of education on the chance of getting reemployed has been estimated by setting the characteristics other than education to population averages and estimate the hazard rate as described above for the different education levels. Contrary to what is true for the risk of entering unemployment, education has a monotonous impact on the hazard of exiting unemployment for employment. The higher the education level is, the higher is the probability to exit unemployment and find a job again, everything else being equal. An explanation for this might be that, following job competition arguments (see section 4.1.1), when unemployed, it is advantageous to have attained a high level of education because it is always possible to apply for

Fig. 4.14. Expected monthly hazard of leaving unemployment for employment

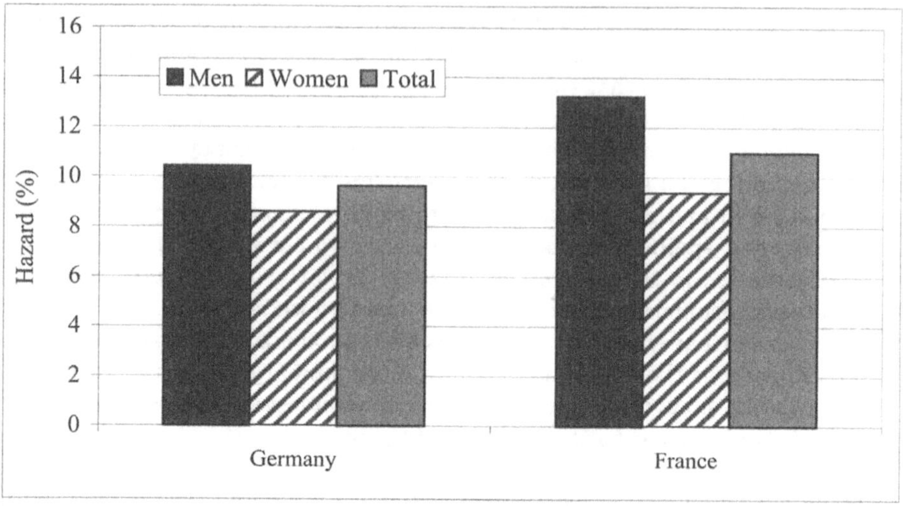

Fig. 4.15. Impact of education on the expected monthly hazard of leaving unemployment for employment

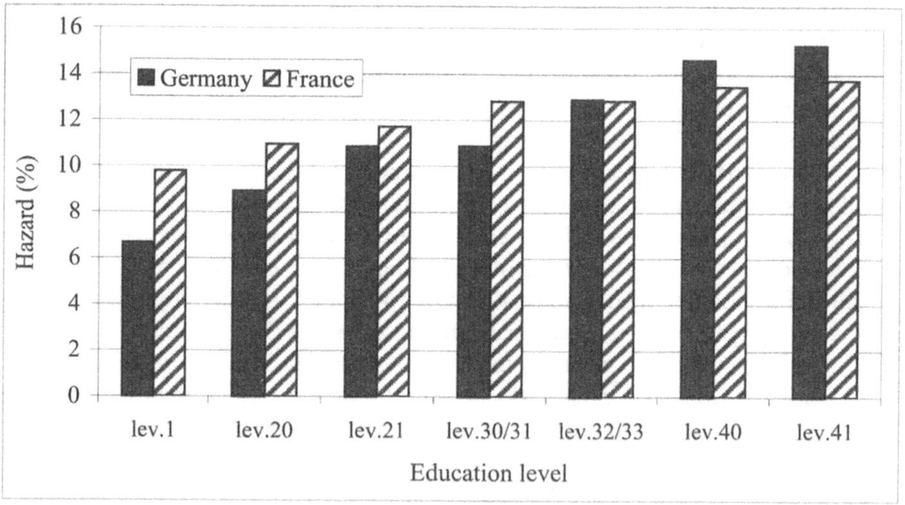

a job below one's qualification level if necessary whereas the reverse is much more difficult.

In particular, in France and in Germany alike, tertiary level education is associated with the best reemployment prospects. In other words, even if advanced vocational qualifications offer a better protection than higher education against the risk of entering unemployment in Germany, as was found out in section 4.5, once unemployed, they are not associated with better reemployment prospects[41]. An explanation for this could be that though specific vocational skills are an efficient protection against the risk of losing one's job, once unemployed, however, it is more advantageous to have more general qualifications. Indeed, general qualifications provide more flexibility in the sense that they are suited to a wider range of jobs for which the unemployed can apply. If the sector the employee was working in faces a crises, for instance, a more generally qualified employee can more easily change his field of work[42]. In contrast, the highly specialised worker will have problems in finding reemployment if the reason why he became unemployed concerns his field of specialisation or sector of activity in general. Thus, if specialised vocational skills make the worker precious to the firm, when the firm happens not to need the specific skills in question, general qualifications permit to adapt more easily to demand conditions when looking for a job.

The differences between France and Germany in the pattern of dependence of the reemployment prospects on education also seem to confirm the interpretation in terms of the balance between vocational and general skills at different levels of the education systems. Indeed, the reemployment prospects are better in France at lower education levels, but for higher education graduates, they are better in Germany[43]. The more practically oriented system of vocational education in Germany offers a better protection against the risk of being made redundant than the more school-based French system, but once unemployed, the French system that lays more emphasis on general education leads to better reemployment prospects, anything else equal. At the higher education level, the same conclusion – in the opposite direction – can be drawn. The French system of higher education, with its practically oriented short tracks and the elite formation of the *Grandes Ecoles* in close collaboration with the economy seems rather efficient in reducing the unemployment risk, but the more academic German system of higher education turns more advantageous when looking for reemployment.

4.6.3 Expected duration of unemployment spells

Drawing on the results of the estimation of the hazard rate from unemployment into either employment or non-employment, one can compute the expected duration of unemployment episodes given certain characteristics. The hazard rates out of unemployment are not unaffected by the time individuals have already been unemployed.

---

[41] Wolbers (2000) finds a similar phenomenon for the Netherlands.

[42] Managing positions, for instance, are relatively little dependent of the sector of activity.

[43] As a result, the level of educational attainment appears to have a stronger discriminating power in Germany than in France, all else equal.

Fig. 4.16. Duration dependence pattern of the expected monthly hazard of leaving unemployment

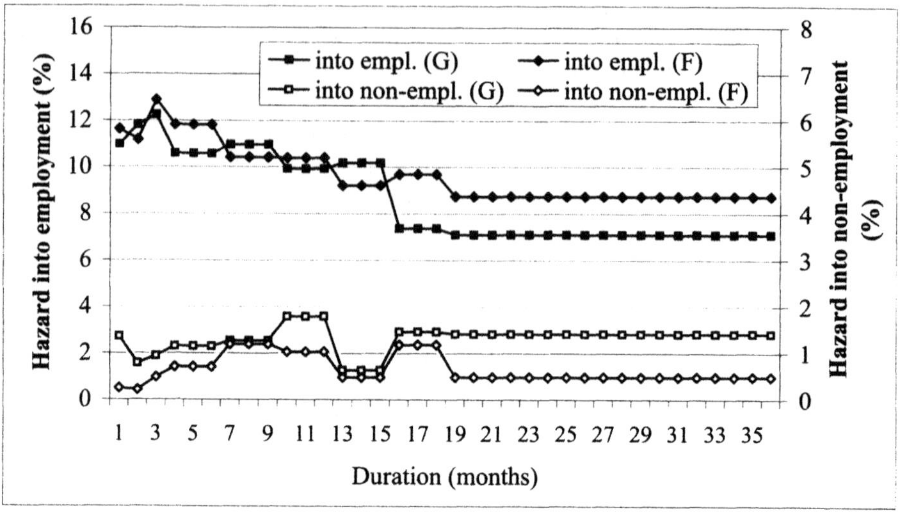

Figure 4.16 illustrates the pattern of duration dependence of the hazard rates out of unemployment, where the characteristics other than current unemployment duration have been set to population averages and the estimated hazards are a weighted average of hazards estimated for each of the heterogeneity groups. The duration dependence is assumed not to depend on other characteristics such as education or gender[44]. The pattern of duration dependence of the hazard from unemployment into employment presents obvious similarities in France and Germany. The longer individuals have already been unemployed, the lower the chance of getting reemployed, even if unobserved individual heterogeneity is controlled for. However, this negative impact of unemployment duration only turns significant for unemployment periods longer than 15 months in Germany and longer than 12 months for France, so, broadly speaking, for the long-term unemployed. The lowering effect of long-term unemployment on the reemployment prospects seems to be stronger in Germany than in France, which points to a higher persistence of unemployment there. As to the hazard from unemployment into non-employment (secondary axis), it is significantly higher in Germany than in France, though it is for both countries much below the hazard of exiting unemployment for employment (see table C.4 in appendix C). Broadly speaking, the duration of unemployment has a slight positive effect on the probability to transit into non-employment but the pattern is rather irregular, which might be due to the small num-

[44] Some attempts were made to interact the baseline hazard dummies with education and/or gender but the too small number of observations makes the results very unrobust.

ber of observations, since the probability of transition from unemployment to non-employment is very low.

Using the information drawn from the estimation results on the hazard rates and the duration dependence of the hazard to the two possible destinations, one can compute the expected duration of an unemployment spell $\widehat{d}^s_{i2}$ as follows:

$$\widehat{d}^s_{i2} = \lim_{T \to +\infty} \sum_{t=1}^{T} (1 - \widehat{h}^s_{i21}(t) - \widehat{h}^s_{i23}(t))^t \tag{4.26}$$

Fig. 4.17. Expected duration of unemployment spells

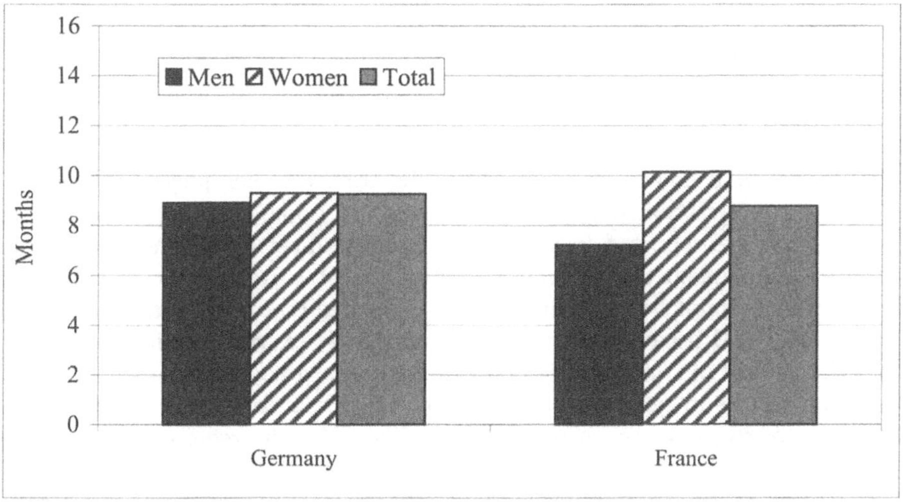

Though the reemployment rate of the unemployed is significantly higher in France than in Germany, the duration of unemployment episodes is only slightly shorter in France (see figure 4.17 and exact figures in table 4.11). This is because in Germany, the exits to non-employment are much more frequent than in France (more than twice as frequent, see table C.4 in appendix C). Indeed, the duration of unemployment does not only depend on the reemployment probability, but also on the probability of transiting into non-employment. Particularly in Germany, the difference across genders is much less marked in terms of unemployment duration than in terms of reemployment prospects. This is because German women quit much more often unemployment for non-employment compared to men, and the gender difference in this respect is much stronger than in France.

Fig. 4.18. Impact of education on expected duration of unemployment spells

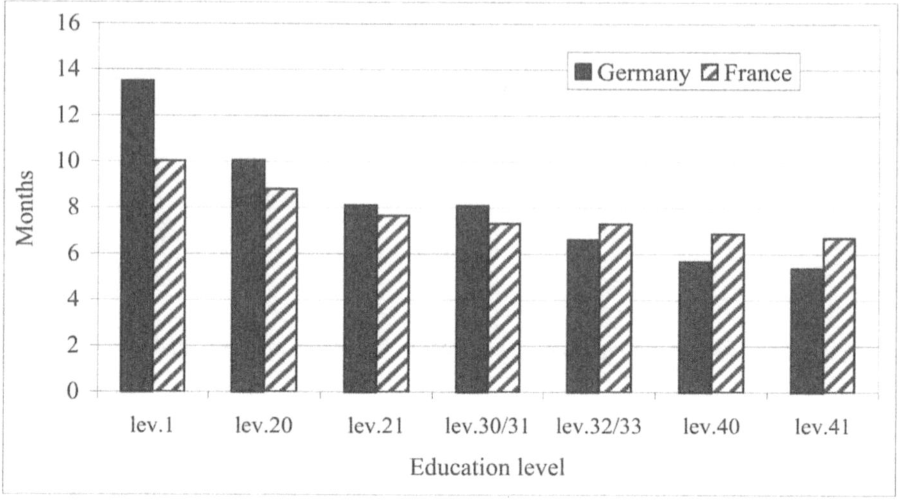

Figure 4.18 depicts the impact of education on unemployment duration, other characteristics being constant and set to population averages. The exact figures are reported in table 4.11. Because most employment spells exit into reemployment rather than non-employment (compare the magnitude of figures in graph 4.14 compared to that of figures reported in table C.4 in appendix C) and because education appears not to exert a significant influence on the hazard of transiting from unemployment to non-employment (see estimation results in table 4.10 as well as the significance tests in table 4.8), the pattern of dependence on education observed for the reemployment hazard basically remains the same when considering overall unemployment duration. Therefore, the conclusions with respect to the role of vocational and general qualifications drawn in section 4.6.2 concerning the reemployment prospects can be transposed to the duration of unemployment spells and will not be further commented here.

4.7 Education and total unemployment risk

In the previous section, I have examined the expected duration of an average unemployment spell after employment has been lost. However, the employees might experience more than one unemployment spell and of course, it makes a difference whether one person expects the unemployment spell duration to occur once or several times. Thus, one needs a measure of the total unemployment risk an employee with given characteristics can expect to face. In this section, the partial analyses on the risk of entering unemployment (section 4.5) and on the duration of unemployment episodes (section 4.6) will be combined to obtain a synthetic indicator of the overall impact of education with respect to the unemployment risk.

4.7.1 Multiple unemployment spells and total unemployment risk

A common approach in the literature to deal with the problem of multiple spells has typically been to consider on the descriptive level the observed duration of unemployment spells and multiply it by the number of unemployment spells incurred by those persons for which unemployment spells are observed (e.g. Karr and John 1989). It would have been possible to follow this approach, differentiating by, say, the education level. However, this approach has several drawbacks. First, because the duration of unemployment spells is computed on the descriptive level, it is underestimated because of the presence of incomplete spells. Moreover, the impact of education would not be cleaned from other factors and what I seek to identify here is the impact of education on the overall expected unemployment duration in a given period of time, other things being constant. This can only be done using the results of a multivariate analysis. Finally, in this approach, the cumulated duration of unemployment is computed only for those people experiencing at least one unemployment spell. It does not measure the total unemployment duration to be expected by *any* individual with given characteristics and neglects the fact that the risk of experiencing at least one unemployment spell might also differ across individuals, in particular with respect to the characteristics to be analysed, here the education level.

Therefore, I follow an alternative approach. The total unemployment risk for an employee with given characteristics is computed as the total number of unemployment months he or she can expect:

$$\begin{aligned} \widehat{d_{i2}} &= \widehat{d^s_{i2}} * \widehat{S_{i2}}(36) \\ &= \widehat{d^s_{i2}} * \overline{\Omega}_{i2}(36) * \widehat{r}_{i12}(36) \end{aligned} \tag{4.27}$$

where $\widehat{d^s_{i2}}$ is the expected duration of unemployment spells computed from the estimation results, rather than the observed duration of unemployment spells, thus taking censoring into account and making it possible to isolate the impact of selected variables. $\widehat{S_{i2}}(36)$ is the expected number of unemployment spells an employee can expect to face within the next three years. $\widehat{S_{i2}}(36)$ is defined as the product of the risk of entering unemployment at least once within the period considered $\widehat{r}_{i12}(36)$, which has been estimated in section 4.5.3, times the average number of unemployment spells then incurred $\overline{\Omega}_{i2}(36)$, obtained from the sample of unemployment spells used for the analysis of exits from unemployment[45]. Multiplying $\widehat{d^s_{i2}}$ by $\overline{\Omega}_{i2}(36)$ yields the

[45] $\overline{\Omega}_{i2}(36)$ is computed on the last 36 months of observations for Germany as well and on the unemployment spells preceded by employment.

Table 4.11. Components of the total unemployment risk

	$\widehat{d^s_{i2}}$ Duration per spell (months)	$\overline{\Omega}_{i2}$ Obs. nb of spells (real)	$\widehat{d^s_{i2}} * \overline{S}_{i2}$ Cumul. duration (months)	$\widehat{r}_{i12}$ Entry risk (%)	$\widehat{S}_{i2}$ Exp. nb of spells (real)	$\widehat{d}_{i2}$ Total risk (months)
			Germany			
Lev. 1	13.49	1.31	17.68	11.95	0.16	2.11
Lev. 20	10.05	1.28	12.83	8.58	0.11	1.10
Lev. 21	8.10	1.19	9.63	7.97	0.09	0.77
Lev. 30/31	8.08	1.16	9.41	6.49	0.08	0.61
Lev. 32/33	6.61	1.19	7.85	6.33	0.08	0.50
Lev. 40	5.67	1.07	6.09	7.11	0.08	0.43
Lev. 41	5.38	1.03	5.56	9.01	0.09	0.50
Men	8.90	1.26	11.25	7.41	0.09	0.83
Women	9.29	1.20	11.19	8.54	0.10	0.96
Total	9.25	1.23	11.42	8.17	0.09	0.93
			France			
Lev. 1	10.03	1.58	15.85	14.44	0.23	2.29
Lev. 20	8.80	1.60	14.04	11.49	0.18	1.61
Lev. 21	7.65	1.67	12.74	10.26	0.17	1.31
Lev. 30/31	7.30	1.61	11.73	8.14	0.13	0.96
Lev. 32/33	7.29	1.59	11.57	8.65	0.14	1.00
Lev. 40	6.87	1.55	10.66	6.62	0.10	0.71
Lev. 41	6.70	1.44	9.64	7.38	0.11	0.71
Men	7.21	1.67	12.00	9.95	0.17	1.19
Women	10.15	1.49	15.12	11.12	0.17	1.68
Total	8.77	1.57	13.74	10.51	0.17	1.44

cumulated unemployment duration that can be expected by those employees who experienced at least one unemployment spell within 3 years[46]. The details of the computation of the total unemployment risk $\widehat{d}_{i2}$, defined as the number of unemployment months to be expected by an employee with given specific characteristics, has been reported in its various components in table 4.11. For the sake of presentation, the estimates of the total unemployment risk $\widehat{d}_{i2}$ have been represented graphically, too (figures 4.19 and 4.20). Further graphs on the cumulated duration of unemployment for the unemployed – the rather typical approach in the literature – as well as on the expected number of unemployment spells can be found in annex C (figures C.13 and C.14 as well as C.15 and C.16 respectively).

[46] This is the measure generally used in the literature on unemployment

Fig. 4.19. Total unemployment risk

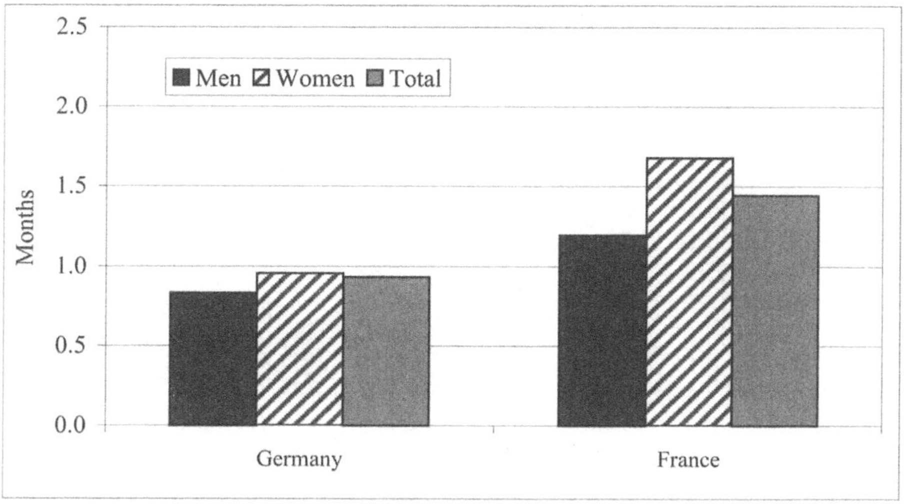

Taking the risk of experiencing unemployment into consideration, the total number of unemployment months to be expected by employees is much higher in France than in Germany. This is because even though the duration of unemployment spells is on average shorter in France (see column $\widehat{d}^s_{i2}$ in table 4.11), the frequency of unemployment spells is significantly higher there (see column $\widehat{S}_{i2}$). Looking at gender differences, the same pattern as that prevailing for the expected duration of one unemployment spell – larger gender differences in France than in Germany due to a lower incidence of non-employment, see section 4.6.3 – is observed for total expected number of unemployment months as well. This is because the expected number of unemployment spells (column $\widehat{S}_{i2}$) proves quite similar for men and women in both countries. This, in turn, is the result of a phenomenon that prevails in both countries. Whereas the risk, when employed, of experiencing unemployment at least once (column $\widehat{r}_{i12}$) is significantly higher for women than for men in both countries, men experience more often than women repeated spells of unemployment (column $\overline{\Omega}_{i2}$).

Concerning the effect of education, however, the pattern changes markedly when observing the total expected number of unemployment months, accounting for the risk of experiencing unemployment, instead of just considering the spell level. The differences between France and Germany are much larger. The total number of unemployment months that employees can expect to face in the next three years is higher in France than in Germany at all education levels. Note, however, that the difference between France and Germany is largest at lower education levels, especially level 2 and 3, while it is smallest at the higher education level. At lower education levels, the expected duration of

Fig. 4.20. Impact of education on total unemployment risk

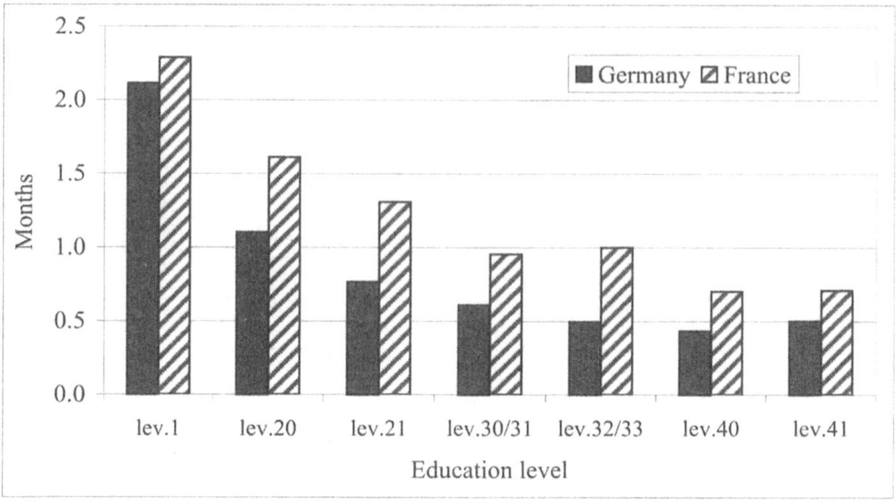

unemployment spells is shorter in France than in Germany, but because the expected number of unemployment spells is very much higher in France (see also figure C.16 in annex C), the gap in total expected unemployment duration turns favourable to Germany. The expected number of unemployment spells is much higher in France than in Germany at lower education levels because of the joint influence of two effects. Not only is the likelihood to experience unemployment at least once higher in France than in Germany, but the French with a low or intermediate education level are also more likely than their German counterparts to face repeated spells of unemployment.

At the tertiary level, the gap in total unemployment risk is much smaller. This is due to the fact that the frequency of unemployment spells for tertiary level graduates does not differ that much. Indeed, even though when French tertiary level graduates experience unemployment, they are more likely than German graduates to face further unemployment episodes, the likelihood that they experience a first unemployment spell is significantly lower, for the reasons explained in section 4.5.2. However, the duration of each unemployment spell is somewhat larger, which explains that French employed tertiary level graduates must expect a higher overall number of unemployment months within the next 3 years.

In terms of total unemployment risk, education proves to have a stronger discriminating power in France than in Germany, due to its particularly strong discriminating impact on the unemployment entry risk. However, as we had seen in section 4.6.3, once unemployed, education is more essential in determining the length of each unemployment episode in Germany than in France.

4.7.2 Concentration of the unemployment problem

The previous steps of the analysis has led to the elaboration of a synthetic indicator $\widehat{d}_{i2}$ of the unemployment outcome of given characteristics (education and gender). The last step of the analysis consists in quantifying the degree of concentration of the unemployment problem on these specific population groups. To this end, a simple concentration index is constructed by relating the share of the employed population represented by the group considered to the share of the total expected unemployment months they cumulate. The larger the index deviates from one, the stronger the concentration of the unemployment on the population group considered.

Table 4.12. Concentration of the unemployment risk on certain population groups

	Germany			France		
	% of employees	% of exp. unempl. duration	Concentration index	% of employees	% of exp. unempl. duration	Concentration index
Level 1	11.1	25.8	2.33	30.6	46.8	1.53
Level 20	27.9	33.8	1.21	21.8	23.5	1.08
Level 21	18.0	15.2	0.85	12.1	10.6	0.87
Level 30/31	16.1	10.8	0.67	6.7	4.3	0.64
Level 32/33	8.0	4.4	0.55	6.2	4.1	0.67
Level 40	6.6	3.1	0.48	11.9	5.6	0.47
Level 41	12.4	6.8	0.55	10.6	5.0	0.48
Men	56.8	53.4	0.94	54.1	45.6	0.84
Women	43.2	46.6	1.08	45.9	54.4	1.19
Total	100.0	100.0	1.00	100.0	100.0	1.00

The results are reported in table 4.12. As can be seen, the unemployment problem is somewhat more concentrated on women than men, particularly in France, but the deviation from one is not very important. However, the concentration of the unemployment problem on specific educational groups is much more important, particularly in Germany. In France, the unemployment risk is concentrated on those individuals without a vocational degree (level 1) essentially. Whereas these represent some 30 percent of the population, they cumulate almost half of the unemployment months. The degree of concentration is even stronger in Germany. The German unemployment problem is highly concentrated on those individuals without a vocational degree, who, though they represent only 11 percent of the population, cumulate more than one quarter of the expected unemployment months. The level 20 (*Hauptschule* degree + apprenticeship) is also disproportionately hit by unemployment. Thus, whereas the unemployment problem is in total, i.e. as measured by $\widehat{d_{i2}}$, less acute in Germany than in France, it is much more unevenly distributed across educational groups.

4.8 Summary and conclusions

This chapter explored the relationship between educational attainment and unemployment risk in France and Germany. France and Germany are both plagued with high levels of unemployment which policy-makers aim to reduce. Because the educational attainment determines to a large extent the employability of individuals, looking at the relative performance of the various qualifications provided by the education systems in terms of unemployment risk, anything else equal, should help finding solutions to the unemployment problem. A cross-country comparison based on France and Germany proved particularly useful for this purpose. Indeed, France and Germany have chosen different options for their education systems, in particular with respect to the degree of consideration of labour market needs at the different levels of the education system. Using the knowledge gained from the previous chapters on the content of the qualifications issued by the respective education systems, an in-depth analysis of the patterns observed both within and across countries made it possible to characterise the nature of the unemployment problem in its various dimensions in either country as well as the role played by education.

The link between education and unemployment has not been as such the object of a single economic theory but some elements of explanation can be derived from different theories, ranging from the human capital theory to job search models. However, the nature of the education-unemployment link is not clear-cut from a theoretical point of view, since opposite effects might be at work. It therefore remains an empirical question. The empirical evidence on this topic available so far, however, does not lead to conclusive results and the findings very much depend on the country examined, the methodology used and the aspect of the unemployment focussed at. The empirical analysis conducted in this chapter therefore aimed to analyse the unemployment problem in all its various dimensions and, using the patterns observed both within and across countries, to draw some conclusions on the strengths and weaknesses of the respective education systems as providers of employment opportunities.

The most widely used indicator of the labour market performance is the unemployment rate. This is why the analysis started with a comparison of the unemployment rate by education level, using national microdata that makes it possible to define these in a comparable way. The unemployment rate appears to be higher in France than in Germany for all education groups, the gap being larger for basic and vocational qualifications. In both countries, it decreases with the education level, but only up to a certain level. Moreover, women face a higher unemployment rate than men in both countries, but the gap is significantly larger in France. The latter can be explained by the much larger extent of labour force non-participation among German women than among French women. Indeed, looking at the employment rate, which relates the number of employees to total population and not only labour force participants shows that the difference between France and Germany in the gender gap is much smaller there than when calculating the unemployment rate among the labour force participants only. Thus, a comparative analysis of unemployment in France and Germany should take the different incidence of non-participation into account.

However, unemployment is a complex problem that should be viewed in dynamic terms rather than just considering the static indicator of the unemployment rate. The econometric analysis therefore focussed on the impact of education on the various dimensions of the dynamics of the unemployment problem: the risk of entering unemployment, the risk once unemployed of remaining unemployed and the risk of recurrence of unemployment episodes. To this end, a discrete time hazard rate model with multiple exit destinations (to isolate the possible effect of differing incidences of non-employment) and nonparametric heterogeneity has been used to model the transitions into and out of unemployment. The formal presentation of the model demonstrates that the multinomial logit framework applied in the recent literature without having been derived formally can be rationalised from an econometric point of view. The model is applied to estimate the monthly hazard of transiting from employment into unemployment as well as the monthly hazard of exiting unemployment for employment, using the retrospective monthly data on the employment status available in the GSOEP and *Emploi* data sets. Drawing on these estimates, the different dimensions of the unemployment risk as well as the impact of education on them can be recovered.

Overall, the risk of losing one's job and enter unemployment in the sequel is higher in France than in Germany, but once unemployed, the reemployment prospects of the French are better. Evidence was found that long-term unemployed have *ceteris paribus* poorer reemployment prospects in both countries, but this negative duration dependence is particularly strong in Germany. Furthermore, not only do French employees have a higher risk of experiencing a first unemployment episode than their German counterparts, but when so, they are also more likely to face repeated unemployment spells. As a result, the number of unemployment episodes they must expect in a given period is much higher in France than in Germany. Thus, the unemployment problem in Germany lies to a greater extent than in France in a comparatively higher persistence of unemployment, while the French unemployment problem rather lies in a greater lack of job security compared to Germany. Overall, the total number of unemployment months an employee can expect to face within the next three years, given the risk of entering unemployment, the risk of recurrence of unemployment and the duration of unemployment spells, is much higher in France than in Germany.

As to gender differences, women prove to have a higher hazard of entering unemployment in both countries, but particularly in Germany. However, because employed women transit more often to non-employment than men, the gender gap is smaller when considering the cumulated risk of transiting to unemployment at least once within a given period, particularly in Germany, where the incidence of non-employment is higher. Not only do women have a higher risk of entering unemployment, when unemployed, they also have poorer reemployment prospects. Here, the gender gap is larger in France. In Germany, however, the unemployment spells are virtually of the same lengths for men and women, but of course, they lead more often to reemployment for men and more often to non-employment for women. Interestingly, the expected number of spells in a given period of three years is similar for men and for women. This is because while women have a higher risk than men of being confronted with unemployment within the period, when it happens, they are less likely to incur repeated unemployment episodes. Overall, the total number of unemployment months employed women must expect given their risk of entering unemployment, of facing recurrent unemployment and the expected duration of unemployment spells is therefore higher for women than for men, but the gender gap is small in Germany and rather large in France.

The relationship between education[47] and risk of entering unemployment appears not to be monotonous. Additional education reduces strongly the risk of entering unemployment, but only up to a certain level (advanced vocational education). Beyond this level, the further advantage of attaining a higher education level is either minor (France) or negative (Germany). For the reemployment prospects of the unemployed, however, the higher the education level, the better. An explanation for this might be that, following job competition arguments, it is always possible to apply for a job below one's qualification level if necessary whereas the reverse is much more difficult. The results seem to indicate that beyond the minimum level of general instruction to be attained, vocational qualifications strongly oriented towards the needs of the labour market offer a better protection against the risk of leaving employment for unemployment than more general education, even of a higher level. However, once unemployed, the level of general education is more important. General qualifications provide more flexibility in the sense that they are suited to a wider range of jobs or sectors of activity for which the unemployed can apply. Thus, though specialised vocational skills make the worker precious to the firm, when the firm happens not to need the specific skills in question, general qualifications permit to adapt more easily to new demand conditions when looking for a job.

This interpretation supports the patterns observed within each country. In Germany, for instance, the best protection against the risk of entering

[47] The impact of education on the various components of the unemployment risk turned out not to vary significantly across genders in neither country. Thus, it seems that the educational degrees of men and women are valued in the same way by the labour market in terms of unemployment risk. We will see in chapter 5 that this is not the case in terms of earnings.

unemployment is given, all else equal, by vocational qualifications of intermediate levels, whereas university graduates face a higher unemployment risk. At the higher education level, upper-tertiary graduates, who receive a more academic training, have a higher unemployment entry risk than lower-tertiary graduates in both countries. The interpretation in terms of general and vocational skills also fits well the patterns observed across countries. The risk of entering unemployment is higher in France than in Germany at lower education levels, but lower for tertiary level graduates, all else equal. In terms of reemployment prospects and of duration of the unemployment spells[48], the chances are better for the French with a lower education level, but French tertiary level graduates have poorer reemployment prospects than their German counterparts. In fact, the German system of vocational education, at the basic and intermediate level, is characterised by its high level of occupational orientation, due to the dual character of the training received, as opposed to the rather theoretical and school-based vocational education in France. At the tertiary level, however, qualifications are more connected to the labour market in France than in Germany, because of the presence of a wide range of *Bac+2* technical tracks at the lower tertiary level and of the *Grandes Ecoles* at the upper tertiary level.

Taking into account the risk of entering unemployment and the recurrence of unemployment spells, the total number of unemployment months an employee can expect within the next three years is higher in Germany than in France at all education levels. However, the gap between France and Germany is largest at the basic and intermediate vocational education level and smallest at the tertiary level. This is because at lower education levels, French workers not only have a higher risk of facing unemployment, but when so, they are confronted to a larger extent than their German counterparts with repeated spells of unemployment. The occurrence of multiple unemployment spells is also higher in France for tertiary level graduates but there, the probability that they incur a first unemployment spell is lower. Based on the total expected number of unemployment months and on a simple index of concentration, the unemployment problem seems altogether to be more acute in France, but is more concentrated on low education groups in Germany. This raises the question whether the level of earnings is not too high, at least in the lower part of the earnings distribution, for poorly qualified people to be competitive on the labour market.

To conclude this chapter, the results indicate that the relationship between education and unemployment is complex when considering all the dimensions of the unemployment problem. If the total expected unemployment risk in the sense defined here is taken as an indicator of the performance of the education system in terms of placement on the labour market, given the prevailing labour

---

48 The duration of the unemployment episode is mainly driven by the reemployment prospects, while the exits to non-employment are more seldom and affect only gender differences but not the pattern of dependence on education.

market conditions and all other factors equal, one can conclude that the German education system is overall more efficient than the French one. How one values the different dimensions of the unemployment risk, however, is largely a matter of political and social preferences. Moreover, the analyses revealed both education systems have their relative strengths and weaknesses depending on the dimension of the unemployment considered. The German system of vocational education proved particularly efficient in protecting against job instability compared to the French one, but less efficient in terms of reemployment prospects. Increasing the general education requirements within the vocational tracks might help improve the reemployment prospects and reduce the duration of unemployment there. At the tertiary level, the risk of entering unemployment is particularly high in Germany, especially for upper tertiary level graduates who typically receive a rather academic education. Improving the connection to the labour market could help reducing the unemployment risk. Besides, one could think of expanding the more practically oriented lower tertiary sector, since, as has been seen in the previous chapter, the lower tertiary sector is rather small and a lower tertiary level definitely practically oriented and significantly below the university level such as the French one is missing. Moreover, it seems important to bring people to reach a minimum education level (the *Realschule* degree in Germany and possibly a basic vocational degree at least), since the unemployment problem is very much concentrated on those people without a vocational degree and in Germany, though to a lesser extent, also on those, though having a basic vocational degree, with a too low level of school education (*Hauptschule* at most).

This chapter was only concerned with one aspect of the labour market value of educational credentials, namely unemployment or access to employment, but says nothing about the quality of the employment the educational degrees give access to. This will be the object of the following chapter, in which the measure used to approximate the quality of employment are the earnings drawn from this employment.

5

Education and earnings in France and Germany

It is one of the essential tasks of the education system to endow youths with qualifications which permit them to insert themselves productively in the labour market. Consequently, the extent to which the various educational qualifications give access to employment or protect against the unemployment risk can be viewed as an indicator of the relative performance of the various parts of the education system with respect to this goal. This issue has been examined in detail in the previous chapter. Now, if individuals find employment for the qualifications they acquired within the education system, the question arises how "good" this employment is. Obviously, the quality of the jobs qualifications give access to is a further dimension of their labour market performance. One might think of different indicators for employment quality: the level of responsibility exercised, the prestige of the occupation or the degree of job satisfaction, for instance. A prominent indicator – and the one chosen here – is the earnings individuals obtain from their labour market activity. Such a quantitative indicator has the merit of producing a single quantitative measure of the quality of employment, thus allowing to establish a clear ranking between the qualifications considered within and across countries, while avoiding any subjective appreciation in its definition. Of course, earnings are only one of the possible indicators of labour market success.

The link between education and earnings has been the object of numerous empirical studies in the past few decades, following the development of the human capital theory and the spread of data sets available for research. Nevertheless, a look at the empirical evidence available so far reveals that there is no really comparative research on this subject for France and Germany. The previous chapters, though, showed that France and Germany are interesting to compare in this regard because they have chosen rather different options for their education systems (see chapter 2), in particular concerning the degree to which labour market aspects are taken into consideration. As an example, the German system of vocational education, with the apprenticeship, is more closely linked to the needs of the labour market than the French one, in which general education has a higher priority. Conversely, at the higher education level, the French system is more oriented towards practice than the German one, with the presence of the *Grandes Ecoles* and a variety of practically oriented short tracks. Chapter 4 showed that this different prioritisation at different levels of the education system had implications in terms of unemployment risk, proved more or less efficient in terms of access to and securing of employment. In this chapter, I examine whether similar effects are observable when considering not only access to employment but also the quality of employment as measured by earnings. This seems an important aspect when evaluating the efficiency of the different education systems as providers of qualifications to be employed successfully on the labour market.

To be more specific, the aim of this chapter is to examine the earnings that can be expected, anything else equal, from the completion of various types and levels of qualification produced by the education system in both countries, not only in terms of expected level of earnings, but also in terms of earnings dispersion. Indeed, the risk associated with the educational investment does not only consist in the risk of unemployment treated in chapter 4, but also in a risk in terms of earnings. The higher the dispersion of earnings to be expected from a given education level, the riskier the corresponding educational investment. For instance, two different degrees might lead to a same level of earnings on average, but with a different earnings dispersion. In that case, individuals will not value these degrees in the same way, depending on their risk-averseness. In this study, the residual earnings dispersion, i.e. the variance in earnings that is not explained by the observables, will be considered as a measure of the remaining earnings uncertainty or briefly speaking, as a measure of earnings risk. Thus, this study aims at examining what an individual can expect to earn additionally from the completion of a higher education level, controlling for other factors, but also the extent to which doing so affects the uncertainty of his or her earnings, as measured by the residual earnings dispersion. Judging from the literature, the latter aspect has gained increasing interest in recent years but the empirical evidence is still scarce at the time being, for France and Germany in particular. Analysing the detailed patterns prevailing both within and across countries of the link between educational attainment and earnings level and dispersion, one can elaborate the picture gained in the previous chapter of the education-employment link and on the strengths and weaknesses of either education systems with respect to their performance as providers of employment opportunities.

A specific modelling design has been developed for this purpose. Basically, the econometric model proposed here is an extension of the Mincerian earnings equation derived from the human capital theory (Mincer 1974) to account for sample selection while allowing for multiplicative heteroscedasticity in the error terms at the same time. This model has the distinct advantage to make it possible to compute comparable estimates of the average earnings premium obtained for detailed levels of educational attainment as well as the effect of the various educational qualifications on the earnings risk as measured by the unexplained variance of earnings, while accounting at the same time for the nonrandom selectivity into paid employment. The results can then be interpreted in the light of the insights gained from the previous chapters concerning the features of the respective education systems, the distribution of qualifications as well as the qualification-specific access to employment. Hereby, as in the previous chapters, a particular focus is laid on the examination of gender differences as well as on the distinction between general and vocational education. We had observed in the previous chapter that vocational education, beyond a minimum level of general education, protects comparatively well against the risk of entering unemployment, whereas a higher level of general or academic education is an advantage when looking for reemployment. How do employers value vocational compared to general education in terms of earnings? Since the unemployment risk differs for vocationally oriented qualifications and more general ones, do we find a similar distinction for the earnings risk? Can similar patterns be identified across countries that would highlight further aspects of the education-earnings link? Do further strengths and weaknesses of either system appear when earnings are considered rather than unemployment? How do gender differences look like as regards the education-earnings (risk) link? These are several of the key questions this study aims to answer.

The chapter is structured as follows. In a first step, section 5.1 provides a review of the literature available on this issue. Hereby, the theoretical framework most empirical studies are imbedded in is first presented, before the evidence available for France and Germany is reviewed. Then, in section 5.2, based on comparable French and German micro data sets, the basic features of the relationship between education and earnings are presented in a descriptive analysis of the distribution of earnings, in terms of levels and dispersion. The study then moves up to the econometric analysis. The modelling framework is presented in section 5.3, laying particular emphasis on modelling the selectivity into paid employment, on the one hand, and the dispersion effects, on the other hand. The data sets used for the application of the model as well as the way the variables have been constructed are explained in section 5.4. Finally, the results of the estimations are presented. The presence, the determinants and the impact of the selectivity on the estimated earnings premium and dispersion effect of education are described in section 5.5, whereas the estimated impact of educational attainment in terms of average earnings premium and residual earnings dispersion are presented in section 5.6. Finally, section 5.7 summarises the key findings and draws some conclusions.

5.1 Education and earnings: overview of the literature

5.1.1 Theoretical and empirical background

Most empirical studies that examine the link between education and private earnings are imbedded in the human capital theoretical framework as pioneered by Becker (1964) and Mincer (1974). The basic idea of the human capital theory is that the acquisition of human capital can be viewed as an investment, in analogy to physical capital, in the sense that a current earnings sacrifice or cost is incurred for a future benefit. By human capital, one understands all the productivity-enhancing skills and knowledge that individuals possess, be it measured by school degrees, qualifications or on-the-job experience. According to this theory, an individual's earnings are proportional to his or her productivity and consequently to his or her stock of human capital. The greater one's human capital accumulation is, the greater one's earnings will be. The factor of proportionality, taking account of the costs incurred by the acquisition of human capital, is a measure of the return to human capital investment (Becker 1964).

The stock of human capital at a given age can be viewed as the sum of all the skills acquired until this age, minus depreciation. The investment decision at one age is not necessarily dichotomous – invest or not invest – but more or less time and effort can be devoted to the acquisition of human capital. Thus, one can go to school full-time, but also part-time, or take an adult education course or train on the job. Ben-Porath (1967) has first tackled the issue of the distribution of the investment in human capital over the life cycle. Essentially, he assumes that individuals behave much like firms in their production decisions. In each year of their life, they invest in human capital up to the point that marginal cost equals the present value of marginal benefit[1] (see also section 3.2.1 as well as section 3.3.1). The costs consist primarily of the foregone earnings arising from the time diverted from the labour market to acquire the incremental human capital unit, but there can also be direct costs (e.g. purchase of books, tuition fees etc.). The benefits are equal to the present value of the stream of extra earnings obtainable from an incremental unit of human capital. The stream of wages goes on until retirement. Due to this finite time horizon, the present value of a unit of human capital is greater for younger than for older workers, since the latter have fewer years left than the formers to reap the benefits of their investments. This leads to a greater human capital accumulation at young ages and hence to a concave earnings profile (Ben-Porath 1967, Polachek and Siebert 1993). In the initial phase of the life-cycle, individuals literally devote all their time to human

[1] Note that not all individuals have the same marginal cost and marginal benefit functions. For instance, more able people will presumably find it less time-consuming and therefore less costly to produce human capital. This implies that human capital investment differs among individuals due to differences in either return or cost conditions, or in the discount rate.

capital investment (schooling stage). This specialisation occurs because the investment is more profitable due to the long remaining time horizon to reap the benefit of the investment as well as because the opportunity costs are particularly low at younger ages since child work is poorly remunerated if not forbidden.

The early empirical studies on education and earnings or on investment in education (e.g. Hanoch 1967) rely on statistical earnings functions, where the earnings are related to schooling and other factors according to a function dictated by the data at the disposal of the researcher. A major development in the literature was brought by Mincer (1974), who sought to establish a theoretical foundation to the empirical earnings function. The aim was to integrate the theories of investment in education and on-the-job training pioneered by Becker (1964) within an empirical framework compatible with more formal models of human capital accumulation such as the Ben-Porath (1967) model. Mincer (1974) derives on theoretical grounds a human capital earnings function which has the advantage of being easily estimable empirically and thereby enhance the empirical content of the theory. The standard Mincer function is of the following form (see the formal presentation in Willis (1986) or in Franz (1999), or Heckman, Lochner and Todd (2003) for alternative presentations of the Mincer earnings equation):

$$\ln y = \beta_0 + \beta_1 s + \beta_2 x + \beta_3 x^2 + u \tag{5.1}$$

where y represents the earnings, s the years of schooling completed and x the years of work experience. Assuming that the whole cost is limited to the opportunity cost of time diverted from the labour market, the schooling coefficient β_1 provides an estimate of the rate of return to education, assumed to be constant in this specification. The concavity of the observed earnings profiles is captured by the quadratic form of the experience variable, the coefficients β_2 and β_3 being positive and negative respectively. Most empirical studies on education and earnings are more or less direct applications of the Mincer's earnings equation. Much effort has been put in dealing with the econometric problems raised by this specification (e.g. Griliches 1977), such as self-selection in education (e.g. Willis and Rosen 1979), the causality problem of the interpretation of the effect of education on earnings (e.g. Card 1998) or more recently the heterogeneity in the return to education (e.g. Belzil and Jörgen 2001).

5.1.2 Empirical evidence for France and Germany

Germany

The empirical literature on the link between education and earnings in Germany until the late 1990s has been reviewed by Lauer and Steiner (1999). In

Germany, the first study directly concerned with the link between education and wages is probably that of Weißhuhn and Clement (1983), who examined the distribution of earnings in connection with the qualification structure. Furthermore, Bellmann, Reinberg and Tessaring (1994) analysed the impact of educational expansion on the distribution of personal income.

As noted in Lauer and Steiner (1999), the bulk of the empirical literature available until the late 1990s does not focus explicitly on the link between education and wages but rather on the wage structure and its determinants as well as on wage differentials between groups of workers or industries. These studies have another focus of interest than education but education appears as one determinant of wages among others. Steiner and Wagner (1998), for instance, analyse changes in earnings inequality in West Germany and thereby comment the impact of human capital variables such as education and labour market experience. The sectoral distribution of wages has also been the object of several studies, such as Hübler and Gerlach (1990) or later on Dustmann and van Soest (1998), who examine wage differentials between private and public sectors. Other papers have a rather methodological focus, like the article by Wagner and Lorenz (1988), who assess the impact of self-election and unobservable heterogeneity on wages.

At the beginning of the 21st century, the link between education and wages seems to have gained renewed interest. Lauer and Steiner (2001), for instance, focus on the returns to education in West Germany, and in a previous paper, Lauer (2000) analyse the extent to which human capital variables contribute to explaining the observed wage differential between West German men and women. The heterogeneity of the returns to education has gained increasing interest in recent years, both from a methodological and from an empirical point of view. Schnabel and Schnabel (2002), for instance use a correlated random-effects model to estimate the average return of a schooling year and its heterogeneity. Thereby, the return itself is modelled as a function of family background. The return to an additional schooling year is found to differ across individuals from different social backgrounds. Prasad (2000) also examines the heterogeneity of the returns to education though based on a different methodology, namely quantile regressions. Generally speaking, the results indicate that the return to one extra schooling year decreases as we move up along the wage distribution. However, differentiating according to educational groups allows for a more differentiated view. The return to a university degree is found to increase along with the wage distribution, whereas the return to a vocational degree seems to decrease as we move up the wage distribution. A further study that uses quantile regression is that of Pereira and Martins (2000), which is mentioned below because it includes France as well as Germany.

France

The empirical literature on the link between education and earnings in France until the late 1990s has been reviewed by Guille and Skalli (1999). In France, the analysis of the relationship between education and wages has a long tradition, not least thanks to the availability of microdata sets suited to such studies (e.g. *Emploi* survey, FQP survey, see description in section 2.3.1). The first extensive analysis based on Mincerian earnings equations was realised by Riboud (1978). The author analyses the role of initial and post-initial education as well as labour market experience and household characteristics as determinants of private earnings and points to some econometric problems associated with the estimation of Mincer-type earnings functions, in particular the possible endogeneity of schooling. Later on, Guillotin and Sevestre (1994) also deal with the problem of the endogeneity of schooling and compare various estimation techniques and their effect on the estimated return to education. They find that the estimated return is higher when correcting for educational endogeneity with instrumental variable techniques. Furthermore, the authors underline the importance of unobserved heterogeneity for the determination of the link between education and earnings. The same conclusion is drawn by Goux and Maurin (1994), who analyse the link between education, experience and wages. As Guillotin and Sevestre (1994), they show that individual fixed effects do not only affect wages, but also condition the impact of observables on wages.

Other French studies have a specific focus of interest. Jarousse and Mingat (1986), for instance, address the question whether the return to education remunerates the skills acquired at school or whether education rather acts as a screening device for the employers to assess the potential of the job applicants (Spence 1973). This issue has also been examined by Skalli (2001)[2]. The authors of both studies find no strong evidence of screening and some evidence of sheepskin effects. Other studies are concerned with differences across groups of workers. Lhéritier (1992), for instance, compares the earnings premium for education for various subsamples of workers depending on personal (e.g. gender) and employers' characteristics (e.g. industry, occupation). Differences between men and women have been the object of a certain number of analyses, e.g. Sofer (1990) or Simonnet (1996). Among the few studies that analyse the link between education and earnings dispersion for France, Atkinson et al. (2001) observe a larger earnings dispersion at both ends of the educational distribution: among the unskilled and among the tertiary education graduates. Thus, the earnings dispersion seems not to be constant across educational groups. This issue, however, has rarely been investigated.

---

[2] Both studies distinguish between the number of schooling years theoretically needed to obtain a degree and the actual number of schooling years needed, the difference providing a signal of ability. They also distinguish between graduating and non-graduating years, the latter enhancing the individual's knowledge but being possibly less remunerated (so-called sheepskin effects).

French-German comparisons

There are very few comparisons of France and Germany on this topic. Among the exceptions, the study of Kaukewitsch and Rouault (1998) should be mentioned, though the analysis is mainly based on earnings functions including occupation levels rather than education levels. Kaukewitsch and Rouault (1998) realise a comparison of wage hierarchies in France and West Germany for 1995. They report that gross average hourly wages are about 25 percent higher in Germany than in France. While French young workers earn less than West German young workers, the opposite is observed for old workers[3]. Compared to their French counterparts, blue-collar workers earn more and white-collar workers less in Germany. The gender wage gap is found to be larger in Germany than in France.

Another comparison of France and Germany is that of Brauns et al. (1997), though it does not deal with earnings but rather with social class position. The authors analyse for Germany, France, the United Kingdom, and Hungary the impact of educational expansion on labour market returns measured by the rate of access to better social class positions. The authors conclude that higher education yields a higher return in France and Germany compared to the UK, where access to tertiary education is less restrictive. The study points to large differences between France and Germany when distinguishing between general and vocational education. In Germany, vocational qualifications appear to be a crucial prerequisite not only to enter the labour market, but also to get employed in skilled work positions, whereas in France, general qualifications on the maturity level at least are essential.

Recently, in the book edited by Harmon, Walker and Westergaard-Nielsen (2001), Guille and Skalli (2001) and Lauer and Steiner (2001) have conducted an analysis of the returns to education in France and Germany respectively, using the same methodology for the purpose of a cross-country comparison of European countries. The results of these studies can be summarised as follows. Based on the most parsimonious specification of Mincer's earnings function[4], the return to education is found to be higher for women than for men in the 1990s, in France and in Germany alike, though the gender gap is larger in Germany. However, the gender gap in the return to education is smaller when controlling for further explanatory factors. Moreover, a declining trend is observed in France since the 1970s, whereas in Germany, the returns to education prove to have remained stable since the mid-1980s.

Concerning the distribution of the returns to education, the only study comparing (among other countries) France and Germany known at this stage is the article by Pereira and Martins (2000), which relies on quantile regressions. Based on a very parsimonious specification of the earnings equation,

[3] This pattern of age-earnings profile seems to be a French peculiarity (see Baudelot and Gollac 1997).

[4] This parsimonious specification makes it possible to estimate exactly the same equation for a wide range of countries.

again, to ensure comparability across countries, the returns to one year of additional schooling appears to increase as we move up the wage distribution in Germany, whereas it is lower at higher quantiles in France. Measuring education in terms of schooling years, however, does not permit to make a differentiated analysis of the link between precise educational attainment and earnings risk.

On the whole, the observation of the empirical evidence available so far reveals that there is no comparative research for France and Germany on the precise link between different types and levels of education and earnings level and dispersion. As argued in the introduction, however, comparing in a detailed manner the way the qualifications produced by the respective education systems in France and Germany are rewarded by the labour market could give further insights with respect to the assessment of their respective performance in terms of employment opportunities. Moreover, most available studies assess the average returns to education and rare are the studies that examine the impact of education in terms of earnings dispersion. The unemployment risk associated with educational achievement has been examined in chapter 4, but educational investments also involve a risk in terms of earnings. The higher the dispersion of earnings to be expected from a given education level, the riskier the corresponding educational investment will be. The present chapter therefore aims at providing some evidence on the relative labour market reward and its riskiness for different types and levels of qualifications, taking France and Germany as benchmarks. Analysing the patterns observed both within and across countries, given the knowledge of the skills produced by both education systems acquired in the previous chapters, is expected to clarify the relationship between types of qualification and labour market success and identify the strengths and weaknesses of either education systems.

Note that the empirical literature traditionally speaks of "return" to education, which is correct only under the assumption that the whole cost of acquiring schooling is reduced to the opportunity cost of time diverted from the labour market. Actually, the acquisition of further education is likely to entail other costs than mere opportunity costs (books, transportation, tuition fees, computer etc.). Therefore, in the remainder of this chapter, I will rather speak of "earnings premium" for education, since this expression does not wrongly suggest that costs have been considered and that the premium can be interpreted as a return.

5.2 Distribution of earnings

To start the empirical analysis, let us first examine the distribution of earnings depending on educational attainment in both countries. The level of educational attainment is defined by a combination of the highest degrees obtained in general and vocational education according to the typology established in section 2.3. As in chapter 4, only a summary table is reported here as a reminder (table 5.1).

Table 5.1. Typology of educational attainment – reminder

	Highest degree obtained
Level 1	**No vocational qualification**
10	No degree
11	Lower secondary education
12	Intermediate secondary education
Level 2	**Basic vocational qualification**
20	No or lower secondary education + basic vocational degree
21	Intermediate secondary education + basic vocational degree
Level 3	**Intermediate qualification**
30	Intermediate vocational degree
31	Vocational maturity certificate
32	General maturity certificate
33	General maturity certificate + vocational degree
Level 4	**Tertiary level qualification**
40	Lower tertiary education
41	Upper tertiary education

Log gross hourly earnings give a measure of how the human capital is rewarded on the labour market, following Mincer (1974). A net measure of earnings would be inappropriate for this study because the aim is here to have an indicator of the individual reward to one's qualification. Thus, an individual measure of earnings is needed here. Net earnings depend instead on the composition of the household since in France like in Germany, the household is the unit of taxation. Moreover, the taxation, and therefore net earnings, also depend on the existence of other sources of income than labour earnings and therefore provide a distorted measure of what employers are ready to pay for the work of individuals. Hourly earnings are considered here, rather than for instance monthly or annual earnings, because the latter measures would introduce a distortion in the measure of the labour market reward of education if the amount of work offered differs across individuals or across countries depending on their education (e.g. if higher educated work more often full-time). Thus, the gross hourly earnings can be considered as a measure of the value employers attach to one hour of work.

For both countries, the gross hourly earnings measure is computed from the gross monthly earnings perceived in the month preceding the interview[5], expressed in Euros, divided by the number of hours worked in that month.

[5] In the *Emploi* survey, gross monthly earnings are given without the social security contributions paid by the employee, unlike in the GSOEP data. In order to make

Irregular payments from the previous year like a 13th month pay or a bonus have been added to the gross earnings proportionally. Following Mincer (1974), the logarithm of this measure of earnings is the outcome of interest in this econometric study.

Table 5.2. Delimitation of the working samples drawn from the GSOEP and the *Emploi* data sets, wave 2000

	Germany		France	
	Observ.	**(%)**	**Observ.**	**(%)**
Total	22,909		121,474	
Without:				
East German	18,942	(-21.9)	-	
Foreigners*	16,742	(-11.6)	115,400	(-5.0)
Beyond 55	12,539	(-25.1)	80,203	(-30.5)
Below 25	10,671	(-14.9)	70,578	(-12.0)
Education missing	10,628	(-0.4)	69,872	(-0.1)
Monthly earnings missing	7,216	(-32.1)	49,678	(-28.9)
Working hours missing	6,818	(-5.5)	45,256	(-8.9)
Working hours > 60	6,777	(-0.6)	44,940	(-0.7)
Working hours < 15	5,219	(-22.1)	43,996	(-2.1)

* Foreigners born abroad only. The sample of foreigners is oversampled in the GSOEP data (see Haisken-DeNew and Frick 2000).

The data sets used for the analysis are the *Emploi* survey for France and the GSOEP data for Germany (see the description of these data sets in section 2.3.1). Table 5.2 reports the original number of observations available in the data for the wave 2000 as well as the remaining number of observations after certain population groups have been successively dropped from the sample. The percentage values in table 5.2 indicate for each step of the sample delimitation by how much the sample has been further reduced by the exclusion of the group considered. The motivation for the exclusion of certain population groups is the same as in section 3.1. The only difference is that I focus here on individuals aged below 55 in order to avoid the problems related to (early) retirement and that those individuals for which the earnings are missing, of course, fall out of the sample. Moreover, I focus on regular employment and therefore exclude the minimally employed (below 15 work hours a week) as well as those individuals who report working more than 60 hours a week as a regular working time since the latter does not seem very plausible.

figures comparable, the French earnings data were augmented by 20 percent, which corresponds to the level of social security contributions (see Kaukewitsch and Rouault 1998).

5.2.1 Structure by education

Figure 5.1 depicts the distribution of average log gross hourly earnings (reported as "mean" in the graph) across education levels in France and Germany as well as their variance ("var", for which the scale is indicated on the secondary axis) in 2000. Figure D.1 and figure D.2 in appendix D give additional details on the developments of earnings by education level over the 1990s, based on the one-digit educational scale[6].

Fig. 5.1. Gross hourly earnings by detailed education level (2000)

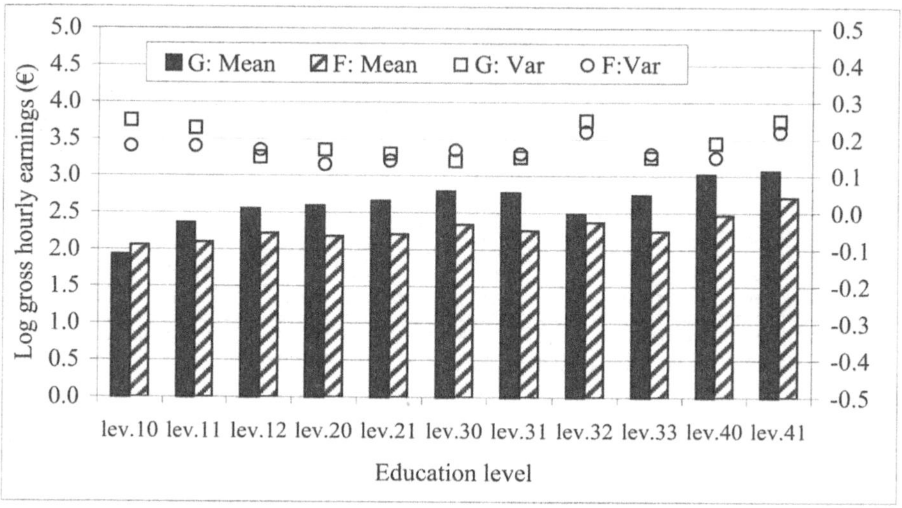

The main elements can be summarised as follows:

- The average earnings are higher in Germany than in France at all education levels.

  The only exception are individuals with level 10 education, i.e. without any degree, for which the earnings are slightly higher in France, though minimally[7]. This might be an effect of the French minimum wage. The gap between German and French earnings is largest at the intermediate education level 3 (except for level 32, i.e. general maturity degree holders) and level 40 (lower tertiary education).

[6] The earnings in the years preceding the introduction of the Euro have been converted in Ecus. The earnings have then been deflated on the basis of the consumer price index so that all earnings are expressed in prices of 2000.

[7] Note, however, that this category comprises almost 18 percent of the population in France in 2000, against less than 1 percent in Germany (see table 3.7 in section 3.1.2).

- The log earnings increase with the education level but irregularly.

  In both countries, individuals with no degree at all (level 10) have the lowest earnings, individuals with a tertiary level degree the highest earnings. Between these extremes, however, the progression of average earnings is not monotonous. The discriminating power of education is stronger in Germany than in France.

- The variance of earnings is higher at low qualification levels but also at university levels, while it is lowest for basic and advanced vocational qualifications.

  This is true in both countries. Interestingly, general maturity graduates who do not possess any vocational qualification show to have a particularly high earnings dispersion in both countries. Thus, it seems that vocational qualifications, as opposed to general qualifications, are associated with a lower variance of earnings. This will be further analysed in the subsequent econometric analysis.

- The variance of earnings tends to be slightly higher in Germany than in France, especially for individuals with a very low qualification level (level 10 or 11).

5.2.2 Gender differences

Let us now have a look at gender differences in the distribution of gross hourly earnings. Figure 5.2 depicts the mean (primary axis) and variance (secondary axis) of log hourly earnings in France and Germany overall as well as separately for men and women. Then, figures 5.3 and 5.4 show for men and women in each country how earnings depend on education. The following features emerge from the graphs:

- Both men and women have higher earnings in Germany than in France, but the country gap is larger for men than for women.

- Men receive overall higher earnings than women in both countries, but the gender gap is significantly larger in Germany than in France.

  As figures D.3 and D.4 in appendix D show, the earnings gap between men and women has remained constant throughout the 1990s in both countries.

- The overall variance of earnings is higher in Germany than in France.

- The variance of earnings is higher for women than for men in both countries, but particularly in Germany.

  As a result, the earnings variance is rather similar for French and German men (it is even slightly higher for French men), but it is much higher for German women than for French women.

Fig. 5.2. Gross hourly earnings by gender (2000)

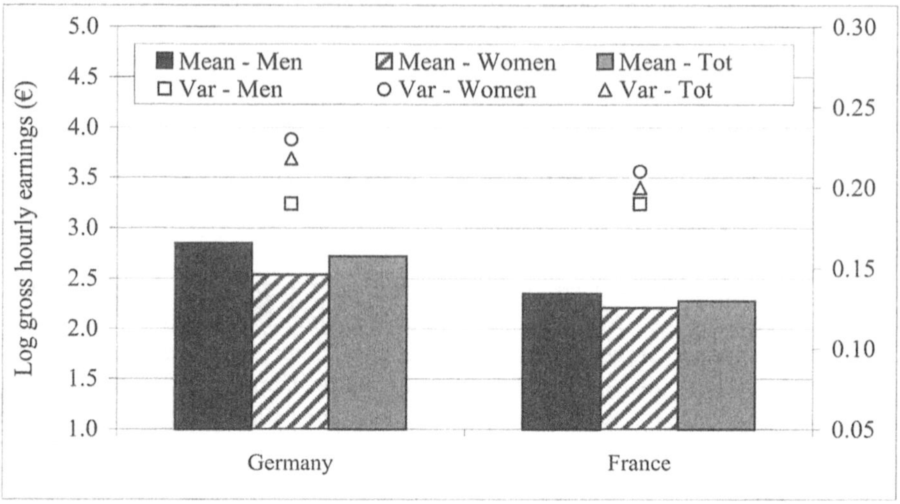

- In both countries, men earn more than women at given education levels but the gender gap is larger in Germany than in France at most levels of educational attainment.

  Thus, part of the overall gender gap earnings is due to differences in the educational attainment[8], part is due to earnings differences by given levels of educational attainment.

- In Germany, women have a higher earnings dispersion than men at lower education levels, but a lower earnings dispersion at higher education levels.

  Thus, poorly qualified women (below level 21, which corresponds to *Realschule* degree plus a basic vocational training) not only perceive lower hourly earnings than their male counterparts but also face a significantly higher earnings dispersion. However, when they have a better education level, in particular beyond the maturity certificate, their earnings dispersion becomes lower than that of men.

- In France, the variance of earnings dispersion of women is close to that of men at most education levels.

  Only for levels 30 and 32/33 (intermediate vocational or general maturity degree) do women enjoy a significantly lower earnings dispersion than men.

[8] Remember from chapter 3 that the advantage of men in terms of educational attainment is much more marked in Germany than in France. For instance, the completion rate of tertiary level degrees widely differs across genders in Germany in favour of men, whereas it is rather close for French men and women (see section 3.1.2).

Fig. 5.3. Gross hourly earnings by education level and gender (2000) – Germany

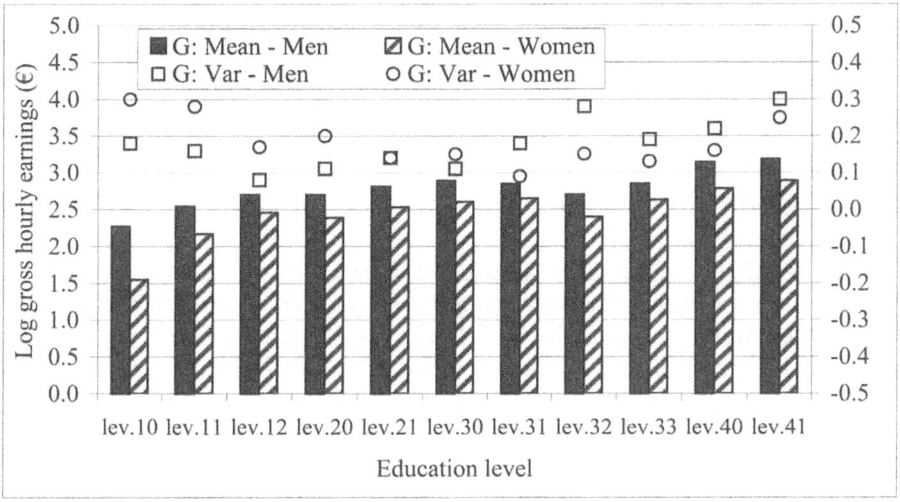

Fig. 5.4. Gross hourly earnings by education level and gender (2000) – France

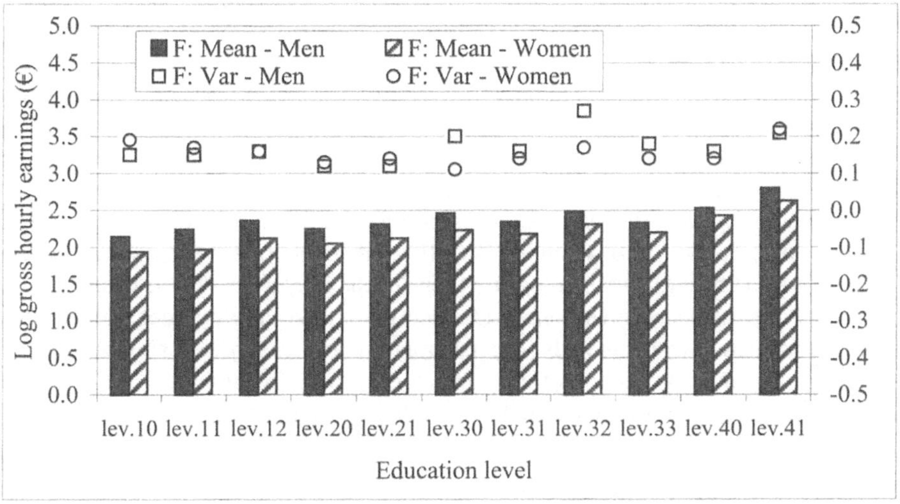

Thus, the overall variance of female earnings observed in figure 5.2 rather stems from a stronger dispersion of the educational attainment than from a higher dispersion of earnings by given education level.

Overall, the descriptive analysis provided first evidence that not only the level of earnings varies across education but also their variance. Moreover, different patterns prevail for men and women in both countries and differences are observed between France and Germany in this respect. Analysing in more detail the similarities and differences in the patterns observed in France and Germany therefore promises to provide further insights into the impact of the different types and levels of education on the level and variance of earnings as well as to uncover more precisely the nature of gender differences in this respect.

5.3 Modelling framework

The descriptive analysis in section 5.2 provided a first overview of the relationship between education, gender and earnings in France and Germany. However, the findings might be driven by some other factors, not accounted for in such a descriptive analysis, that affect both earnings and education. The next step of the study is therefore to investigate how educational attainment is rewarded by the labour market as measured by gross hourly earnings, abstracting from the other factors that might affect earnings and education. Doing so, one can try and isolate what I call here the earnings premium for education, i.e. the effect of attaining a specific education level on the earnings prospects, anything else being equal. Particular efforts have been put in modelling not only the average effect of education on earnings, but also its impact in terms of earnings dispersion. The latter aspect, as has been mentioned in section 5.1.2, has been relatively little investigated in the literature until now.

Besides, chapter 4 has shown that there are substantial differences between France and Germany in the access to employment, regarding both labour force participation and the incidence of unemployment. Moreover, the way labour force participation and unemployment incidence depend on education and gender proved to differ too. As a result, the employment propensity of French and German men and women with different levels of educational attainment exhibits a different pattern (see further details in chapter 4 and in section 5.5). Therefore, neglecting the effect of selectivity into employment, which conditions whether we observe labour earnings, could bias the estimated earnings premium for education or its effect on earnings dispersion. This is why the selectivity into employment will be explicitly modelled here.

5.3.1 A sample selection model

The first step of the model development consists in using a standard extension of Mincer's model (Mincer 1974) presented in equation (5.1) so as to take selectivity into employment into account. Let the model be defined as follows:

$$\begin{aligned} \ln y_{1i} &= x_i\beta + \varepsilon_{1i} && \text{if} \quad y_{2i}^* > 0 \\ \ln y_{1i} &= \text{not observed} && \text{if} \quad y_{2i}^* \leq 0 \end{aligned} \tag{5.2}$$

$$\begin{aligned} y_{2i}^* &= z_i\gamma + \varepsilon_{2i} \\ y_{2i} &= 1 \quad \text{if} \quad y_{2i}^* > 0 \\ y_{2i} &= 0 \quad \text{if} \quad y_{2i}^* \leq 0 \end{aligned} \tag{5.3}$$

y_{1i} is the variable indicating the earnings perceived by individual i, $i \in \{1...N\}$. y_{1i} is assumed to be a linear function of some human capital variables contained in the vector x_i[9] and some unobserved component ε_{1i}. β is the vector of coefficients – to be estimated – that describe the way the explanatory variables affect the expected earnings. The earnings can only be observed for people who actually receive earnings, which is indicated by the binary variable y_{2i}, which takes the value 1 if the earnings of individual i are observed and 0 otherwise. y_{2i}^* is the corresponding latent – continuous – variable which describes the propensity to be selected in the sample of observations for which earnings are observed. The selection propensity depends in a linear way on some variables contained in the vector z_i, the effect of which being captured by the coefficient vector γ, and on some unobserved factors ε_{2i}.

What I am interested in here is the earnings premium for education, i.e. how much additional earnings a randomly chosen individual with a specific educational attainment would earn, had he attained another – higher – education level, given other characteristics contained in vector x_i. Thus, one can compute for each possible education level the average earnings premium to be expected from attaining this level rather than the level of reference. However, it is unknown what individuals whose earnings we do not observe would earn given their education level and constant other characteristics, would they be working. A problem arises if the population of working people is not a random sample of the whole population. Estimating the earnings premium for different levels of education on the sole basis on the sample of those people for which we actually observe earnings would yield biased estimates in the extent to which this sample is not a random sample of the whole population.

To illustrate this more formally, let us express the conditional expectation of y_{1i}, for all $i \in \{1...N\}$, given x_i and given that y_{1i} is observed, as:

$$E[y_{1i}|x_i, y_{2i}^* > 0|z_i] = x_i\beta + E[\varepsilon_{1i}|\varepsilon_{2i} > -z_i\gamma] \tag{5.4}$$

From this expression, it is obvious that estimating β by ordinary least squares (OLS) yields unbiased results only if $E[\varepsilon_{1i}|\varepsilon_{2i} > -z_i\gamma] = 0$, i.e. if ε_{1i} and ε_{2i} are independent from each other, i.e. only if the selection process is random. If this is not the case, however, the OLS estimates will be biased.

9 Note that this is already an extension of Mincer's original model which assumed that human capital consists of schooling and work experience only. Here, it is assumed that other human capital variables enter the earnings equation in a linearly additive way. Mincer himself applied a similar extension of his own model, included further human capital variables in the earnings equation such as training (Mincer 1989), even if this means that the equation estimated is not strictly derived from the theory.

Therefore, instead of assuming the independence of the error terms of the selection and of the wage equation, I will assume, in the spirit of Heckman (1979), that they are jointly distributed with a bivariate normal distribution of the following form:

$$\begin{pmatrix} \varepsilon_{1i} \\ \varepsilon_{2i} \end{pmatrix} \sim \mathcal{N}\left(\begin{pmatrix} 0 \\ 0 \end{pmatrix}, \begin{pmatrix} \sigma_{1i}^2 & \varrho\sigma_{1i} \\ \varrho\sigma_{1i} & \sigma_{2i}^2 \end{pmatrix} \right) \tag{5.5}$$

where $\mathcal{N}$ denotes the bivariate normal distribution function. ϱ measures the correlation between ε_{1i} and ε_{2i}. This correlation is assumed to be constant across individuals[10]. It can be shown that, given assumption (5.5), the conditional expectation of ε_{1i} given that y_{1i} is observed, is:

$$\begin{aligned} E[\varepsilon_{1i}|\varepsilon_{2i} > -z_i\gamma] &= x_i\beta + \varrho\sigma_{1i}\frac{\phi(-z_i\gamma/\sigma_{2i})}{1-\Phi(-z_i\gamma/\sigma_{2i})} \\ &= x_i\beta + \varrho\sigma_{1i}\frac{\phi(z_i\gamma/\sigma_{2i})}{\Phi(z_i\gamma/\sigma_{2i})} \end{aligned} \tag{5.6}$$

Thus, the OLS regression line of y_1 will be biased upward if $\varrho\sigma_1$ is positive and downward if $\varrho\sigma_1$ is negative, since the ratio $\phi(z_i\gamma/\sigma_{2i})/\Phi(z_i\gamma/\sigma_{2i})$, which is also called the inverse Mills ratio and represents the non-selection hazard, is always positive. The size of the bias depends on the magnitude of the correlation, on the relative variance of the disturbance σ_1, and on the severity of the truncation. There is no bias if the correlation ϱ is zero.

Heckman (1979) suggests a two-step method to estimate such selection models, also called limited information maximum likelihood (LIML). The method consists in first estimating the selection equation using a probit model, then computing a fitted value of the index function of the latent variable $z_i\widehat{\gamma}$. The inverse Mills ratio is then derived as $\phi(z_i\widehat{\gamma}/\widehat{\sigma}_{2i})/\Phi(z_i\widehat{\gamma}/\widehat{\sigma}_{2i})$ and included as an additional regressor in a second-step earnings regression. The coefficient estimated for the inverse Mills ratio is then a measure of $\varrho\sigma_{1i}$ and an estimate of the correlation ϱ can be recovered from this coefficient and the estimated variance of the disturbance $\widehat{\sigma}_{1i}$. The resulting estimates are consistent but not asymptotically efficient. The conventional standard error estimates are inconsistent. Moreover, the normality assumption is necessary to ensure consistency, therefore, this estimator is not more robust than the one-step maximum likelihood estimator or full information maximum likelihood (FIML). Thus, LIML requires the same level of restrictive assumptions than FIML but is not as efficient.

For this reason, it seems preferable to opt for the FIML estimation and this is the approach adopted here. Two types of observations enter the likelihood function of the model described by equations (5.2) and (5.3): first, the observations for which no earnings are observed, second, the observations for which

[10] This assumption will be somewhat relaxed since the correlation will be allowed to differ between men and women (see section 5.5).

earnings are observed. The probability of the former type of observations is given by:

$$Pr(y_{2i}^* \leq 0|z_i) = Pr(\varepsilon_{2i} > -z_i\gamma) \\ = \Phi(-z_i\gamma/\sigma_{2i}) \\ = 1 - \Phi(z_i\gamma/\sigma_{2i}) \tag{5.7}$$

The probability of the latter type of observations is:

$$Pr(y_{1i}|x_i, y_{2i}^* > 0|z_i) = f(y_{1i})Pr(y_{2i}^* > 0|y_{1i}, x_i, z_i) \tag{5.8}$$

$$= f(y_{1i})Pr(\varepsilon_{2i} > -z_i\gamma|\varepsilon_{1i}, x_i, z_i)$$
$$= \frac{1}{\sigma_{1i}}\phi\left(\frac{y_{1i} - x_i\beta}{\sigma_{1i}}\right)\Phi\left(\frac{z_i\gamma + (\varrho/\sigma_{1i})(y_{1i} - x_i\beta)}{\sqrt{\sigma_{2i}^2 - \varrho^2}}\right)$$

Therefore, the likelihood for the complete sample of observations is:

$$\mathcal{L} = \tag{5.9}$$
$$\prod_{i=1}^{n_0} 1 - \Phi(z_i\gamma/\sigma_{2i}) \prod_{i=n_0+1}^{N} \frac{1}{\sigma_{1i}}\phi\left(\frac{y_{1i} - x_i\beta}{\sigma_{1i}}\right)\Phi\left(\frac{z_i\gamma + (\varrho/\sigma_{1i})(y_{1i} - x_i\beta)}{\sqrt{\sigma_{2i}^2 - \varrho^2}}\right)$$

where there are n_0 observations for which earnings are not observed and $N - n_0$ observations for which earnings are observed. The log-likelihood function is thus given by:

$$\ln \mathcal{L} = \sum_{i=1}^{n_0} \ln(1 - \Phi(z_i\gamma/\sigma_{2i})) \tag{5.10}$$
$$+ \sum_{i=n_0+1}^{N} \left[-\ln \sigma_{1i} + \ln \phi\left(\frac{y_{1i} - x_i\beta}{\sigma_{1i}}\right) + \ln \Phi\left(\frac{z_i\gamma + (\varrho/\sigma_{1i})(y_{1i} - x_i\beta)}{\sqrt{\sigma_{2i}^2 - \varrho^2}}\right)\right]$$

5.3.2 Modelling the effect of education on residual earnings dispersion

The sample selection model described above, either in its two-step form originally suggested by Heckman (1979) or the one-step FIML estimator preferred here, requires some further assumptions on the variances in order to be identifiable and estimable empirically. A widely used assumption in the empirical literature is the homoscedasticity of the disturbances, both for the selection and for the main equation. As a result, σ_{1i} simplifies to σ_1 and σ_{2i} to σ_2. Moreover, σ_2 is typically normalised to 1, without loss of generality, because in the probit equation, γ and σ_2 are not separately identified but only the ratio γ/σ_2 is identified.

This makes the estimation far easier from a practical point of view but the homoscedasticity assumption gives rise to some problems in the context of the present study. First, it is well known that in the linear model, the OLS estimator is unbiased and consistent even in the presence of heteroscedasticity, but it is then inefficient and the OLS standard errors computed for the coefficients are incorrect. Therefore, the conventional test statistics based on them are invalid (see among others Johnston and DiNardo (2001), chapter 6). Moreover, here, the earnings equation is not estimated by OLS but the whole model – including both the selection and the earnings equation – is estimated simultaneously by maximum likelihood. As soon as the model is nonlinear, the coefficients themselves are biased in the presence of heteroscedasticity, not only the standard errors. If we take, as an example, the case of the probit equation defined by equation (5.3) and express the scedastic term as a function of the parameters $\sigma_{2i} = \sigma_2 g(z_i)$, then we have:

$$Pr(y_{21} = 1) = \Phi\left(\frac{z_i\gamma/g(z_i)}{\sigma_2}\right) \tag{5.11}$$

It appears clearly that the coefficient vector that would be estimated by a simple probit assuming homescedastic disturbance would mix up the mean effect of the variables z_i captured by γ and the effect that the z_i exert through the scedastic function $g(z_i)$.

One might argue that in most cases, it does not matter whether the variables z_i affect the probability through the regression function or through the scedastic function (Johnston and DiNardo 2001). In the present study, however, it does matter since I precisely aim at distinguishing the effect of the education variables on mean earnings and on the residual variance of earnings. Therefore, the assumption of homoscedasticity of the disturbances will not be made, neither in the selection nor in the earnings equation. Instead, the specification of the model will be adapted to allow the disturbances to be heteroscedastic.

Basically, two types of parametric heteroscedastic models are encountered in the literature: the random coefficient or additive heteroscedasticity model (in the line of Hildreth and Houck 1968) and the multiplicative heteroscedasticity model (building on the original work by Harvey 1976). The random coefficient heteroscedasticity is assumed to be of the form:

$$\sigma_i^2 = t_i\alpha \tag{5.12}$$

Here, the multiplicative heteroscedasticity model is used, which Greene (2000) finds to be a very flexible and general model[11]. Thus, the heteroscedasticity is assumed to be of the form:

[11] The estimation of random coefficients models proves to be extremely time-consuming and therefore only tractable for one random coefficient in practice

$$\sigma_{1i}^2 = exp(x_i^h \beta^h) \qquad (5.13)$$
$$\sigma_{2i}^2 = exp(z_i^h \gamma^h)$$

or equivalently:

$$\ln \sigma_{1i}^2 = x_i^h \beta^h \qquad (5.14)$$
$$\ln \sigma_{2i}^2 = z_i^h \gamma^h$$

The vector x_i^h includes a constant term β_0^h. Thus, if x_i^h contains a set of dummy variables, one of which – the base group – having been left out, then, $exp(\beta_0^h)$ provides an estimator of the disturbance variance for the base group and the other coefficients of β^h indicate in which direction and how far the disturbance variance of the other categories deviates from that of the reference group. For σ_{2i}^2 to be normalisable to 1 – failing which the model is not identified – z_i^h should not include a constant term. σ_{1i}^2 and σ_{1i}^2 can be replaced by the expressions (5.14) in the log-likelihood function defined in equation (5.10).

The maximisation of the resulting log-likelihood function permits to get estimates of all the parameters of this model[12]. In particular, it permits to compute estimates of the average earnings premium for education (see further details in section 5.6.2). Indeed, if a set of dummy variables describing the level of educational attainment is comprised in the vector of explanatory variables x_i, the corresponding parameter estimates will give an estimate of the average premia obtained for the respective educational attainment compared to a reference educational group. Moreover, the model makes it possible to account for two types of heterogeneity in the earnings premium for education. First, the heterogeneity due to observable characteristics can be captured by interacting the education dummies contained in x_i with the relevant characteristics[13]. Second, the heterogeneity due to unobserved factors can be captured by including the education variables in the scedastic function. This way, one can estimate how the residual earnings dispersion varies across education levels[14]. Thus, the model allows us to calculate the average earnings premia drawn from different education levels as well as the effect of education on unexplained earnings dispersion, while differentiating both aspects according to selected observed characteristics such as gender.

(see Harmon, Hogan and Walker (2003) for an application of a random coefficients model for the United Kingdom to estimate the level and the dispersion of the return to one year of schooling). Because I want to differentiate between different education levels and also across genders, I prefer the multiplicative heteroscedasticity model here.

12 See in Gould and Sribney (1999) how to programme maximum likelihood estimations with the software package Stata.

13 Here, the heterogeneity across genders in the average earnings premium for education will be tested formally.

14 Here also, the differences between men and women in the impact of education on residual earnings dispersion will be tested formally. See further details in section 5.6.3

5.4 Data and variables

As mentioned at the beginning of section 5.2, the empirical analysis is based on a sample of individuals (nationals or born in the respective country) aged 25 to 55 drawn from the *Emploi* survey for France and from the GSOEP data for Germany (see further details on sample delimitation in section 5.2 and a description of the GSOEP and *Emploi* data sets in section 2.3.1). The econometric analysis uses the waves 1991 to 2000, since no continuous measure of earnings is available before this date in the French data set[15]. The estimation sample contains about 38,800 observations (8,000 individuals) for Germany, of which approximately 23,700 have earnings (4,900 individuals). For France, the sample entails 654,700 observations on 330,283 individuals. Of the total number of observations, 405,000 contain information on labour earnings, which covers about 219,400 individuals (see statistics reported at the bottom of table 5.4 and table 5.6 as well as in table 5.2).

The dependent variable for equation (5.2) is the logarithm of the gross hourly earnings such as defined at the beginning of section 5.2. The dependent variable for equation (5.3) is a binary variable which takes the value 1 if the information on gross hourly earnings is not missing and 0 otherwise.

Table 5.3 provides a synthetic overview of the explanatory variables used for the econometric analysis, distinguishing between variables included in both the selection and the earnings equation, variables included only in the earnings equation and variables included only in the selection equation. Special attention has been paid to using the same variables for both countries and defining them in a way as similar as possible. Summary statistics for all the variables used are provided in appendix (table D.1, appendix D).

The primary explanatory variable of interest here is of course the education level, since the aim is to estimate the effect of education on average earnings as well as earnings dispersion. The education variable is defined as a set of dummy variables, as explained in section 5.2 (see the reminder table 5.1 and additional information in chapter 2). Individuals with an educational attainment of level 10 or 11 (no degree at all or only a school degree of the lowest level) constitute the reference category. Another variable of crucial interest for the present analysis is the sex of individuals, since differences between men and women in the earnings premium for education and in the effect of education on unexplained earnings dispersion shall be examined. Thus, education and gender, as well as interactions between them, are the key variables

[15] Because both the GSOEP and the *Emploi* survey are longitudinal data sets, one might think of exploiting the repeated observations on the same individuals over time to isolate individual effects. However, random effects estimates are inconsistent because the individual effects are correlated with the regressors and fixed effect or first differences estimators cannot be used because gender and education are basically time-invariant. If one assumes that the unobserved individual factors have a similar effect in both countries, however, the comparison of the results across countries should be hardly affected.

Table 5.3. Explanatory variables

Variables	Definition
Variables common to both the selection and the earnings equation	
Education level	10 categories: level 10/11; level 12; level 20; level 21; level 30; level 31; level 32; level 33; level 40; level 41 (see table 5.1)
Sex	2 categories: female; male
Age	polynome: age; age squared
Current quarter	Germany: 3 categories: 1st quarter (January to March); 2nd quarter (April to June); 3rd/4th quarter (July to December) France: 2 categories: 1st quarter (January to March); 2nd/4th quarter (April to December)
Time trend	10 year dummies: 1991 to 2000
Variables specific to the earnings equation	
Tenure	polynome: years of tenure; years of tenure squared
Firm size	6 categories: <5 employees; 5-19 employees; 20-199 employees; 200-1,999 employees; $\geq 2{,}000$ employees; missing
Industry	9 categories: industry (mechanical and electrical engineering, stone, iron, steel and chemical industry, paper, textile, food industry, other); agriculture/energy (agriculture, forestry, fishing, energy, mining); construction; trade (wholesale and retail); banking (banking, insurance, real estate); transports (transports and communications); private services (personal services, eating and drinking, other services to professionals or private households); public services (welfare services, government, non-profit institutions, other); missing
Fixed-term contract	2 categories: not fixed term; fixed term
Part-time employment	2 categories: full-time; part-time
Public employment	2 categories: private employment; public employment
Father's occupation	7 categories: worker; farmer; self-employed; senior manager; middle-level manager; employee; missing
Variables specific to the selection equation	
Marital status	2 categories: married; not married
Number and age of children below 18	10 categories: no children; 1 child aged 6-17; 1 child aged 3-5; 1 child aged 0-2; 2 children, youngest aged 6-17; 2 children, youngest aged 3-5; 2 children, youngest aged 0-2; more than 2 children, youngest aged 6-17; more than 2 children, youngest aged 3-5; more than 2 children, youngest aged 0-2

to be continued...

...table 5.3 continued

Variables	Definition
Variables specific to the selection equation (continued)	
Partner's education	4 categories: level 1; level 2; level 3; level 4 (see table 5.1)
Partner's earnings	gross monthly earnings (prices of 2000)
No info on partner's earnings	2 categories: information; no information
No partner	2 categories: partner; no partner
Home ownership	2 categories: owner of the house/appartment living in (himself or spouse); not owner
City size	3 categories: fewer than 20,000 inhabitants; between 20 and 100,000 inhabitants; 100,000 inhabitants or more

included in the earnings equation, both in the main equation to determine the average earnings premium for education and in the scedastic equation to examine how the unexplained earnings variance depends on education and whether this effect depends on gender. Further key variables, age and a yearly trend, have been added in the scedastic function to clean the estimates from these effects[16].

Further control variables have been included in the earnings equation in order to control for observed heterogeneity and isolate the labour market reward of education if everything else is equal. In particular, the tenure in the firm, firm size and industry branch as well as the type of working contract (part-time or full-time, fixed-term or unlimited duration, private or public employment) are expected to capture the variation in earnings due to job-related factors. Likewise, the age of the individual as well as the year and the quarter under observation since there might be some seasonal effects[17] should also be accounted for. Moreover, a set of dummy variables depicting father's occupation is intended to capture further heterogeneity in the earnings[18] and

[16] In principle, one could include all explanatory variables of the main equation in the scedastic equation as well, but the number of variables should not be too high to leave enough variation in the scedastic terms. Several experiments with more variables in the scedastic equation showed that the estimates of the impact education are hardly affected, but the estimates become less robust if the number of variables is too high, especially for Germany.

[17] Note that in France, the bulk of the interviews takes place in March or in the first quarter and only a few individuals are interviewed in the second quarter (1.65 percent). In Germany, the majority of interviews takes place in the first quarter also, but a substantial part (about 25 percent) is interviewed in the second quarter and a nonnegligible part (about 8 percent) is interviewed in the second half of the year (see descriptive statistics in table D.1, appendix D).

[18] Schnabel and Schnabel (2002) find out that family background is an important source of heterogeneity in earnings.

to reduce the problems arising from the possible endogeneity of the education variable[19]. These variables have been constructed as defined in table 5.3 and will not be commented further here.

Some of the variables in the earnings equation have also been included in the selection (into employment) equation since they are expected to exert a direct influence on the selection outcome: the education level, the sex and age of the individual as well as the quarter and year under observation. In addition, specific variables on the household composition (marital status as well as number and age of the children below 18 in the household), on the partner (level of education and earnings when there is a partner), on wealth (as proxied by home ownership) and on the local context (city size) have been included as further variables to explain the probability to be involved in paid employment. The validity of these exclusion restrictions will be tested. All the variables are defined in a strictly comparable way for France and Germany, as reported in table 5.3. Many of these variables have also been used in chapter 4 and are defined here in the same way. As for the earnings equation, the model allows for multiplicative heteroscedasticity in the selection equation, whereby the variance in the selection propensity may vary according to the education level of the individuals, possibly in a different way for men and women. Thus, the education dummies, gender, and interactions between gender and education have been included in the scedastic equation of the selection equation, too.

Let us now turn to the estimation results. Both equations (5.3) and (5.2) have been estimated simultaneously as well as the correlation between them through the maximisation of the log-likelihood function (5.10), where both the level and the variance of earnings is allowed to differ by education and gender according to the function (5.14) as described in section 5.3.2. The correlation is allowed to be different for men and women.

5.5 Selectivity into paid employment

In a first step (section 5.5), the results concerning selectivity into paid employment will be presented. Hereby, the aim is less to make a detailed analysis

[19] The endogeneity of schooling in earnings equations and the correction of the bias caused by it has been the object of numerous studies (e.g. Card 2000). However, the literature leads to controversial conclusions as to the optimal correction of the endogeneity problem, one important problem lying in the nonavailability of valid instruments (see Lauer and Steiner 2001; Card 2000; Heckman et al. 2003). Therefore, like in Harmon et al. (2003) education is considered exogenous, conditional on the other explanatory variables. This should be a minor problem here since the focus of the analysis is on comparing the hierarchy and the dispersion of the earnings premia for different education levels across countries rather than determining their absolute levels.

of the patterns of (non-)employment[20] but rather to examine the extent of selectivity and its pattern of dependence on education and gender in so far as this is relevant for the estimates of the link between education and earnings, presented in details in section 5.6.

5.5.1 Specification tests

Table 5.4 presents overall statistics as well as the results of specification tests with respect to the choice of the variables to be included in the selection equation. In this table, only the results of the χ^2-tests[21] conducted jointly on a set of variables[22] have been reported. The statistical significance of separate variables has also been tested in a systematic way but the results appear in the table 5.5.

First of all, the presence of gender differences in the impact exerted by all the variables on the selection into employment has been systematically tested. To this end, the specification was augmented with interaction terms between gender and the explanatory variables. The statistical significance of these interactions has then been tested. As can be seen, most interaction terms with gender are significant for both countries, which means that the determinants of selection into employment differ between men and women. Considering that the extent of labour force participation as well as the incidence of unemployment have been found to differ widely across genders in both countries (see chapter 4), it is not surprising that also the determinants of the employment propensity differ across genders. Looking more into detail, the only sets of interaction terms which were not significant at the 10 percent statistical level at least were those with partner's education, but also with quarter and year under observation for Germany. These interactions have therefore been dropped from the corresponding equation. Further joint tests have been run on the sets of variables themselves and the results reported in table 5.4 indicate that all the variables are highly significant in statistical terms and contribute to explain the selection propensity.

Then, the presence of heteroscedasticity as well as the variables it depends upon have been tested. The test on the null hypothesis of homoscedasticity, i.e. on the hypothesis that all coefficients of all the variables included in the scedastic function are not statistically different from zero, in which case the variance would be normalisable to 1, is strongly rejected for both countries. The education dummy variables are highly significant, but also the female dummy (see table 5.5) as well as the interactions between the female dummy and the education variables. Thus, not only does the average work propensity

[20] An extensive analysis of the education-(un)employment link is the object of chapter 4.

[21] The formula of the χ^2-tests is given in equation (4.13), chapter 4.

[22] The null hypothesis tested here is that the set of variables taken jointly are not significantly different from zero. The figure in parentheses gives the probability to which the null hypothesis can be rejected.

Table 5.4. Joint tests results for selection equation and overall statistics

Null hypothesis	Germany χ^2	Germany $p > \chi^2$	France χ^2	France $p > \chi^2$
Tests on gender interactions (mean effects)				
Female * Education = 0	103.24	(0.00)	1,073.05	(0.00)
Female * Age = 0	23.35	(0.00)	749.56	(0.00)
Female * Number and age children = 0	115.63	(0.00)	1,466.13	(0.00)
Female * Partner's education = 0	1.56	(0.67)	44.76	(0.00)
Female * City size = 0	22.89	(0.00)	39.57	(0.00)
Female * Quarter = 0	3.37	(0.18)		
Female * Year = 0	7.69	(0.57)	30.51	(0.00)
Tests on specific coefficients (mean effects)				
Education = 0	83.50	(0.00)	229.26	(0.00)
Age = 0	63.68	(0.00)	1,813.71	(0.00)
Number and age children = 0	19.48	(0.02)	99.14	(0.00)
Partner's education = 0	16.46	(0.00)	253.11	(0.00)
City size = 0	21.76	(0.00)	1,020.24	(0.00)
Quarter = 0	78.25	(0.00)		
Year = 0	106.19	(0.00)	85.35	(0.00)
Tests on scedastic term (dispersion effects)				
Homoscedasticity: all coefficients = 0	265.71	(0.00)	1,162.98	(0.00)
Female * Education = 0	79.24	(0.00)	167.99	(0.00)
Education = 0	107.77	(0.00)	367.09	(0.00)
Validity of exclusion restrictions				
R^2 test	0.47		0.39	
Overall Wald test	15,452.40	(0.00)	2.2e+05	(0.00)
Wald test selection equation	347.31	(0.00)	11,283.92	(0.00)
Observations	38,756		654,686	
Number of individuals	8,041		330,283	
Log-likelihood	-27,463.72		-540,776.61	

differ across educational groups and genders, anything else being equal, but also the variance of this work propensity.

The overall Wald test, which tests the hypothesis that all the slope coefficients of both equations are jointly insignificant, is strongly rejected. The specific Wald tests for the selection equation also indicate that the variables included in this equation are altogether highly significant. The value of these test statistics is much higher for France, like the log-likelihood in absolute terms, because of the much larger number of observations in the French sample.

Finally, the validity of the exclusion restrictions should be tested. As a matter of fact, there might be some collinearity problems if the variables used for determining the selection into employment are not adequate instruments.

The test used here is the R^2 of an estimation of the inverse Mill's ratio (computed as $\phi(z_i\gamma/\sigma_{2i})/\Phi(z_i\gamma/\sigma_{2i})$ such as in equation (5.6)) on the regressors of the earnings equation. If the R^2 appears to be too high (at levels above 0.70 for instance), this is an indication of the weakness of the exclusion restrictions. Here, the values obtained for R^2 seem reasonable (see Puhani 2000).

5.5.2 Impact of education and gender on the selection into paid employment

Table 5.5 reports the full estimation results for the selection equation. In the upper part of the table, the mean effects are reported, i.e. the coefficients estimated for vector γ (see equation (5.3)). The lower part of the table reports the dispersion effects, i.e. the coefficients estimated for the scedastic function (vector γ^h, see equation (5.13)). Since the focus of the study is on education, this section concentrates on the impact of education, differentiated by gender, on the propensity of selection into paid employment. The effect of the other variables can be read from table 5.5 and will not be further commented here.

Generally speaking, the work propensity seems to increase along with the education level, since the significant coefficients are positive and rather increasing with the education level. As has been shown in section 5.5.1, the effect of educational attainment on the propensity to be engaged in paid employment differs between men and women.

For men, the effect of education can be read directly from the coefficients of the education variables reported in table 5.5. The coefficients are to be interpreted relative to the reference category of men with poor educational attainment (level 10 or 11). In Germany, the probability of being employed for men with level 12 education (*Realschule* degree) does not differ significantly from that of the reference group, but from this level onwards, the work propensity rather increases with education. Anything else equal, it is rather similar for men with a basic or intermediate vocational degree (education level 20 to 30). The attainment of the maturity certificate as the highest degree, being the vocational one (*Fachhochschulreife*) or the general one (*Abitur*) is not associated with a higher employment propensity for men. However, men with a vocational degree in addition to their general maturity certificate are more likely to be observed to work, and even more so men with a tertiary level degree, in particular a university degree. In France also, the work propensity of men rather tends to increase with education. Thus, poorly qualified men (level 10 and 11) have the lowest, tertiary level graduates the highest selection propensity. However, the coefficients are smaller in scope for French men compared to their German counterparts, which indicates that education is less discriminatory as regards access to employment there. Looking more into detail, the employment probabilities of men with education level 12 to 33 turn out to be slightly higher than that of the poorly educated men of the reference group but they do not differ much among each other. Furthermore, there is a kind of threshold at the tertiary level. Higher education male graduates

Table 5.5. Determinants of selection into paid employment

Variable	Germany coef.	(s.e)	France coef.	(s.e)
Mean effects (γ):				
Education (ref.: Level 10/11)				
Level 12	-0.07	(0.07)	0.08**	(0.03)
Level 20	0.34**	(0.09)	0.00	(0.01)
Level 21	0.29**	(0.10)	0.09**	(0.02)
Level 30	0.39**	(0.11)	0.00	(0.04)
Level 31	0.18	(0.11)	0.09*	(0.04)
Level 32	-0.37	(1.25)	0.11**	(0.04)
Level 33	0.64*	(0.25)	0.08	(0.09)
Level 40	0.75**	(0.18)	0.34**	(0.04)
Level 41	0.86**	(0.22)	0.16**	(0.02)
Female * Level 12	1.20**	(0.12)	0.21**	(0.03)
Female * Level 20	0.11	(0.09)	0.23**	(0.01)
Female * Level 21	0.46**	(0.10)	0.32**	(0.02)
Female * Level 30	0.55**	(0.12)	0.36**	(0.04)
Female * Level 31	0.42**	(0.13)	0.50**	(0.04)
Female * Level 32	0.24	(2.27)	0.35**	(0.04)
Female * Level 33	0.07	(0.30)	0.48**	(0.10)
Female * Level 40	0.61**	(0.21)	0.49**	(0.05)
Female * Level 41	0.14	(0.21)	1.00**	(0.04)
Female	-1.61**	(0.50)	-2.75**	(0.10)
Age and marital status				
Age/10	0.24†	(0.12)	0.13**	(0.04)
Age squared/100	-0.07**	(0.02)	-0.01*	(0.00)
Female * Age/10	1.06**	(0.27)	1.23**	(0.05)
Female * Age squared/100	-0.14**	(0.03)	-0.16**	(0.01)
Married	0.13**	(0.04)	0.22**	(0.01)
Female * Married	-0.55**	(0.08)	-0.42**	(0.01)
Number and age of children (ref.: No children)				
One child aged 6-17	-0.05	(0.04)	0.04**	(0.01)
One child aged 3-5	-0.06	(0.06)	0.05**	(0.01)
One child aged 0-2	-0.09	(0.06)	0.09**	(0.01)
Two children, youngest 6-17	-0.07	(0.05)	0.04**	(0.01)
Two children, youngest 3-5	0.00	(0.06)	0.07**	(0.01)
Two children, youngest 0-2	0.02	(0.07)	0.09**	(0.01)
More children, youngest 6-17	-0.22**	(0.08)	0.07**	(0.01)
More children, youngest 3-5	-0.23**	(0.09)	0.06**	(0.02)
More children, youngest 0-2	-0.26**	(0.09)	0.09**	(0.02)
Female * One child aged 6-17	-0.48**	(0.07)	-0.13**	(0.01)
Female * One child aged 3-5	-1.10**	(0.13)	-0.17**	(0.02)

to be continued...

...table 5.5 continued

Variable	Germany coef.	(s.e)	France coef.	(s.e)
Female * One child aged 0-2	-2.22**	(0.22)	-0.29**	(0.02)
Female * Two children, youngest 6-17	-0.77**	(0.10)	-0.27**	(0.01)
Female * Two children, youngest 3-5	-1.66**	(0.17)	-0.43**	(0.02)
Female * Two children, youngest 0-2	-2.86**	(0.27)	-0.68**	(0.02)
Female * More children, youngest 6-17	-1.26**	(0.16)	-0.71**	(0.02)
Female * More children, youngest 3-5	-1.91**	(0.22)	-0.97**	(0.03)
Female * More children, youngest 0-2	-2.88**	(0.31)	-1.26**	(0.04)
Partner's education (ref.: Level 1)				
Level 2	0.06*	(0.03)	0.03**	(0.01)
Level 3	0.04	(0.03)	-0.06**	(0.01)
Level 4	-0.08†	(0.04)	-0.12**	(0.01)
Female * Level 2			-0.02†	(0.01)
Female * Level 3			0.01	(0.01)
Female * Level 4			-0.08**	(0.01)
Partner's earnings				
Gross monthly earnings/1,000	0.01	(0.02)	0.02**	(0.00)
Female * Gross monthly earnings/1,000	-0.05**	(0.02)	-0.02**	(0.00)
No information on partner's earnings	-1.05**	(0.09)	-0.45**	(0.01)
Ownership status (ref.: Not owner)				
Owner	0.19**	(0.03)	0.04**	(0.01)
Female * Owner	-0.31**	(0.05)	-0.15**	(0.01)
City size (ref.: <20,000 inh.)				
20-100,000 inhabitants	0.14**	(0.03)	0.15**	(0.01)
≥100,000 inhabitants	0.14**	(0.03)	0.20**	(0.01)
Female * 20-100,000 inhabitants	-0.22**	(0.05)	-0.06**	(0.01)
Female * ≥100,000 inhabitants	-0.12*	(0.05)	-0.04**	(0.01)
Current quarter (ref.: 1st quarter)				
2nd quarter	-0.20**	(0.03)	-0.11**	(0.02)
3rd/4th quarter	-0.35**	(0.04)		
Female * 2nd quarter			0.19**	(0.03)
Year (ref.: 2000)				
1991	0.46**	(0.05)	-0.08**	(0.01)
1992	0.43**	(0.05)	-0.08**	(0.01)
1993	0.49**	(0.06)	-0.09**	(0.01)
1994	0.47**	(0.05)	-0.09**	(0.01)
1995	0.43**	(0.05)	-0.08**	(0.01)
1996	0.46**	(0.05)	-0.08**	(0.01)
1997	0.45**	(0.05)	-0.08**	(0.01)
1998	0.45**	(0.05)	-0.06**	(0.01)
1999	0.53**	(0.06)	-0.06**	(0.01)

to be continued...

...table 5.5 continued

Variable	**Germany** coef.	(s.e)	**France** coef.	(s.e)
Female * 1991			0.00	(0.02)
Female * 1992			0.02	(0.02)
Female * 1993			0.05**	(0.02)
Female * 1994			0.05**	(0.02)
Female * 1995			0.04*	(0.02)
Female * 1996			0.05**	(0.02)
Female * 1997			0.03†	(0.02)
Female * 1998			0.02	(0.02)
Female * 1999			0.03†	(0.02)
Constant	-0.04	(0.35)	1.10**	(0.07)
Dispersion effects (γ^h):				
Education (ref.: Level 10 or 11)				
Level 12	-0.86**	(0.20)	0.60**	(0.08)
Level 20	0.45*	(0.18)	0.02	(0.04)
Level 21	0.25	(0.21)	0.42**	(0.07)
Level 30	0.52*	(0.21)	0.67**	(0.14)
Level 31	0.04	(0.26)	0.51**	(0.10)
Level 32	2.58	(5.31)	0.93**	(0.12)
Level 33	1.06*	(0.43)	0.96**	(0.28)
Level 40	0.78**	(0.29)	1.08**	(0.09)
Level 41	1.11**	(0.31)	0.73**	(0.07)
Female * Level 12	0.78**	(0.27)	-0.51**	(0.09)
Female * Level 20	-1.01**	(0.22)	-0.09†	(0.05)
Female * Level 21	-0.97**	(0.24)	-0.35**	(0.08)
Female * Level 30	-0.82**	(0.26)	-0.74**	(0.17)
Female * Level 31	-0.10	(0.32)	-0.34**	(0.12)
Female * Level 32	-1.74	(5.33)	-0.67**	(0.13)
Female * Level 33	-1.04*	(0.46)	-0.46	(0.31)
Female * Level 40	-0.46	(0.37)	-0.30**	(0.10)
Female * Level 41	-0.62†	(0.35)	-0.55**	(0.10)
Female	0.97**	(0.21)	0.34**	(0.05)
Age/10	0.01	(0.02)	-0.06**	(0.01)
Trend	-0.02**	(0.00)	0.01**	(0.00)
Correlation selection / earnings equation (ϱ):				
Female	-0.25**	(0.06)	-0.14**	(0.02)
Male	-0.57**	(0.06)	-0.40**	(0.01)
Tests on correlation				
ϱ: Male = Female	14.89	(0.00)	154.10	(0.00)
$\varrho = 0$	97.60	(0.00)	1,318.85	(0.00)

Significance level : † : 10% * : 5% ** : 1%

have a significantly higher probability to be in paid employment than their more poorly educated counterparts, though the effect is not as strong as in Germany.

Overall, the fact of being a woman strongly reduces the probability of being employed in France and in Germany alike, everything else being equal, as can be seen from the negative sign of the female dummy. In both countries, however, the interactions between the female dummy and the education dummies are significant and positive. This means that education has more discriminatory power for women than for men in terms of access to employment. Moreover, the coefficients of the interactions are larger in magnitude for France than for Germany. Thus, the effect of being a woman is as such more strongly negative in France than in Germany, but education increases more strongly the employment participation of women in France[23]. In particular, French women with a university degree of upper tertiary level (level 41) are much more likely to be in paid employment than more poorly educated women.

Education does not only play a role in terms of average propensity to work, but also in terms of remaining or unexplained dispersion of this work propensity, after observable characteristics have been controlled for. Here, the effects are very much different for men and women (see bottom of table 5.5). For men, attaining a higher level of educational attainment increases the unexplained dispersion in the participation propensity, everything else being equal. This is true in both France and Germany. In particular, men with an education level beyond the maturity certificate have a significantly higher residual dispersion in employment participation than more poorly educated men. Being a woman is associated with a higher unexplained dispersion of the propensity to work compared to men, especially in Germany. However, contrary to men, attaining a higher level of educational attainment reduces the unexplained dispersion in the work propensity among women.

To sum up the results, education increases the average propensity of working for men and even more for women, though women have on the whole a lower employment propensity than men, anything else equal. At the same time, education also increases the unexplained variance in the employment propensity of men, whereas it reduces the dispersion for women, though, on the whole, women have a higher unexplained dispersion in their employment propensity.

5.5.3 Presence and impact of selectivity

Since the primary focus of this chapter is on the link between education and earnings (employment issues have been treated in chapter 4), the modelling of

[23] Note that the relative educational attainment of women compared to men is better in France than in Germany (see chapter 3), which contributes to explaining that the labour force participation of women is overall higher in France than in Germany (see also chapter 4).

the selection into paid employment is only of interest if selectivity is at work. This is why the presence of selectivity has been tested. If the selection into paid employment proved not to have an impact on the determinants of earnings, then, the earnings equation could (and should, for efficiency reasons) be estimated on its own. As is reported at the bottom of table 5.5, the hypothesis that the correlation ϱ between the unobserved factors of the selection equation and the earnings equation is zero, i.e. the hypothesis that there is no selectivity effect, is strongly rejected. Thus, it is important to model the selection into employment together with the earnings, otherwise the coefficients might be biased.

Moreover, the correlation between selection into paid employment and earnings was allowed to differ between men and women, since the labour force participation decision is known to differ widely across genders and there is therefore no a priori reason to assume that the correlation with earnings should be the same for men and women. As a matter of fact, a further test shows that the correlation does differ for men and women. This is why a gender specific correlation term has been estimated for both countries. The correlation proves to be highly significant and negative for both men and women and stronger for women than for men in both countries.

Given that there is evidence of selectivity effects affecting the determination of earnings, the question which arises now is whether this selectivity affects the estimates of the effects of education on earnings. To address this issue, the earnings equation has been estimated again without correcting for selectivity bias. The whole estimation results are given in table D.4 in appendix D and will not be further commented here. Then, the average earnings premia and the earnings dispersion effects of education, as well as their standard errors have been computed in the same way as in sections 5.6.2 and 5.6.3 on the basis of the coefficients of the earnings equation estimated without correcting for selectivity bias. The estimated average earnings premia and earnings dispersion effects of education with and without correction for selectivity are reported in table D.2 in appendix D and the difference between them indicates the extent to which the selectivity bias affects these estimates.

As can be seen, even if selectivity does not affect much the qualitative interpretation of the results, it has an impact on the magnitude of the estimates. The estimated earnings premia for education are slightly higher when one does not correct for the selectivity bias due to nonrandom selection into paid employment. For France, however, the difference is rather small, especially for men. For Germany, the difference is a little bit higher, but this is also because the estimates are somewhat less precise due to a smaller number of observations. The effect of education on earnings dispersion also tend to be larger when omitting to correct for the selectivity bias. Here, however, the effect is more marked for men than for women in both countries. The following results are based on the selectivity-corrected equations since these are the correct ones.

5.6 The earnings premium for education

This section presents the results of the estimation for the earnings equation, corrected for selectivity into paid employment.

5.6.1 Tests and estimation results

Table 5.6. Joint tests results for the earnings equation

Null hypothesis	Germany χ^2	Germany $p>\chi^2$	France χ^2	France $p>\chi^2$
Tests on gender interactions (mean effects)				
Female * Education = 0	90.06	(0.00)	305.01	(0.00)
Female * Age = 0	11.96	(0.00)	1,321.29	(0.00)
Female * Tenure = 0	7.64	(0.00)	1,544.39	(0.00)
Female * Firm size = 0	32.03	(0.00)	837.62	(0.00)
Female * Industry = 0	131.20	(0.00)	413.46	(0.00)
Female * Father's occupation = 0	22.05	(0.00)	82.42	(0.00)
Female * Quarter = 0	1.44	(0.49)	2.13	(0.16)
Female * Year = 0	8.12	(0.52)	52.35	(0.00)
Tests on specific coefficients (mean effects)				
Education = 0	1,812.73	(0.00)	31,158.54	(0.00)
Age = 0	360.67	(0.00)	8,221.81	(0.00)
Tenure = 0	310.72	(0.00)	6,177.22	(0.00)
Firm size = 0	896.33	(0.00)	1,985.40	(0.00)
Industry = 0	446.89	(0.00)	2,262.03	(0.00)
Father's occupation = 0	264.22	(0.00)	1,796.23	(0.00)
Quarter = 0	135.59	(0.00)		
Year = 0	397.71	(0.00)	884.75	(0.00)
Tests on scedastic term (dispersion effects)				
Homoscedasticity: all coefficients = 0	792.76	(0.00)	7,073.68	(0.00)
Female * Education = 0	205.79	(0.00)	584.76	(0.00)
Education = 0	353.20	(0.00)	3,450.18	(0.00)
Wald test earnings equation	13,410.06	(0.00)	1.8e+05	(0.00)
Non-censored observations	23,661		404,976	
Number of individuals	4,928		219,420	

As for the selection equation, the first step consists here also in determining which variables should be included in the earnings equation. To this end, the statistical significance of the variables has been tested in a systematic way. Here again, only the results of the joint tests are reported in table 5.6, whereas the test results on the statistical significance of separate variables appear directly with the estimation results in table 5.7.

Table 5.7. Determinants of earnings (corrected for selectivity)

Variable	Germany coef.	Germany (s.e)	France coef.	France (s.e)
Mean effects (β):				
Education (ref.: Level 10/11)				
Level 12	0.13**	(0.03)	0.18**	(0.00)
Level 20	0.05**	(0.01)	0.09**	(0.00)
Level 21	0.21**	(0.01)	0.17**	(0.00)
Level 30	0.17**	(0.01)	0.28**	(0.01)
Level 31	0.17**	(0.02)	0.27**	(0.00)
Level 32	0.06	(0.08)	0.32**	(0.01)
Level 33	0.13**	(0.02)	0.29**	(0.01)
Level 40	0.43**	(0.02)	0.41**	(0.00)
Level 41	0.51**	(0.02)	0.70**	(0.00)
Female * Level 12	0.06†	(0.04)	-0.02**	(0.01)
Female * Level 20	0.12**	(0.02)	0.01**	(0.00)
Female * Level 21	0.08**	(0.02)	0.01†	(0.01)
Female * Level 30	0.10**	(0.02)	0.01	(0.01)
Female * Level 31	0.07*	(0.03)	0.00	(0.01)
Female * Level 32	0.31**	(0.10)	0.01	(0.01)
Female * Level 33	0.23**	(0.03)	0.01	(0.01)
Female * Level 40	0.03	(0.03)	0.08**	(0.01)
Female * Level 41	0.08**	(0.03)	0.03**	(0.01)
Female	-0.52**	(0.10)	0.13**	(0.03)
Age/10	0.41**	(0.03)	0.34**	(0.01)
Age squared/100	-0.04**	(0.00)	-0.03**	(0.00)
Female * Age/10	0.03	(0.05)	-0.18**	(0.01)
Female * Age squared/100	-0.01	(0.01)	0.02**	(0.00)
Tenure/10	0.11**	(0.01)	0.13**	(0.00)
Tenure squared/100	-0.02**	(0.00)	-0.02**	(0.00)
Female * Tenure/10	0.04*	(0.02)	0.07**	(0.00)
Female * Tenure squared/100	-0.01*	(0.01)	-0.00**	(0.00)
Firm size (ref.: <5 employees)				
5-19 employees	0.14**	(0.01)	-0.04**	(0.00)
20-199 employees	0.23**	(0.01)	-0.01**	(0.00)
200-1,999 employees	0.28**	(0.01)	0.02**	(0.00)
≥2,000 employees	0.33**	(0.01)	0.05**	(0.00)
Missing information	0.11**	(0.04)	0.10**	(0.00)
Female * 5-19 employees	0.07**	(0.02)	0.07**	(0.00)
Female * 20-199 employees	0.08**	(0.02)	0.05**	(0.00)
Female * 200-1,999 employees	0.10**	(0.02)	0.04**	(0.00)
Female * ≥2,000 employees	0.11**	(0.02)	0.03**	(0.00)
Female * Missing information	0.09	(0.06)	-0.07**	(0.01)

to be continued...

...table 5.7 continued

Variable	Germany coef.	Germany (s.e)	France coef.	France (s.e)
Industry branch (ref.: Industry or missing)				
Agriculture, energy	-0.01	(0.01)	-0.08**	(0.00)
Construction	-0.01	(0.01)	-0.06**	(0.00)
Trade	-0.12**	(0.01)	-0.06**	(0.00)
Banking	0.05**	(0.01)	0.04**	(0.00)
Transports	-0.16**	(0.01)	-0.02**	(0.00)
Private services	-0.25**	(0.03)	-0.05**	(0.00)
Public services	-0.09**	(0.01)	-0.09**	(0.00)
Missing information	-0.02	(0.03)	-0.18**	(0.01)
Female * Agriculture, energy	-0.04	(0.03)	0.02**	(0.01)
Female * Construction	-0.01	(0.03)	0.06**	(0.01)
Female * Trade	0.03*	(0.01)	0.01**	(0.00)
Female * Banking	0.06**	(0.02)	0.02**	(0.01)
Female * Transports	0.12**	(0.02)	0.02**	(0.01)
Female * Private services	-0.01	(0.03)	-0.03**	(0.00)
Female * Public services	0.17**	(0.02)	0.04**	(0.00)
Female * Missing information	-0.06	(0.04)	0.06**	(0.01)
Type of employment				
Fixed-term contract	-0.19**	(0.01)	-0.14**	(0.00)
Female * Fixed-term contract	0.01	(0.02)	0.05**	(0.01)
Part-time employment	0.11**	(0.02)	0.12**	(0.00)
Female * Part-time employment	-0.15**	(0.02)	-0.10**	(0.00)
Public employment	-0.03**	(0.01)	0.03**	(0.00)
Female * Public employment	0.07†	(0.02)	0.06**	(0.00)
Father's occupation (ref.: Worker)				
Farmer	-0.04**	(0.01)	-0.04**	(0.00)
Self-employed	0.03**	(0.01)	0.04**	(0.00)
Senior manager	0.07**	(0.01)	0.09**	(0.00)
Middle manager	0.06**	(0.01)	0.06**	(0.00)
Employee	0.04**	(0.01)	0.03**	(0.00)
Missing information	-0.06**	(0.01)	-0.01**	(0.00)
Female * Farmer	0.04**	(0.03)	0.02**	(0.00)
Female * Self-employed	0.03†	(0.02)	0.00	(0.00)
Female * Senior manager	-0.02	(0.02)	-0.01**	(0.00)
Female * Middle manager	-0.02	(0.01)	-0.01*	(0.00)
Female * Employee	0.03	(0.02)	0.00	(0.00)
Female * Missing information	0.02†	(0.01)	0.04**	(0.01)
Current quarter (ref.: 1st quarter)				
2nd quarter	0.05**	(0.01)	0.02**	(0.01)
3rd/4th quarter	0.07**	(0.01)		
Year (ref.: 2000)				
1991	-0.11**	(0.01)	-0.03**	(0.00)

to be continued...

...table 5.7 continued

	Germany		France	
Variable	**coef.**	**(s.e)**	**coef.**	**(s.e)**
1992	-0.10**	(0.01)	-0.02**	(0)
1993	-0.05**	(0.01)	0.04**	(0.00)
1994	-0.04**	(0.01)	0.02**	(0.00)
1995	0.02†	(0.01)	0.01**	(0.00)
1996	0.02†	(0.01)	0.01**	(0.00)
1997	-0.03**	(0.01)	-0.01**	(0.00)
1998	-0.04**	(0.01)	-0.03**	(0.00)
1999	-0.02*	(0.01)	-0.02**	(0.00)
Female * 1991			0.00	(0.01)
Female * 1992			0.00	(0.01)
Female * 1993			-0.01**	(0.00)
Female * 1994			-0.02**	(0.00)
Female * 1995			-0.01*	(0.00)
Female * 1996			-0.01†	(0.00)
Female * 1997			0.00	(0.00)
Female * 1998			-0.01	(0.00)
Female * 1999			0.01*	(0.00)
Constant	1.54**	(0.07)	1.23**	(0.02)
Dispersion effects (β^h):				
Education (ref.: Level 10 or 11)				
Level 12	0.13*	(0.06)	0.09**	(0.01)
Level 20	-0.15*	(0.06)	-0.07**	(0.01)
Level 21	-0.10**	(0.04)	-0.05**	(0.01)
Level 30	-0.02	(0.07)	0.07**	(0.03)
Level 31	0.32**	(0.08)	0.01	(0.02)
Level 32	0.53**	(0.16)	0.34**	(0.02)
Level 33	0.17†	(0.09)	0.11**	(0.04)
Level 40	0.30**	(0.08)	0.08**	(0.01)
Level 41	0.63**	(0.07)	0.60**	(0.01)
Female * Level 12	-0.46**	(0.15)	-0.08**	(0.02)
Female * Level 20	-0.40**	(0.08)	-0.07**	(0.01)
Female * Level 21	-0.43**	(0.08)	-0.20**	(0.02)
Female * Level 30	-0.63**	(0.09)	-0.40**	(0.04)
Female * Level 31	-0.93**	(0.12)	-0.27**	(0.02)
Female * Level 32	-0.73**	(0.21)	-0.33**	(0.02)
Female * Level 33	-0.37**	(0.11)	-0.32**	(0.05)
Female * Level 40	-0.44**	(0.11)	-0.31**	(0.02)
Female * Level 41	-0.72**	(0.09)	-0.18**	(0.02)
Female	0.90**	(0.07)	0.16**	(0.01)
Age	0.07**	(0.01)	0.19**	(0.01)
Trend	0.02**	(0.00)	-0.02**	(0.00)
Constant	-2.54**	(0.06)	-2.20**	(0.01)

Significance level : † : 10% * : 5% ** : 1%

To test the presence of gender differences in the impact of the variables on earnings, interactions between the variables and a female dummy have been included as additional regressors beside the variables themselves. The results of the joint tests show that all the gender interaction terms are significant in statistical terms except those with the quarter and the year under observation for Germany. The latter interactions have therefore been dropped from the German earnings equation. Thus, the impact on earnings of almost all explanatory variables differs across genders. Looking at the variables themselves (not only the interactions), the sets of dummy variables all prove extremely significant and so do the variables taken separately (see tables 5.6 and 5.7 respectively). This explains the high value found for the Wald test statistic, which tests the hypothesis, strongly rejected, that all variables of the earnings equation taken together are not statistically different from zero.

Further tests are about the impact of education and gender on the variance of earnings. The hypothesis of a homoscedastic variance of earnings is strongly rejected for both countries since the variables included in the scedastic function taken jointly turn out to be significantly different from zero. The education dummies are extremely significant, as well as the female dummy and the interactions between gender and education. Thus, the level of educational attainment does not only affect the expected level of earnings, but also the dispersion of earnings, and this in a different way for men and women.

Table 5.7 reports the whole estimation results of the earnings equation. The next sections will present in detail the effect of education, differentiating between men and women, both in terms of levels (section 5.6.2) and in terms of dispersion (5.6.3). The impact of the variables other than education can be read from the table and will not be further commented here, since this is not the primary focus of this study.

5.6.2 Effect of education on earnings level

In this part, the mean effect of education on earnings is examined, drawing on the coefficients estimated and presented in table 5.7. The aim is here to get an estimate of the average earnings premium for education. In other words, what I aim to find out is how much additional earnings is associated, on average, with the attainment of a higher level of education, if anything else is equal.

5.6.2.1 Computation

Let us specify the model presented in section 5.3 in the following way. The vector of explanatory variables x_i and the corresponding coefficient vector β can be defined as:

$$\begin{aligned} x_i &= [1, educ, educ \times female, female, \tilde{x}_i] \\ \beta &= [\beta_0, \beta_1, \beta_2, \beta_3, \tilde{\beta}] \end{aligned} \tag{5.15}$$

where $female$ is a dummy variable taking the value 1 if the individual is a woman and 0 otherwise, and *educ* is a vector depicting educational attainment as a set of dummy variables. The vector *educ* is defined as:

$$educ = [level\ 12,\ level\ 20,\ level\ 21,\ level\ 30,\ level\ 31,\ level\ 32,\ level\ 33,\ level\ 40,\ level\ 41] \tag{5.16}$$

where the *level* variables are dummy variables taking the value 1 if the person has attained the corresponding education level and 0 otherwise. $educ \times female$ is the vector of interactions between $female$ and *educ*. $\tilde{x}_i$ is the vector comprising all other explanatory variables, and $\tilde{\beta}$ is the corresponding coefficients vector.

Thus, equations (5.2) can be rewritten as:

$$\begin{aligned} \ln y_{1i} &= \beta_0 + \beta_1 educ + \beta_2 educ \times female + \beta_3 female \\ &\quad + \tilde{x}_i \tilde{\beta} + \varepsilon_{1i} \quad \text{if} \quad y_{2i}^* > 0 \\ \ln y_{1i} &= \text{not observed} \quad \text{if} \quad y_{2i}^* \leq 0 \end{aligned} \tag{5.17}$$

The coefficients of the education variables in equation (5.17) give a measure of the reward in terms of earnings of the respective level of educational attainment compared to the reference group of individuals with poor education, i.e. with level 10 or 11 education. This earnings reward for a specific education level compared to the reference group is called here the average earnings premium for the education level considered. The vector of average earnings premia for all the education levels included in *educ* is called AEP and the vector of corresponding standard errors $SE(AEP)$.

For men, AEP and $SE(AEP)$ can be read directly from the coefficients and standard errors reported in table 5.7:

$$\begin{aligned} AEP_{men} &= \hat{\beta}_1 \\ SE(AEP)_{men} &= \sqrt{var(\hat{\beta}_1)} \end{aligned} \tag{5.18}$$

For women, there is on the one hand an overall effect of being a woman, irrespective of the education level attained and anything else equal, captured by the coefficient $\hat{\beta}_3$ with a standard error amounting to $\sqrt{var(\hat{\beta}_3)}$. On the other hand, the earnings premium obtained for a same education level on average might differ between men and women. For women, the average earnings premia for education cannot be read directly from the coefficients reported in table 5.7, but can be computed in the following way:

$$\begin{aligned} AEP_{women} &= \hat{\beta}_1 + \hat{\beta}_2 \\ SE(AEP)_{women} &= \sqrt{var(\hat{\beta}_1) + var(\hat{\beta}_1) + 2cov(\hat{\beta}_1, \hat{\beta}_2)} \end{aligned} \tag{5.19}$$

The overall vector of earnings premia for the various education levels, regardless of gender, can therefore be computed as:

$$AEP_{all} = \hat{\beta}_1 + \overline{female}\,\hat{\beta}_2 \qquad (5.20)$$
$$SE(AEP)_{all} = \sqrt{var(\hat{\beta}_1) + \overline{female}^2 var(\hat{\beta}_1) + 2\,\overline{female}\,cov(\hat{\beta}_1, \hat{\beta}_2)}$$

where $\overline{female}$ is the proportion of females in the sample.

5.6.2.2 Results

The exact figures computed for each element of AEP and $SE(AEP)$ for men, women and altogether, based on the estimates obtained from the selectivity-corrected earnings equation with heteroscedastic variances as reported in table 5.7 are given in table D.2 in appendix D[24]. For illustration purposes, the average earnings premium for education is represented graphically here (please consult table D.2 to see the standard errors of the estimated earnings premia).

Fig. 5.5. Average earnings premium for education (Ref.: Level 10/11)

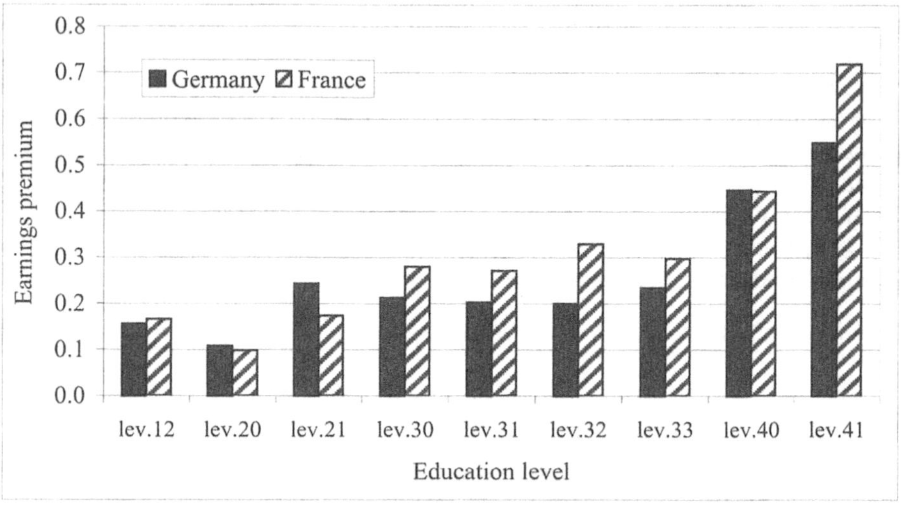

Figure 5.5 pictures the average earnings premia for the various education levels in France and Germany, irrespective of gender, calculated on the basis of equation (5.20). As can be seen, attaining a higher education level than the reference level 10 or 11 yields a positive earnings premium in both countries. Though broadly speaking, the higher the education level, the higher the reward in terms of earnings, the education-earnings link is not monotonous. Looking into detail, one can see that a level 20 qualification (no or lower

[24] For comparison, the estimates computed on the basis of the regression without selectivity correction have been reported, too.

secondary education + basic vocational degree) yields a smaller earnings premium than level 12 qualification (intermediate secondary education without any vocational qualification) in Germany and in France alike. Thus, it seems that the employers attach more value to the attainment of a minimum level of general education than to the acquisition of a vocational qualification. A reason for this might be that the quality of the completed vocational training might depend on the level attained in general education or that a minimum level of general education is necessary to show enough learning flexibility in the job. In any case, it is, on average, more worth it in terms of earnings to strive for attaining at least an intermediate level of general education rather than, having a poor general education, to opt for a basic vocational degree. Failing to attain at least this minimum level of general education cannot be compensated by completing a vocational qualification, though the vocational qualification as such has a positive impact on earnings, at least for people with only a poor general education.

In France, there is not much difference in the earnings premium for education level 12 and for education level 21, i.e. whether individuals with an intermediate secondary education have or do not have a basic vocational degree. This means that in France a basic vocational degree has some value only if one has an extremely poor level of secondary education (i.e. a basic vocational degree is "better than nothing"), but as soon as one has attained intermediate secondary schooling, this becomes irrelevant. This is different in Germany, where *Realschule* graduates (i.e. intermediate secondary schooling) enjoy a positive earnings premium for completing a basic vocational qualification, as can be seen from the significantly higher earnings premium for level 21 than for level 12. Thus, the skills provided by the vocational education system seem to be more highly valued by the labour market in Germany than in France. This confirms the results found in chapter 4. Not only does the completion of basic vocational education (level 2) better protect against the unemployment risk in Germany than in France, but when employment is found, it also leads to a higher earnings premium on average. Again, this might be explained by the fact that vocational education in Germany is more tightly linked to the needs of the labour market while it remains rather theoretical in France and less connected to the job market. In this context, it becomes more essential to reach a minimum level of general education based on which one can train more easily on the job.

In Germany, the completion of an intermediate level qualification (level 3) does not yield any additional earnings premium. Thus, advanced vocational qualifications bring a further advantage in terms of employment (see chapter 4), but less so in terms of earnings. By contrast, in France, intermediate vocational qualifications bring about an additional earnings premium compared to basic ones, though it makes no difference if these have the status of a maturity certificate (level 31) or not (level 30). Moreover, unlike in Germany, the completion of the general maturity certificate (*Baccalauréat Général*, level 32 and 33) as such is rewarded in terms of earnings, though the additional premium obtained for it is rather small. This confirms the high status of the *Baccalauréat* in France.

In both countries, higher education degrees yield a high earnings premium on average, anything else being equal. Thus, there is a large gap between the average earnings premium of tertiary level degrees and that of qualifications below this level. Level 40 degrees, i.e. lower tertiary level degrees yield a similar reward in France and Germany, though in the classification of educational degrees, the requirement level of these level 40 degrees is lower in France (2 years after *Baccalauréat*) than in Germany (4 years after *(Fach)Hochschulreife*), see chapter 2. The earnings premium for upper tertiary education is much higher in France than in Germany, though study duration is typically shorter. This is most probably the effect of the presence of the *Grandes Ecoles*, which comprise about 30 percent of higher education graduates and are specifically designed to meet the demand of the economy for high-level positions (see chapter 2).

Let us now have a look at gender differences in the average earnings premium for education. Judging from the coefficient of the female dummy in table 5.7, being a woman rather than a man has as such a negative impact on earnings in Germany, whereas it affects earnings positively in France if anything else is held constant. This means that if they had the same characteristics as men and the same rewards of these characteristics, French women would receive slightly higher earnings than their male counterparts on average, while German women would earn less. Thus, part of the larger gender gap in gross hourly earnings in Germany, observed in section 5.2, can be explained by this differing gross effect of being a woman in either country, assuming that everything else is equal.

We know from chapter 3 that the educational attainment of women is poorer than that of men in Germany and to a lesser extent also in France. However, looking at figure 5.6 and figure 5.7, it appears that, on the whole, attaining a same level of educational attainment, rather than the reference level 10/11, is more highly rewarded for women than for men in terms of earnings. This is true in both countries, though the gender gap in the average earnings premium for education is significantly larger in Germany than in France. Thus, the level of education has more discriminating power among women than among men as regards the determination of the earnings level. This is somewhat paradoxical considering that one might expect women to invest more than men in their education if they enjoy a higher return to investment. Particularly in Germany, women are more poorly endowed in human capital – at least as measured by educational attainment – but they enjoy a significantly more favourable reward of their education.

The gender gap in the average earnings premium for education does not have the same extent for all education levels. In Germany, women have a higher premium than men for all education levels, but the gap is particularly large for level 32 and level 33, i.e. for holders of the general maturity certificate (*Abitur*). It is much less pronounced for tertiary education graduates. In France, the earnings premia for basic and advanced vocational qualifica-

Fig. 5.6. Average earnings premium by gender (Ref.: Level 10/11) – Germany

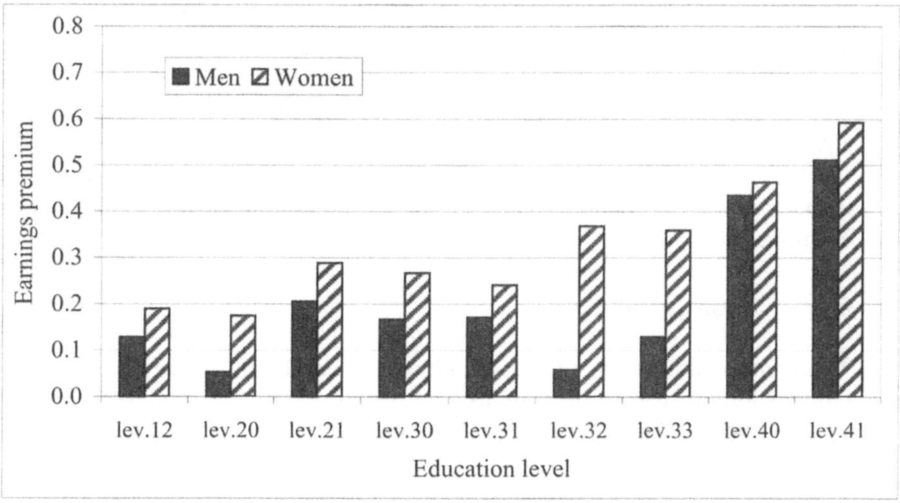

Fig. 5.7. Average earnings premium by gender (Ref.: Level 10/11) – France

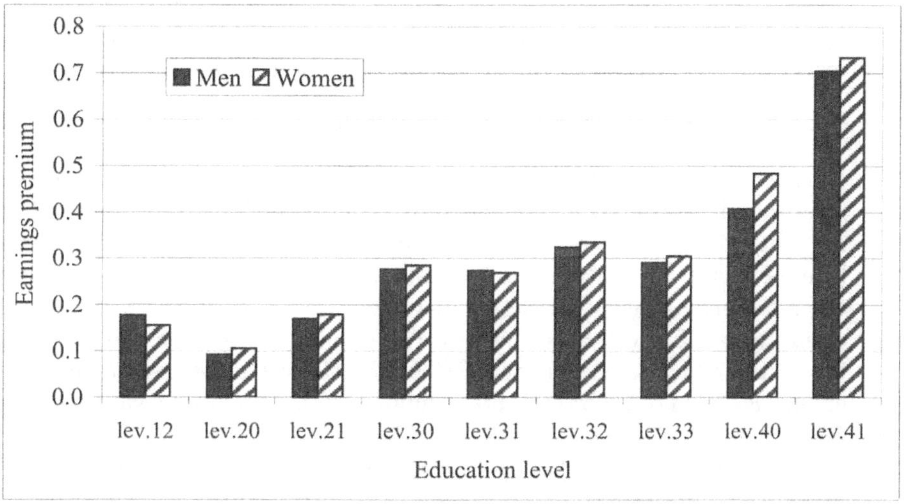

tions are nearly the same for French men and women. However, there is a significant gap in favour of women in the earnings premium for tertiary level qualifications, especially lower tertiary ones.

5.6.3 Effect of education on unexplained earnings dispersion

This section is concerned with the effect of education on the residual earnings dispersion, i.e. on the remaining earnings dispersion after observable factors have been controlled for. The previous section showed what earnings premium can be expected from investing in a certain education level, anything else equal. However, it also matters whether the educational investment affects the unexplained earnings dispersion to be expected. Indeed, the residual earnings dispersion can be seen as a measure of the remaining earnings uncertainty or earnings risk.

5.6.3.1 Computation

The computation of the effect of education on the unexplained earnings dispersion follows the same principle as presented in section 5.6.2. The vector x_i^h and the corresponding coefficient vector β^h defined in section 5.3 can be expressed as:

$$\begin{aligned} x_i^h &= [1, educ, educ \times female, female, \tilde{x}_i^h] \\ \beta^h &= [\beta_0^h, \beta_1^h, \beta_2^h, \beta_3^h, \tilde{\beta}^h] \end{aligned} \tag{5.21}$$

where *educ*, *female* and *educ* × *female* are defined as in section 5.6.2 and $\tilde{x}_i^h$ and $\tilde{\beta}^h$ are vectors comprising the remaining variables and coefficients respectively. Then, the scedastic equation (5.14) can be rewritten as:

$$\ln \sigma_{1i}^2 = \beta_0^h + \beta_1^h educ + \beta_2^h educ \times female + \beta_3^h female + \tilde{x}_i^h \tilde{\beta}^h \tag{5.22}$$

The coefficients of the education variables in equation (5.22) are to be interpreted in reference to the group of individuals with poor (level 10 or 11) education. Thus, the coefficients measure the effect of attaining a specific level of education in terms of unexplained earnings dispersion compared to the reference category, in short, they measure the earnings dispersion effect of education. Let EDE be the vector of earnings dispersion effects estimated for all the education levels and $SE(EDE)$ the vector of associated standard errors. EDE and $SE(EDE)$ are computed in an analogous way as in section 5.6.2.

For men, the earnings dispersion effects of attaining a specific education level rather than level 10/11 can be read directly from the coefficients and standard errors reported at the bottom of table 5.7 under the heading "dispersion effects":

$$\begin{aligned} EDE_{men} &= \hat{\beta_1^h} \\ SE(EDE)_{men} &= \sqrt{var(\hat{\beta_1^h})} \end{aligned} \tag{5.23}$$

For women, again, there is first an overall earnings dispersion effect of being a woman, irrespective of the education level and all other characteristics being equal, that is captured by the coefficient $\hat{\beta_3^h}$ with a standard error amounting to $\sqrt{var(\hat{\beta_3^h})}$. In addition to this overall effect of being a woman, there is an additional effect of being a woman that goes through the effect of education. For women, the effect of education on unexplained earnings dispersion can be be computed as:

$$\begin{aligned} EDE_{women} &= \hat{\beta_1^h} + \hat{\beta_2^h} \qquad (5.24) \\ SE(EDE)_{women} &= \sqrt{var(\hat{\beta_1^h}) + var(\hat{\beta_1^h}) + 2cov(\hat{\beta_1^h}, \hat{\beta_2^h})} \end{aligned}$$

The overall effect of education on unexplained earnings dispersion, irrespective of gender, can therefore be expressed as:

$$\begin{aligned} EDE_{all} &= \hat{\beta_1^h} + \overline{female}\,\hat{\beta_2^h} \qquad (5.25) \\ SE(EDE)_{all} &= \sqrt{var(\hat{\beta_1^h}) + \overline{female}^2 var(\hat{\beta_1^h}) + 2\,\overline{female}\,cov(\hat{\beta_1^h}, \hat{\beta_2^h})} \end{aligned}$$

5.6.3.2 Results

The estimated earnings dispersion effects for each level of educational attainment relative to the reference level 10/11 as well as the associated standard errors are given in table D.3 in the appendix D. Here, the estimates of the elements of EDE are represented graphically, without the standard errors.

Fig. 5.8. Earnings dispersion effect of education (Ref.: Level 10/11)

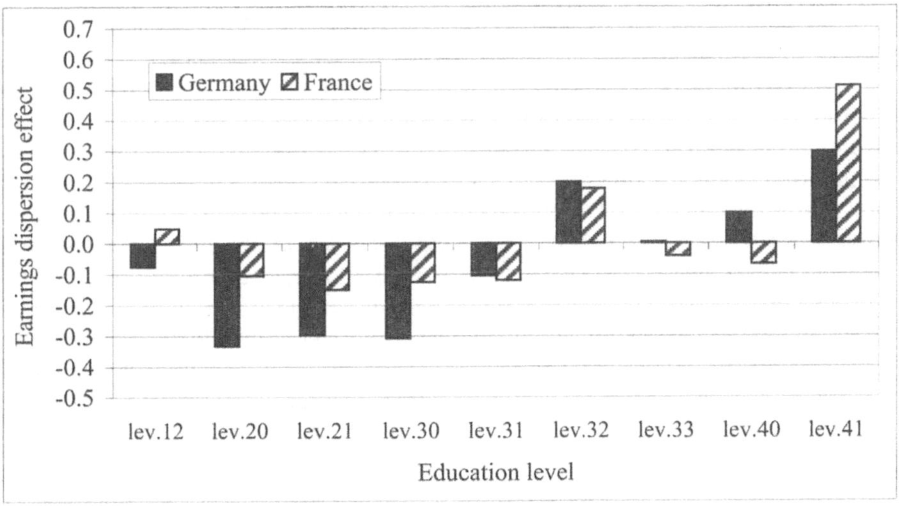

Figure 5.9 shows for France and Germany the effect that is caused, irrespective of gender, by the attainment of a specific education level rather than

no or only a low level school degree, computed on the basis of formula (5.25). As can be seen, the pattern of earnings dispersion effects of education exhibit some similarities in France and Germany. In both countries, attaining level 12 (i.e. intermediate secondary schooling) has only a small effect, negative[25] in Germany and positive in France, in terms of earnings dispersion compared to having a poorer education. However, the completion of vocational qualifications (level 20 to level 31) significantly reduces the earnings risk as measured by the residual earnings dispersion. Thus, not only the risk in terms of unemployment is reduced by the acquisition of vocational education but also the earnings risk. In Germany, this is particularly true for basic and advanced vocational training while it is less so for the vocational maturity certificate (level 31). Maybe this is because the vocational maturity certificate is less closely connected to the labour market than dual qualification forms. The effects of vocational education on earnings dispersion are larger in magnitude in Germany than in France[26]. Thus, the completion of a vocational qualification not only yields an earnings premium, anything else equal, but also reduces the earnings risk significantly, particularly in Germany.

A further commonality is that in France and in Germany alike, individuals having at most the general maturity certificate (level 32) face a comparatively higher earnings dispersion. This might be due to the fact that this qualification level certifies the acquisition of general skills which might lead to very different types of occupations that are likely to bring about different levels of earnings. This interpretation is consistent with the observation that on the whole, no significant effect regarding earnings dispersion, compared to the reference group, is found for those who completed a vocational qualification in addition to the general maturity certificate (level 33). The dispersion-enhancing effect of the general maturity certificate level is offset by the dispersion-reducing effect of a vocational qualification.

Upper tertiary level graduates are those who face the highest earnings dispersion, especially in France. Interestingly, they face a higher earnings risk than the lower tertiary level graduates. Again, this might be due to the fact that lower tertiary qualifications are typically rather focussed on the needs of the labour market. By contrast, the upper tertiary level includes on the one hand some general study tracks that are not really designed to meet the needs of employers and the graduates of which might experience difficulties in finding a job[27] or at least a well rewarded job. On the other hand, this category also includes those highly skilled workers whose skills are highly demanded by the economy. Thus, the group of upper tertiary level graduates is likely to be a much more heterogeneous group in terms of jobs occupied and this could

[25] Judging from the standard error reported in table D.3, the small effect found for Germany is hardly significant in statistical terms.

[26] Note, however, that the standard errors are also larger.

[27] Chapter 4 seems to confirm this since upper tertiary graduates face a higher unemployment risk than lower tertiary graduates.

explain that they face a higher earnings dispersion, even though they have on average the highest earnings premium (see section 5.6.2). The higher earnings dispersion effect found for level 41 graduates in France compared to Germany might have its cause in the definition of this education level. Indeed, due to data limitations, this category also includes tertiary level qualifications that require three years of study after the completion of the maturity certificate. This category is therefore broader than for Germany, where the upper tertiary level consists of university graduates who study for at least four years (see chapter 2).

Let us now examine gender differences in unexplained earnings dispersion and in the impact of education on it. First, the estimation results reported in table 5.7 show that anything else equal, the sole fact of being a woman implies a higher earnings dispersion, judging from the positive and significant effect found for the female dummy in the scedastic function of the earnings equation. Not only do women have lower earnings on average, these earnings are also less easily predictable. This overall dispersion-enhancing effect of being a woman is stronger in Germany than in France. Moreover, in both countries, the level of educational attainment has a different impact on unexplained earnings dispersion for men and for women. As figure 5.9 and figure 5.10 show, the gender differences in the earnings dispersion effect of education are substantial. The pattern of earnings dispersion effects presents some similarities across countries, though there are differences in some particular areas and in the magnitude of the effects.

In Germany and France alike, the completion of a vocational degree reduces significantly the unexplained earnings dispersion for women compared to their counterparts with no vocational degree, whereas it is much less so for men, for which the effects observed are very small in scope. This dispersion-reducing effect is much stronger for German than for French women. Looking more into detail, it appears that for German women, there is no significant difference in the earnings dispersion effect of level 20 and level 21, which indicates that the vocational degree matters more with respect to earnings dispersion than the distinction between low and intermediate school degrees. This is different in France, where women with an intermediate school degree in addition to their basic vocational education (level 21) face a lower earnings dispersion than those with a lower school level. However, there, the intermediate school degree alone (level 12) does not lead to any significant reduction in unexplained earnings dispersion, contrary to what is observed for German women. An advanced vocational qualification reduces further the earnings risk faced by French and German women, anything else equal, though the additional effect is quite small, especially for level 31 qualifications (vocational maturity degree).

From the general maturity certificate onwards, the pattern of earnings dispersion effects changes. For German women, the residual earnings dispersion is still lower than for the reference group of poorly educated women, but only slightly. The higher the educational level attained beside the general maturity

Fig. 5.9. Earnings dispersion effect of education by gender (Ref.: Level 10/11) – Germany

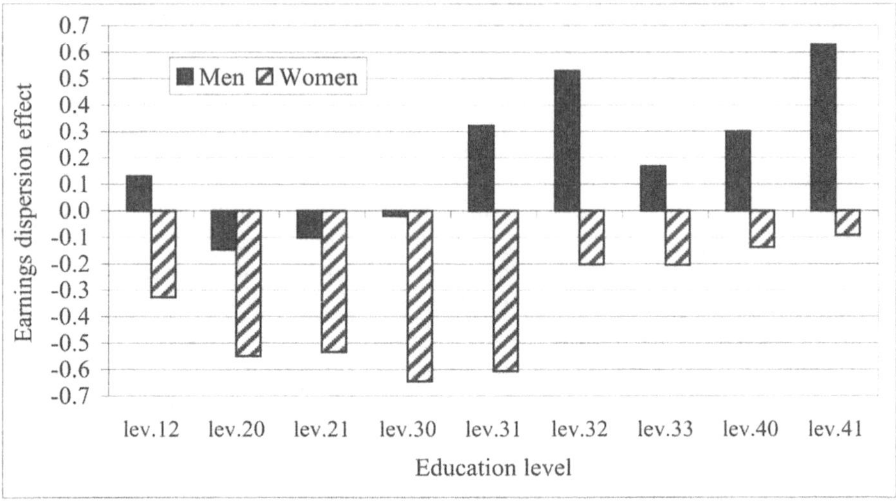

Fig. 5.10. Earnings dispersion effect of education by gender (Ref.: Level 10/11) – France

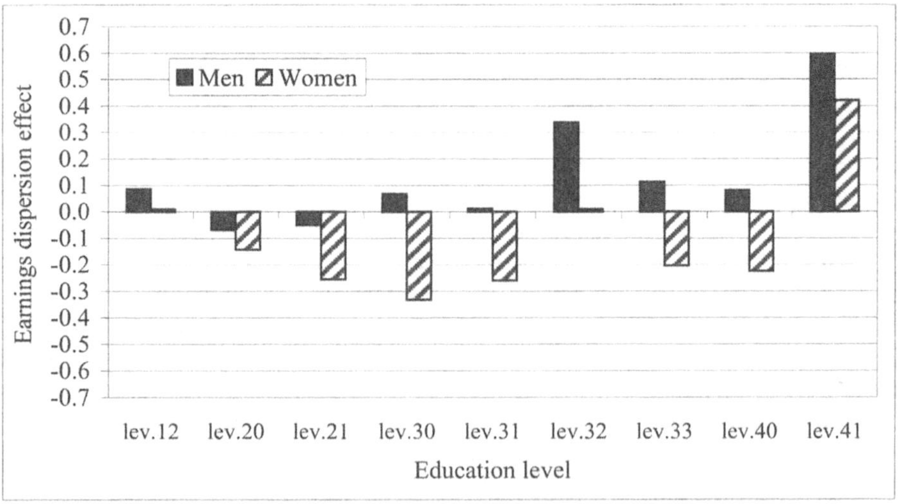

certificate, the smaller the earnings dispersion effect[28]. For men, in contrast, the effects go in the opposite direction. Qualifications above the vocational maturity level (level 31) in Germany and above the general maturity level in

[28] Note that for French women, having the general maturity certificate has no effect in terms of earnings dispersion compared to the reference group.

France (level 32) are associated with a higher earnings dispersion. Interestingly, in both countries, the unexplained earnings dispersion is particularly high for male holders of the general maturity certificate and for male university graduates. However, whereas French women also face a strong dispersion enhancing effect for being a university graduate, like their male counterparts though not to the same extent, no such effect is observable in Germany.

On the whole, the completion of a higher level of education does not only yield a higher earnings premium for women than for men on average, but also leads to a reduction in their earnings risk, if the latter is measured by the earnings dispersion unexplained by the other observable characteristics.

5.7 Summary and conclusions

In this chapter, the way the qualifications acquired within the French and the German education systems are rewarded in terms of labour market earnings has been thoroughly analysed. To be more specific, the study assesses for both countries the earnings premium an individual can expect from attaining a specific education level rather than a reference level, but also the impact of attaining such an education level on the unexplained earnings dispersion. The latter can be viewed as a measure of earnings uncertainty or earnings risk. A look at the literature reveals indeed that even though the link between education and earnings has been extensively analysed internationally following the development of the human capital theory, there is very little comparative work on France and Germany in this area. Such a comparison, however, provides useful insights into the relative performance of two quite different education systems as providers of qualifications for the labour market. Moreover, there is very little evidence on the impact of education on earnings dispersion and this chapter is also a contribution in this respect. The observation of the patterns prevailing both within and across countries enables me to highlight further aspects of the relationship between education and individual labour market success in France and Germany.

The first step of the empirical analysis consists in examining on a descriptive level the basic relationship between educational attainment and the level and dispersion of gross hourly earnings. The earnings are on average higher in Germany than in France, and this at all education levels. In both countries, men have higher earnings than women at all education levels, but the gender gap is larger in Germany. In both countries also, the variance is found to be higher at low education levels as well as among university graduates, while it is lowest for basic and advanced vocational qualifications. In France, the variance of earnings at a given education level is rather similar for men and women, whereas in Germany, women with a poor education face a higher unexplained earnings dispersion than their male counterparts, while the reverse is true at higher education levels.

In order to isolate the effects of education in terms of earnings level and dispersion, however, one has to abstract them from other factors that might drive the bivariate relationships observed. An econometric model has been formulated with a design suited to the specific purposes of this study. First, since chapter 4 has shown that there are substantial differences between France and Germany in the access to employment, the selection into paid employment has been explicitly modeled. Because the selection into employment is known to be gender-specific, the estimated correlation between the selection propensity and the earnings equation has been allowed to differ for men and women. Second, gender differences are accounted for by the inclusion of interaction terms of the variables with gender, the significance of which having been tested in a systematic way. Finally, the assumption of homoscedastic variances is relaxed, and for both the selection and the earnings equation, the residual variance is allowed to vary across education levels and genders. This model has been estimated by means of maximum likelihood procedures and the results permit to compute estimates of the average earnings premia obtained from the completion of various levels of educational attainment as well as estimates of their effect on earnings dispersion, differentiated for men and women.

The key findings of the econometric analysis can be summarised as follows. First, evidence is found that selectivity effects are at work and differ for men and women, judging from the fact that the correlation between the selection and the earnings equation is significant and that it is found to differ significantly across genders. Therefore, omitting to model the selection process would result in biased estimates of the parameters of the earnings equation. Indeed, though the bias is not important enough in magnitude to affect much the qualitative interpretation of the results, the estimates of the average earnings premia for education as well as of the effect on earnings dispersion are affected by the selectivity bias.

Based on this selectivity-corrected model with multiplicative heteroscedasticity, the effects of education on earnings in terms of level and dispersion have been computed from the estimation results. Broadly speaking, as expected, the higher the educational attainment is, the higher the expected level of earnings, anything else constant. However, the relationship between education and level of earnings is not monotonous when considering detailed levels of education. Several interesting features emerge from the analysis. First, the attainment of a minimum level of instruction seems to be valued by the employers in both countries and the completion of a vocational degree is not as well rewarded in terms of earnings as the achievement of this minimum (intermediate) level of general education. Thus, concentrating the efforts on fostering the achievement of at least an intermediate level of general instruction seems to be a good policy with a view to improving the employment prospects, both regarding unemployment risk (see chapter 4), and the access to a higher level of earnings.

Second, basic vocational education – at least after an intermediate school degree – does not only better protect against the unemployment risk in Germany than in France as has been seen in chapter 4, but when employment is found, it also leads to a higher earnings premium on average. This confirms the better external efficiency of the German system of vocational education as opposed to the low-status vocational education in France, which remains rather theoretical, less connected to the job market, and signals failure in general education (see chapter 2). In Germany, however, there is no additional earnings premium for attaining qualifications at the maturity level, unlike in France, where the completion of the *Baccalauréat* or other qualifications, even vocational, at this level, is rewarded in the form of an earnings premium. Finally, the completion of higher education yields a particularly high earnings premium in both countries. The earnings premium for upper tertiary qualifications is significantly higher in France, though study duration is typically shorter. This is most probably the effect of the presence of the *Grandes Ecoles*, which comprise about 30 percent of higher education graduates and are specifically designed to produce graduates for high-level positions.

Looking at gender differences, it appears that whereas the gender gap in unemployment was larger in France than in Germany (though less so the gap in employment, due to a higher labour force participation in France, see chapter 4), the gender earnings gap is much larger in Germany than in France. In both countries but especially in Germany, women have a lower educational attainment than men (see chapter 3) but enjoy a higher earnings premium for education, anything else equal. Thus, the level of educational attainment is a more discriminating factor in the determination of the earnings level among women than among men.

Education is found not only to affect the expected level of earnings, but also the earnings dispersion. Thus, there is population heterogeneity in the earnings premium for education. The residual earnings dispersion, after observed factors have been controlled for, may be viewed as a measure of earnings risk in the sense that the earnings are less reliably predictable if they have a high dispersion. Interestingly, the effects of education on the unexplained earnings dispersion or earnings risk is found to present some obvious similarities in France and Germany. In both countries, overall, the completion of vocational qualifications reduces significantly the unexplained earnings dispersion, but the effect is particularly strong in Germany. By contrast, more general qualifications, like the general maturity certificate, are associated with a comparatively stronger earnings dispersion. Upper tertiary level graduates are those who face the highest unexplained earnings dispersion in both countries, particularly in France, due to a larger heterogeneity in the qualifications considered to be of upper tertiary level.

Looking at the effect of gender reveals further common patterns. First, being a woman implies as such a higher unexplained earnings dispersion, controlling for other factors, especially in Germany. Moreover, the effect of education on the residual earnings dispersion appears to differ dramatically across genders in both countries. As a matter of fact, the completion of basic or advanced vocational qualifications turns out to reduce substantially the unexplained earnings dispersion for women, particularly for German women, whereas no such effect is observed for men. The attainment of a level of education beyond the maturity still reduces the earnings risk of women – with the exception of French upper tertiary education graduates – though not to the same extent as vocational qualifications of lower level. For men, by contrast, the attainment of a higher level of education *increases* the earnings dispersion risk instead of reducing it like for women. Thus, not only do women, on average, enjoy a higher earnings premium than men for investing in education, but it also reduces their earnings risk to a larger extent than for men.

Thus, the findings show that examining solely the effect of education in terms of earnings level illustrates only one aspect of the relationship between education and earnings. The level of education attained is not neutral with respect to earnings dispersion, even after controlling for gender-specific selection into employment and a large number of explanatory factors. The results confirm the findings of chapter 4 that the labour market requires the attainment of a minimum of general instruction. The greater labour market efficiency of the German system of vocational education found in terms of unemployment risk in chapter 4 is confirmed when looking at the earnings premium and the earnings risk. Regarding upper tertiary education, it yields a higher earnings premium on average in France, but this higher earnings premium is associated with a larger uncertainty. The latter risk is counterbalanced by the comparatively lower risk incurred by French university graduates of entering unemployment, as observed in chapter 4, but adds to their higher risk of long-term unemployment.

6

Conclusion

This study is an in-depth analysis of the distribution of educational attainment and its impact on individual labour market outcomes in France and Germany. To finalise the study, I will draw some conclusions from the key findings that emerge from the various analyses and identify areas where there seems to be scope for further research. The qualifications of workers have gained increasing importance as a factor of productivity in modern economies. Analysing a country's endowment in education compared to its competitors provides insights into an essential aspect of its long-term competitiveness and growth capacity. At the individual level, education determines to a large extent people's employment prospects, even though it is complemented by other skills acquired during subsequent life in the form of further training or informal learning. After the publication of the results of the PISA study, Germany showed very much concern about the poor educational performance of German pupils compared to pupils in other European countries in 2000. French pupils, for instance, performed significantly better than their German counterparts. Not only did the performance of German students appear to be comparatively low on average, but the dispersion of the test results also proved particularly high. The German education system has been accused of producing more social inequalities than other education systems, in the sense that children from poorer family background are suspected to have significantly poorer educational prospects. This seems to appear in the PISA test results, though not much research has been performed on this data to date. A too low level of educational achievement and large social inequalities are two undesirable outcomes that have repercussions on a wide range of other social and economic outcomes in the long-run.

A first objective of this study was therefore to examine how educational attainment is distributed in Germany and whether social inequalities in educational prospects are particularly pronounced in comparison to France, one of its major competitors. Instead of looking at the test scores of 15 year-olds in three general subjects (mathematical, reading and scientific literacy), educational attainment is defined here by the highest credentials obtained in general and vocational education. These certify and provide information on all the skills acquired within the course of the educational career. On a practical level, this is the information contained in the data sets available for this research. The first step was therefore to find a measure of educational attainment that accounts for the hierarchies of credentials within each country while being suited to highlight differences and similarities across France and Germany in the subsequent empirical analyses, based on the available data. This requires a good knowledge of the educational institutions and of the nature of skills certified by the credentials.

This is why chapter 2 started with a detailed presentation of the education systems in either country. It appeared that France provides a good benchmark for comparison with Germany because the German and the French education systems differ – among others – precisely in the features that are typically mentioned as potential causes of the German poor educational achievement observed in PISA. For instance, the comparatively late age of enrolment in primary school as well as the half-day character of German education as opposed to full-day schooling in countries such as France are typically viewed as features explaining the poor performance of German students. Moreover, as a rule, German pupils are streamed at an early stage of their educational career into different schools or at least classes according to their learning ability. The aim of this streaming of education is to provide an education adapted to the needs and abilities of the pupils. Nevertheless, this early and rather strict segregation of pupils is suspected to foster social inequalities and to explain the strong dependence of educational achievement on social origin. This thought is consistent with the French view that keeping all pupils in a single structure up to secondary education should contribute to reducing social inequalities in educational opportunities. Chapter 3 therefore examined whether educational attainment measured by the educational credentials obtained indeed turn out to be more tightly linked to social background in Germany than in France.

Though PISA test scores were more dispersed in Germany than in France, the distribution of degrees proved less dispersed. This is true when considering attainment in general secondary education, but also for final educational attainment. This suggests that the test scores for given degrees have a particularly large variance in Germany. The question therefore arises how skills are certified by credentials in both countries. Indeed, many more people in France have no degrees at all, while much fewer people have low scores. This holds for school degrees but also for vocational degrees. One explanation is that the requirements in general subjects for obtaining a vocational or a low-level school degree are substantially higher in France. This explains why many more French people fail to obtain a vocational degree. Considering that employers in Germany often deplore the lack of writing and mathematical skills of their trainees, there seems to be scope for further research on the correspondence between skill requirements and degrees. Indeed, it is important that degrees certify skills in a reliable way and the requirements should be adapted to the needs of the economy. In a knowledge-based society, one might consider revising the requirements in general subjects for obtaining vocational degrees, even if that means that the rate of failure, which is currently very low in Germany, would increase.

A further topic of chapter 3 was whether social inequalities in educational attainment with respect to family background are more pronounced in Germany than in France, as could be expected from the PISA results and from the characteristics of the education systems. To analyse this, a model of educational attainment first needed to be developed. The model developed here provides an economic rationale to the interpretation of the empirical estimations. Moreover, the multivariate ordered probit design of the model makes it possible to analyse the impact of certain factors at different stages of the educational career. Though the PISA test scores proved to vary more strongly by family background in Germany than in France, the findings here show that family background has a surprisingly similar impact on educational attainment in both countries. Again, this suggests that the German education system might be more lenient than the French one with students having poor results in general subjects, who typically come from disadvantaged social groups. This question deserves further research. Another finding is that most social inequalities already arise at school, whereas family background has a weaker impact on post-secondary education. Thus, measures designed to reduce social inequalities in educational achievement should be directed towards early stages of the educational process.

Furthermore, another German peculiarity appeared. Whereas the impact of family background on educational attainment proved similar in France and Germany, inequality with respect to gender turned out to be much larger in Germany, particularly in general secondary education. Whereas French women have a better schooling achievement than men, for a given generation and social background, the reverse is true in Germany. There, much fewer women than men have completed the maturity certificate, which gives access to higher education. Why this is so and whether it is so in the youngest generation despite better test results of girls at PISA is scope for further research. In particular, the streaming of German boys and girls into the different types of secondary schools, given their abilities, is worth being further analysed. For post-secondary education, however, men performed better than women in both countries but here also, gender differences turned out to be far more pronounced in Germany.

Thus, educational attainment is more highly dispersed in Germany than in France. It depends in a similar way on family background in both countries but gender differences are significantly stronger in Germany. In a second step, the study analysed how educational attainment determines the employment prospects of individuals in both countries. The objectives were twofold. First, through the analysis of the patterns prevailing both within and across countries, one can assess how successful two education systems with quite different options are as providers of qualifications to be used on the labour market. This way, one can identify some strengths and weaknesses in either education system, which should help to gain insights in the way to design the own education system more efficiently. Moreover, the analysis relies on a differentiated measure of educational attainment in terms of type and level. Drawing some conclusions from the patterns observed within and across countries contributes to characterise more precisely the link between education and labour market outcomes in some new aspects as will appear below, in general and specifically for France and Germany.

The labour outcomes examined here are the unemployment risk and earnings. These outcomes can be taken as indicators of the labour market value of educational qualifications, anything else constant. France and Germany are both plagued with high rates of unemployment. As education is the main determinant of employment prospects, looking at the details of the education-unemployment link helps to identify the relative performance of the various qualifications produced by the education system. This was the object of chapter 4. The unemployment rate is higher in France than in Germany at all education levels. However, unemployment is dynamic in nature and this study distinguishes the various dimensions of unemployment dynamics: the risk of entering unemployment, the risk of remaining in unemployment or unemployment duration, and finally the risk of recurrence of unemployment. Based on a discrete time competing risks hazard rate model, the first step consisted in estimating the impact of education on the risk of entering unemployment on the one hand, and on the chance of finding reemployment once unemployed on the other hand.

The analyses showed that the unemployment problem lies to a greater extent in a lack of job security in France, while the persistence of unemployment is a larger problem in Germany. A central finding emerging from the analysis is that the link between education and risk of entering unemployment is not monotonous as one might have expected. Attaining a higher education level reduces the risk of entering unemployment, but only up to a certain level. Beyond this level, the further advantage of having attained a higher level of education is minor in France or negative in Germany. Thus, tertiary education graduates in Germany have for instance a higher risk of experiencing unemployment than workers with an intermediate vocational qualification below the maturity level. For the reemployment prospects of the unemployed in both countries, however, the higher the education level, the better. An interpretation for this is that vocational qualifications strongly oriented towards the needs of the labour market offer a better protection against the risk of losing one's job and becoming unemployed than more general education, even of a higher level. This is because highly specialised vocational skills make the worker precious to the firm. However, when it turns out that the firm does not need the specific skills any more and the worker becomes unemployed, the level of general education proves more important. This might be because general qualifications provide more flexibility in the sense that they are suited to a wider range of jobs or sectors of activity for which the unemployed can apply. Thus, the unemployed with a high level of general education can adapt more easily to new demand conditions when looking for a job.

This interpretation in terms of labour market orientation of qualifications is consistent with the patterns observed both within and across countries. For instance, in each country, the lower tertiary qualifications, which are generally directed to the needs of the labour market, are associated with a lower risk of entering unemployment than the more academic upper tertiary qualifications, but with poorer reemployment prospects. Moreover, comparing France and Germany, it appears that the German system of vocational education proves particularly efficient in protecting against the risk of entering unemployment compared to the French one, but less efficient for reemployment prospects. By contrast, tertiary level qualifications better protect against the unemployment entry risk in France but are associated with poorer reemployment prospects than in Germany. As a matter of fact, as chapter 2 showed, the German dual system of vocational education is characterised by a high degree of labour market orientation compared to the more theoretical and school-based system in France. At the tertiary level, however, education is more linked to the labour market in France, with the presence of the *Grandes Ecoles* at the upper tertiary level and of a wide range of practical short tracks at the lower tertiary level.

Based on the estimates of the risk of entering and exiting unemployment, the impact of education on unemployment duration could be computed. Transitions from unemployment into non-employment occur significantly more often in Germany than in France, because of the much lower labour force participation rate of German mothers compared to their French counterparts. Therefore, even though the reemployment prospects of the unemployed are significantly poorer in Germany than in France, the duration of unemployment episodes is only slightly longer in Germany. Taking the incidence of repeated episodes of unemployment into account, a synthetic indicator of total unemployment risk could be computed, which expresses the number of unemployment months an employee is expected to face in the next three years. The total unemployment risk is higher in France than in Germany at all education levels, anything else constant, but the gap is largest for basic and advanced vocational qualifications and smallest for tertiary level qualifications. This is because even if the duration of each unemployment episode is a bit longer in Germany, vocational qualifications protect better against the risk of facing unemployment and in particular of facing repeated unemployment episodes than in France. For tertiary level graduates, the French education system proves a bit more efficient in endowing students with qualifications that protect them against the risk of losing their job and when unemployed of remaining unemployed for a long time. However, when they have been unemployed once, they are more likely than in Germany to incur repeated unemployment episodes.

Finally, a simple indicator of the degree of concentration of the unemployment problem on certain population groups has been constructed. It appears that the unemployment problem is concentrated on low educated groups in both countries, but this concentration is particularly strong in Germany. Individuals with a very low qualification have by far the highest risk of becoming unemployed, a higher risk of facing repeated episodes of unemployment and once unemployed, they also have far poorer prospects of getting reemployed in both countries. This raises the question whether the level of earnings in the lower part of the earnings distribution is not too high for poorly qualified individuals to be competitive on the labour market. Research in this area indicates that this might be the case. It seems of crucial importance to induce individuals to reach a minimum level of education if they are to find a job. This seems to be a major challenge for policy makers. A further axis of research could focus on the link between skills produced by the education system and the unemployment risk, for both cognitive skills such as those tested in PISA and more vocational ones. This would make it possible to find out how to revise the content of the qualifications issued by the education system with a view to increasing the chances of employment of individuals in the context of rapid technological change.

If individuals manage to find for their qualifications a productive use in the labour market, the question arises how much the labour market is ready to pay for them. The earnings can be viewed as a measure of the labour market value of the qualifications. Chapter 5 therefore looked at the link between educational attainment and earnings, taking the risk of non-employment or unemployment into account. To be more specific, it examined the earnings premium an individual with given characteristics can expect to gain from the attainment of a specific education level. It also examined how education affects the uncertainty of earnings. Indeed, the risk associated with the educational investment does not only consist in an unemployment risk but also in an earnings risk. Here, the unpredictability of earnings is viewed as a measure of the earnings risk. To analyse this issue, a specific econometric model has been designed. This model consists in extending standard earnings equation in the tradition of Mincer (1974) to control for non-random and gender-specific selectivity into paid employment while allowing for multiplicative heteroscedasticity at the same time. This way, the effect of education on the expected earnings level but also on the unexplained earnings variance could be computed, controlling for other factors.

The results indicate that selectivity effects are at work and that they are gender-specific, as the statistical difference in the correlation between employment propensity and earnings equations showed. The non-random selectivity affects the estimates of the earnings premium and risk associated with various levels of education, though the results are not much affected in qualitative terms. The estimates of the average earnings premia show that the completion of a minimum level of general instruction is valued by employers in both countries and the completion of a basic vocational degree is not as well rewarded as the attainment of this minimum level of general education. The completion of a basic vocational degree is only rewarded if an intermediate school degree is attained. Thus, not only does the completion of an intermediate school degree reduce the unemployment risk, but it also improves significantly the earnings prospects. Therefore, it seems advisable on a policy level to direct the efforts to fostering the achievement of at least an intermediate level of general instruction.

Beyond this minimum level of general education, basic vocational education yields a higher average earnings premium in Germany than in France. Thus, the German dual system of vocational education is more efficient than the French one not only because it protects better against unemployment but also because it gives access to comparatively better employment. However, in Germany, there is no further earnings gain for attaining an advanced qualification instead of a basic one. This implies that the education-earnings link is not monotonously increasing when education is defined in a differentiated way. However, in France, the completion of qualifications at the maturity level gives access to better paid positions, which is not the case in Germany. Thus, the key position of the *Baccalauréat* is reflected by higher earnings. A common feature between France and Germany is that completing higher education gives access to substantially better paid jobs. The earnings premium for tertiary education is higher in France, though study duration is typically shorter. This is most probably the effect of the presence of the *Grandes Ecoles* which are specifically designed to produce graduates for high-level positions.

Another key finding is that education also affects earnings dispersion or to be more specific the predictability of earnings. Interestingly, there are obvious similarities between France and Germany. In both countries, the completion of vocational qualifications not only reduces the unemployment risk, but also reduces the earnings risk substantially. This effect is particularly marked in Germany. By contrast, more general qualifications such as the general maturity certificate lead to a lesser predictability of earnings. In both countries, upper tertiary level graduates are those who face the highest unexplained earnings dispersion. Thus, education is not neutral with respect to earnings dispersion, even after controlling for selectivity into employment and a wide range of other explanatory factors. Only looking at the average earnings effect of education would neglect an important aspect of the labour market value of education.

Furthermore, gender differences in the labour market outcomes of education have been analysed thoroughly. As mentioned above, in the population observed, women lag behind in terms of educational achievement, especially in Germany. This has as such consequences on their labour outcomes. Adding to this, women prove to have, given their education level and anything else equal, a higher risk of unemployment and poorer reemployment prospects than men. Their unemployment spells end more often in non-employment than for men, especially in Germany. As a result, the duration of unemployment episodes is only slightly longer for women than for men in Germany, whereas the gender gap in the duration of unemployment episodes remains quite large in France. In both countries, women have a higher risk than men of facing unemployment at least once but when so, they are less likely to face repeated episodes of unemployment. Overall, they have a higher total unemployment risk than men in both countries but the gender gap is larger in Germany. In contrast, the earnings gap in favour of men is significantly larger in Germany than in France. Thus, inequalities across genders concern to a greater extent access to employment in France, whereas they are more present in terms of earnings in Germany.

The effect of education on labour market outcomes described above applies in a similar way to men and women concerning unemployment. This is not the case for earnings. Whereas women face overall lower earnings than men, they enjoy significantly higher earnings premia for education than men, even after controlling for gender-specific selectivity into employment. Moreover, there are spectacular gender differences concerning the effect of education on unexplained earnings dispersion. Women face a higher earnings uncertainty than men, ceteris paribus. However, investing in vocational education reduces the earnings uncertainty for women, not for men. This is true for both countries. Further investing in education increases again the unexplained dispersion for both men and women, but for women, the earnings risk remains below that prevailing in the absence of basic education. Thus, not only do women enjoy a higher average earnings premium than men but investing in education also reduces their earnings risk, whereas it *increases* the earnings risk of men.

Overall, this analysis of the link between education and labour outcomes in France and Germany shows that useful insights could be gained from the comparison between France and Germany. First, the comparison made it possible to assess the position of each country compared to its main competitor with respect to an essential factor of productivity and its efficient use in the labour market. Moreover, the observations of commonalities across countries enabled me to characterise more precisely the education-labour market relationship in some aspects less investigated in the literature such as the impact of type and level of education on various dimensions of the unemployment risk or on the earnings uncertainty. Analysing the patterns prevailing both within and across countries helped reveal some relative strengths and weaknesses of two education systems with different options and priorities. Besides, the distinction of the outcomes observed across genders revealed some tremendous differences between France and Germany. This is an invitation to make further research on what drives these differences which are particularly large in Germany, at least compared to France. In particular, not much research has been done on gender differences in educational attainment and where it comes from so far. The link between tested ability, school allocation and degrees obtained seems worth being further analysed.

Moreover, the relationship between education and labour market outcomes proved to be more complex than one might assume and than seems to be the case when education is measured in a less precise way. In particular, it appeared essential not only to measure the level of education but also the type of education completed. This study, by distinguishing between general and vocational qualifications at the different education levels to the extent that the data allowed it, is a first step in this direction. As a matter of fact, it appeared that the type of qualification matters a lot, be it for the study of educational achievement or for that of education-related labour market outcomes. Therefore, further research could be directed at a more detailed analysis of the link between the content of the qualifications, or at least specific skills, and labour market outcomes such as the unemployment risk or the earnings prospects. The educational credentials are supposed to certify some sets of skills, but as has been mentioned above, the correspondence between skills and credentials also seems worth being analysed. Moreover, it might be useful to analyse the labour market impact of specific skills rather than of the sets of skills certified by the credentials. This requires, of course, the availability of appropriate data.

Appendix

A

Glossary

Note: F=France, G=Germany

Abendschule, Abendkolleg (G)	Night school
Abitur (G)	High school (*Gymnasium*) degree
Abschluss (G)	Degree, certificate, diploma
Académie (F)	Educational jurisdiction
Allgemeine Hochschulreife (G)	General university entrance qualification
Apprentissage (F)	Apprenticeship
Bac, Baccalauréat (F)	High school degree
Bac Géné, Baccalauréat Général (F)	General high school degree
Bac Pro, Baccalauréat Professionnel (F)	Vocational high school degree
Baccalauréat ES (F)	*Bac Géné*, economic and social section
Baccalauréat L (F)	*Bac Géné*, literary section
Baccalauréat S (F)	*Bac Géné*, scientific section
BAFöG, Bundesausbildungsförderungsgesetz (G)	Federal Training Assistance Law
BE, Brevet d'Enseignement (F)	Vocational certificate
BEA, BE Agricole (F)	Vocational certificate, agriculture
BEC, BE Commercial (F)	Vocational certificate, commerce
BEH, BE Hôtelier (F)	Vocational certificate, hotel management
BEI, BE Industriel (F)	Vocational certificate, industry
BEP, Brevet d'Etudes Professionnelles (F)	Vocational studies certificate
BEPC, Brevet d'Etudes du Premier Cycle (F)	*Collège* certificate
Berufsaufbauschule (G)	Vocational extension school
Berufschule (G)	Part-time vocational school
Berufsfachschule (G)	Full-time vocational school
BES, BE Social (F)	Vocational certificate, social
BLK, Bund-Länder-Kommission für Bildungsplanung und Forschungsförderung (G)	*Bund-Länder* Commission for Educational Planning and Research Promotion
Brevet National (F)	National certificate, see *BEPC*
BP, Brevet Professionnel (F)	Master craftsmen certificate

BT, Brevet de Technicien (F)	Technical certificate
BTn, Baccalauréat Technologique (F)	Technological high school degree
BTn SMS, Sciences Médico-Sociales (F)	BTn, medical and social sciences
BTn STAE, Sciences et Technologies de l'Agronomie et de l'Environnement (F)	BTn, agricultural and environmental sciences and technologies
BTn STI, Sciences et Technologies Industrielles (F)	BTn, industrial sciences and technologies
BTn STL, Sciences et Technologies de Laboratoire (F)	BTn, laboratory sciences and technologies
BTn STPA, Sciences et Technologies du Produit Agro-Alimentaires (F)	BTn, farm-produce industry sciences and technologies
BTn STT, Sciences et Technologies Tertiaires (F)	BTn, tertiary sciences and technologies
BTS, Brevet de Technicien Supérieur (F)	Advanced technical certificate
Bund (G)	Federation
CAP, Certificat d'Aptitude Professionnelle (F)	Vocational aptitude certificate
CEP, Certificat d'Etudes Primaires (F)	Primary school certificate
CES, Contrat-Emploi-Solidarité (F)	Solidarity-employment contract
CFA, Centre de Formation des Apprentis (F)	Apprenticeship training centre
CFES, Certificat de Fins d'Etudes Secondaires (F)	Upper secondary education certificate
CFI, Crédit Formation Individualisé (F)	Individualised training credit
Collège (F)	Lower secondary school
CPGE, Classe Préparatoire aux Grandes Ecoles (F)	Preparatory class for entrance examinations for admission to *Grandes Ecoles*
DEA, Diplôme d'Etudes Approfondies (F)	Advanced research studies certificate, *Bac+5*
DESS, Diplôme d'Etudes Supérieures Spécialisées (F)	Advanced specialised studies, *Bac+5*
DEUG, Diplôme d'Etudes Universitaires Générales (F)	First cycle university degree, *Bac+2*
DEUST, Diplôme d'Etudes Universitaires Scientifiques et Techniques (F)	Scientific and technical studies certificate, *Bac+2*
DFEO, Diplôme de Fin d'Etudes Obligatoires (F)	Compulsory education certificate
Diplom (G)	Academic examination
Diplomprüfung (G)	*Diplom* examination
Doctorat (F)	Doctorate, *Bac+8*
Duales System (G)	Apprenticeship system in Germany
DUT, Diplôme Universitaire Technologique (F)	Technical university degree, *Bac+2*
Ecole élémentaire (F)	Primary school
Ecole maternelle (F)	Nursery school
Ecolc Polytechnique (F)	Name of a specific graduate school of engineering

Ecoles d'ingénieurs (F)	Graduate schools for engineering
Ecoles de commerce et de gestion (F)	Graduate schools for business
ENA, Ecole Nationale d'Administration (F)	Graduate schools for public administration
Enquête Emploi (F)	Employment Survey
ENS, Ecole Normale Supérieure (F)	Name of a specific scientific graduate school administration
ENV, Ecole Nationale Vétérinaire (F)	Name of a specific graduate school for veterinary
Fachgebundene Hochschulreife (G)	Subject-specific university entrance qualification
Fachgymnasium, berufliches Gymnasium (G)	Specialized *Gymnasium*
Fachhochschule (G)	Higher technical college
Fachoberschule (G)	Technical secondary school
Fachschule (G)	Technical college
Formation en alternance (F)	Part-time training
FQP, Enquête Formation et Qualifications Professionnelles (F)	Education and Qualification Survey
Gesamtschule (G)	Comprehensive school
Grande Ecole (F)	Graduate school
Grundgesetz (G)	Basic Law
Grundschule (G)	Primary school
Grundstudium (G)	Basic university studies cycle
GSOEP (G)	German Socio-Economic Panel
Gymnasium (G)	High school
Gymnasiums-Oberstufe (G)	Gymnasium, 2nd stage
Hauptschule (G)	Lower secondary school
Hauptstudium (G)	Advanced university studies cycle
Hochschulprüfung (G)	Academic examination
Hochschulrahmengesetz (G)	Framework law governing the general principles for higher education
IEP, Institut d'Etudes Politiques (F)	Institute for political studies
IUFM, Institut Universitaire de Formation des Maîtres (F)	Teacher training university institute
IUP, Institut Universitaire (F) Professionnel (F)	Vocational university institute
IUT, Institut Universitaire Technologique (F)	Technical university institute
Kindergarten (G)	Nursery school
Kirchliche Prüfung (G)	Church examination
KMK, Ständige Kultusministerkonferenz (G)	Standing Conference of the *Länder* Ministers of Education and Cultural Affairs
Land, Länder (G)	Federal state(s)
Lehre, Lehrausbildung (G)	Apprenticeship
Licence (F)	University degree, *Bac+3*
Lycée (F)	Upper secondary school

Lycée d'enseignements général et technologique (F)	General and/or technological *Lycée*
Lycée professionnel (F)	Vocational *Lycée*
MA, Magister Artium (G)	Initial or post-graduate university degree combining several subjects
Maîtrise (F)	University degree, *Bac+4*
Meisterbrief (G)	Master craftsmen certificate
Promotion (G)	Doctorate
Realschule (G)	Intermediate secondary school
Sonderschule (G)	Special school
Sozialbeitrag (G)	Social contribution
Staatsexamen (G)	State examination
STS, Section de Techniciens (F) Supérieurs (F)	Higher technical classes
Studentenwerksbeitrag (G)	Contribution to the student administration
Vordiplomprüfung (G)	Intermediate university examination
Vorschule (G)	Pre-school class at primary school
Zwischenprüfung (G)	see *Vordiplomprüfung*

B

Further tables for chapter 3

Table B.1. Distribution of degrees among higher education graduates (Level 4) in France, 1985 and 2000

Education level	Men 1985	Men 2000	Women 1985	Women 2000	All 1985	All 2000
40 Lower tertiary	100	100	100	100	100	100
400 DEUG	28.3	18.8	33.3	21.4	31.3	20.3
401 BTS/DUT	59.3	72.7	25.1	45.1	38.8	56.8
402 Paramedical	12.5	8.5	41.5	33.5	30.0	23.0
41 Upper tertiary	100	100	100	100	100	100
University	56.8	60.2	87.9	85.0	68.3	71.6
410 Bac+3/4	24.1	32.5	48.5	56.8	33.1	43.7
411 Bac+5	32.7	27.7	39.4	28.2	35.2	27.9
Grande Ecole	43.2	39.8	12.1	15.0	31.7	28.4
412 Grande Ecole	30.7	33.3	9.1	12.7	22.7	23.8
413 Top Grande Ecole*	12.5	6.5	3.0	2.4	9.0	4.6

*Note: Here is the list of the *Grandes Ecoles* reported as the most prestigious in the *Emploi* survey: Centrale, Ecole de l'Air, Ecole de la Magistrature, ESSEC, ENA, ENGREF, ENSAE, Génie Maritime, HEC, INA ("Agro"), Mines, Navale, Normale Sup, Polytechnique, Ponts, Saint-Cyr, Sciences Po Paris, Sup-Aéro and Télécom.

Table B.2. Distribution of attainment in general secondary education, 1985-2000 (in percentage of population)

	No degree			Low level			Interm. level			High level		
	M	W	All	M	W	All	M	W	All	M	W	All
							Germany					
1985	0.5	0.6	0.5	62.3	66.0	64.2	22.3	25.1	23.8	14.9	8.4	11.5
1986	0.4	0.6	0.5	61.1	64.7	62.9	22.8	25.5	24.2	15.7	9.2	12.4
1987	0.6	0.6	0.6	60.3	63.9	62.2	23.5	25.5	24.5	15.6	10.0	12.7
1988	0.5	0.6	0.6	60.0	63.2	61.6	23.8	26.0	24.9	15.7	10.2	12.8
1989	0.9	0.7	0.8	57.7	61.6	59.7	24.7	26.8	25.8	16.7	10.9	13.8
1990	1.1	0.8	0.9	56.7	60.0	58.4	24.9	28.1	26.5	17.3	11.2	14.2
1991	1.3	0.9	1.1	55.5	57.2	56.3	24.8	29.6	27.3	18.4	12.3	15.3
1992	1.8	1.0	1.4	54.8	55.1	54.9	24.6	31.3	28.0	19.0	12.6	15.7
1993	2.0	1.4	1.7	53.4	53.4	53.4	25.0	31.7	28.4	19.6	13.6	16.5
1994	2.1	1.7	1.9	52.0	51.3	51.7	26.2	32.2	29.3	19.7	14.8	17.2
1995	2.1	1.9	2.0	50.6	49.7	50.1	27.5	32.6	30.1	19.8	15.9	17.8
1996	2.3	2.0	2.2	48.9	48.2	48.6	29.0	33.8	31.4	19.7	16.0	17.8
1997	2.5	2.2	2.3	48.7	46.6	47.7	28.8	35.2	32.0	20.0	16.1	18.0
1998	2.7	2.0	2.3	47.4	45.7	46.5	29.9	35.7	32.8	20.0	16.6	18.3
1999	2.4	2.2	2.3	47.8	45.7	46.7	28.8	34.9	31.9	20.9	17.3	19.1
2000	2.4	2.3	2.3	46.3	43.5	44.9	29.6	35.6	32.6	21.7	18.6	20.1
							France					
1985	29.9	28.0	28.9	40.8	39.1	39.9	15.0	18.5	16.8	14.3	14.5	14.4
1986	29.8	27.4	28.6	39.6	38.1	38.8	16.2	19.5	17.9	14.5	15.0	14.7
1987	30.7	27.8	29.2	37.9	36.7	37.2	16.6	20.2	18.4	14.8	15.4	15.1
1988	30.2	27.2	28.7	36.7	35.4	36.0	17.3	21.0	19.2	15.7	16.5	16.1
1989	30.1	27.1	28.6	36.0	34.2	35.1	18.1	21.6	19.9	15.7	17.1	16.4
1990	31.8	28.0	29.9	32.9	32.0	32.4	19.0	22.5	20.8	16.3	17.6	17.0
1991	33.4	29.0	31.1	31.3	30.4	30.9	19.2	22.8	21.0	16.2	17.8	17.0
1992	34.4	29.9	32.1	29.0	28.6	28.8	19.6	22.8	21.3	17.0	18.7	17.9
1993	33.5	28.5	30.9	28.5	27.6	28.1	20.2	23.4	21.8	17.9	20.4	19.2
1994	32.9	27.7	30.3	27.2	26.5	26.9	21.0	24.1	22.6	18.9	21.7	20.3
1995	33.0	27.1	30.0	26.0	25.4	25.7	21.5	24.8	23.2	19.5	22.7	21.1
1996	33.8	27.2	30.5	24.6	24.1	24.3	21.5	25.0	23.3	20.2	23.7	22.0
1997	33.5	27.4	30.4	23.4	22.6	23.0	21.8	25.4	23.6	21.2	24.6	22.9
1998	33.2	26.9	30.0	22.4	21.7	22.1	22.9	26.0	24.4	21.6	25.4	23.5
1999	32.8	26.7	29.7	21.2	20.5	20.9	23.6	26.6	25.1	22.5	26.2	24.3
2000	32.2	25.9	29.0	20.3	20.0	20.1	24.0	26.8	25.4	23.5	27.4	25.5

Note: M=Men, W=Women.

Table B.3. Detailed shares of population with no vocational degree (Level 1), 1985-2000 (in percentage of total population)

	Level 10			Level 11			Level 12			Tot. Level 1		
	M	W	All	M	W	All	M	W	All	M	W	All
							Germany					
1985	0.3	0.5	0.4	10.4	32.6	22.1	0.8	3.6	2.3	11.5	36.7	24.7
1986	0.2	0.5	0.4	10.1	31.0	21.0	0.8	3.4	2.2	11.1	34.9	23.5
1987	0.3	0.5	0.4	9.8	30.1	20.3	1.0	3.3	2.2	11.2	33.9	22.9
1988	0.3	0.5	0.4	9.7	29.1	19.8	1.0	3.6	2.3	10.9	33.2	22.5
1989	0.4	0.6	0.5	9.5	27.3	18.7	1.2	3.6	2.4	11.1	31.4	21.6
1990	0.5	0.6	0.6	9.5	25.5	17.7	1.2	3.8	2.5	11.3	30.0	20.9
1991	0.9	0.7	0.8	9.9	23.3	16.9	1.2	3.9	2.6	11.9	28.0	20.3
1992	0.9	0.8	0.8	10.0	22.7	16.6	1.1	3.9	2.5	12.0	27.4	20.0
1993	0.9	0.9	0.9	9.4	21.8	15.8	1.1	3.8	2.5	11.4	26.5	19.2
1994	1.1	1.2	1.2	9.3	20.6	15.1	1.3	3.7	2.5	11.6	25.5	18.8
1995	0.6	1.3	1.0	9.6	20.0	15.0	1.3	3.7	2.5	11.5	25.0	18.5
1996	0.9	1.4	1.2	8.3	18.0	13.3	1.3	3.8	2.6	10.5	23.2	17.1
1997	1.1	1.4	1.3	9.7	17.1	13.5	1.5	4.0	2.8	12.3	22.6	17.5
1998	1.2	1.3	1.2	9.5	16.5	13.1	1.6	4.6	3.1	12.2	22.3	17.4
1999	0.9	1.4	1.2	9.3	15.4	12.5	1.5	4.9	3.2	11.7	21.7	16.9
2000	0.7	0.8	0.7	9.0	13.6	11.3	1.4	4.9	3.5	11.6	19.3	15.5
							France					
1985	22.5	24.0	23.3	22.9	28.8	25.9	6.2	8.5	7.4	51.6	61.2	56.5
1986	21.9	23.3	22.6	22.0	27.7	24.9	6.5	8.6	7.6	50.4	59.6	55.1
1987	21.8	23.2	22.5	20.7	26.2	23.5	6.3	8.5	7.5	48.9	57.9	53.5
1988	21.1	22.3	21.7	19.8	25.1	22.5	6.4	8.9	7.7	47.3	56.3	51.9
1989	20.5	21.8	21.2	19.0	24.4	21.7	6.6	9.4	8.1	46.1	55.6	50.9
1990	21.3	22.4	21.9	17.4	22.7	20.1	6.6	9.4	8.0	45.3	54.5	50.0
1991	21.6	22.7	22.2	16.1	21.4	18.8	6.4	8.8	7.7	44.2	52.9	48.6
1992	22.0	22.9	22.4	14.7	19.9	17.4	6.2	8.6	7.4	42.9	51.4	47.2
1993	20.7	21.4	21.1	14.1	19.1	16.6	6.4	8.9	7.7	41.2	49.5	45.4
1994	20.0	20.6	20.3	12.9	18.1	15.6	6.5	9.0	7.8	39.4	47.7	43.6
1995	19.6	20.1	19.8	12.2	17.3	14.8	6.4	9.2	7.8	38.1	46.5	42.4
1996	19.7	19.6	19.7	11.4	16.2	13.8	6.5	9.0	7.7	37.5	44.8	41.2
1997	19.2	19.5	19.3	11.0	15.3	13.2	6.2	8.9	7.6	36.4	43.6	40.0
1998	18.6	18.7	18.7	10.2	14.5	12.4	6.3	8.6	7.5	35.1	41.8	38.5
1999	18.1	18.4	18.2	9.6	13.6	11.6	6.3	8.5	7.4	34.0	40.5	37.3
2000	17.7	17.6	17.6	9.0	12.9	11.0	6.2	8.5	7.4	32.8	39.0	36.0

Note: M=Men, W=Women.

Table B.4. Detailed shares of the population with at most a basic vocational degree (Level 2), 1985-2000 (in percentage of total population)

	Level 20			Level 21			Tot. Level 2		
	M	W	All	M	W	All	M	W	All
					Germany				
1985	44.2	31.3	37.4	9.3	13.8	11.6	53.5	45.0	49.0
1986	43.7	31.8	37.5	9.8	14.5	12.2	53.5	46.3	49.8
1987	43.6	32.3	37.7	10.2	14.2	12.3	53.8	46.5	50.0
1988	43.4	32.2	37.6	10.5	14.1	12.4	53.9	46.3	50.0
1989	42.5	32.3	37.3	10.9	14.6	12.8	53.5	47.0	50.1
1990	41.7	32.4	36.9	11.3	14.8	13.1	53.0	47.2	50.0
1991	40.1	31.6	35.7	10.8	16.4	13.7	50.9	47.9	49.4
1992	39.4	30.2	34.6	10.7	17.6	14.3	50.1	47.8	48.9
1993	39.4	30.3	34.7	10.5	17.8	14.2	49.8	48.1	48.9
1994	37.5	29.4	33.4	11.2	18.7	15.1	48.8	48.2	48.5
1995	36.2	28.2	32.0	12.3	18.6	15.5	48.4	46.7	47.5
1996	36.1	28.7	32.3	12.9	19.7	16.4	49.0	48.4	48.7
1997	34.3	28.2	31.2	13.1	20.5	16.8	47.4	48.7	48.1
1998	33.2	27.9	30.5	14.0	19.9	17.1	47.1	47.9	47.5
1999	33.1	29.1	31.1	13.3	18.8	16.2	46.4	48.0	47.2
2000	33.0	28.3	30.6	13.3	21.3	17.4	46.2	49.7	48.0
					France				
1985	21.9	12.4	17.0	4.1	5.3	4.7	26.0	17.7	21.7
1986	22.2	12.7	17.4	4.6	5.7	5.2	26.8	18.5	22.5
1987	22.9	13.1	17.9	4.9	6.2	5.6	27.7	19.3	23.4
1988	23.0	13.4	18.1	5.2	6.5	5.9	28.2	19.9	24.0
1989	23.9	13.6	18.6	5.7	6.7	6.2	29.5	20.3	24.8
1990	24.1	14.0	18.9	6.2	7.2	6.7	30.3	21.1	25.6
1991	24.7	14.5	19.5	6.2	7.6	6.9	30.9	22.0	26.4
1992	24.8	14.8	19.7	6.6	7.8	7.2	31.4	22.6	26.9
1993	25.1	14.7	19.8	7.4	8.4	7.9	32.4	23.1	27.7
1994	25.2	14.7	19.9	8.1	9.0	8.6	33.3	23.7	28.5
1995	25.2	14.4	19.7	8.5	9.5	9.0	33.7	23.8	28.7
1996	25.3	14.7	19.9	8.4	9.7	9.1	33.7	24.5	29.0
1997	24.9	14.5	19.6	8.8	10.0	9.4	33.7	24.6	29.1
1998	24.8	14.4	19.5	9.0	10.3	9.7	33.9	24.7	29.2
1999	24.3	14.1	19.2	9.3	10.6	10.1	33.7	24.8	29.1
2000	24.1	14.3	19.1	9.8	10.7	10.3	33.9	25.0	29.4

Note: M=Men, W=Women.

Table B.5. Detailed shares of the population with at most an intermediate qualification (Level 3), 1985-2000 (in percentage of total population)

	Level 30			Level 31			Level 32			Level 33			Tot. Level 3		
	M	W	All	M	W	All	M	W	All	M	W	All	M	W	All
							Germany								
85	14.9	7.5	11.0	2.0	1.6	1.8	0.5	0.7	0.6	2.1	2.1	2.1	19.6	11.8	15.5
86	14.7	7.3	10.8	2.3	1.9	2.1	0.8	0.6	0.7	2.2	2.2	2.2	19.9	11.9	15.8
87	14.6	7.3	10.8	2.0	2.1	2.1	0.8	0.7	0.8	2.1	2.3	2.2	19.5	12.4	15.9
88	14.5	7.9	11.1	2.1	1.9	2.0	0.8	0.7	0.8	1.9	2.4	2.1	19.2	13.0	16.0
89	14.3	8.0	11.0	2.4	2.2	2.3	0.9	0.7	0.8	1.9	2.8	2.4	19.4	13.7	16.5
90	13.5	8.5	10.9	2.6	2.2	2.4	1.3	0.8	1.0	2.1	3.1	2.6	19.5	14.6	17.0
91	13.5	8.5	10.9	2.8	2.5	2.7	1.1	1.0	1.0	2.5	3.4	3.0	19.9	15.3	17.5
92	13.3	8.9	11.0	3.0	2.7	2.8	1.2	1.1	1.1	2.5	3.2	2.9	20.0	15.9	17.8
93	13.2	9.0	11.1	3.4	2.4	2.9	1.4	1.3	1.4	2.9	3.5	3.2	20.9	16.2	18.5
94	13.7	7.9	10.7	3.4	3.0	3.2	1.4	1.2	1.3	2.4	4.1	3.3	20.9	16.2	18.5
95	13.1	8.2	10.6	4.1	3.3	3.6	1.5	1.2	1.4	3.0	4.5	3.8	21.7	17.2	19.4
96	12.9	7.8	10.3	3.9	3.5	3.7	1.9	1.3	1.6	3.2	5.2	4.3	21.9	17.9	19.8
97	13.0	7.7	10.3	3.8	3.8	3.8	1.8	1.4	1.6	3.3	5.8	4.6	21.9	18.6	20.2
98	13.6	7.5	10.4	3.6	4.1	3.8	1.1	1.3	1.2	3.4	5.6	4.6	21.6	18.4	20.0
99	13.7	7.8	10.7	3.2	4.0	3.7	1.2	1.0	1.1	3.6	5.9	4.8	21.7	18.7	20.2
00	13.0	8.3	10.6	3.6	3.6	3.6	1.5	1.1	1.3	3.8	5.3	4.6	21.8	18.4	20.0
							France								
85	2.6	1.7	2.1	2.1	1.6	1.8	3.7	4.9	4.3	1.0	1.1	1.1	9.4	9.2	9.3
86	2.6	1.7	2.1	2.2	1.9	2.1	3.9	5.0	4.4	0.9	1.1	1.0	9.6	9.6	9.6
87	2.6	1.7	2.2	2.3	2.0	2.2	3.9	5.1	4.5	0.9	1.1	1.0	9.8	10.0	9.9
88	2.6	1.7	2.2	2.6	2.1	2.3	4.2	5.4	4.8	0.9	1.1	1.0	10.2	10.3	10.3
89	2.5	1.7	2.1	2.7	2.2	2.4	4.2	5.6	4.9	0.8	1.0	0.9	10.1	10.5	10.3
90	2.6	1.8	2.2	2.5	2.5	2.5	4.1	5.4	4.7	0.7	1.0	0.9	9.9	10.6	10.3
91	2.4	1.5	1.9	3.0	3.0	3.0	3.9	5.3	4.6	0.6	0.9	0.8	9.9	10.7	10.3
92	2.0	1.4	1.7	3.4	3.3	3.3	4.0	5.5	4.7	0.6	0.9	0.7	9.9	11.0	10.5
93	2.0	1.4	1.7	3.4	3.4	3.4	3.9	5.5	4.7	0.5	0.9	0.7	9.8	11.1	10.5
94	1.9	1.4	1.6	3.4	3.4	3.4	4.1	5.7	4.9	0.6	0.9	0.7	10.0	11.3	10.6
95	1.9	1.3	1.6	3.5	3.4	3.4	4.2	5.9	5.1	0.6	0.9	0.7	10.2	11.4	10.8
96	1.9	1.3	1.6	3.5	3.5	3.5	4.2	6.3	5.3	0.7	0.9	0.8	10.3	12.0	11.1
97	1.9	1.3	1.6	3.7	3.6	3.7	4.4	6.4	5.4	0.7	0.9	0.8	10.7	12.2	11.5
98	1.8	1.5	1.7	4.0	3.8	3.9	4.6	6.7	5.7	0.7	0.9	0.8	11.2	12.9	12.1
99	1.9	1.6	1.6	4.3	4.0	4.1	4.7	6.9	5.8	0.7	0.9	0.8	11.6	13.3	12.5
00	1.9	1.6	1.8	4.2	4.0	4.1	5.0	7.0	6.0	0.8	1.1	0.9	11.9	13.6	12.8

Note: M=Men, W=Women.

Table B.6. Detailed shares of the population with a higher education degree (Level 4), 1985-2000 (in percentage of total population)

	Level 40			Level 41			Tot. Level 4		
	M	W	All	M	W	All	M	W	All
				Germany					
1985	5.4	2.2	3.7	10.0	4.4	7.1	15.4	6.6	10.8
1986	5.4	2.2	3.7	10.0	4.7	7.3	15.5	6.9	11.0
1987	5.6	2.3	3.9	10.0	5.0	7.4	15.5	7.3	11.3
1988	5.4	2.4	3.8	10.6	5.1	7.8	16.0	7.5	11.6
1989	5.8	2.4	4.0	10.2	5.6	7.8	16.0	8.0	11.8
1990	5.7	2.7	4.2	10.5	5.6	8.0	16.2	8.3	12.1
1991	6.0	2.8	4.3	11.3	6.0	8.5	17.3	8.8	12.9
1992	5.9	2.9	4.3	12.0	6.1	8.9	17.9	9.0	13.3
1993	5.5	2.7	4.1	12.3	6.6	9.4	17.9	9.2	13.4
1994	5.6	2.6	4.1	13.1	7.5	10.2	18.7	10.1	14.3
1995	5.9	2.9	4.3	12.6	8.2	10.3	18.4	11.1	14.6
1996	6.0	2.5	4.2	12.6	8.0	10.2	18.6	10.5	14.4
1997	6.2	2.8	4.5	12.3	7.3	9.7	18.4	10.1	14.2
1998	6.5	3.3	4.9	12.5	8.1	10.2	19.0	11.4	15.1
1999	6.9	3.2	5.0	13.3	8.4	10.8	20.2	11.6	15.7
2000	7.2	3.5	5.2	12.8	9.7	11.2	20.0	13.1	16.4
				France					
1985	5.1	7.4	6.3	7.9	4.5	6.2	13.1	11.9	12.4
1986	5.3	7.6	6.5	7.9	4.7	6.3	13.2	12.3	12.7
1987	5.5	7.9	6.8	8.1	4.9	6.5	13.6	12.9	13.2
1988	5.7	8.1	6.9	8.7	5.3	7.0	14.3	13.5	13.9
1989	5.7	8.3	7.0	8.5	5.4	6.9	14.3	13.7	14.0
1990	5.8	8.4	7.1	8.7	5.4	7.0	14.5	13.8	14.1
1991	6.1	8.7	7.4	8.9	5.7	7.3	15.0	14.4	14.7
1992	6.7	9.0	7.8	9.1	6.1	7.6	15.8	15.1	15.4
1993	7.0	9.7	8.4	9.6	6.6	8.1	16.6	16.3	16.5
1994	7.3	10.3	8.8	10.0	7.0	8.5	17.3	17.3	17.3
1995	7.8	10.8	9.3	10.2	7.4	8.8	18.0	18.2	18.1
1996	8.1	11.0	9.5	10.4	7.8	9.1	18.5	18.8	18.6
1997	8.4	11.3	9.9	10.9	8.3	9.6	19.2	19.6	19.4
1998	8.7	11.9	10.3	11.1	8.7	9.9	19.8	20.6	20.2
1999	9.2	12.2	10.7	11.6	9.2	10.4	20.8	21.5	21.1
2000	9.4	12.5	11.0	11.9	9.8	10.9	21.4	22.4	21.9

Note: M=Men, W=Women.

Table B.7. Definition of father's occupation

Father's occupation	Germany	France
Worker	Untrained worker Semi-trained worker Trained worker Worker in agriculture	Untrained worker Driver, packer Qualified worker Worker in agriculture
Farmer	Self-employed farmer	Self-employed farmer
Self-employed	Self-employed (<10 workers) Self-employed (≥10 workers) Help in family business	Artisan Tradesman Self-employed (≥10 workers)
Senior manager	Liberal profession, academic Professional position Managerial position High-level civil servant Executive-level civil servant	Liberal profession High-level civil servant Scientific professions Professional position Managerial position
Middle manager	Semi-trained employee Farm foreman or overseer Master craftsman Middle-level civil servant	Semi-trained employee Teachers, health professions Technicians Master craftsman Middle-level civil servant
Employee	Industry foreman Untrained employee Low-level civil servant	Employee Police, military Low-level civil servant
Missing	Retired Not employed (in training, unempl., sick, prisoner, military) Dead, do not know	Not employed Missing

Table B.8. Descriptive statistics (sample of simultaneous estimation, in %)

		Germany	France
Secondary education	Low	56.95	59.88
	Middle	27.74	17.98
	High	15.32	22.14
Final education	No vocational degree	24.07	45.80
	Basic voc. degree	45.42	26.78
	Intermediate qualif.	17.15	10.73
	Lower tertiary	4.26	7.59
	Upper tertiary	9.09	9.09
Post-school education of:			
Low second. leavers	No vocational degree	27.82	62.55
	Basic voc. degree	60.60	32.94
	Intermediate qualif.	10.28	3.35
	Higher education	1.31	1.06
Middle second. leavers	No vocational degree	8.05	37.71
	Basic voc. degree	46.55	31.87
	Intermediate qualif.	32.44	18.37
	Higher education	12.96	12.05
High second. leavers	No higher education	28.08	34.27
	Lower tertiary	9.03	26.47
	Upper tertiary	62.89	39.26
Sex	Male	50.04	49.07
	Female	49.96	50.93
Birth cohort	1929-38	22.95	19.95
	1939-48	23.75	22.10
	1949-58	23.07	28.95
	1959-68	30.23	29.00
End of primary (G) / lower secondary (F) education	1939-50	29.48	19.02
	1951-55	10.58	10.80
	1956-60	11.69	12.45
	1961-65	10.83	16.27
	1966-70	13.21	15.60
	1971-75	15.00	16.18
	1976-78	9.22	9.68

to be continued...

...table B.8 continued

		Germany	**France**
End of secondary education	1945-50	13.58	11.92
	1951-55	14.39	9.42
	1956-60	10.65	9.33
	1961-65	11.16	13.29
	1966-70	10.48	14.32
	1971-75	11.53	14.42
	1976-80	15.48	14.64
	1981-86	12.73	12.67
Mother's education	No vocational degree	43.98	82.88
	Basic voc. degree	36.66	7.16
	Intermediate qualif.	3.39	4.29
	Higher education	1.16	3.54
	Missing	14.80	2.14
Father's education	No vocational degree	12.39	72.07
	Basic voc. degree	52.88	11.94
	Intermediate qualif.	12.63	5.14
	Higher education	6.90	6.74
	Missing	15.20	4.12
Father's occupation	Worker	35.62	33.23
	Farmer	5.57	12.96
	Self-employed	7.95	11.20
	Senior manager	10.41	7.26
	Middle manager	13.34	9.91
	Employee	4.07	9.00
	Missing	23.03	16.43

C

Further tables and figures for chapter 4

Table C.1. Regression results: earnings equation

Variable	**Germany** coef.	(s.e)	**France** coef.	(s.e)
Education level (ref.: Level 10)				
Level 12	0.26**	(0.02)	0.27**	(0.01)
Level 20	0.18**	(0.01)	0.18**	(0.00)
Level 21	0.24**	(0.01)	0.31**	(0.00)
Level 30	0.40**	(0.01)	0.42**	(0.01)
Level 31	0.32**	(0.02)	0.41**	(0.01)
Level 32	-0.16**	(0.02)	0.46**	(0.01)
Level 33	0.32**	(0.01)	0.41**	(0.01)
Level 40	0.53**	(0.01)	0.61**	(0.00)
Level 41	0.63**	(0.01)	0.77**	(0.00)
Female	-0.56**	(0.00)	-0.40**	(0.00)
Age				
Age/10	0.23**	(0.03)	0.58**	(0.01)
Age squared/100	0.02**	(0.00)	0.05**	(0.01)
Children<6	-0.02**	(0.01)	0.04**	(0.00)
City size (ref.: <20,000 inh.)				
20-100,000 inh.	0.05**	(0.01)	0.04**	(0.00)
≥100,000 inh.	0.10**	(0.01)	0.05**	(0.00)
Regional dummies	Yes		Yes	
Year dummies	Yes		Yes	
Constant	6.98**	(0.06)	7.68**	(0.03)
Observations	53,486		151,839	
R^2	0.32		0.33	

Significance level : † : 10% * : 5% ** : 1%

Table C.2. Regression results: unemployment compensation equation

Variable	Germany coef.	Germany (s.e)	France coef.	France (s.e)
Education level (ref.: Level 10)				
female	-0.38**	(0.01)	-0.18**	(0.01)
Level 12	0.12**	(0.02)	0.13**	(0.02)
Level 20	0.06**	(0.01)	0.09**	(0.02)
Level 21	0.16**	(0.01)	0.17**	(0.02)
Level 30	0.18**	(0.02)	0.29**	(0.06)
Level 31	0.26**	(0.02)	0.20**	(0.03)
Level 32	0.01	(0.05)	0.26**	(0.03)
Level 33	-0.04	(0.02)	0.28**	(0.06)
Level 40	0.27**	(0.02)	0.29**	(0.02)
Level 41	0.21**	(0.02)	0.45**	(0.03)
Female	-0.38**	(0.01)	-0.18**	(0.01)
Age				
Age/10	0.27**	(0.05)	0.21**	(0.06)
Age squared/100	0.03**	(0.01)	0.04**	(0.01)
Children<6	-0.02**	(0.01)	0.06**	(0.01)
City size (ref.: <20,000 inh.)				
20-100,000 inh.	0.02†	(0.01)	-0.02	(0.02)
≥100,000 inh.	0.04**	(0.01)	0.01	(0.01)
Unemployment duration				
(ref.: Germany:<12 months, France:1 month)				
2 months			0.17**	(0.02)
3-5 months			0.34**	(0.02)
6-11 months			0.33**	(0.02)
12-17 months	0.00	(0.01)	0.28**	(0.02)
18-23 months	-0.07**	(0.02)	0.18**	(0.03)
24-35 months	-0.20**	(0.02)	0.12**	(0.02)
≥36 months	-0.44**	(0.02)	-0.10**	(0.02)
Regional dummies	Yes		Yes	
Year dummies	Yes		Yes	
Constant	6.46**	(0.09)	8.24**	(0.12)
Observations	11,083		11,604	
R^2	0.25		0.15	

Significance level : † : 10% * : 5% ** : 1%

Fig. C.1. Unemployment rate by education level – Germany

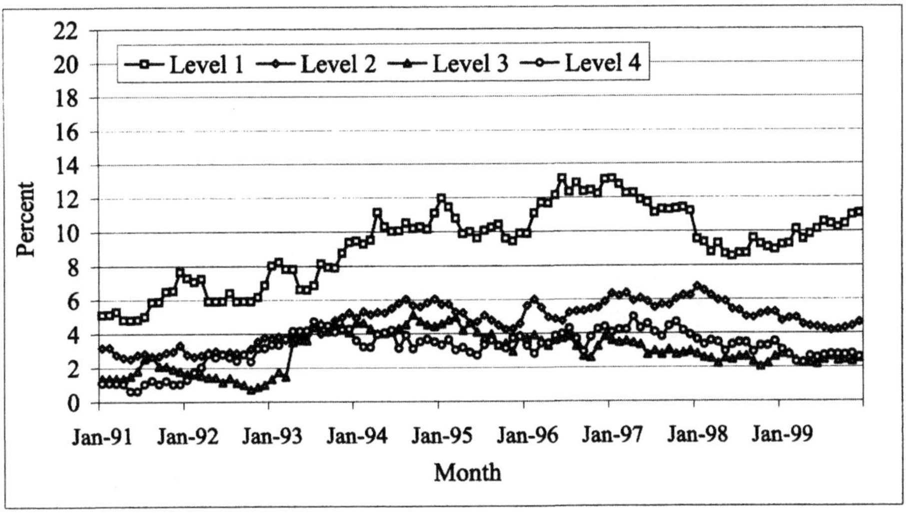

Fig. C.2. Unemployment rate by education level – France

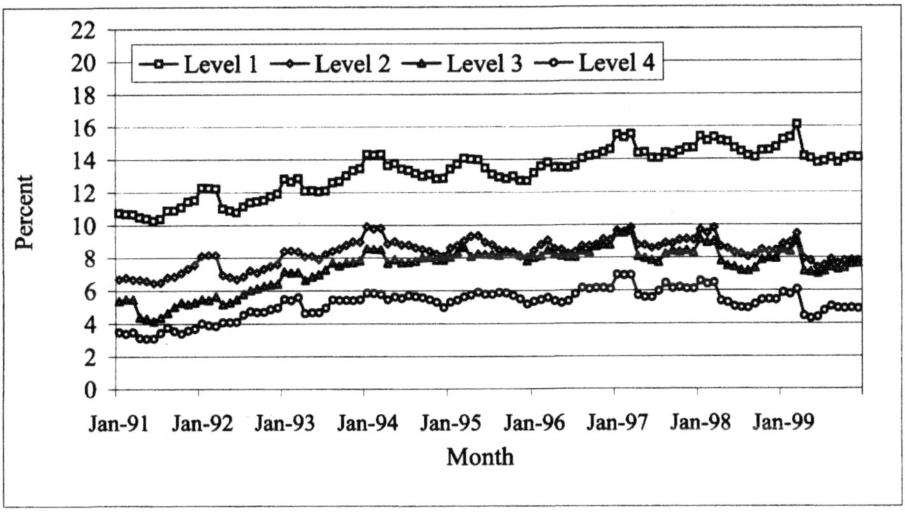

Fig. C.3. Unemployment rate by gender – Germany

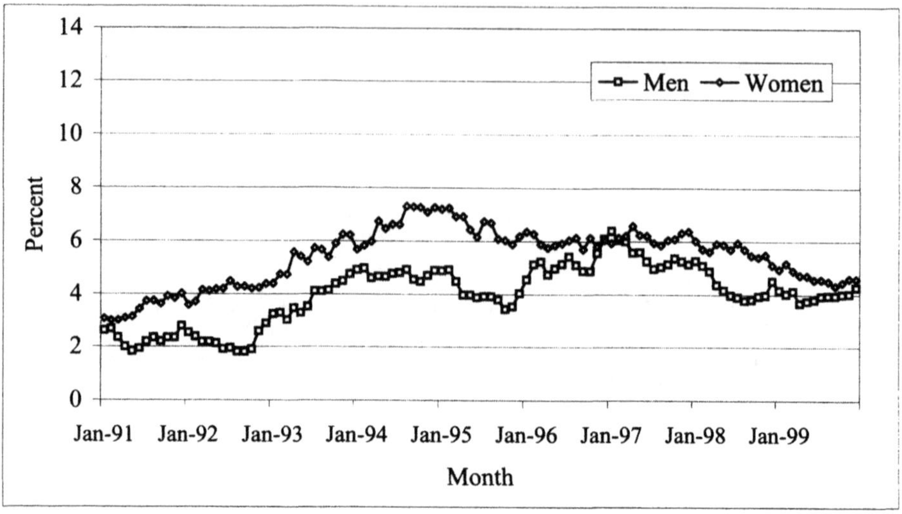

Fig. C.4. Unemployment rate by gender – France

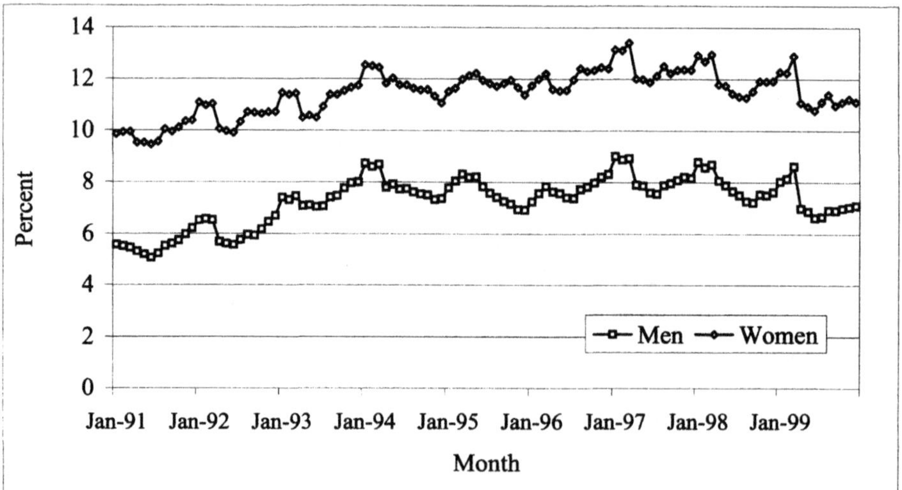

Fig. C.5. Non-employment rate by education level – Germany

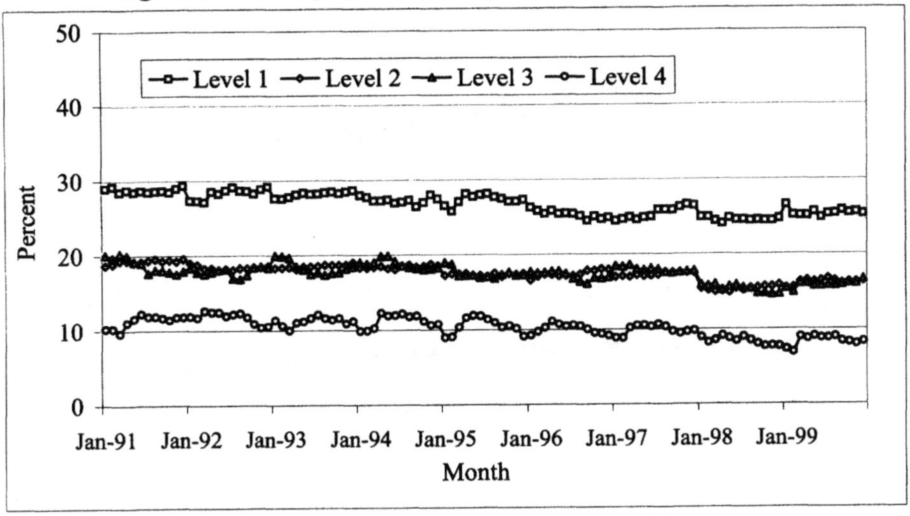

Fig. C.6. Non-employment rate by education level – France

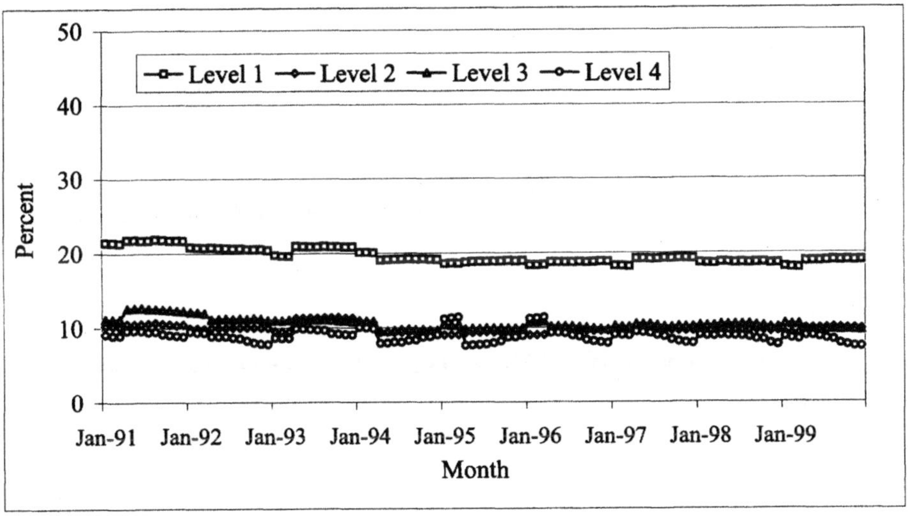

Fig. C.7. Non-employment rate by gender – Germany

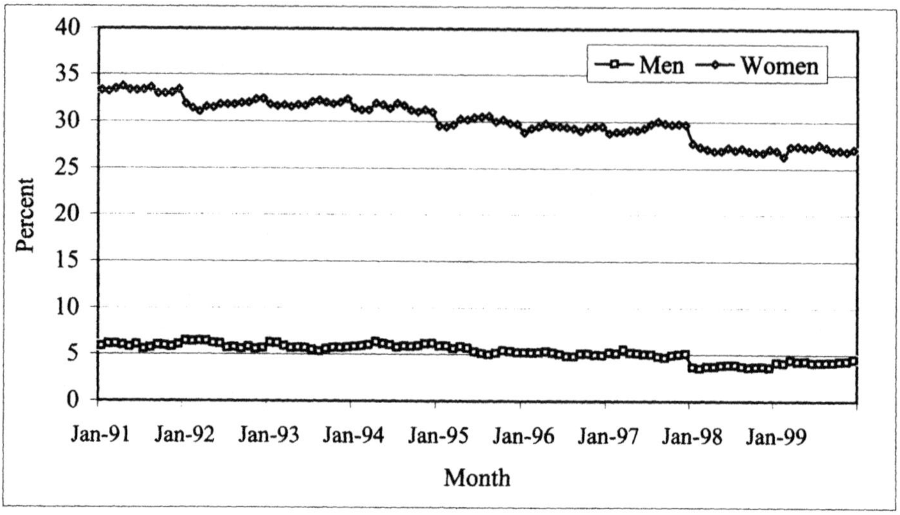

Fig. C.8. Non-employment rate by gender – France

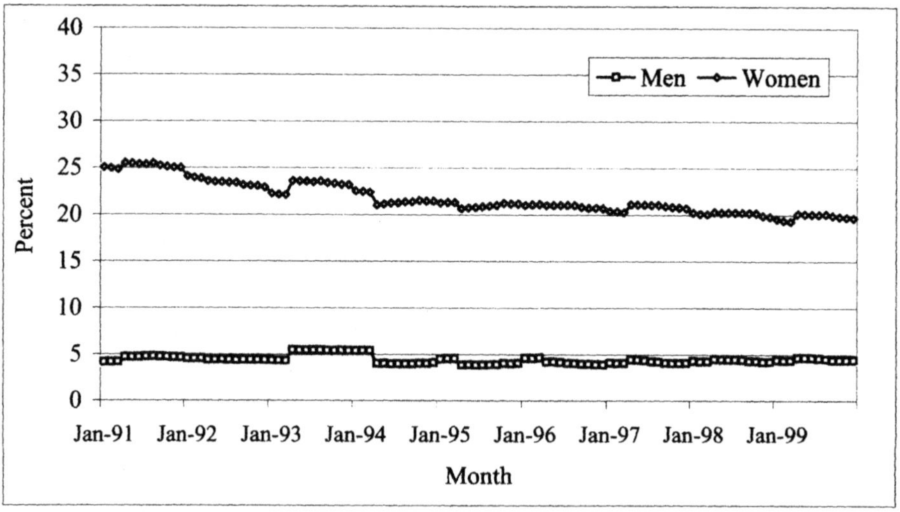

Fig. C.9. Employment rate by education level – Germany

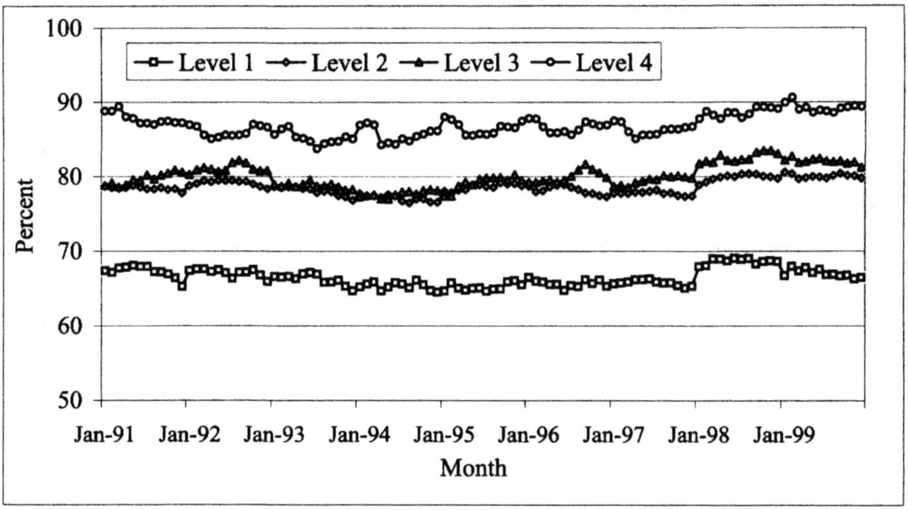

Fig. C.10. Employment rate by education level – France

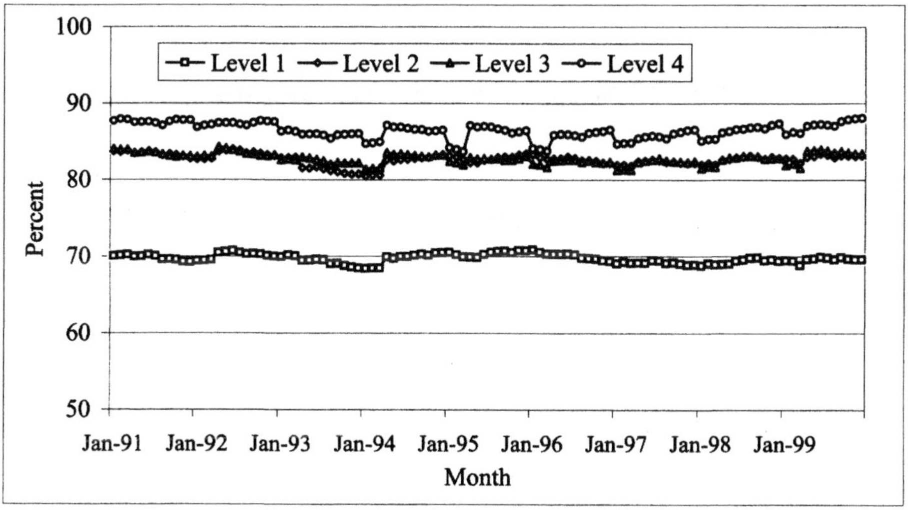

Fig. C.11. Employment rate by gender – Germany

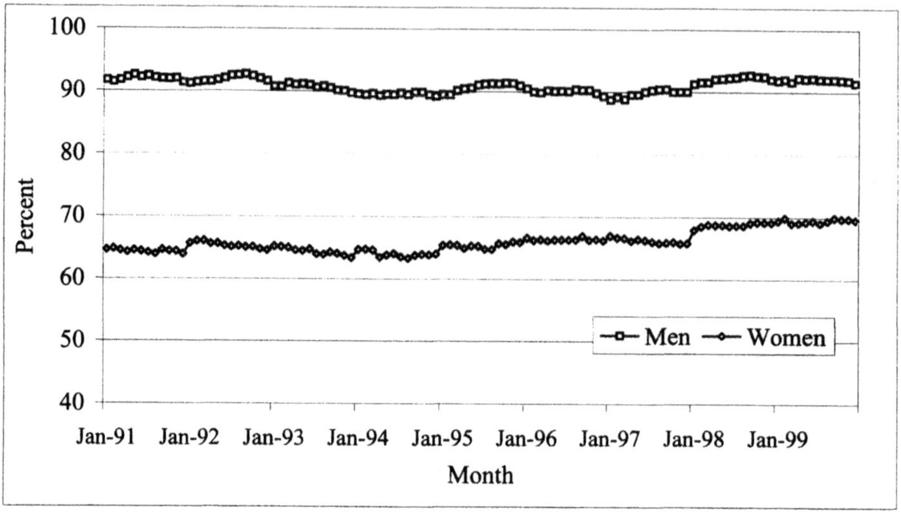

Fig. C.12. Employment rate by gender – France

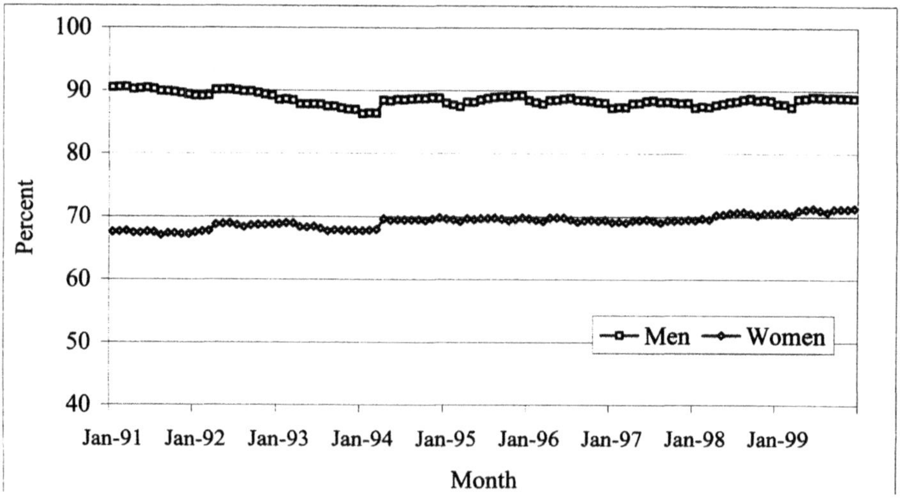

Table C.3. Descriptive statistics for the estimation samples (%)

	Spells of:	Employment Germany	Employment France	Unemployment Germany	Unemployment France
Education level	Level 1	11.1	30.6	25.4	45.8
	Level 20	27.9	21.8	32.8	19.5
	Level 21	18.0	12.1	15.0	10.3
	Level 30 or 31	16.1	6.7	9.3	4.9
	Level 32 or 33	8.0	6.2	4.6	6.8
	Level 40	6.6	11.9	3.4	7.3
	Level 41	12.4	10.6	9.5	5.4
Sex	Male	56.8	54.1	49.4	40.2
	Female	43.2	45.9	50.6	59.8
Duration	1 month			11.9	14.6
	2 months			10.0	11.7
	3 months			8.5	9.8
	4-6 months			18.8	21.1
	7-9 months			13.0	14.2
	10-12 months			9.2	10.3
	13-15 months			6.2	6.2
	16-18 months			4.5	4.3
	≥19 months			18.1	7.7
Tenure	<1 year	8.1	1.4		
	1-1.5 years	6.1	3.7		
	1.5-2 years	5.5	3.5		
	2-3 years	8.7	7.8		
	3-4 years	6.2	4.4		
	4-7 years	16.3	11.5		
	7-10 years	14.4	12.1		
	10-15 years	12.5	13.3		
	≥15 years	22.0	38.9		
	Missing	0.3	0.0		
Firm size	<5 employees	13.4	29.1		
	5-19 employees	16.2	10.0		
	20-199 employees	25.2	14.0		
	200-1,999 employees	21.2	19.9		
	≥2,000 employees	23.8	22.7		
	Missing	0.9	4.3		

to be continued...

...table C.3 continued

	Spells of:	Employment		Unemployment	
		Germany	France	Germany	France
Industry branch	Industry	31.6	17.6		
	Agriculture, energy	3.0	8.2		
	Construction	5.7	5.8		
	Trade	12.7	11.9		
	Banking	9.0	4.3		
	Transports	5.4	4.4		
	Private services	3.4	16.3		
	Public services	27.9	31.3		
	Missing	1.10	0.2		
Previous empl. status	Employed			77.0	82.8
	Unemployed	4.6	5.2		
	Non-employed	6.2	1.7	23.0	17.2
	Left-censored	89.2	93.1		
Marital status	Married	69.6	68.9	54.3	49.3
	Not married	30.4	31.1	45.7	51.7
Children<6	0 child	81.4	82.6	79.7	81.5
	1 child	13.9	13.7	14.7	15.3
	2 child	4.4	3.5	5.0	2.9
	3 child	0.3	0.2	0.5	0.3
	4 child	0.0	0.0	0.1	0.0
Home ownership	Owner	48.7	70.0	25.9	47.5
	Not owner	51.3	30.0	74.1	52.5
Age	Age 25-30	19.0	11.3	27.7	22.0
	Age 31-35	21.1	14.4	21.2	19.1
	Age 36-40	19.2	18.0	16.2	16.8
	Age 41-45	16.4	20.1	11.8	16.4
	Age 46-50	14.4	20.5	11.2	12.8
	Age 51-55	9.9	15.7	11.9	12.9
City size	<20,000 inh.	43.6	49.8	41.8	0.44
	20-100,000 inh.	27.6	11.9	24.5	14.8
	≥100,000 inh.	28.8	38.2	33.7	41.0
Unemployment rate		9.3 (2.1)*	11.7 (3.0)*	9.1 (2.4)*	12.6 (3.3)*
IRR				33.9 (7.2)*	44.8 (9.5)*
Current quarter	1st quarter	21.7	27.8	24.6	30.3
	2nd quarter	26.3	24.4	23.4	20.0
	3rd quarter	26.2	24.1	25.0	22.9
	4th quarter	25.8	23.7	26.6	26.9

to be continued...

...table C.3 continued

	Spells of:	Employment		Unemployment	
		Germany	France	Germany	France
Quarter of spell begin	1st quarter			21.4	18.9
	2nd quarter			12.4	33.0
	3rd quarter			14.4	24.3
	4th quarter			51.7	23.9
Year	1991			2.2	
	1992			5.3	
	1993			9.5	
	1994			12.7	
	1995			12.8	
	1996	11.7		14.5	
	1997	11.5		16.2	11.0
	1998	12.9	40.5	14.1	33.4
	1999	12.5	47.7	12.7	43.2
	2000		11.8		12.0

*For metric variables, the figure in parentheses refers to the standard error.

Table C.4. Expected monthly hazard of entering non-employment (%)

	From employment		From unemployment	
	Germany	France	Germany	France
Level 1	0.41	0.18	1.27	0.56
Level 20	0.40	0.20	1.22	0.54
Level 21	0.26	0.16	1.18	0.53
Level 30/31	0.53	0.12	1.18	0.51
Level 32/33	0.40	0.16	1.13	0.51
Level 40	0.28	0.14	1.10	0.50
Level 41	0.30	0.09	1.08	0.50
Men	0.15	0.10	0.81	0.34
Women	1.13	0.27	2.01	0.78
Total	0.36	0.16	1.21	0.54

Fig. C.13. Expected cumulated duration of unemployment for those who experienced unemployment

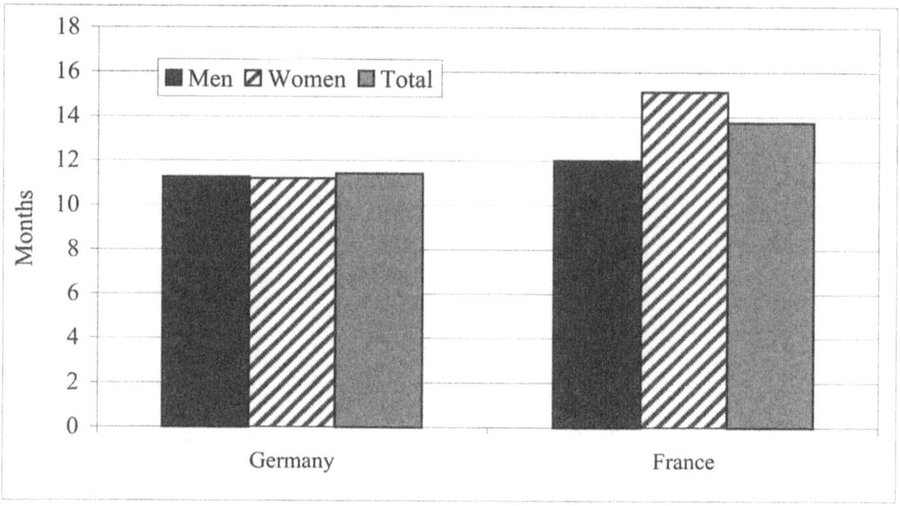

Fig. C.14. Impact of education on expected cumulated duration of unemployment for those who experienced unemployment

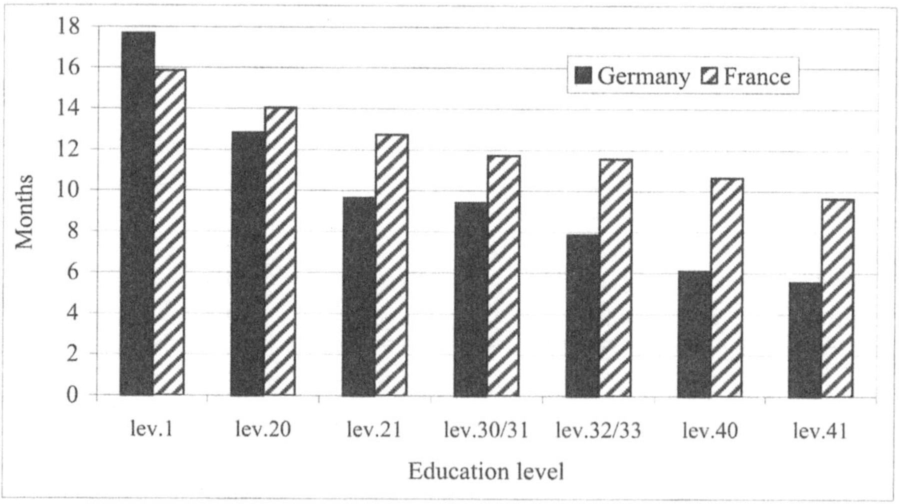

Fig. C.15. Expected number of unemployment spells

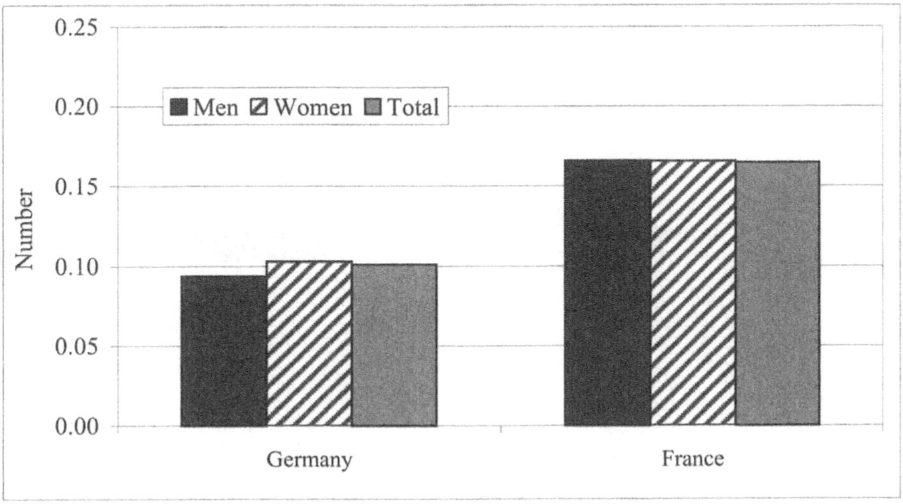

Fig. C.16. Expected number of unemployment spells by education level

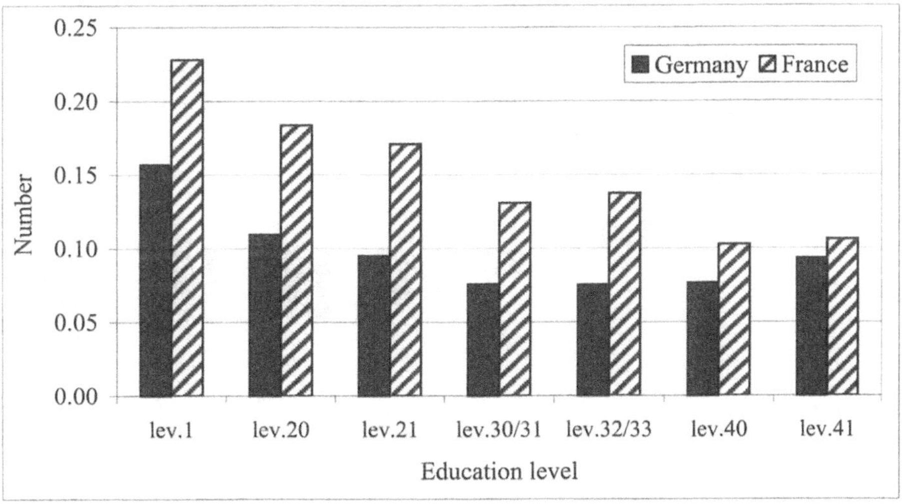

Fig. C.17. Concentration of unemployment with respect to gender

Fig. C.18. Concentration of unemployment with respect to education

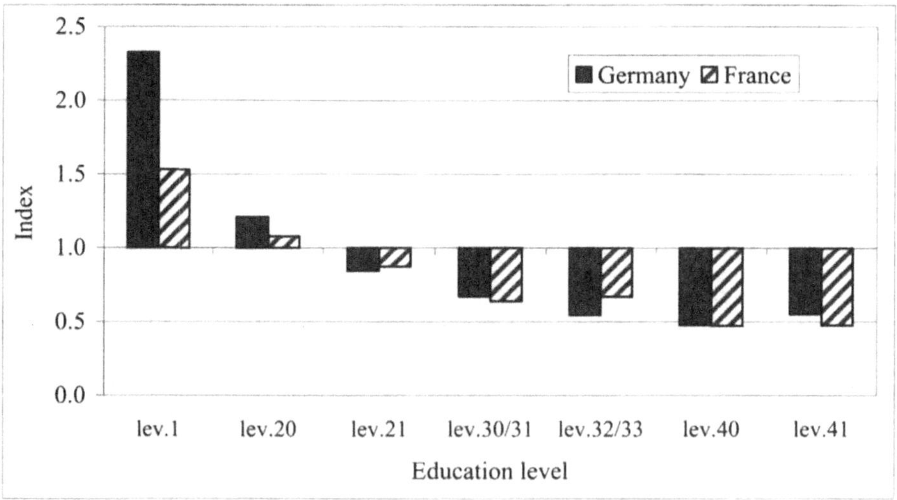

D

Further tables and figures for chapter 5

Table D.1. Descriptive statistics for sample of simultaneous estimation (%)

		Germany	France
Education level	Level 10 or 11	11.01	28.26
	Level 12	3.00	7.99
	Level 20	31.39	20.71
	Level 21	17.02	10.28
	Level 30	11.68	1.62
	Level 31	4.06	4.11
	Level 32	1.78	5.59
	Level 33	5.07	0.86
	Level 40	4.40	10.59
	Level 41	10.60	10.00
Female		52.55	52.20
Age (years)		39.70	39.89
		(8.67)*	(8.43)*
Married		76.32	69.33
Number/age of children	No children below 18	51.70	43.17
	1 child aged 6-17	15.52	16.13
	1 child aged 3-5	4.21	4.07
	1 child aged 0-2	4.92	4.50
	2 children, youngest 6-17	9.08	12.76
	2 children, youngest 3-5	4.49	5.15
	2 children, youngest 0-2	3.92	4.33
	≥3 children, youngest 6-17	2.25	4.22
	≥3 children, youngest 3-5	2.24	3.08
	≥3 children, youngest 0-2	1.66	2.60

to be continued...

...table D.1 continued

		Germany	France
Partner's education	Level 1	14.39	36.48
	Level 2	47.94	31.77
	Level 3	22.70	12.19
	Level 4	14.97	19.55
Partner's gross monthly income (Euros)		1,356.37	1001.70
		(169.21)*	(304.34)*
No info on partner's income		18.32	27.75
No partner		11.23	17.16
Owner		48.95	59.15
City size	<20,000 inhabitants	39.58	45.66
	20-100,000 inhabitants	27.98	13.24
	≥100,000 inhabitants	32.45	41.10
Current quarter	1st quarter	65.66	98.35
	2nd quarter	25.92	1.65
	3rd/4th quarter	8.42	
Year	1991	8.91	9.14
	1992	8.69	9.45
	1993	8.56	9.97
	1994	9.38	10.25
	1995	9.81	10.24
	1996	9.84	10.24
	1997	9.73	10.13
	1998	10.70	10.19
	1999	10.17	10.18
	2000	14.21	10.21
In paid employment (selected)		60.06	61.86
Log hourly wage (Euros)		2.71	2.26
		(0.45)*	(0.45)*
Tenure (years)		10.46	11.02
		(8.83)*	(9.13)*
Firm size	<5 employees	6.21	27.84
	5-19 employees	13.11	9.85
	20-199 employees	25.90	15.52
	200-1,999 employees	24.43	20.84
	≥2,000 employees	28.80	20.80
	Missing	1.55	5.16

to be continued...

...table D.1 continued

		Germany	**France**
Industry branch	Industry	32.67	20.84
	Agriculture, energy	2.12	3.51
	Construction	4.43	5.21
	Trade	12.29	11.56
	Banking	8.00	4.84
	Transports	5.44	4.73
	Private services	2.01	16.71
	Public services	30.72	31.90
	Missing	2.32	0.71
Type of employment	Fixed-term contract	4.16	3.91
	Part-time employment	20.00	17.63
	Public employment	30.64	34.71
Father's occupation	Farmer	4.18	11.05
	Self-employed	6.25	10.60
	Senior manager	10.91	7.66
	Middle manager	15.87	11.94
	Employee	4.54	15.12
	Worker	38.23	40.36
	Missing	20.02	3.28

*For metric variables, the figure in parentheses refers to the standard error.

Fig. D.1. Gross hourly earnings by education level – Germany

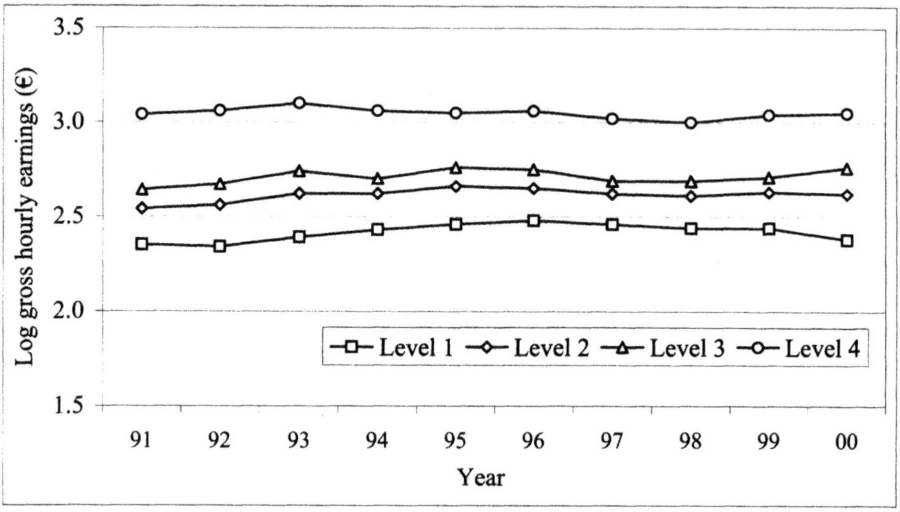

Fig. D.2. Gross hourly earnings by education level – France

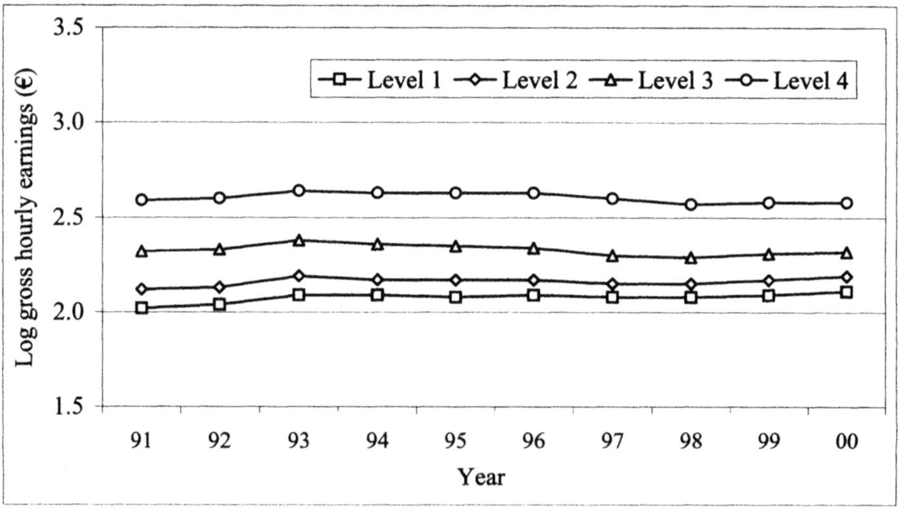

Fig. D.3. Gross hourly earnings by gender – Germany

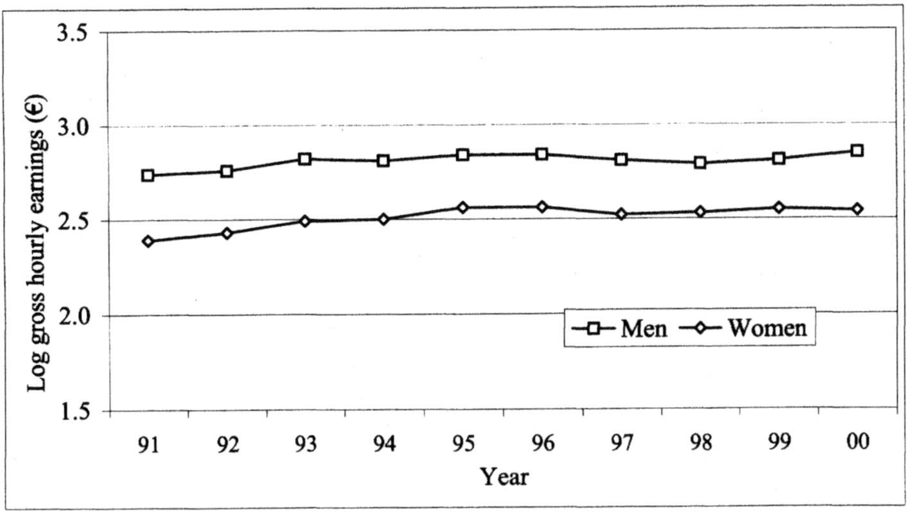

Fig. D.4. Gross hourly earnings by gender – France

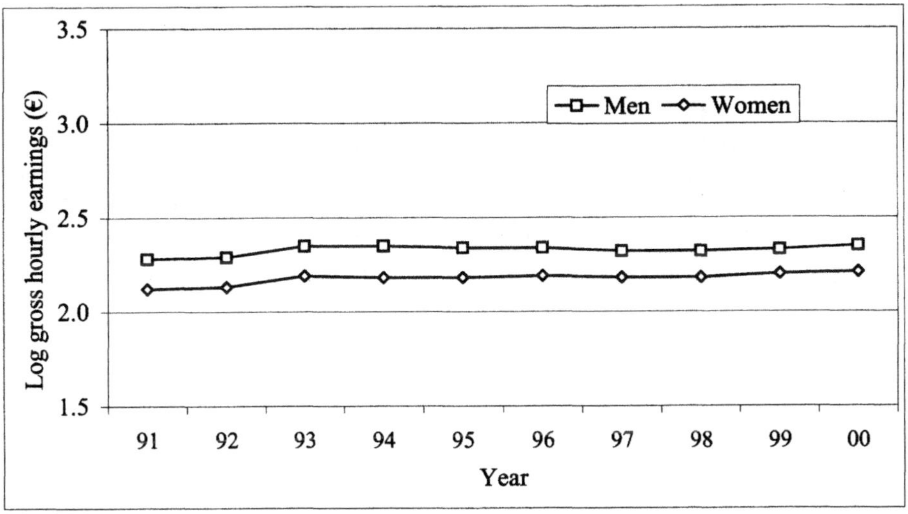

Table D.2. Average earnings premium for education (ref.: Level 10/11)

		Germany		France	
Selectivity correction:		**With**	**Without**	**With**	**Without**
Men	Level 12	0.13 (0.03)	0.10 (0.02)	0.18 (0.00)	0.19 (0.00)
	Level 20	0.05 (0.01)	0.07 (0.01)	0.09 (0.00)	0.10 (0.00)
	Level 21	0.21 (0.01)	0.22 (0.01)	0.17 (0.00)	0.18 (0.00)
	Level 30	0.12 (0.01)	0.19 (0.01)	0.28 (0.01)	0.29 (0.01)
	Level 31	0.17 (0.02)	0.18 (0.02)	0.27 (0.00)	0.29 (0.00)
	Level 32	0.06 (0.08)	0.11 (0.05)	0.32 (0.01)	0.34 (0.00)
	Level 33	0.13 (0.02)	0.17 (0.01)	0.29 (0.01)	0.31 (0.01)
	Level 40	0.43 (0.02)	0.47 (0.01)	0.41 (0.00)	0.43 (0.00)
	Level 41	0.51 (0.02)	0.54 (0.01)	0.70 (0.00)	0.69 (0.00)
Women	Level 12	0.19 (0.02)	0.23 (0.02)	0.16 (0.00)	0.17 (0.00)
	Level 20	0.17 (0.02)	0.19 (0.01)	0.11 (0.00)	0.12 (0.00)
	Level 21	0.29 (0.02)	0.31 (0.01)	0.18 (0.00)	0.20 (0.00)
	Level 30	0.27 (0.02)	0.30 (0.02)	0.28 (0.01)	0.31 (0.01)
	Level 31	0.24 (0.02)	0.27 (0.02)	0.27 (0.00)	0.30 (0.00)
	Level 32	0.37 (0.05)	0.37 (0.05)	0.33 (0.00)	0.36 (0.00)
	Level 33	0.36 (0.02)	0.39 (0.02)	0.30 (0.01)	0.33 (0.01)
	Level 40	0.46 (0.02)	0.50 (0.02)	0.48 (0.00)	0.52 (0.00)
	Level 41	0.59 (0.02)	0.63 (0.02)	0.73 (0.01)	0.76 (0.00)
All	Level 12	0.16 (0.02)	0.16 (0.02)	0.17 (0.00)	0.18 (0.002)
	Level 20	0.11 (0.01)	0.13 (0.01)	0.10 (0.00)	0.11 (0.001)
	Level 21	0.24 (0.01)	0.26 (0.01)	0.17 (0.00)	0.19 (0.001)
	Level 30	0.21 (0.01)	0.24 (0.01)	0.28 (0.00)	0.30 (0.004)
	Level 31	0.20 (0.01)	0.22 (0.01)	0.27 (0.00)	0.29 (0.002)
	Level 32	0.20 (0.05)	0.23 (0.04)	0.33 (0.00)	0.35 (0.002)
	Level 33	0.23 (0.01)	0.27 (0.01)	0.30 (0.01)	0.32 (0.005)
	Level 40	0.45 (0.01)	0.48 (0.01)	0.44 (0.00)	0.47 (0.002)
	Level 41	0.55 (0.01)	0.58 (0.01)	0.72 (0.00)	0.73 (0.002)

Table D.3. Dispersion of the earnings premium for education (ref.: Level 10/11)

		Germany		France	
Selectivity correction:		**With**	**Without**	**With**	**Without**
Men	Level 12	0.13 (0.06)	0.18 (0.12)	0.09 (0.01)	0.13 (0.01)
	Level 20	-0.15 (0.06)	-0.18 (0.10)	-0.07 (0.01)	-0.06 (0.01)
	Level 21	-0.10 (0.04)	-0.14 (0.06)	-0.05 (0.01)	-0.02 (0.01)
	Level 30	-0.02 (0.07)	0.06 (0.06)	0.07 (0.03)	0.11 (0.02)
	Level 31	0.32 (0.08)	0.36 (0.07)	0.01 (0.02)	0.05 (0.02)
	Level 32	0.53 (0.16)	0.59 (0.15)	0.34 (0.02)	0.39 (0.02)
	Level 33	0.17 (0.09)	0.20 (0.08)	0.11 (0.04)	0.17 (0.04)
	Level 40	0.30 (0.08)	0.39 (0.07)	0.08 (0.01)	0.14 (0.01)
	Level 41	0.63 (0.07)	0.75 (0.06)	0.60 (0.01)	0.64 (0.01)
Women	Level 12	-0.33 (0.07)	-0.39 (0.07)	0.01 (0.01)	0.01 (0.01)
	Level 20	-0.55 (0.05)	-0.55 (0.05)	-0.14 (0.01)	-0.14 (0.01)
	Level 21	-0.53 (0.05)	-0.55 (0.05)	-0.25 (0.01)	-0.25 (0.01)
	Level 30	-0.65 (0.06)	-0.64 (0.06)	-0.33 (0.03)	-0.33 (0.03)
	Level 31	-0.61 (0.08)	-0.60 (0.08)	-0.26 (0.02)	-0.25 (0.02)
	Level 32	-0.20 (0.09)	0.21 (0.13)	0.01 (0.01)	0.02 (0.01)
	Level 33	-0.20 (0.07)	-0.21 (0.07)	-0.20 (0.03)	-0.19 (0.03)
	Level 40	-0.14 (0.08)	-0.13 (0.08)	-0.22 (0.01)	-0.21 (0.01)
	Level 41	-0.09 (0.06)	-0.08 (0.06)	0.42 (0.01)	0.44 (0.01)
All	Level 12	-0.08 (0.06)	-0.12 (0.07)	0.05 (0.01)	0.07 (0.01)
	Level 20	-0.33 (0.04)	-0.30 (0.04)	-0.10 (0.01)	-0.10 (0.01)
	Level 21	-0.30 (0.04)	-0.28 (0.04)	-0.15 (0.01)	-0.13 (0.01)
	Level 30	-0.31 (0.05)	-0.26 (0.04)	-0.13 (0.02)	-0.10 (0.02)
	Level 31	-0.10 (0.06)	-0.08 (0.05)	-0.12 (0.01)	-0.10 (0.01)
	Level 32	0.20 (0.09)	0.19 (0.10)	0.18 (0.01)	0.21 (0.01)
	Level 33	0.00 (0.07)	0.03 (0.05)	-0.04 (0.03)	-0.01 (0.02)
	Level 40	0.10 (0.05)	0.16 (0.05)	-0.07 (0.01)	-0.03 (0.01)
	Level 41	0.30 (0.05)	0.37 (0.04)	0.51 (0.01)	0.54 (0.01)

Table D.4. Determinants of earnings (uncorrected for selectivity)

	Germany		France	
Variable	**coef.**	**(s.e)**	**coef.**	**(s.e)**
Mean effects (β):				
Education (ref.: Level 10/11)				
Level 12	0.10**	(0.02)	0.19**	(0.00)
Level 20	0.07**	(0.01)	0.10**	(0.00)
Level 21	0.22**	(0.01)	0.18**	(0.00)
Level 30	0.19**	(0.01)	0.29**	(0.00)
Level 31	0.18**	(0.02)	0.29**	(0.00)
Level 32	0.11*	(0.05)	0.34**	(0.00)
Level 33	0.17**	(0.01)	0.31**	(0.01)
Level 40	0.47**	(0.01)	0.43**	(0.00)
Level 41	0.54**	(0.01)	0.69**	(0.00)
Female * Level 12	0.14**	(0.03)	-0.02**	(0.00)
Female * Level 20	0.11**	(0.02)	0.02**	(0.00)
Female * Level 21	0.09**	(0.02)	0.02**	(0.00)
Female * Level 30	0.10**	(0.02)	0.02*	(0.01)
Female * Level 31	0.09**	(0.03)	0.01†	(0.01)
Female * Level 32	0.26**	(0.07)	0.02**	(0.01)
Female * Level 33	0.22**	(0.02)	0.02**	(0.01)
Female * Level 40	0.03	(0.03)	0.08**	(0.00)
Female * Level 41	0.08**	(0.02)	0.07**	(0.01)
Female	-0.49**	(0.10)	0.11**	(0.00)
Age/10	0.41**	(0.03)	0.35**	(0.01)
Age squared/100	-0.04**	(0.00)	-0.03**	(0.00)
Female * Age/10	0.02	(0.05)	-0.18**	(0.01)
Female * Age squared/100	0.00	(0.01)	0.02**	(0.00)
Tenure/10	0.11**	(0.01)	0.13**	(0.00)
Tenure squared/100	-0.02**	(0.00)	-0.02**	(0.00)
Female * Tenure/10	0.04*	(0.02)	0.07**	(0.00)
Female * Tenure squared/100	-0.01†	(0.01)	-0.00**	(0.00)
Firm size (ref.: $<$5 employees or missing)				
5-19 employees	0.14**	(0.01)	-0.04**	(0.00)
20-199 employees	0.23**	(0.01)	-0.01**	(0.00)
200-1,999 employees	0.29**	(0.01)	0.02**	(0.00)
$\geq$2,000 employees	0.34**	(0.01)	0.06**	(0.00)
Missing information	0.12**	(0.04)	0.10**	(0.00)
Female * 5-19 employees	0.07**	(0.02)	0.07**	(0.00)
Female * 20-199 employees	0.08**	(0.02)	0.05**	(0.00)
Female * 200-1,999 employees	0.09**	(0.02)	0.04**	(0.00)
Female * $\geq$2,000 employees	0.11**	(0.02)	0.03**	(0.00)
Female * Missing information	0.08	(0.06)	-0.07**	(0.00)

to be continued...

...table D.4 continued

Variable	Germany coef.	Germany (s.e)	France coef.	France (s.e)
Industry branch (ref.: Industry or missing)				
Agriculture, energy	-0.01	(0.01)	-0.08**	(0.00)
Construction	-0.01	(0.01)	-0.06**	(0.00)
Trade	-0.11**	(0.01)	-0.06**	(0.00)
Banking	0.05**	(0.01)	0.05**	(0.00)
Transports	-0.16**	(0.01)	-0.02**	(0.00)
Private services	-0.27**	(0.03)	-0.05**	(0.00)
Public services	-0.09**	(0.01)	-0.09**	(0.00)
Missing information	-0.03	(0.03)	-0.18**	(0.01)
Female * Agriculture, energy	-0.04	(0.03)	0.02**	(0.01)
Female * Construction	-0.01	(0.03)	0.06**	(0.01)
Female * Trade	0.04*	(0.01)	0.01**	(0.00)
Female * Banking	0.06**	(0.02)	0.02**	(0.01)
Female * Transports	0.12**	(0.02)	0.02**	(0.01)
Female * Private services	0.01	(0.03)	-0.03**	(0.00)
Female * Public services	0.17**	(0.02)	0.04**	(0.00)
Female * Missing information	-0.05	(0.04)	0.06**	(0.01)
Type of employment				
Fixed-term contract	-0.19**	(0.01)	-0.14**	(0.00)
Female * Fixed-term contract	0.00	(0.02)	0.05**	(0.01)
Part-time employment	0.09**	(0.02)	0.12**	(0.00)
Female * Part-time employment	-0.15**	(0.02)	-0.10**	(0.00)
Public employment	-0.03**	(0.01)	0.03**	(0.00)
Female * Public employment	0.07†	(0.02)	0.06**	(0.00)
Father's occupation (ref.: Worker)				
Farmer	-0.04**	(0.01)	-0.04**	(0.00)
Self-employed	0.03**	(0.01)	0.04**	(0.00)
Senior manager	0.07**	(0.01)	0.09**	(0.00)
Middle manager	0.06**	(0.01)	0.06**	(0.00)
Employee	0.04**	(0.01)	0.03**	(0.00)
Missing information	-0.06**	(0.01)	-0.02**	(0.00)
Female * Farmer	0.06*	(0.03)	0.02**	(0.00)
Female * Self-employed	0.03†	(0.02)	0.00	(0.00)
Female * Senior manager	-0.02	(0.02)	-0.01**	(0.00)
Female * Middle manager	-0.02	(0.01)	-0.01**	(0.00)
Female * Employee	0.03	(0.02)	-0.00	(0.00)
Female * Missing information	0.02	(0.01)	0.04**	(0.01)
Current quarter (ref.: 1st quarter)				
2nd quarter	0.04**	(0.01)	0.02**	(0.01)
3rd/4th quarter	0.05**	(0.01)		
Year (ref.: 2000)				
1991	-0.10**	(0.01)	-0.03**	(0.00)
1992	-0.08**	(0.01)	-0.02**	(0.00)

to be continued...

...table D.4 continued

Variable	Germany coef.	Germany (s.e)	France coef.	France (s.e)
1993	-0.03**	(0.01)	0.04**	(0.00)
1994	-0.02**	(0.01)	0.02**	(0.00)
1995	0.04**	(0.01)	0.01**	(0.00)
1996	0.04**	(0.01)	0.01**	(0.00)
1997	-0.01	(0.01)	-0.01**	(0.00)
1998	-0.02**	(0.01)	-0.03**	(0.00)
1999	0.00	(0.01)	-0.02**	(0.00)
Female * 1991			0.00	(0.01)
Female * 1992			0.01	(0.00)
Female * 1993			-0.01*	(0.00)
Female * 1994			-0.01**	(0.00)
Female * 1995			-0.01†	(0.00)
Female * 1996			-0.01	(0.00)
Female * 1997			-0.00	(0.00)
Female * 1998			-0.00	(0.00)
Female * 1999			0.01*	(0.00)
Constant	1.45**	(0.06)	1.16**	(0.02)
Dispersion effects (β^h):				
Education (ref.: Level 10/11)				
Level 12	0.18	(0.12)	0.13**	(0.01)
Level 20	-0.18	(0.10)	-0.06**	(0.01)
Level 21	0.14**	(0.06)	-0.02†	(0.01)
Level 30	0.06	(0.06)	0.11**	(0.02)
Level 31	0.36**	(0.07)	0.05**	(0.02)
Level 32	0.59**	(0.15)	0.39**	(0.02)
Level 33	0.20	(0.08)	0.17**	(0.04)
Level 40	0.39**	(0.07)	0.14**	(0.01)
Level 41	0.75**	(0.06)	0.64**	(0.01)
Female * Level 12	-0.40**	(0.14)	-0.11**	(0.02)
Female * Level 20	-0.47**	(0.07)	-0.08**	(0.01)
Female * Level 21	-0.45**	(0.08)	-0.23**	(0.02)
Female * Level 30	-0.70**	(0.08)	-0.44**	(0.04)
Female * Level 31	-0.96**	(0.10)	-0.30**	(0.02)
Female * Level 32	-0.88**	(0.20)	-0.38**	(0.02)
Female * Level 33	-0.48**	(0.10)	-0.36**	(0.05)
Female * Level 40	-0.53**	(0.10)	-0.36**	(0.02)
Female * Level 41	-0.83**	(0.08)	-0.21**	(0.02)
Female	1.04**	(0.06)	0.22**	(0.01)
Age	0.09**	(0.01)	0.22**	(0.01)
Trend	0.03**	(0.00)	-0.02**	(0.00)
Constant	-2.70**	(0.05)	-2.29**	(0.01
Observations	23,661		404,976	
Log-likelihood	-6,126.685		-1.367e+05	

Significance level : † : 10% * : 5% ** : 1%

List of figures

List of tables

References

Aghion, P. and Howitt, P. (1998). *Endogenous Growth Theory.* Cambridge, Mass.: MIT Press.

Allison, P. (1982). Discrete-Time Methods for the Analysis of Event Histories. In S. Leinhardt (Ed.), *Sociological Methodology* (p. 61-97). San Fransisco: Jossey-Bass.

Amemiya, T. (1986). *Advanced Econometrics.* Oxford: Basil Blackwell Ltd.

Artelt, C., Baumert, J., Klieme, E., Neubrand, M., Prenzel, M., Schiefele, U., Schneider, W., Schümer, G., Stanat, P., Tillmann, K.-J. and Weiß, M. (Eds.). (2001). *PISA 2000: Zusammenfassung zentraler Befunde. Schülerleistung im internationalen Vergleich.* Berlin: Max-Planck-Institut für Bildungsforschung.

Ashenfelter, O. and Ham, J. (1979). Education, Unemployment and Earnings. *Journal of Political Economy, 87*, 99-116.

Atkinson, T., Glaude, L., Olier, L. and Piketty, T. (2001). *Inégalités économiques.* Paris: La Documentation Francaise.

Baker, M. and Melino, A. (2000). Duration Dependence and Nonparametric Heterogeneity: A Monte Carlo Study. *Journal of Econometrics, 96*, 357-393.

Baudelot, C. and Gollac, M. (1997). Le salaire du trentenaire: question d'âge ou de génération? *Economie et Statistique, 304/305*, 17-36.

Bauer, M. and Bertin-Mourot, B. (1995). Le recrutement des élites économiques en France et en Allemagne. In E. Suleiman and H. Mendras (Eds.), *Le recrutement des élites en Europe* (p. 91-112). Paris: La Découverte.

Baur, R. (1972). *Elternhaus und Bildungschancen. Eine Untersuchung über die Bedeutung des Elternhauses für die Schulwahl nach der 4. Klasse Grundschule.* Weinheim: Beltz.

Becker, G. S. (1964). *Human Capital: A Theoretical and Empirical Analysis, with Special Reference to Education.* New York: Columbia University Press.

Becker, G. S. (1965). A Theory of the Allocation of Time. *Economic Journal, 75*, 493-517.

Becker, G. S. and Tomes, N. (1986). Human Capital and the Rise and Fall of Families. *Journal of Labor Economics, 4*(3), 1-39.

Bellmann, L., Reinberg, A. and Tessaring, M. (Eds.). (1994). *Bildungsexpansion, Qualifikationsstruktur und Einkommensverteilung* (Vol. 221). Berlin: Duncker und Humblot.

Belzil, C. and Jörgen, H. (2001). *Heterogeneous Returns to Human Capital and Dynamic Self-Selection* (Discussion Paper No. 272). IZA.

Bender, S. and Seifert, W. (1996). Zuwanderer auf dem Arbeitsmarkt: Nationalität und geschlechtsspzifische Unterschiede. *Zeitschrift für Soziologie, 25*(6), 473-495.

Ben-Porath, Y. (1967). The Production of Human Capital and the Life Cycle of Earnings. *Journal of Political Economy, 75*, 352-365.

Blau, P. M. and Duncan, O. D. (1967). *The American Occupational Structure.* New York: Wiley.

Blossfeld, H.-P. (1993). Changes in Educational Opportunities in the Federal Republic of Germany. In Y. Shavit and H.-P. Blossfeld (Eds.), *Persistent Inequality. Changing Educational Attainment in Thirteen Countries* (p. 51-74). Boulder: Westview Press.

Bonnal, L. and Fougère, D. (1990). Les déterminants individuels des durées de chômage. *Economie et Prévision, 5*, 45-82.

Bonnal, L., Mendès, S. and Sofer, C. (2002). School-To-Work Transition: Apprenticeship versus Vocational School in France. *International Journal of Manpower, 23*(5), 426-442.

Boudon, R. (1973). *L'inégalité des chances.* Paris: Armand Colin.

Boudon, R. (1974). *Education, Opportunity and Social Inequality.* New York: Wiley.

Bourdieu, P. and Passeron, J. (1970). *La reproduction.* Paris: Les éditions de Minuit.

Brauns, H., Gangl, M. and Scherer, S. (1999). *Education and Unemployment* (Working Paper No. 6). MZES.

Brauns, H., Müller, W. and Steinmann, S. (1997). *Educational Expansion and Returns to Education, A Comparative Study on Germany, France, the UK and Hungary* (Working Paper No. I/23). MZES.

Büchel, F. and Wagner, G. (1996). Soziale Differenzen der Bildungschancen in Westdeutschland unter besonderer Berücksichtigung von Zuwandererkindern. In W. Zapf (Ed.), *Lebenslagen im Wandel. Sozialberichterstattung im Längsschnitt.* Frankfurt: Campus.

Cameron, S. V. and Heckman, J. J. (1998). Life Cycle Schooling and Dynamic Selection Bias: Models and Evidence for Five Cohorts of American Males. *Journal of Political Economy, 106*(2), 262-333.

Card, D. (1998). *The Causal Effect of Education on Earnings* (Working Paper No. 2). Center for Labor Economics, University of California.

Card, D. (2000). *Estimating the Return to Schooling: Progress on Some Persistent Econometric Problems* (Working Paper No. 7769). NBER.

Cases, C. and Lollivier, S. (1994). Estimation d'un modèle de sortie de chômage à destinations multiples. *Economie et Prévision, 113-114*(2/3), 177-187.

Cohen, D., Lefranc, A. and Saint-Paul, G. (1997). French Unemployment: A Transatlantic Perspective. *Economic Policy, 25*, 267-291.

D'Addio, A. C. (1998). *Unemployment Durations of French Young People: the Impact of Individual, Family and Other Factors on the Hazard Rate* (CORE Discussion Paper No. 9851). Université Catholique de Louvain.

De Graaf, P. (1988). Parents' Financial and Cultural Resources, Grades and Transition to Secondary School in the Federal Republic of Germany. *European Sociological Review, 4*(3), 209-221.

Dormont, B., Fougère, D. and Prieto, A. (2001). L'effet de l'allocation unique dégressive sur la reprise d'emploi. *Economie et Statistique, 3*, 3-28.

Duru-Bellat, M., Jarousse, J.-P. and Mingat, A. (1993). Les scolarités de la maternelle au lycée. *Revue Francaise de Sociologie, 34*, 43-60.

Duru-Bellat, M. and Mingat, A. (1987). Facteurs institutionnels de la diversité des carrières scolaires. *Revue Francaise de Sociologie, 25*, 233-254.

Dustmann, C. (2001). *Parental Background, Primary to Secondary School Transition and Wages* (Discussion Paper No. 367). IZA.

Dustmann, C. and van Soest, A. (1998). Public and Private Sector Wages of Male Workers in Germany. *European Economic Review, 42*(8), 1417-1441.

Ermisch, J. F. and Francesconi, M. (2001). Family Matters: Impacts of Family Background on Educational Attainments. *Economica, 68*, 137-156.

European Communities. (1998). *A Guide to Higher Education Systems and Qualifications in the EU and EEA Countries.* Brussels: Office for Official Publications of the European Communities.

European Communities. (2002). *Key Data on Education in the European Union.* Brussels: Office for Official Publications of the European Communities.

Eurybase. (2003). *http://www.eurydice.org/eurybase.html.* Eurydice.

Eurydice/Cedefop. (1995). *Structures of the Education and Initial Training Systems in the European Union.* Brussels: Office for Official Publications of the European Communities.

Fahrmeir, L. and Tutz, G. (2001). *Multivariate Statistical Modelling Based on Generalized Linear Models* (2 ed.). New York: Springer Verlag.

Flinn, C. J. and Heckman, J. J. (1983). Are Unemployed and Out of the Labor Force Behaviorally Distinct Labor Force States? *Journal of Labor Economics, 1*(1), 28-42.

Florens, J.-P., Fougère, D., Kamionka, T. and Mouchart, M. (1995). La modélisation économétrique des transitions sur le marché du travail. *Economie et Prévision, 116*, 181-217.

Florens, J.-P., Gérard-Varet, L.-A. and Werquin, P. (1989). L'impact de l'indemnisation sur la durée et l'ancienneté du chômage. *Economie et Prévision, 87*(1), 93-104.

Forgeot, G. and Gautié, J. (1997). Insertion professionnelle des jeunes et processus de déclassement. *Economie et Statistique, 4*(5), 53-74.

Fougère, D., Kramarz, F. and Magnac, T. (2000). Youth Employment Policies in France. *European Economic Review, 44*(4/6), 928-942.

Franz, W. (1982). *Youth Unemployment in the Federal Republic of Germany: Theory, Empirical Results and Policy Implications.* Tübingen: Mohr und Siebeck.

Franz, W. (1999). *Arbeitsmarktökonomik.* Berlin, Heidelberg: Springer-Verlag.

Franz, W., Inkmann, J., Pohlmeier, W. and Zimmermann, V. (2000). Young and Out in Germany: On Youths' Chances of Labor Market Entrance in Germany. In D. Blanchflower (Ed.), *Youth Employment and Joblessness in Advanced Countries* (p. 381-425). Chicago: University of Chicago Press.

Franz, W. and Zimmermann, V. (2002). The Transition from Apprenticeship Training to Work. *International Journal of Manpower, 23*(5), 411-425.

Gang, I. N. and Zimmermann, K. F. (1999). *Is Child like Parent? Educational Attainment and Ethnic Origin* (Discussion Paper No. 57). IZA.

Gottschall, K. and Hagemann, K. (2002). Die Halbtagsschule in Deutschland. *Aus Politik und Zeitgeschichte, B*(41), 12-22.

Gould, W. and Sribney, W. (1999). *Maximum Likelihood Estimation with Stata.* College Station: Stata Press.

Gouriéroux, C. (1989). *Econométrie des variables qualitatives* (2nd ed.). Paris: Economica.

Goux, D. and Maurin, E. (1994). Education, expérience et salaire: tendances récentes et évolutions de long-terme. *Economie et Statistique, 116*, 155-178.

Goux, D. and Maurin, E. (1997). Destinées sociales: le rôle de l'école et du milieu d'origine. *Economie et Statistique, 306*(6), 13-26.

Goux, D. and Maurin, E. (1998). From Education to First Job: The French Case. In W. Müller and Y. Shavit (Eds.), *From School to Work: A Comparative Study of Educational Qualifications and Occupational Destinations* (p. 114-142). Oxford: Oxford University Press.

Greene, W. H. (2000). *Econometric Analysis* (4th ed.). London: Prentice Hall International.

Griliches, B. Z. (1977). Estimating the Returns to Schooling: Some Econometric Problems. *Econometrica, 45*(1), 1-22.

Guille, M. and Skalli, A. (1999). Returns to Human Capital: A Review of the French Empirical Literature. In R. Asplund and P. T. Pereira (Eds.), *Returns to Human Capital in Europe, A Literature Review* (p. 85-124). Helsinki: Taloustieto Oy.

Guille, M. and Skalli, A. (2001). France. In C. Harmon, I. Walker and N. Westergaard-Nielsen (Eds.), *Education and Earnings in Europe – A*

Cross-Country Analysis of the Returns to Education. Cheltenham (UK): Edward Elgar.

Guillotin, Y. and Sevestre, P. (1994). Estimations des fonctions de gains sur données de panel. *Economie et Prévision, 116*, 119-135.

Haisken-DeNew, J. and Frick, J. (Eds.). (2000). *Desktop Companion to the German Socio-Economic Panel (GSOEP) Study.* Berlin: DIW.

Han, A. and Hausman, J. (1990). Flexible Parametric Estimation of Duration and Competing Risks Models. *Journal of Applied Econometrics, 5*, 1-28.

Hanoch, G. (1967). An Economic Analysis of Earnings and Schooling. *Journal of Human Resources, 2*, 310-329.

Hanushek, E. A. (1992). The Trade-Off Between Child Quantity and Quality. *Journal of Political Economy, 100*(1), 84-117.

Harmon, C., Hogan, V. and Walker, I. (2003). Dispersion in the Economic Return to Education. *Labour Economics, 10*(2), 205-241.

Harmon, C., Walker, I. and Westergaard-Nielsen, N. (2001). *Education and Earnings in Europe – A Cross-Country Analysis of the Returns to Education.* Cheltenham (UK): Edward Elgar.

Harvey, A. (1976). Estimating Regression Models with Multiplicative Heteroscedasticity. *Econometrica, 44*(3), 461-465.

Hausman, J. and McFadden, D. (1984). A Specification Test for the Multinomial Logit Model. *Econometrica, 52*, 1219-1240.

Haveman, R. and Wolfe, B. (1995). The Determinants of Children's Attainments: A Review of Methods and Findings. *The Journal of Economic Literature, 33*(4), 1829-1878.

Heckman, J. J. (1976). A Life-Cycle Model of Earnings, Learning and Consumption. *Journal of Political Economy, 84*(4), 11-44.

Heckman, J. J. (1979). Sample Selection Bias as a Specification Error. *Econometrica, 47*, 153-161.

Heckman, J. J., Lochner, L. J. and Todd, P. E. (2003). *Fifty Years of Mincer Earnings Regressions* (Working Paper No. 9732). NBER.

Heckman, J. J. and Singer, B. (1984). Econometric Duration Analysis. *Journal of Econometrics, 24*, 63-132.

Hildreth, C. and Houck, J. P. (1968). Some Estimators for a Linear Model with Random Coefficients. *Journal of the American Statistical Association, 63*(322), 584-595.

Hübler, O. and Gerlach, K. (1990). Sectoral Wage Patterns, Individual Earnings and the Efficiency Wage Hypothesis. In H. König (Ed.), *Economics of Wage Determination* (p. 56-83). Berlin, Heidelberg: Springer Verlag.

Hunt, J. (1999). *Determinants of Non-Employment and Unemployment Durations in East Germany* (Working Paper No. 7128). NBER.

International Labour Office (Ed.). (1989). *Employment, Unemployment, Wages and Hours of Work.* Geneva: ILO.

Jarousse, J.-P. and Mingat, A. (1986). Un réexamen du modèle de Mincer. *Revue Economique, 37*, 999-1030.

Jenkins, S. (2002). *Survival Analysis.* Colchester: mimeo.

Jenkins, S. P. (1995). Practitioner's Corner – Easy Estimation Methods for Discrete-Time Duration Models. *Oxford Bulletin of Economics and Statistics, 57*(1), 129-138.

Johnston, J. and DiNardo, J. (2001). *Econometric Methods* (4th ed.). New York: MacGraw-Hill.

Joutard, X. and Ruggiero, M. (2000). Recherche d'emploi et risque de récurrence du chômage - Une analyse des qualifications. *Annales d'Economie et de Statistique, 2000*(1), 239-265.

Jovanovic, B. (1979). Job Matching and the Theory of Turnover. *Journal of Political Economy, 5.*

Judge, G., Hill, C., Griffiths, W. and Lee, T. (1985). *The Theory and Practice of Econometrics.* New York: Wiley.

Juhn, C., Murphy, K. M. and Pierce, B. (1993). Wage Inequality and the Rise in Returns to Skill. *Journal of Political Economy, 101*(3), 410-441.

Kalbfleisch, J. and Prentice, R. (1980). *The Statistical Analysis of Failure Time Data.* New York: Wiley.

Karr, W. and John, K. (1989). Mehrfacharbeitslosigkeit und kumulative Arbeitslosigkeit. *Mitteilungen aus der Arbeitsmarkt- und Berufsforschung, 22*, 1-32.

Katz, L. and Murphy, K. (1992). Changes in Relative Wages 1963-1987 – Supply and Demand Factors. *Quarterly Journal of Economics, 107*(Feb.), 35-78.

Kaukewitsch, P. and Rouault, D. (1998). Les structures des salaires en France et en Allemagne en 1995: une analyse statistique comparative des hiérarchies salariales. *Economie et Statistique, 315*(5), 3-27.

Kettunen, J. (1997). Education and Unemployment Duration. *Economics of Education Review, 16*(2), 163-170.

Kodde, D. A. (1988). Unemployment Expectations and Human Capital Formation. *The European Economic Review, 32*(8), 1645-1660.

König, W., Lüttinger, P. and Müller, W. (1988). *A Comparative Analysis of the Development and Structure of Educational Systems : Methodological Foundations and the Construction of a Comparative Educational Scale (CASMIN)* (Working Paper No. 12). University of Mannheim.

Kristen, C. (1999). *Bildungsentscheidungen und Bildungsungleichheit – Ein Überblick über den Forschungsstand* (Working Paper No. 5). MZES.

Kristen, C. (2000). *Ethnic Differences in Educational Placement: The Transition from Primary to Secondary Schooling* (Working Paper No. 92). MZES.

Lancaster, T. (1990). *The Econometric Analysis of Transition Data.* Cambridge: Cambridge University Press.

Lauer, C. (2000). *Gender Wage Gap in West Germany: How Far Do Gender Differences in Human Capital Matter?* (Discussion Paper No. 00-7). ZEW.

Lauer, C. and Steiner, V. (1999). Returns to Human Capital in Germany: Review of the Empirical Literature. In R. Asplund and P. T. Pereira

(Eds.), *Returns to Human Capital in Europe, A Literature Review* (p. 125-146). Helsinki: Taloustieto Oy.

Lauer, C. and Steiner, V. (2001). Germany. In C. Harmon, I. Walker and N. Westergaard-Nielsen (Eds.), *Education and Earnings in Europe. A Cross-Country Analysis of the Returns to Education* (p. 102-128). Cheltenham (UK): Edward Elgar.

Lauer, C. and Weber, A. M. (2003). *Employment of Mothers After Childbirth: A French-German Comparison* (Discussion Paper No. 03-50). ZEW.

Layard, R., Nickell, S. and Jackman, R. (1991). *Unemployment.* New York: Oxford University Press.

Lhéritier, J. (1992). Les déterminants du salaire. *Economie et Statistique, 257*, 9-22.

Maddala, G. S. (1983). *Limited-Dependent and Qualitative Variables in Econometrics.* Cambridge: Cambridge University Press.

Magnac, T. (1998). *State Dependence and Heterogeneity in Youth Employment Histories* (Working Paper No. 9747). CREST.

Magnac, T. and Visser, M. (1999). Transition Models with Measurement Errors. *The Review of Economics and Statistics, 81*(3), 466-474.

Manski, C. F. and Wise, D. A. (1983). *College Choice in America.* Cambridge, Mass.: Harvard University Press.

Mare, R. D. (1980). Social Background and School Continuation Decisions. *The Journal of American Statistical Association, 75*(370), 295-305.

Marry, C., Kieffer, A., Brauns, H. and Steinmann, S. (1998). France-Allemagne: Inégales avancées des femmes. *Revue Française de Sociologie, 39*(2), 353-389.

Mincer, J. (1974). *Schooling, Experience and Earnings.* New York: NBER.

Mincer, J. (1989). *Job Training: Costs, Returns and Wage Profiles* (Working paper No. 3208). NBER.

Mincer, J. (1991a). *Education and Unemployment of Women* (Working Paper No. 3837). NBER.

Mincer, J. (1991b). *Education and Unemployment* (Working Paper No. 3838). NBER.

Moebus, M. and Verdier, E. (1997). La construction des diplômes professionnels en Allemagne et en France. *Céreq Bref, 130.*

Mortensen, D. (1976). Job Matching under Imperfect Competition. In O. Ashenfelter and J. Blum (Eds.), *Evaluating Labor-Market Effects of Social Programs* (p. 194-232).

Mortensen, D. (1986). Job Search and Labor Market Analysis. In O. Ashenfelter and R. Layard (Eds.), *Handbook of Labor Economics* (p. 849-919). Amsterdam: North-Holland.

Müller, W. (1990). *Does Education Matter? Evidence from Cross-National Comparisons.* Stanford: Center for Advanced Study in the Behavioral Science.

Müller, W. and Haun, D. (1994). Bildungsexpansion und Bildungsungleichheit. In W. Glatzer (Ed.), *Einstellungen und Lebensbedingungen in Europa* (p. 225-268). Frankfurt: Campus.

Müller, W., Steinmann, S. and Ell, R. (1998). Education and Labour-Market Entry in Germany. In W. Müller and Y. Shavit (Eds.), *From School to Work* (p. 143-188). Oxford: Oxford University Press.

Muysken, J. and Ter Weel, B. (2000). Overeducation and Crowding Out of Low-Skilled Workers. In L. Borghans and A. de Grip (Eds.), *The Overeducated Worker? The Economics of Skill Utilisation* (p. 109-132). Cheltenham (UK): Edward Elgar.

Narendranathan, W. and Stewart, M. (1993). How Does the Benefit Effect Vary as Unemployment Spells Lengthen? *Journal of Applied Econometrics, 8*, 361-381.

Nicaise, I. (2001). Human Capital, Reservation Wages and Job Competition: Heckman's Lambda Re-Interpreted. *Applied Economics, 33*, 309-315.

Nickell, S. (1979). Education and Lifetime Patterns of Unemployment. *Journal of Political Economy, 87*(5), 117-131.

OECD. (2002). *Knowledge and Skills for Life: First Results from PISA 2000.* Paris: OECD.

OECD. (2003). *Education at a Glance: OECD Indicators.* Paris: OECD.

Pereira, P. T. and Martins, P. S. (2000). *Does Education Reduce Wage Inequality? Quantile Regressions Evidence from Fifteen European Countries* (Discussion Paper No. 709). ETLA.

Petersen, T. (1995). Analysis of Event Histories. In *Handbook of Statistical Modeling for the Social and Behavioural Sciences.* New York: Plenum Press.

Pissarides, C. (1990). *Equilibrium Unemployment Theory.* Cambridge (MA): Basil Blackwell Ltd.

Plaßmann, G. (2002). *Der Einfluss der Arbeitslosenversicherung auf die Arbeitslosigkeit in Deutschland* (Beiträge zur Arbeitsmarkt- und Berufsforschung No. 255). IAB, Bundesanstalt für Arbeit.

Polachek, S. and Siebert, W. (1993). *The Economics of Earnings.* Cambridge: Cambridge University Press.

Prasad, E. (2000). *The Enbearable Stability of the German Wage Structure: Evidence and Interpretation* (Working Paper No. 00-22). IMF.

Puhani, P. A. (2000). The Heckman Correction for Sample Selection and its Critique. *Journal of Economic Surveys, 14*, 53-68.

Reize, F. (2002). *Leaving Unemployment for Self-Employment.* Doctoral dissertation, University of Mannheim.

Riboud, M. (1978). *Accumulation du capital humain.* Paris: Economica.

Romer, P. M. (1990). Endogenous Technological Change. *Journal of Political Economy, 98*(5), 71-102.

Ronning, G. (1991). *Mikroökonometrie.* Berlin, Heidelberg: Springer Verlag.

Rosenzweig, M. R. and Wolpin, K. I. (1993). Intergenerational Support and the Life-Cycle Incomes of Young Men and Their Parents: Human Capital Investments, Coresidence and Intergenerational Financial Transfers. *Journal of Labor Economics, 11*(1), 84-112.

Rothe, G. (1995). *Die Systeme beruflicher Qualifizierung Frankreichs und Deutschlands im Vergleich* (Beiträge zur Arbeitsmarkt- und Berufsforschung No. 190). IAB, Bundesanstalt für Arbeit.

Schmidt, C. M. (1999). *Persistence and the German Unemployment Problem: Empirical Evidence on German Labor Market Flows* (Discussion Paper No. 31). IZA.

Schnabel, R. and Schnabel, I. (2002). *Family and Gender Still Matter: The Heterogeneity of Returns to Education in Germany* (Discussion Paper No. 02-67). ZEW.

Shavit, Y. and Blossfeld, H.-P. (1993). *Persistent Inequality – Changing Educational Attainment in Thirteen Countries.* Boulder: Westview Press.

Simonnet, V. (1996). Mobilité professionnelle et salaire: des différences entre hommes et femmes. *Economie et Statistique, 269*, 59-72.

Skalli, A. (2001). The Role of Schooling: Screening Versus Human Capital. In R. Asplund (Ed.), *Education and Earnings. Further Evidence from Europe.* Helsinki: Taloustieto Oy.

Small, K. A. and Hsiao, C. (1985). Multinomial Logit Specification Tests. *International Economic Review, 26*(3), 619-627.

Sofer, C. (1990). La répartition des emplois par sexe: capital humain ou discrimination? *Economie et Prévision, 92/93*, 77-86.

Spence, M. (1973). Job Market Signalling. *Journal of Labor Economics, 87*, 355-374.

Steiner, V. (1997). *Extended Benefit Entitlement Periods and the Duration of Unemployment* (Discussion Paper No. 97-14). ZEW.

Steiner, V. (2001). Unemployment Persistence in the West German Labour Market: Negative Duration Dependence or Sorting? *Oxford Bulletin of Economics and Statistics, 63*(1), 91-113.

Steiner, V. and Wagner, K. (1998). Has Earnings Inequality Changed in the 1980s. *Zeitschrift für Wirtschafts- und Sozialwissenschaften, 118*, 29-59.

Taubman, J. (1976). The Determinants of Earnings: Genetics, Family and Other Environments: A Study of White Male Twins. *American Economic Review, 66*, 858-870.

Thélot, C. and Vallet, L.-A. (2000). La réduction des inégalités sociales devant l'école depuis le début du siècle. *Economie et Statistique, 334*, 3-32.

Thurow, L. (1975). *Generating Inequality.* New York: Basic Books.

van den Berg, G. J. and van der Klaauw, B. (2001). Combining Micro and Macro Unemployment Duration Data. *Journal of Econometrics, 102*(2), 271-309.

Veil, M. (2002). Ganztagsschule mit Tradition: Frankreich. *Aus Politik und Zeitgeschichte, B*(41), 29-37.

Wagner, J. and Lorenz, W. (1988). The Earnings Function Under Test. *Economics Letters, 27*(1), 95-99.

Weißhuhn, G. and Clement, W. (1983). *Ausbildung und Einkommen in der Bundesrepublik Deutschland* (Beiträge zur Arbeitsmarkt- und Berufsforschung No. 80). IAB.

Wiese, W. (1982). Elternstatus, Lehrerempfehlung und Schullaufbahn. *Zeitschrift für Soziologie, 11*(1), 49-63.

Willis, R. J. (1986). Wage Determinants: A Survey and Reinterpretation of Human Capital Earnings Functions. In O. Ashenfelter and R. Layard (Eds.), *Handbook of Labor Economics* (p. 525-602). Elsevier Science Publishers.

Willis, R. J. and Rosen, S. (1979). Education and Self-Selection. *Journal of Political Economy, 87*(5), 7-36.

Wilson, K. (2001). The Determinants of Educational Attainment: Modeling and Estimating the Human Capital Model and Education Production Functions. *Southern Economic Journal, 67*(3), 518-551.

Wolbers, M. H. (2000). The Effects of Level of Education on Mobility Between Employment and Unemployment in the Netherlands. *European Sociological Review, 16*(2), 185-200.

Wurzel, E. (1993). *An Econometric Analysis of Unemployment Duration in West Germany*. Heidelberg: Physica-Verlag.

Zimmermann, V. (2000). *Arbeitsmarktprobleme Jugendlicher: eine empirische Untersuchung ihres Weges in die Beschäftigung*. Baden-Baden: Nomos.